How to Make It Big in the Seminar Business

How to Make It Big in the Seminar Business

Second Edition

Paul Karasik

McGraw-Hill

New York   Chicago   San Francisco
Lisbon   London   Madrid   Mexico City
Milan   New Delhi   San Juan   Seoul
Singapore   Sydney   Toronto

1 2 3 4 5 6 7 8 9 0 DOC/DOC 0 9 8 7 6 5 4

ISBN 0-07-142683-3

This publication is designed to provide accurate and authoritative information in regard to the subject matter covered. It is sold with the understanding that neither the author nor the publisher is engaged in rendering legal, accounting, or other professional service. If legal advice or other expert assistance is required, the services of a competent professional person should be sought.

—From a Declaration of Principles jointly adopted by a Committee of the American Bar Association and a Committee of Publishers

McGraw-Hill books are available at special quantity discounts to use as premiums and sales promotions, or for use in corporate training programs. For more information, please write to the Director of Special Sales, McGraw-Hill, 2 Penn Plaza, New York, NY 10121-2298. Or contact your local bookstore.

 This book is printed on recycled, acid-free paper containing a minimum of 50% recycled de-inked fiber.

*To Saul Ellenbogen, Alan Gompers, Moss Jacobs,
Marilyn Portnoy, and Gary Karasik, my best
friends. You always had faith in me and the
work. And to all those who want to improve the
lives of others through education.*

Contents

Part 4. The Seminar Business Yellow Pages   173

Preface

It was a warm August afternoon when I walked into my boss's office to drop the bomb. Commencement day had finally arrived. The words were simple and direct, "I quit." The implications for both my boss and myself were not.

For me, leaving my well-paying position was the biggest professional risk I had ever taken. I had spent two years building an extremely profitable division of his company and I would be giving up a great deal of security. For my boss, my leaving meant the loss of considerable revenue. Although he mouthed the words, "Good luck," I knew his heart was saying, "Paul, are you sure you know what you're doing?"

Neither friends nor family could believe I was leaving a secure job to pursue seminar leadership professionally. In fact, most of them didn't know what a professional seminar leader was.

It Started on a Dare

The path that led me to the seminar business actually began about 22 years before, when I was 15 years old and became a professional musician. This was when I first experienced the exhilaration of applause and accolades from an audience.

The love of performance and the media led me to pursue a major in communications at Temple University. But after college, I found myself pursuing music again.

This was during the early 1970s and the "personal-growth" seminar trend was taking hold throughout America. Thanks to a friend who was promoting speakers, seminars, and personal-growth conferences in New York City, I began to subsidize my music career with talks and seminars on personal-development topics. I thoroughly enjoyed delivering these seminars, but the idea of doing it full-time never occurred to me.

Although I sold a number of my songs to major publishers, signed a modest recording contract, and produced a moderately successful record, enduring success proved elusive. Making it in the music business was far more difficult than I had imagined.

My desire for a more stable lifestyle and steady income led me to pursue sales and marketing. For the next five years I achieved financial success, but felt something was missing. I did not have any passion for what I was doing day to day.

Coincidentally, at this time, my friend Jennifer invited me to accompany her to a seminar. At first I refused. "I know all that stuff," I told her, "I used to give those seminars myself a few years back." She insisted, so finally I caved in and went to the seminar.

Soon after it began, the seminar leader asked if anyone in the audience wanted to do something different with their life. She then looked at *me* and said, "What do *you* want to do?" Without missing a beat—and without thinking—I jokingly said, "I want to do what you do."

Not to be outdone, the seminar leader said, "Then why don't you come up here and do it."

Accepting her challenge, I said, "OK, I will!"

The audience of more than 500 people gasped in unison as I made my way to the front of the room. The seminar leader stood on the side and watched with delight as I answered questions from the audience, which seemed somewhat intoxicated by the sight of one of their own fulfilling his dream right there. After about ten minutes, I thanked the seminar leader for the opportunity and returned to my seat. I sat down knowing what I needed to do. My personal mission became totally clear. It was that evening that I heard my "calling" to be a seminar leader.

Growth as a Seminar Leader and the Launching of the American Seminar Leaders Association

Since that auspicious moment, I have delivered hundreds of seminars and speeches throughout the world. Many times, before I am about to walk up to the front of a room and stand before an audience, I am overwhelmed with the deepest sense of gratitude. I feel blessed to have found a profession that allows me to help others while receiving so much inner satisfaction and financial reward.

The seminar business is a creative wonderland. It offers unlimited opportunities to design and deliver new programs, as well as create profitable products such as books and audio and video programs.

In just the few short years I have been in this business, I have created 12 seminars, 8 different audio programs, 2 video programs, and authored 2 other books. My most recent book, *Sweet Persuasion*, has been published by Simon & Schuster and is being distributed worldwide. In addition, Simon & Schuster purchased the film rights and released a training film by the same name.

I have had the honor of appearing on programs with such notable people as ex-President Ronald Reagan, Dr. Norman Vincent Peale, and many of the gurus from the world of business. In fact, I feel that in a sense, I am a guru of sorts. My specialty is a motivational program called "Winning." It is a unique multimedia program with music, a customized slide show, humor, and strategies and techniques for achieving peak performance. Recently I had the unique pleasure of presenting this "Winning" program as a one-man show on Broadway in New York City.

I truly believe that what I have achieved is attainable for you too, for almost anyone. The purpose of this book is to guide you toward success in the seminar business.

Soon after entering the seminar business, I began to tell others about all the rewards it offered. Often I would spend hours offering advice to individuals who had an interest in pursuing seminars. Then, in order to help others more efficiently, I organized the information into a program called, "How to Create Your Own Successful Seminar/Workshop Business." It has been extremely successful, and I continue to present it on a regular basis throughout America.

At the end of this program participants would often ask for a follow-up seminar or meeting. To fill this need, I sent out an announcement to all the alumni of the seminar inviting anyone who was seriously interested in the seminar business to attend. About 20 people showed up and we made a commitment to meet monthly.

The meeting in New York became the first official gathering of what soon came to be known as the American Seminar Leaders Association or ASLA. We agreed on a mission statement. "ASLA is an organization of professional seminar and workshop leaders who seek to enhance their professional skills and market their services and products more successfully."

ASLA has grown rapidly and currently provides a national newsletter, books, tapes, regional and national educational programs, certification for seminar leaders, and professional services that produce brochures and audio and video products for seminar leaders.

How This Book Evolved and How It Will Benefit You

How to Make It Big in the Seminar Business is a natural continuation of my national seminar and the work of the American Seminar Leaders Association. It is in the true spirit of my role as an "information entrepreneur."

Before I wrote this book, I carefully evaluated hundreds of "how-to" books to determine the approach and format that would be most useful to both the entry-level and the advanced seminar leader. In addition, I reviewed any existing material that related to the seminar business. My aim was to create the most comprehensive and beneficial book ever written on this subject.

In order to achieve that aim, I have provided you with the rules, strategies, techniques, guidelines, and methodologies that will make your journey to success as problem-free as possible. None of the information contained in this book is theoretical. Instead, I have provided you with information that works when applied. Throughout the book and in the Yellow Pages section, you are provided with resources and specific contacts that will connect you to the business of developing, marketing, and presenting seminars.

We have entered the information age. There are unlimited opportunities for qualified seminar leaders. By helping you I help myself. As the seminar business grows and the quality of seminar leaders improves, there will be more and more opportunities for everyone.

Ultimately the role of the seminar leader is to help others, to educate them, and to make the world a better place to live. There can never be too many competent and inspired presenters, as long as the information is needed. It is in this spirit that I offer you this book.

May your continued success be filled with joy, satisfaction, and unlimited financial rewards.

Paul Karasik
Manhatton Beach, CA

Preface to the Second Edition

It's hard to believe it has been 12 years since I wrote the first edition of this book. In some ways it seems it was just yesterday, but as I reflect on all that has changed I must admit it does feel like a very long time ago.

What has not changed for me is my conviction that I am doing exactly what I am supposed to be doing. This knowing provides me with a sense of purpose and instills my life with meaning that has become even more elusive to many people since I wrote the first edition.

Today more than ever I am convinced that educating others, regardless of the topic and market, provides a connection to life that is absolutely priceless. When asked the question, "What do you do?" I use a variety of titles including consultant, seminar leader, author, and industry expert. But to myself (or as I recently answered my young daughter when she asked me) I just say, "I'm a teacher." It is so simple and at the same time so profound to see and think of myself in this light.

If you are contemplating or are currently pursuing the seminar business as a career, I encourage you to jump in and stay committed. This business offers a powerful combination of both monetary and personal rewards. You will enjoy a freedom and an entrepreneurial excitement that is truly a gift that I continue to be grateful for practically every day.

This process of designing, marketing, and presenting information and education to groups was the centerpiece of the first edition, and it remains the unique focus point of this edition also.

Yet the need to revise the book was overwhelming. Since the publication of the first edition the microchip revolutionized the world. It's quite amazing for me to reflect on the fact that the first edition was pre-Internet! Contacts and resources have been revised and new information has been added. And obviously, the most critical pieces of contact information—Web sites—are included throughout this edition.

This edition offers advice and information regarding the opportunities of the new digital world of the DVD, compact disc, and PowerPoint presentation. You will also learn how to conduct money-making tele-seminars and "Webinars" in the comfort of your home office.

Yes, the microchip has provided the world unlimited free access to an almost infinite amount of information. But ironically, it has provided seminar leaders with even more opportunities to make money and thrive. Information has become plentiful, but good advice has become harder to find.

For those of you who will follow the directions provided in this book and offer your programs and advice in multiple formats, the business environment of today offers more creative ways to serve others while simultaneously creating lucrative income for yourself.

My own seminar business has grown largely because of these changes and innovations. Today a greater portion of my work is coaching and consulting. It is both profitable and personally rewarding to get more deeply involved with my clients. The portion of my income derived from digital products and Web-based seminars continues to grow each year. I have embraced the opportunities highlighted in this edition and I hope you will also.

I don't believe in accidents. If you've got this book in your hands there is a reason. Every year since the first edition was published I've heard from individuals who have followed their dream and achieved success. This is my sincerest wish for you too.

Stay focused on what you want and you are destined to achieve it.

Paul Karasik
www.paulkarasik.com
paul@paulkarasik.com

Acknowledgments

J. B., Rob Gibert, Jeff Herman, Donna Libby, Lynne Lindahl, Lisa Merrill, Deirdre MacLean, and Marsha Tolkin. You helped by planting the seeds, cultivating the soil, carrying the water, and shedding the light that produced this beautiful flower.

And special thanks to Samantha, my lifelong muse and the two primary sources for inspiration, my children Sky and Star.

How to Make It Big in the Seminar Business

PART 1

How to Put Together a Dynamic Seminar

Introduction

Welcome to the Profitable World of Seminars

You probably already have some idea of the rewards available in doing seminars if you are reading this book. You may even be sharing in these rewards already. Just in case you are not familiar with the scope of the seminar business, let's take a minute to expand your view of this incredible business.

According to *Training* magazine, a periodical of the corporate seminar business, American businesses currently spend more than $44 billion a year on educational programs. In addition to that, the personal-growth seminar market is estimated to be between $10 to $20 billion a year. In the United States today, there are thousands of seminar companies and countless seminar leaders who are sharing a piece of the seminar pie.

If you possess knowledge or information that can be of value to someone else, then you qualify to share in the profits currently being reaped in the seminar business. Whether you decide to go into seminars part-time or full-time, the good news is that you can become part of this profitable business starting right now.

Besides money, you will receive recognition, perhaps even fame. Yes, the seminar business has its stars too. By choosing to become a seminar leader, you will gain attention, respect, and recognition from others. By positioning yourself as the expert in your field, you will become the guru that others admire. There is a feeling of intoxication that comes with this territory, a kind of addiction that develops once you have a taste of what it's like to be an information entrepreneur.

The third reward you will reap from the seminar business occurs on an inner level. Each of us has the capacity to fulfill a deeper purpose, to make a contribution to this world, and to help others enjoy a better life. The seminar business offers a direct way to share a part of yourself and to influence the lives of others in a positive manner.

As Ralph Waldo Emerson said, "It is one of the most beautiful compensations of this life, that no man can sincerely try to help another without helping himself." Although there may be many endeavors that are more altruistic in nature, giving seminars provides the opportunity to help others and thereby to help yourself.

What Exactly Is a Seminar?

A seminar is an exchange of information that is confined to a specific topic. This information answers questions and usually solves specific problems. It can affect the personal or professional life of the participants. Seminars generally last from one hour to a few days in length. They don't usually take as long or go into the same depth as a college course.

There are a few similar kinds of information exchanges worth noting for comparison:

A *speech* is a session that usually lasts for less than two hours and can be used to inform, inspire, or entertain.

A *workshop* is similar to a seminar, although it is more likely to involve some hands-on experience. For example, a computer software workshop might include sitting down at the computer and actually using the software.

A *training program* is a seminar designed to develop specific skills that are applied in a business or professional setting to increase effectiveness or productivity.

For the sake of simplicity, I will refer to any short, concise, benefit-oriented program as a seminar.

What Are the Two Major Seminar Markets?

The seminar business can be divided into two markets. It is important for anyone trying to break into the seminar business to become familiar with each and to understand their similarities and differences. You should also know their advantages and disadvantages, so you can decide which one is best for you.

Public Seminars

First let's examine the *public* seminar market. This is the market with which people are most familiar. A public seminar refers to any seminar that is given in a public gathering place, such as a hotel, and can be attended by anyone willing to pay the seminar tuition. There are numerous public seminar companies that offer programs nationwide on a variety of topics. Some of the most popular public seminar companies include: American Management Association, Dun & Bradstreet, Career-Track, Keye Productivity Center, and National Seminar Group. In Part 4, "The Seminar Business Yellow Pages," you will find a list of public seminar companies.

Many public seminars are on a general topic, such as management skills for the new manager or selling skills. In many cases these seminars are focused on special interest groups, such as bankers, insurance agents, or accountants, and the participants are sent by their employer or perhaps by an organization to which they belong.

The most popular form of promotion for the public seminar is direct mail, although there are certain kinds of seminars that lend themselves to newspaper advertisements or radio spots.

Public seminars have the potential for enormous profits, but they require a substantial investment for promotion. In addition, the potential for mistakes in choosing the correct mailing lists or advertising vehicles makes the public seminar a high-risk venture.

The specific strategies for marketing public seminars with the least amount of risk are discussed in detail in later chapters of this book that focus on marketing techniques.

One example of an extremely successful public seminar was Dr. Norman Vincent Peale's program. His organization consistently sold 1000 or more seats in each of the cities he visited regularly.

There are a few reasons for Dr. Peale's success. First, he had a number of best-selling books, including the classic, *The Power of Positive Thinking*. This book positioned him as an authority and gave him celebrity status.

Second, he worked with highly skilled promoters. A direct-mail campaign was launched about a month before the seminar. In addition, the promoters initiated a telemarketing campaign. They telephoned the recipients of the brochure and personally invited them to the seminar. Finally, teaser ads were run in the major local newspaper about a week before the seminar. These ads were inquiry generators and resulted in additional registrations.

In most cases a minimum of a few thousand dollars is required for the promotion of a public seminar. On the other hand, if you win, you stand a chance to win big. Public seminars can be powerful income generators. In addition, income from selling books, tapes, CDs, and other spinoff products can add up to a small fortune in a multicity rollout of a good seminar. In fact, public seminars are often loss leaders for the "real money" that is generated from "back-of-the-room sales." The art of back-of-the-room sales is discussed in detail in Chapter 16.

In-House Seminars

The second market is the *in-house* seminar. This is the hidden seminar market. An in-house seminar is sponsored by one organization—a corporation, a professional association, or a nonprofit group, such as a church, synagogue, civic club, chamber of commerce, and so forth. The seminar is focused on providing benefits to the members of the sponsoring organization. The organization usually pays the seminar leader a set fee and pays the marketing expenses. This program is not open to the general public, and many times it is delivered on location, hence the name *in-house* or *on-site*.

An example of an in-house seminar is a selling skills seminar for salespeople at a company that manufacturs copiers. The company might have 20 salespeople in a given office. The seminar will be delivered at the company's office, and only those 20 salespeople will be invited.

Another example of an in-house program is a seminar at a multiday conference for chiropractors on techniques for building a professional practice. The professional association of chiropractors provides the city, the room, and the audience. The seminar leader merely shows up, delivers the seminar, and gets paid.

Other examples of in-house, or sponsored, programs are corporate training programs for the development of employees and adult education evening classes at a local college.

The primary disadvantage of developing, promoting, and delivering in-house programs is that there is usually a ceiling on your income as a seminar leader. Although in many cases you can prearrange for additional money if the program draws more than a certain number of participants, generally your fee will be predetermined.

The good news is that your fee can be more than generous if you are able to provide immediate solutions to an organization's problems. While you might deliver an evening seminar for an adult education program and receive a few hundred dollars, a similar program for a corporation or a trade or professional association can be worth a few thousand dollars. In addition, you might be able to profit further from the sale of books and tapes if you have them.

The greatest advantage of in-house seminars is that there is little risk involved in promoting them. Low-cost marketing techniques are employed, and there is no major investment needed.

By focusing your energies on providing a special interest group with information that will contribute to the success of its members, you can begin to make money in the seminar business immediately.

In the beginning you need to establish your credibility, but once you have a track record, you will be able to market your program easily and inexpensively. Chapter 13 is devoted to marketing in-house seminars.

There are some companies that specialize in providing in-house programs. These companies are listed in Part 4 under "Corporate Training Companies."

To Sponsor or Not to Sponsor Seminars

How to Make It Big in the Seminar Business is designed to give you all the information you need to understand the opportunities, challenges, and rewards of the seminar business.

Do you want to sponsor your own public seminars? Or would you rather market in-house programs to corporations and other organizations?

Or perhaps you might like to get a job delivering a program for one of the major seminar companies. You will find a list of public seminar companies and corporate training companies in Part 4. Chapter 15, "How to Get a Job with a Seminar Company," explains the steps you must take to land a job with one of these companies.

You might want to investigate all of these opportunities and then make your decision based upon your investigation. This book provides the information you need to be successful, regardless of the path you choose.

The Two Secrets for Success in the Seminar Business

In public and in-house seminars alike, your ultimate success will be guaranteed if you devote your efforts to mastering both ends of the business: the "front end" and the "back end."

The front end involves standing in front of a room full of people. It includes the program itself (its content and structure) and your delivery of it. It is always far easier to sell quality. Ultimately the most effective marketing strategy is to design and deliver a fantastic seminar. If you do so, your reputation will precede you. Quality will earn you sponsors, seminar registrants, repeat business, and referrals.

The back end of the business includes everything involved in getting you to the front of the room. It is the marketing of the seminar. The greatest seminar in the world is worthless if there is nobody in the room to receive the information.

You must make a commitment to mastering this back end of the seminar business. Initially, you must focus your efforts equally on front-end and back-end issues. If you correctly and diligently follow the "front-end/back-end" philosophy, you are assured a piece of the seminar pie and will have no trouble making it big in the seminar business.

How to Use This Book

The purpose of this book is to provide you with the opportunity to achieve success in the seminar business. *How to Make It Big in the Seminar Business* is based upon two proverbs. The first is knowledge is power. To this end, Parts 1 and 3 provide the information you need to design and deliver a money-making seminar. Part 2 focuses on seminar marketing strategies and techniques.

The second proverb this book is based upon is it's not what you know, it's who you know. To address this issue in a comprehensive way, important contacts are provided throughout this book. In addition, Part 4 is a Yellow Pages for the seminar business. No other book on the seminar business has as many contacts as you will find in *How to Make It Big in the Seminar Business*.

A conscientious effort has been made to make sure all addresses and phone numbers are up to date. However, because of constant changes in the business world, there are bound to be some that are inaccurate. These inaccuracies are beyond our control, and we apologize. Future editions will be updated to keep *How to Make It Big in the Seminar Business* the classic how-to business book that it is meant to be.

1

How to Choose a Winning Topic

A winning seminar topic is one that will attract lots of people who are willing to spend their time and money to attend your seminar.

The Four Critical Features of a Winning Topic

Choose a Topic That You Love

What do you love to talk about? What is your passion? What topic do you find fascinating? What valuable information would you love to share with others?

The eminent educator Dale Carnegie addressed this aspect of the business well: "You never achieve real success unless you like what you're doing."

It is important for you to choose a topic that excites you. No one else will get excited about your topic unless and until you do. When you get excited, your enthusiasm becomes infectious and your program much more motivational. Motivation is an essential ingredient of any truly dynamic seminar and will usually make the difference between just good evaluations and excellent ones.

!!! **Caution.** Ultimately it is the public, not you, who decides if a seminar topic is good or not.

Related to choosing a topic that you love is teaching what you yourself want to learn. When you approach your topic with curiosity, you will naturally stay current and well informed about it. When you are well informed, you will deliver your seminar in a more relaxed and confident manner. The result will be a relaxed, receptive audience that will be inspired by your program.

Choose a Topic That Provides Hard-to-Find Information That Can Be Applied Immediately

We live in an age and culture in which the speed at which information is distributed continues to accelerate. Fax machines, modems, computers, cellular phones, voice mail—all have created an atmosphere of instant information in our society.

People will pay big money for immediate answers and instant relief to their problems.

There is one simple measure of a winning topic: Are people willing to pay to attend a seminar on your topic? You must be able to answer this question with a resolute yes. If you can't, you probably have a marketing problem on your hands.

If you don't know, do some research. Are there similar seminars currently being presented? Have there been seminars presented on your topic in the past? Is it a topic of current interest that is receiving a lot of media attention?

Chances are, if the program has been delivered successfully in the recent past, it can be presented again with similar success.

Choose a Topic That Has a Laser Beam Focus

You have two ways in which you can focus your seminar: by topic and by audience. You can focus by topic alone, by audience alone, or by topic and audience. For example, let's assume you have decided you would like to do a financial-planning seminar. This is a broad topic.

Now, let's see how the audience can be focused by topic and by audience. To focus your financial-planning seminar by topic, choose only one aspect of financial planning, such as tax planning or retirement planning. To focus by audience, you might choose women. A more focused audience might be recently divorced or widowed women. A laser beam focus might be recently widowed or divorced women under the age of 35 who earn $50,000 or more a year and have one or two children.

If you have already decided whom you would like to market your seminar to, one of the easiest ways to focus your topic and organize your seminar is by using a questionnaire or survey. If you have an idea for a seminar, ask a sampling of your prospective audience if they would attend a seminar on this topic. If you need an idea for a seminar, ask your prospective audience what kind of seminar they would be willing to attend.

Figure 1-1 is an example of a survey you might want to customize for your audience.

Aside from helping you identify your topic, a seminar questionnaire provides you with valuable marketing information. The questionnaire enables you to discover specific needs and to uncover problems you will

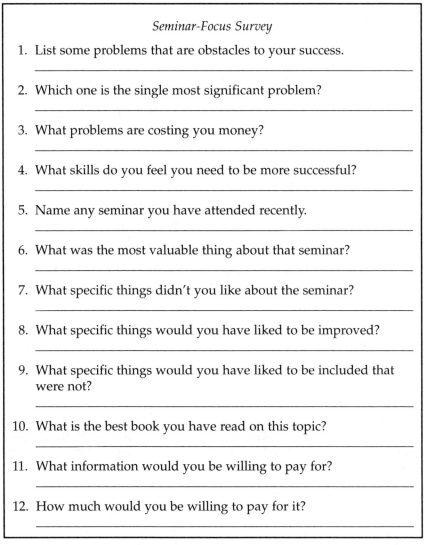

Seminar-Focus Survey

1. List some problems that are obstacles to your success.

   _____

2. Which one is the single most significant problem?

   _____

3. What problems are costing you money?

   _____

4. What skills do you feel you need to be more successful?

   _____

5. Name any seminar you have attended recently.

   _____

6. What was the most valuable thing about that seminar?

   _____

7. What specific things didn't you like about the seminar?

   _____

8. What specific things would you have liked to be improved?

   _____

9. What specific things would you have liked to be included that were not?

   _____

10. What is the best book you have read on this topic?

    _____

11. What information would you be willing to pay for?

    _____

12. How much would you be willing to pay for it?

    _____

Figure 1-1. A questionnaire will help you focus your seminar on the needs of the audience.

want to address in your seminar. Take care of the needs of your audience, and your audience will take care of you.

If you have an idea for a seminar but are not sure who your audience should be, try a few direct-mail tests. Judging from the response you get from a mailing to a few of your proposed audience members, you will quickly and fairly cheaply determine if you have identified a good audience for your seminar. There is more information on how to do this in Chapter 9.

Choose a Topic That Provides Substantial Perceived Benefits

People seek benefits. They spend a greater part of every day trying to gain rewards or avoid punishment. People do not buy seminars; they buy the benefits the seminars offer. Therefore, you should market benefits, not seminars.

Here are samples of the kinds of benefits on which you could focus your marketing efforts.

Rewards people want to gain:

To be loved	To win the praise and admiration of peers
To make money	
To gain recognition	To be healthy
To feel secure	To live in comfort
To advance in their careers	To maintain a positive self-image
To experience pleasure	To save time
To achieve success	To have fun
To be accepted socially	To improve themselves

Punishments people want to avoid:

To feel pain	To be insecure
To be unhealthy	To be lonely
To waste or lose money	To die
To waste time	

The bottom line is that you must correctly identify the specific benefits your target audience is seeking and then provide them with those benefits. The most commonly offered topics for both public and in-house seminars are listed in Figures 1-2 and 1-3.

Business and Professional Topics

Accounting	Executive	Outplacement
Affirmative Action	Development	Performance
Alcoholism	Family	Appraisal
Assertiveness	Financial Planning	Problem Solving
Assessment	First Aid	Productivity
(Employee)	Future Trends	Project Management
Attitude Automation	Goal Setting	Public Relations
Behavioral Theories	Graphic Design	Public Speaking
Body Language	Group Dynamics	Purchasing
Brain Theory	Hiring	Quality
Budgeting	Health Issues	Reading (Remedial)
Career Development	Industrial Relations	Retirement
Change	Internet Marketing	Robotics
Chemical	Interviewing	Safety
Dependency	Inventory Control	Sales Management
Clerical Skills	Labor Relations	Sales Training
Counseling Skills	Language (Foreign)	Security
Computers	Legal Issues	Sensitivity Training
Conflict	Leadership	Sexual Harassment
Management	Listening Skills	Statistical Analysis
Creativity	Management Skills	Strategic Planning
Credit	Marketing	Stress Management
Crime in the Work-	Mathematics	Succession Planning
place	Media Relations	Supervising
Crisis Management	Meeting Planning	Team Building
Cross-Cultural Skills	Memory	Technical Skills
Customer Service	Development	Technology
Data Processing	Mergers/	Applications
Delegation	Acquisitions	Telemarketing
Disabilities	Motivation	Telephone Skills
Discipline	Needs Analysis	Time Management
Drug Abuse	Negotiation	Web site Design
Engineering	Nutrition	Women's Issues
Ergonomics	Office Automation	Word Processing
Ethics	OSHA	Writing Skills

Figure 1-2. Listing of the most commonly offered business and professional seminar topics.

Personal-Development Topics

Acting	Dance	Losing Your Foreign
Art	Desktop Publishing	Accent
Body Building	Drawing	Meeting People
Body Massage	Fencing	Modeling
Bridge	Finding a Mate	Photography
Calligraphy	Flirting	Procrastination
Career Alternatives	Flower Arranging	Psychic Development
Charisma	Gift Baskets	Real Estate Investing
Classical Music	Home Repair	Reflexology
Clutter	Horseback Riding	Scuba Diving
Color Analysis	Hypnosis	Self-Esteem
Comedy	Ice Skating	Swimming
Creative Visualization	Image	Taxes
Creative Writing	Jewelry Making	Voice
Credit	Karate	Weight Control
Cross-Country Skiing	Knitting	Wine Tasting

Figure 1-3. Listing of the most commonly offered personal-development seminar topics.

2

What You Need to Succeed in the Seminar Business

There are three prerequisites for success in the seminar business. You will need knowledge, the right attitude, and skills. In some of these areas you might have the necessary qualifications. The purpose of this chapter is to help you make an honest self-assessment. Let's look at each prerequisite in more detail.

Knowledge

You must know your subject completely. In fact, you must be able to position yourself as one of the leading authorities on your particular topic. To put it bluntly, *do your homework*.

Although you probably have direct experience and possibly all the right credentials, you must work continually to expand your frame of reference. You must become a veritable repository of information on your topic. As a seminar leader, you are an information entrepreneur. You must keep updating your stock. There are six simple steps you must take to become a true authority:

1. Identify the top 10 books written on your topic and read them. Make sure to include all of the classics in your field.

2. If there are any audio- or videocassettes available, listen to and watch them.

3. Locate any seminars on your topic and go to them. You can learn a lot from your colleagues and competitors.

4. Subscribe to any periodicals that have up-to-date information on your topic.

5. Join any organizations that focus on your topic. For example, if your

topic is computers, there are a number of professional associations to which computer consultants belong.

6. Position yourself as one of the experts. Personally introduce yourself to as many notable people in your field, both locally and nationally, as you can. You'll be amazed how quickly and easily you'll be received by the so-called gurus on your topic. The "great ones" always seem to want to help those who are sincerely interested and dedicated to the topic. After all, teaching or mentoring is a large part of what being a guru means. Remember that. You may be a guru yourself someday.

As an illustration of step 6, let me share a personal experience.

Not too long ago, I was consulting for an individual who wanted to give seminars on stress management. She came to my office holding a book that she felt contained the most valid and essential information on this topic. The author was a personal idol of hers.

Although she was thoroughly knowledgeable about her topic, she had not yet empowered herself as an authority. I asked her if she would like to become a colleague of the author. She replied, "Of course." I looked up the author's telephone number, picked up the phone, and dialed it. When he answered, I handed the phone to my client.

She almost panicked, but she took the phone. She apologized for bothering him, nervously introduced herself, and subsequently had a long conversation that initiated a relationship that, to my knowledge, is still alive today.

Now when my client is delivering her seminar, she refers to the well-known author as a personal friend and associate. She also has developed a very real and direct connection to one of the most respected people in her field and a pipeline to the most current information on her topic.

When you give a seminar, you will invariably be asked a variety of questions. If you do your homework, you will always be able either to answer the question, fully or in part, or, at the very least, to provide direction to where the questioner might find the answer.

!!! Contacts.   See Part 4 in this book under "Professional Associations for Networking and Education."

Attitude

There are six essential personal qualities that winners possess. You probably possess all of them to one degree or another, but there is no one who can't benefit from improvement in one or several of these areas. Identify the traits or qualities you need to enhance or develop.

1. *Commitment.*   As in all areas of endeavor, until you commit your-

self—in this case to the seminar business—you will achieve very little. You will lack effectiveness. Commitment helps you overcome any fears or misgivings you might have. Commitment is the mind-set, the wellspring for the resources and creative ideas, that is so essential in the seminar business.

Regardless of the professional path you choose to take in the seminar business, commitment will help you overcome the obstacles that are bound to occur.

2. *Confidence.* Confidence is not only a feeling but also the outward expression of commitment. Whether you are promoting or presenting, exhibiting confidence is critical in gaining the support of others.

It is not always possible to feel confident, but it is always possible to exhibit confidence. An excellent exercise is to practice exhibiting confidence under all conditions. To do this, you reverse cause and effect, working backward from the outward manifestation to the feeling itself. You'll be amazed what happens. In many cases, the result is that you will feel confident!

3. *Sense of mission.* When you feel a sense of mission, or purpose, you will automatically possess the positive mental attitude you need to create, market, and present your program. Speakers with a mission are charismatic and almost always effective. If you feel that presenting seminars is a way to help others and that it is, therefore, more of a calling than a job, your potential for achieving success is unlimited.

4. *Persistence.* Let's face it, everything is not going to go your way all the time. Sure, you're likely to catch a lot of breaks along the way, but you're also likely to catch an equal number of challenges. If you can't accept failure, you've got a big problem. Every new undertaking requires the ability to bounce back and stay on course with positive expectancy. As Calvin Coolidge said,

> Nothing in the world can take the place of persistence.
> Talent will not; nothing is more common than unsuccessful men with talent.
> Genius will not; unrewarded genius is almost a proverb.
> Education will not; the world is full of educated derelicts.
> Persistence and determination are alone supreme.

5. *Goal orientation.* If you don't know what you want, you're not very likely to get it. It is important to make goal setting a habit, not just an occasional practice. Your goals should be divided into three categories: short-term, medium-range, and long-term. Setting goals means writing them down, with target dates for achieving them. Start right now if you haven't already.

Here is an example of short-term, medium-range, and long-term goal setting.

Long-Term Goal
Sell 50,000 copies of my book to target market   5 years

Medium-Range Goals
Complete the writing of the book   2 years
Secure a publishing contract   1 year

Short-Term Goals
Complete the book proposal   90 days
Write two or three sample chapters   60 days
Begin to outline the book   30 days

   In this case, your long-term goal might be to sell 50,000 books to your target market. Completing the book is a necessary step toward achieving this goal. Breaking this goal into bite-sized pieces makes success not only possible but also probable.
   6. *High energy (enthusiasm).*   The seminar business requires energy, lots of it, and in many forms.
   Creative energy is needed to put your program together. Good seminar programs are continually updated and revised to keep them current for the audience and interesting for you as a presenter.
   Mental energy is needed to research and replenish your information pool, as well as to market your program and run your business.
   Physical energy is needed to keep up hectic travel schedules and to present your seminar enthusiastically. Success requires stamina to endure long hours on your feet and many long hours in preparation.
   Emotional energy is needed to really care about the participants who have spent their time and money to attend your program. You will also need emotional strength to deal with the successes and disappointments that come with the turf.

Skills

Although you might have the luxury of hiring others with the following five skills, more than likely you will need to develop them personally. All of these skills range from necessary to highly desirable if you are to achieve your greatest potential as a seminar leader.

Writing Skills

Although the spoken word is your basic communicating and money-making tool in the seminar business, writing skills are also needed if you want to ease your path to glory. You needn't be a Hemingway, but you will need effective business writing skills.
   If you don't already possess the ability to write persuasively and you

want to develop better writing skills, start by reading one of the many good books available on the topic or by attending classes at your local college or university. Classes in business and professional writing are proliferating currently. Your options have never been better.

But the real secret to becoming an effective writer is *to write*. Start writing now. As with most skills, you will improve faster with practice.

Our culture practically worships the written word. Therefore, you will gain respect and influence people if your letters, workbooks, resource guides, articles, and proposals are powerful, clear, and of high quality. Ultimately, you will *want* to be the person who *"wrote* the book." Chapter 16 provides valuable information and resources to help you get out your written word.

Telephone Skills

The most valuable business tool of the twenty-first century remains the telephone. You need to be able to secure speaking opportunities and enroll participants using the convenience of the telephone. Even if you are already comfortable and fairly proficient doing business on the phone, work to increase your effectiveness. It will increase your profits. There are three key principles to remember when using the telephone.

1. Always set measurable goals for yourself when you use the telephone. For example, if you are marketing your in-house seminar, you can set a goal of 10 calls per day to prospective organizations.

2. Always develop a script from which to work in order to keep control of the conversation. This script should include your opening and closing, as well as answers to possible questions you might be asked.

3. Never sound as though you are using a script. Each call should maintain a conversational tone. Even though you might be answering the same question for the one hundredth time, it should sound fresh. This might be difficult at first, but you will quickly master it if you make this one of your skill development goals.

Selling Skills

Your ability to sell your program will largely determine your success, like it or not. You will be selling your seminar, your books, your tapes, your ideas, and, of course, yourself. As I have already mentioned, the greatest seminar in the world is of no value without people in the room.

Selling is a learned discipline, but it is simple once you know how. You should never have to use a hard sell. In fact, the hard sell will do you and your business more harm than good. As a first step, you must learn the art of selling as a way of serving. If you believe in your seminar and your products, you will find this kind of selling a very simple and natural process.

There are a few important ideas to always keep in mind when you sell.

1. Take the time to develop rapport and establish a relationship with the person to whom you are selling. In this way, you will always be setting up long-lasting relationships. Once you have sold yourself as a resource, the chances are excellent the person will come back.

2. Identify the needs of the person you are selling to, and sell the benefits that relate to those needs. For instance, let's say you want to enroll someone in your time-management seminar. If you determine that your prospect is seeking to achieve more balance between his or her business and personal life, focus your sales presentation on how your seminar will provide answers to this specific problem.

3. Never forget to ask for exactly what you want. If you want the people in your seminar to purchase your book or tapes, say clearly, "My books and tapes are on sale in the back of the room. I accept all major credit cards." There have been numerous studies done of professional salespeople in which a large percentage of them never asked for the order. Don't forget to ask for the order!

!!! **Resource.** An excellent and inexpensive publication designed to help you develop effective selling skills is *Selling Power* magazine and online. It is well written, educational, and motivational as well.

Selling Power
P.O. Box 5467
Fredericksburg, VA 22406
Phone: (800) 752-7355
Fax: (540) 752-7001
www.sellingpower.com

Presentation Skills

Your ability to present information effectively is a necessary skill. One of your most powerful marketing strategies is repeat business and referrals. In order to get this business, you need highly evolved speaking skills.

Professional presentation skills in the seminar business go beyond standing in the front of the room and delivering a lecture like a college professor. You need to add humor, audiovisuals, and a level of drama to the presentation.

Perhaps you possess very good speaking skills already. That's fine, but don't stop with very good. Make one of your goals to improve continually as a speaker, to set yourself far above the crowd.

Computer Skills

The primary need for computer skills is to take advantage of the computer's word processing capabilities. There are letters to write, proposals to generate, and lots of handouts and workbooks to create. The computer will save you time and money in the long run. Along with the computer, you need basic typing skills.

The second and equally vital importance of your computer is to maintain your own mailing list. This is a list or combination of lists of people who are good prospects for your seminars or individuals with whom you have already done business.

There are a variety of easy-to-use and inexpensive software programs that can be used to create your database for future business opportunities. Your database should be easy to maintain and will be a powerful ongoing marketing resource.

These programs also allow you to maintain history records and notes on each entry and schedule future calls as needed. They all offer valuable sales and marketing features that will assist you in your business.

!!! **Resource.** Here are two excellent software programs you can use. They are both excellent, widely used, and you are likely to find technical support for both of them locally. If not, both have support hotlines and provide upgrades.

Act!   Goldmine
Best Software Small Business Division   Goldmine Software
(877) 501-4496   (800) 654-3526
www.Act.com   www.goldminesw.com

!!! **Contacts.** Two organizations will provide you with invaluable assistance in developing your professional skills. They both offer books, tapes, seminars, newsletters, networking opportunities, and lots of other resources.

American Seminar Leaders   National Speakers Association
    Association   1500 South Priest Drive
2405 E. Washington Blvd.   Tempe, AZ 85281
Pasadena, CA 91104   Phone: (480) 968-2552
Phone: (800) 801-1886   Fax: (480) 968-0911
Fax: (626) 798-0701   www.nsaspeaker.org
www.asla.com

3

How to Design a Money-Making Seminar

In order to create a truly successful seminar, you must follow Karasik's axiom.

> Focus on the needs of your audience, and your audience will focus on you.

Strategies for Putting Your Seminar Together

Designing a great seminar is simple if you follow this three-part process.

1. *Focus on where your participants are right now.* What is their level of expertise on the topic before taking your seminar: beginner, intermediate, or advanced? Among the most common mistakes a seminar leader makes is to create a seminar that is either too elementary or too advanced. In either case, your participants do not get what they came for or what they need.

For example, if you are delivering a sales seminar to brand-new salespeople, your content should be very broad. They need an understanding and an overview of the selling process itself, the basics. On the other hand, if your audience consists of experienced salespeople, they will be bored with material they've heard before.

2. *Focus on where they want to go.* Focus on the benefits your participants expect. In the case of the sales seminar, the participants will probably want to make more money by closing more sales. If you construct a seminar that focuses on helping them achieve their goals, you are guaranteed rave reviews.

3. *Focus on what your audience needs to learn to get where they want to go.* Again, using the example of the sales seminar, the audience might want to learn how to prospect for new clients, how to handle objections, and how to prequalify leads. The information or skills your audience needs are known as objectives. By achieving the objectives above, the salespeople will get where they want to go—they will make more money.

The One Technique Essential for a Perfect Seminar

The first step you must take in creating a perfect seminar for your participants is to *ask them what they need to know.* You can accomplish this with a written questionnaire or by interviewing on the telephone.

If you are designing a new seminar and have identified your target audience, you can reach them easily enough. For example, if your seminar is for secretaries, you can call up a few secretaries at random, tell them what you're doing, and ask them for a few minutes of interviewing time.

Another good technique for finding out the needs of your potential audience is to call an association made up of your potential audience. For example, let's say your target audience is nurses. There are many national nursing associations you can contact to pinpoint the problems they would like you to solve. You can locate the names and telephone numbers of the associations that would be helpful to you by referring to the pages in Chapter 13 that deal with trade and professional associations.

Once you have begun to deliver your program, you will be able to refine the design of your seminar with the information you receive from participants. You get this information from informal interviews conducted after each program and from formal written evaluations filled out after the seminar.

Whether you are asking your audience on the phone, in person, or by means of a written questionnaire, the answers to the following two questions will become the basis for your seminar:

1. What three things would you most like to see covered in this seminar?
2. If you could have only one of these covered, which would it be?

The answers to these two questions will provide you with your seminar modules. It's almost as if you've created a series of miniseminar topics. Designing a comprehensive seminar becomes much easier when you break your seminar down into bite-sized pieces.

Answers to the second question will help you prioritize your modules. By knowing which modules are most important to your audience, you will be able to devote the appropriate amount of time to each module.

Why Use the Modular Design Approach (MDA)?

The quick answer to this question is very simple. You use it because it works. But here are several of the reasons why it works so well.

1. It allows you to arrange or rearrange the flow of the seminar easily and quickly.

2. You can customize your seminar according to the specific needs of a given group. For example, if your sales group does not need information on prospecting, it becomes very simple to drop this module without affecting the integrity of the rest of the seminar.

3. Researching your material is much easier when you have organized your seminar in a modular fashion. If you develop each module as if it were a miniseminar, your seminar will be filled with lots of variety. Each module will have its own opening, middle, and closing.

4. It makes it easier to transpose your seminar into other media. For example, the modules can easily become a series of printed monographs, chapters of a book, or sections in an audio or video program.

5. You will be able to create spin-off programs based on the needs of your audience. For example, a time-management module could be expanded into a full stand-alone seminar, such as time-management techniques for salespeople.

6. Participants appreciate the feeling of completion as you progress from one module to the next. Because modules make it possible to digest larger bodies of information, attendees literally get more for their money using an MDA. Think of it this way: Most of us cut up our food and chew it a while before we swallow it.

If you have identified the needs of your audience and designed modules to address those needs, your seminar is practically guaranteed to be effective.

An Example of MDA

Let's say you have decided to do a three-hour seminar called "How to Run Your First Marathon without Killing Yourself." Here is a step-by-step application of the MDA in putting together an effective seminar.

The first step is to interview members of the local running clubs who are training for a marathon, members of the local track team, Sunday joggers, or anyone else who might be interested in running a marathon. Ask them what a person needs to know to run his or her first marathon. Have them identify the one thing with which they are most concerned.

Let's say you get a random list that looks like this:

- Type of shoes to train in
- Foods to eat during training and marathon
- Training schedule
- Clothes to wear during marathon
- Time needed to train for the marathon
- What to do on marathon day
- How to choose the best marathon to run
- Protection from getting injured
- How to stay motivated
- How to avoid "hitting the wall"
- Special running gear
- Pain and difficulty in running a marathon

Suppose you found that the topic people identified most as their first priority was training.

With this information in hand, the modules for your seminar would be arranged as follows:

A. How to choose the best marathon to run

B. Shoes and running gear

C. Training schedule for your first marathon

D. Injuries, how to avoid them, and what to do

E. Peak performance and self-motivation techniques

F. What to do the day of the marathon

As you can see, these modules are the logical building blocks for the seminar. You can research each topic independently and develop each module with appropriate case studies, stories, participatory exercises, and so forth. For example, Module F could be broken down like this:

F. What to do the day of the marathon
   1. Wake-up time
   2. Physical and mental preparation
      a. Participatory exercise

3. Pacing yourself correctly
   a. The first few miles
   b. Predicting your finishing time
4. How to avoid "hitting the wall"
   a. Personal story
   b. Precautionary technique
   c. What to do if you do "hit the wall"
   d. Walking, water, and stretching
5. Recovering after the run

As you can see from this example, the modular design approach makes building a comprehensive and effective seminar a simple process. Master the MDA methodology, and you will be able to create new seminars quickly and easily.

!!! **Resource.**   If you want to deliver an outstanding seminar that has been designed and packaged with workbooks, visuals, and leader's guide, contact Sandy Karn with Creative Results Sources, Inc. You can choose from a wide variety of business and personal development topics. Optional programs are held throughout the country to teach you how to deliver the seminars.

To obtain more information on these "prepackaged" seminars, contact:

Sandy Karn, President
Creative Results Sources, Inc.
P.O. Box 405
Wheaton, IL 60189
Phone: (630) 668-2726 (Ask for Dept. 101 for special discounts)
www.resultsinfo.com

PART 2

How to Make Big Money in the Seminar Business

4

Your Passport to Marketing Success—TADA

Most seminar marketing plans don't work for one simple reason: failure to define accurately the target market. When I ask a potential seminar leader or promoter who his or her audience is, and that person replies, "Everybody," I know we're in big trouble. In most cases, marketing a program to *everybody* presents a monumental, usually insurmountable problem.

TADA—The Magic Marketing Formula

TADA stands for target audience design approach. TADA is the guiding light for successful seminar marketing. It is the reference point for developing a marketing plan. TADA will help you make decisions such as site selection, workbook design, fees, refreshments, advertising methods, brochure style, mailing-list selection, and practically anything else.

Successful program marketing depends upon making correct decisions, not arbitrary ones. Using your target audience as a reference point, you will automatically make the right choices.

It is easy to design a concise and efficient marketing plan based upon your target audience. For example, let's say you have a seminar called "How to Hire the Right People." It would be safe to say that the human resources department of small- to medium-sized companies would be the market. Since the average salary of a director of human resources for a company of this size is not in a high range, traveling from a great distance to attend this seminar is unlikely. Because of the nature of the seminar, industries that have a high employee turnover rate, such as retail sales, might be good candidates.

In the above example, the target audience was defined by a number of factors: industry, company size, department, position, and salary range.

How to Use the Target Audience Design Approach

With the above information in hand, you can now make educated marketing decisions. Using TADA, you can easily locate mailing lists of directors of human resources of large retail operations.

You might also examine the possibility of using advertising vehicles, such as trade magazines that your prospective audience might read. (In this case, you would use the trade magazine of the National Retail Merchants Association.) Of course, your seminar brochure would be designed with your target audience in mind, written in the language of the retail industry.

When you apply TADA to market your seminar, you spend your marketing dollar wisely. Use TADA to make all marketing decisions, and you can't lose.

Creating a Ten-Factor Profile of Your Target Audience

Here are ten criteria by which you can define your audience. For each category, try to think of the requirements that need to be met when pitching your seminar.

1. *Sex.* You will want to identify the ratio of men to women. If your audience is all or primarily men, an advertisement in the sports section of the Sunday newspaper might be an effective marketing vehicle. Similarly, if you are marketing a weight loss seminar to an audience that is primarily women, the life-style section of the newspaper would be the proper place for an ad.

2. *Age.* What age group are you targeting? When you are writing copy for your brochure, certain words and phrases will mean different things to different age groups. What might be perfect for baby boomers could be totally ineffective with the generation that precedes them.

3. *Place of residence.* Where does your target audience live? If your audience is urban, posters put up around town could work well. This marketing strategy would be much less effective in the suburbs.

4. *Industry.* Specific industries require specific seminars. A great example of this is the overnight shipping industry. Because of the constant time pressure employees feel, companies such as Federal Express provide an assortment of stress management seminars. Industries such as this

might also be a fertile market for seminars on similar topics, such as time management.

5. *Occupation.* Some occupations require specific ingredients in order to be successful. For example, seminars for chief executive officers (CEOs) might require exotic locations, such as Bermuda or Hawaii. Similarly, seminars for law enforcement officers might do best broken up into small segments or held on weekends.

6. *Education.* Although you might possess an MBA from Harvard Business School, your target audience might not have more than a high school diploma. Sometimes marketing material completely misses its mark because it fails to speak the language of the target audience.

7. *Position.* If you can identify the exact position of your target audience, you will be able to pinpoint the correct and most profitable mailing lists. For example, if you have a seminar for reducing business overhead, purchasing agents of large companies might be the mailing list to purchase.

8. *Income level.* Lots of seminar leaders who give programs on financial investment want to market their seminar to very wealthy people. The problem is that few people in this income group attend public seminars. Therefore, if you are seeking to market to this target audience, you must develop more creative strategies. One seminar leader on this topic travels to the various high-price health spas and does his program on this topic for "free." He walks away with valuable clients, which pays huge dividends.

9. *Career experience.* Is your program for entry-level employees or for those with more experience? One of the popular programs the American Management Association offers is geared for the newly appointed manager. By focusing their program on a specific experience level, they have tapped a lucrative market.

10. *Career skill needed for professional success.* Perhaps you know your market is for receptionists. Market telephone skills, and you will hit a valuable marketing "hot" button.

In many cases, one or two of these factors will weigh more heavily than the others. Use any or all, but make sure you use the laser beam marketing strategy of TADA.

$$$ **Saver.** Your most important money-saving strategy is TADA. With it you will avoid wasting marketing dollars. You will minimize risk when you advertise or use direct mail. In general, you will be able to make the best choices when it comes to promoting your seminar.

5
Choosing the Best Month, Day, and Time

It is crucial for you to choose the date and time for your seminar very carefully. Timing will have an immense impact on the attendance of your seminar.

Rules of Thumb When Choosing Your Month and Day

Although there are exceptions to every rule, follow these general guidelines when you are planning dates for your seminar.

1. *Avoid holidays of any kind.* This includes both national and religious holidays, as well as the vacation periods that normally fall around them. People get wrapped up in the preparations for holidays, are distracted by them, or travel to visit friends and family during holiday periods. For example, you should avoid the Friday after Thanksgiving and the days before Christmas and just after New Year's Day.

2. *Avoid major national events.* Although many of these events are of no interest to you personally, they preoccupy many members of your potential audience. Some examples of this type of event are the Super Bowl, the World Series, political conventions and elections, and even TV broadcasts like the Academy Awards.

3. *Avoid major local events.* Don't try to compete with such local events as county fairs and festivals and local sporting events. If a home-town college football team is playing a big game, be careful; you don't want to compete with this type of event.

4. *Be careful about weather conditions.*   Winter months, especially in certain regions, can pose threats to the success of your seminar. Particularly in urban areas, snow is seen as a major obstacle. It can cause a poor turnout of preregistered participants and wipe out most of your on-site registrations. To avoid a case such as this, you might want to schedule your event before or after the time period when you are most likely to get snowstorms.

5. *Remember TADA.*   Timing should take into account the requirements of your target audience as defined in the preceding chapter. For example, if you are planning a seminar for doctors, make sure the American Medical Association is not holding a convention or major meeting at the same time. Similarly, don't plan a seminar for accountants during the first part of April.

The Best (and Worst) Months of the Year to Hold and Promote Your Seminar

If you are promoting seminars, there are a few important guidelines to consider when choosing the date.

1. September and October are generally the best attended months for seminars. Perhaps it is a holdover from the school-year schedule that seminars seem to do best in the fall, the back-to-school time of year.

2. Early November works well, but be careful to avoid the week of Thanksgiving for reasons already explained.

3. The winter months of January, February, and March are good, except where weather conditions could make travel difficult. As mentioned, in areas such as the Northeast there is often hesitation, cancellation, or drop-off due to bad weather. Also, avoid the beginning of January, since it falls right after a holiday.

4. April and May are also generally good months for promoting seminars. There are no major holiday conflicts except for Memorial Day and Easter.

5. June, July, and August are not the best months for promoting seminars because many people take their vacations during these months.

6. Although very early December can work well, December is the least favorable month because of the preoccupation with the Christmas holiday.

)

The Best (and Worst) Days of the Week to Hold and Promote Your Seminar

In addition to the considerations already mentioned, here are guidelines for choosing the best day of the week to promote your seminar.

1. Tuesday, Wednesday, and Thursday are generally very good days to give seminars of any kind. The primary reason is that people often take three-day weekends and might be unavailable on Mondays and Fridays. Chances are good most people will be available during the heart of the workweek.

2. Friday is an excellent day to promote business seminars, especially if the fee is paid by the participant's business. Seminar registrants usually take advantage of a Friday seminar schedule to make their weekend begin early.

3. Saturday is an excellent day for personal-development seminars, since it avoids conflicts with business hours.

4. Sunday tends to be considered a family day or "day of rest" for many people. It can work for personal-development seminars, but the better choice is Saturday.

5. Monday is a get-back-to-work day. Most time-management research has proved that Mondays are stress filled and very busy. Consequently, you should avoid trying to put one more item on people's agendas. As a general rule, avoid Monday if you can.

Guidelines for Choosing the Best Time of Day

One final bit of fine tuning is in order when thinking about optimal timing. There are a few basic guidelines for choosing the time of the day to hold your seminar.

1. Traffic patterns must be considered. Make allowances for rush hour in major metropolitan areas.

2. Remember TADA. For example, if your audience consists of secretaries or receptionists, an 8 a.m. start is feasible, since they are accustomed to this hour. If your audience consists of homemakers with children, a 9 a.m. start would probably fit into their schedule more conveniently. They need the early morning hours to get children off to school and complete daily household chores.

3. Half-day seminars should be scheduled between the hours of 8 a.m. and 12:30 p.m. or 12:30 p.m. and 5 p.m.

4. Full-day seminars should start no later than 9 a.m. and end preferably before 5 p.m. People like to get a jump on traffic. Starting at about 4 p.m. they begin to fidget in their seats or apologetically start to leave early, no matter how good you are.

5. If you are promoting a multiday program, there will probably be participants using air transportation. You can end the first day between 4 p.m. and 5 p.m., but plan to end the final day by 4 p.m. at the latest so that people will have time to get to the airport and make their plane connections.

6. Evening seminars should be scheduled between 6 p.m. and 10 p.m. The best hours in the evening are between 6:30 p.m. and 9:30 p.m. Most people need time to grab some dinner after work and travel to the seminar location and would prefer not to return home too late in the evening.

7. It is always preferable to reduce the number of days for which a program is scheduled and extend the hours. There are two reasons for this strategy. First, many participants find it difficult to devote a number of days to attending a seminar. Second, you will want to use your time efficiently. Whether you spend 2 hours or 6 hours on a given day at a seminar, you essentially spend the whole day. Therefore, two 6-hour days is more efficient than four 3-hour days.

8. If you are presenting your seminar to a local audience and your TADA profile reveals that participants will not be traveling great distances, do not present multiday evening seminars on consecutive nights. If you do, there is an increased chance that participants will have schedule conflicts. Book your seminar on alternate weekday evenings or on the same day on consecutive weeks.

9. Personal-development seminars are best presented in the evening hours to avoid conflicts with work. Your participants are less likely to get time off for a seminar that is not work-related.

10. Finally, schedule business seminars to end early in the afternoon. For those who are busy and conscientious, they will have time to get back to their office or job. For those who are looking for a reason to end the day a little early, your seminar might be just the right ticket.

6
How to Choose the Best Seminar Site

The All-Important Question

What site will increase your attendance or make your seminar most profitable?

Here we come back to TADA. Choose a site with your target audience in mind. Are your attendees high-level executives who not only can afford but also expect to spend their time in an attractive, upscale, possibly exotic location? Are you marketing a seminar to an audience who would be more likely to attend if your program was conveniently located in the center of the city? Or would your audience be more drawn to a beautiful, natural setting?

Assuming you are familiar with your target audience, you probably have some good ideas about what type of location would be most likely to appeal to them.

!!! **Contacts.** The Yellow Pages in Part 4 of this book contains a list of over 1200 hotels in major seminar markets that are equipped for seminars. They have facilities that are designed to accommodate your needs.

Most seminars are held in meeting rooms at hotels throughout the world, but some seminars are routinely held at resort settings such as Club Med, on Caribbean cruise ships, and at retreat centers in mountain wilderness areas. To find out about these exotic sites, you might have to do some research on the Internet.

In the past 20 years, a new type of seminar location has evolved—the conference center. These facilities are specially built to accommodate meetings and seminars. They have been designed to maximize program effectiveness and convenience. The accommodations, business services, audiovisual equipment, and facility location provide the perfect environment for holding seminars.

!!! **Contact.** For a list of conference centers and for more information on the conference center concept, you can contact:

The International Association of Conference Centers
243 North Lindbergh Blvd.
St. Louis, MO 63141
Phone: (314) 993-8575
Fax: (314) 993-8919
www.iacconline.com

Criteria for Choosing a Seminar Location

1. *Population.* As in any form of marketing, you want to choose locations with significant populations. There is no magic size for a city to qualify as a good location for a seminar, but generally any city with a population of a million or more is a viable site.

Of course, there are many excellent cities for seminars that have populations of fewer than a million. Usually these cities draw from a greater metropolitan area. San Francisco and northern New Jersey are good examples of densely populated areas that fit this description.

2. *Accessibility to transportation.* If your audience will be arriving by plane, it is important to choose a city with daily, nonstop flights. Air access is especially important if you have to attract an audience from diverse parts of the country. However, surveys show that the majority of seminar participants travel 100 miles or less. Therefore, you should consider locations that have easy and convenient access by car or public transportation.

3. *Economic conditions.* Although you might choose an area or city that has a substantial population, it is important to consider the community's economic base. The presence of the following institutions or conditions are favorable signs: Fortune 500 companies, large universities and colleges, a wide variety of first-class hotels, an active chamber of commerce and/or convention center, and low unemployment.

4. *Charisma.* Ask yourself this question, "When I think of this city what do I think of?" Your answer to this simple question will give you a good idea of what others will think when you advertise your seminar in this location. Bayonne, New Jersey, is my hometown, but, although it is quite a beautiful place, thanks to lots of Johnny Carson jokes very few people view it as such. Similarly, cities such as Miami or Las Vegas evoke images that will have either a positive or negative effect on your marketing efforts, depending on your target audience. Availability of entertainment, such as sporting events, theater, and other cultural activities, contribute to the charisma of a city and should also be considered when choosing a city as a seminar location.

Guidelines for Evaluating a Facility

The seminar facility you choose can help to make or break the success of your seminar. You will want to choose a location that will provide your participants with a location that is both convenient and comfortable. In addition, you will want to choose a facility that is cost-effective without sacrificing quality. The simplest way to evaluate and choose a facility for your seminar is to ask the following questions.

Site Location

1. How far is the facility from the airport, both in traveling time and in distance? If people will be flying from other cities to attend your seminar, you will want to choose a facility that is easy to reach from the airport where they will arrive. (See the Yellow Pages in Part 4 for locations close to the airports in most of the major seminar cities across the United States.)

2. Is direct transportation available to the facility from the airport? Many hotels and conference centers will provide shuttle service to the facility free of charge. When you are calling or visiting a location, be sure to ask if they provide this service. It may help you to make your final decision.

3. Is there convenient and adequate on-site parking available? If people will be driving to the location, you will want to provide easy parking. Although many facilities will provide parking, many do not. If on-site parking is not adequate, you will need to direct your participants to nearby, reasonably priced parking.

Site Facilities and Services

4. Is there an adequate number of sleeping rooms available? If your seminar site is a meeting room in a hotel, there will probably be lots of sleeping rooms. However, if there is another big meeting at the hotel or if there is a major convention in town, there may not be any rooms available. In these instances, you might not be able to accommodate the people who will be attending your event. Find out.

5. Does the facility have recreational facilities, such as a pool, health club, golf course, and tennis courts, to help attract participants? Many people view seminars as an opportunity to get away from work, and they look forward to spending some fun time while they are away. All other things being equal, a facility that offers these activities is preferred.

6. Are the sleeping rooms well furnished and do they have room to spread out? Many hotels that cater to business groups have rooms large enough for spreading out papers or provide a desk area with Internet connection where work can be done. If your seminar is a multiday program with homework, room size might be important.

7. Is room service available? If your participants will be arriving late in the evening after the restaurants are closed, this can be especially important. Also, many people prefer room service when they are traveling alone.

8. Are the public areas neat and clean? Like it or not, the cleanliness of the facility is a reflection on you. Often, participants will spend more time in the public areas than in their sleeping rooms. When you are performing a site inspection, observe these public areas carefully.

9. Are the front desk personnel and bellhops courteous and efficient? Once again, the staff members at the site location are part of your team. Make sure they reflect positively on you.

10. Are the elevators quick and large enough? Elevators that are slow or inadequate could result in delays that affect your program schedule.

11. Are there other events, seminars, or conferences scheduled before, during, or after your program? A very busy seminar site can put a strain on the overall service.

12. Is the sales or banquet office service-oriented and, in general, helpful? You will be able to get a good idea of the kind of overall service available by the way the people you contact at the sales office treat you.

13. Are there a variety of meeting rooms to choose from? If you get a larger number of registrants than you projected, it is comforting to know that there will be a larger meeting room available.

14. Is there storage available if you want to ship materials ahead? If you have a considerable amount of material to ship ahead, make sure the facility has adequate storage space.

The Meeting Room

15. Are the heating and cooling systems in the meeting rooms efficient? Find out how the temperature is controlled. Make sure it is easy to adjust the temperature, if necessary.

16. Are the meeting rooms sufficiently soundproof? The easiest way to check this out is to turn on a portable radio or CD player in the meeting room adjacent to the one you are considering for rental. You'll know how soundproof your room is by listening to the volume level from your room.

17. Are the ceilings high enough in the meeting rooms? Meeting rooms with low ceilings can be claustrophobic, especially if there will be a large group of people attending your program.

Audiovisual Equipment

18. What audiovisual equipment is included with the room rental? Many meeting facilities provide some simple audiovisual equipment with the room. Ask before you rent the room. This complementary equipment can result in hundreds of dollars of savings to you.

19. Does the facility provide its own audiovisual equipment, or do they use an outside vendor? If the facility provides the equipment, it will be easier to make last-minute changes in equipment. In some cases, rentals can be less expensive when the facility provides the equipment.

20. What is the full menu of audiovisual equipment available on-site, and what are the charges? Ask for a complete price list for equipment rental. Certain equipment, such as video projectors, might be extremely expensive. In such cases, it might be more cost-effective to bring your own.

Additional Amenities

21. Are any added conveniences, such as pencils, pads, water setups, and mints, provided in the meeting rooms? Sometimes it's the little things that make the big impression.

22. What specific food and beverages are available for meals and breaks, and what are the costs? You will need to know what is available and the costs in order to budget your expenses.

23. Does the facility have a good restaurant on-site, or are some located nearby? This is especially important if your program is one day or more in length.

24. Do the meeting rooms have comfortable chairs and well-designed tables for working on and taking notes?

25. Is there easy access to telephones and other business equipment, such as fax and copy machines?

What About Meals and Refreshments?

There is no conclusive evidence that including meals or refreshments will increase registrations. But there are some general guidelines that can help you make your decision.

1. If networking and sharing are important to the participants, including lunch or dinner could increase the profitability of the seminar.

2. People expect coffee and tea at seminars that start first thing in the morning. It is best to include these beverages. Be sure to mention it in your brochure.

3. Order your coffee by the gallon; it will save you money.

4. If you order soft drinks or juices for afternoon refreshments, ask to be charged by consumption.

5. Making meals an option may work the best. Some people would rather use lunch to make telephone calls, take a walk, or spend one-on-one time with another participant.

6. Lunch generally costs between $15 and $20. If you decide to include lunch, make the proper adjustments when you are pricing your program.

7. When you are ordering food of any kind, give regard to the current trends in eating habits. In general, people are eating with more attention to health and nutrition. Many people are vegetarians, avoid soft drinks, and drink decaffeinated coffee. When you order food of any kind, include the healthy alternatives. If you don't, resentments can develop.

Rules to Guarantee the Best Meeting Room Price

1. *Follow the principle of buy small, sell big.*   This rule says that when you are buying a product or service, you should always appear small while negotiating for the best price. Don't puff yourself up or try to impress the hotel or facility staff when you are reserving space. Instead, say "Well, I'm planning a little meeting. I'm not really sure how many people we're going to get..." On the other hand, when you are selling your seminar, emphasize your credibility and how big you are.

2. *Emphasize the fact that if things go well, you will be a repeat customer.* Although staff members at many hotels constantly change, the fact that they might be able to book you again will appeal to them and give them the justification they need to reduce the rate.

3. *Utilize the sleeping rooms and catering department at the hotel.*   Your leverage will increase if you rent sleeping rooms or buy food. The more you spend in these two areas, the lower your room rental will be. In fact, it is not unusual to get your meeting room *free of charge* if your expenditures in these other areas are significant. If you know your group will be occupying a considerable number of rooms, open your negotiations with this fact.

4. *Remember, there is no set price.*   There is an old adage that says that you can negotiate anything. In the business of contracting a facility for your seminar, this is the rule, not the exception. In most cases, the facility would rather reduce the room rental rate than leave the rooms empty. Correspondingly, during a busy period, you will have more difficulty negotiating.

!!! **Resources.**   The following two resources are excellent sources for information on new sites and on developments in the meeting industry.

Meeting Professionals International
4455 LBJ Freeway—Ste 1200
Dallas, TX 75244
Phone: (972) 702-3000
Fax: (972) 702-3070
www.mpiweb.org

Successful Meetings
770 Broadway
New York, NY 10003
Phone: (646) 654-4400
www.successmtgs.com

Meeting Professionals International (MPI) is an organization of professional meeting planners. It provides a wide variety of educational programs and an extremely sophisticated magazine. There is an annual national convention, and local chapters exist in all major cities.

Successful Meetings is a monthly publication that provides valuable current information relevant to the meeting industry.

After You Have Booked Your Meeting Room

You will want to send out a confirmation agreement to describe and confirm the arrangements you have made on the phone. In addition, it is a good idea to include a simple layout of the exact setup you would like. See Figure 19-1 in Chapter 19 for an example of a sample layout.

Figure 6-1 illustrates a basic confirmation form. This form will act as a letter of agreement. It will eliminate any chance for confusion in your verbal negotiations and can help minimize problems the day of your event. You can customize this agreement to suit your specific needs.

Meeting Facility Confirmation
(Your Letterhead)

To: _____(Contact name)_____

_____(Facility)_____

_____(Address)_____

_____

Meeting date(s) _____

Meeting hours _____

List meeting as _____

Food and beverage service:

Date	Time	Refreshment	Quantity
_____	_____	_____	_____
_____	_____	_____	_____
_____	_____	_____	_____

Please refresh the water and the room at __(Time).__

Please set up the room for _____ people. (See attached diagram for the setup.)

Please provide the following audiovisual equipment.

No.   Description

_____ Microphone _____

_____ Overhead projector _____

_____ Slide projector _____

_____ Flipchart _____

_____ LCD projector _____

_____ Screen _____

_____ Video monitor _____

_____ Audiocassette monitor _____

_____ Other _____

As per our agreement, charges will be:

Room rental $_____

Food and beverage service $_____

Audiovisual $_____

Guest room rental $_____

Please feel free to call me with any questions.

Thank you.

Sincerely,

Figure 6-1. Sample of a meeting facility confirmation letter.

7

How to Set Your Fee and Get It

Guidelines for Setting Your Fee

Here are the basic factors you must consider when you set your fee. Of course, with experience, your fee can easily be adjusted and fine-tuned for optimum profitability.

1. *Research the competition.* Identify seminars that are being offered to the same target audience or on the same topic as yours. Study their pricing schedules. Do as many comparison studies as you can. Make sure you are using established seminars. Otherwise, it might be a case of the inexperienced leading the inexperienced.

2. *Give perceived value.* If you are offering enough perceived added value, you can increase your fee proportionately. You can add value with take-home manuals, reference materials, books, tapes, and follow-up consulting.

3. *Use the target audience design approach.* Consider the financial situation of your target audience. For example, if you are promoting seminars on telephone skills for receptionists, you might not be able to charge as much as you could if you are promoting seminars on the development of an international marketing plan for business executives.

4. *Establish the participant-to-profitability factor.* Let's say your seminar fee is $50 and you attract 100 people. If you increase your fee to $100, you attract only 60 people. Even though you have reduced the number of participants by 40 percent, your gross has increased by 20 percent. In this case, it would be more profitable to double the fee.

5. *Play the numbers game.* Sometimes the number of participants is more important than seminar fee profits. If your real profits come from spin-off products and services, it would be better to lower the seminar fee.

The game of selling is largely a numbers game. If you are selling books, tapes, consulting service, or more intensive seminars, you'll want to play the numbers game.

Many seminar leaders conduct introductory seminars for free or for $10 or $20 and use that technique to introduce themselves and their program to their target audience. At the introductory event, they offer another more intensive—and usually more expensive—program. In effect, they are marketing one seminar with another seminar. The introductory event is an investment for the second seminar. (There is more about this two-step promotion strategy in Chapter 12.)

6. *Test your price.* Try two different prices for your seminar and see which price works better. It's easy to do. First print two sets of brochures that are identical except for the price. Then mail to your target audience using different mailing lists, or use the same mailing list and distinguish among the different zip codes. Use the results of this test to help determine your fee.

7. *Measure success by the ratio of return on your marketing dollar.* Your fee and your gross receipts are important, but they do not measure your profitability. Your success is determined by the ratio of return on your marketing dollar. A return of $3 for every $1 spent is considered good. A return of $4 is great.

Group Discounts

Group discounts are excellent incentives for increasing seminar enrollment. Here are a few ways to take advantage of this strategy:

- Offer a discount to participants when they enroll in groups of two or more. For example, if the seminar fee is $100 and two people sign up together, you can drop the tuition to $90 per person.

- Offer one free registration to any organization or individual who signs up three or more people. In effect, you are offering a scholarship program. In doing so, you are creating an incentive program for seminar enrollment.

- When appropriate, offer discounts to couples.

Don't Forget Early Bird Specials

The best way to start seeing a quick return on your investment is to offer discounts for early registration. It will be well worth the 10 percent or 15 percent off to get some money coming back to you as soon as possible. For example, if your registration fee is $195, offer it for $175 to anyone who registers two weeks or more in advance.

Using the Magic-9 Technique

Have you ever wondered why so many products and services are priced at $9.95, $99, or $195? The answer is simple. It works.

Human behavior is fascinating to study. Just think how different you feel about these two numbers: $99.95 and $100.10. Marketing research has proved a substantially larger number of people will buy at the $99.95 price. The difference is only 15 cents, but the cost is perceived to be more than that.

It's a good idea to price your seminar using the magic-9 technique.

Special Pricing Issues for In-House Seminars

Setting fees for in-house seminars is really a matter of what the traffic will bear. Corporations, businesses, and large organizations generally pay between $1500 and $3500 for a full day seminar. Local adult education programs are accustomed to paying considerably less, usually a few hundred dollars.

Sometimes an organization will promote your seminar, but they are unsure how successful it will be. In these cases you can ask for a minimum payment with the stipulation that you will get a bonus if the seminar draws *more than* a certain number of participants. To determine the fee you will be able to charge there are three helpful questions you can ask the sponsor.

1. "How many people will be attending?" Generally, the larger the anticipated audience, the bigger the budget is likely to be.

2. "What have you paid your seminar leaders in the past?" Whatever people have paid in the past they are likely to pay again in the future.

3. "What are the participants paying for the program?" If the organization sponsoring the seminar is charging a fairly high fee, it will likely mean more money for you. Conversely, if you have been asked to speak at a local chapter of a professional association, the fee is more likely to be modest.

How to Negotiate the Highest Fee for Your In-House Seminar

You should have a published fee schedule. The published fee is the price you charge to give your seminar.

The price for a full-day seminar and a half-day should not be that far apart. For example, you might charge $3000 for a half-day seminar and

$3500 for a full-day seminar. The logic for this close pricing is very simple. If you do a half-day seminar in Columbus, Ohio, it is unlikely you will be able to deliver another program that day. Even though you have only spoken for a half day, your whole day has been consumed.

You need a second published price for local programs. For programs you can drive to and return home the same day, a price schedule might be $2000 for a half-day seminar and $2500 for a full-day seminar. You can afford to charge less for local programs because you will not have to spend as much time traveling. You also avoid the inconvenience of air travel.

Sometimes the organization that wants you to speak will pay the fee without hesitation, and other times they will be unable to pay your fee. Expect both reactions.

When they can't pay your published fee, ask, "What are you prepared to pay?" At this point negotiations have begun, and you will have to decide how much you want to take the assignment. Until you are established, it is always best to try to take every program you possibly can.

As your reputation and credibility grow, you will negotiate less often and receive your published fee on a more regular basis.

Aside from the fee, make sure the sponsoring organization pays for all travel expenses. *Fees should always be separate from your expenses.* The reason is very simple. You can quickly lose a large share of your fee if you are paying your own way.

When delivering an in-house seminar, you can add profits by charging for your workbooks. Depending upon the quality of your materials, you can charge anywhere from $10 to $100 per person. If you have a book available, you can offer to provide it to all the participants as seminar materials. Even a small markup of $2 or $3 can add up to $500 or $1000 for the day if there are 200 or 300 participants at your program.

If you have a handout of a few pages, the best policy is to offer the masters to the program director and allow the organization to reproduce the handout at their cost.

After you have agreed upon all the financial details, send a contract or letter of agreement. Figure 7-1 illustrates a sample letter of agreement that works well.

Company and Personal Checks

It is difficult, if not impossible, to be in the seminar business without taking checks. Many times you will not be able to wait for them to clear. In most cases this will not be a problem; the vast majority of checks will be fine.

If businesses are sending people to your seminar, you will probably have to bill them and wait. Although sometimes it seems like forever, you will usually get your check within 30 to 60 days. If you don't, give them a call. Your billing or your check probably got lost somewhere, possibly in the mail.

Why You *Must* Accept Credit Cards

Statistics show that as much as 50 percent of your registrations may be paid by credit cards. As a general rule, accepting credit cards will increase your enrollments by up to 20 percent. You cannot afford not to take credit cards.

Credit cards will also help you capture much of the spin-off business in products and services at the seminar itself, when participants are most inspired to make purchases. Many participants attend a seminar without their checkbooks, but few will be there without their credit cards.

Another advantage of accepting credit cards is that they serve as a guarantee for check payments. When you take a check, write the applicant's credit card number on it.

The most common credit cards are Visa, MasterCard, and American Express. So be prepared to accept these three cards for payment.

Opening a Credit Card Merchant's Account—It's Simple

In order to take credit card payments, you will need to open a merchant's account. For Visa and MasterCard, first check with your local bank. Many banks have been the victims of credit card fraud and consequently are reluctant to give you a merchant's account. You might have to get on the phone and start checking around at other banks. Each bank has its own criteria for determining whether you qualify.

One important criteria for determining whether or not you qualify to receive a merchant's account is that you do no mail-order business. I repeat *no mail order*. Mail order has been one of the major areas where the credit card companies have been ripped off and they don't want to get burned any more.

In recent years many companies have risen to meet the demand for small business credit card processing services. Most of these companies provide you with the opportunity to offer all of the major credit cards.

It is worth your time to do some comparison shopping. The difference in processing charges can mean substantial amounts of money to you. Here are some companies you can explore.

LETTER OF AGREEMENT
Between
Paul Karasik Associates and XYZ Company

Dear _____:

Subject: Sweet-Persuasion Selling Seminar

Paul Karasik will speak to your group on _____. The location
                                              (Date)
will be _____ in _____ , _____.
      (Hotel or training facility)   (City)   (State)

This presentation will be _____ in length. It will
begin at _____ and end at _____.

The fee for this presentation will be _____ plus expenses, which include round-trip air fare from Newark International Airport in Newark, New Jersey (it may not be necessary to include the state); hotel; meals; and ground transportation.

You will receive one master copy of the handout material, which will be tailored to your organization's program. This will be mailed 30 days prior to the program date. This master copy will then be reproduced by you in sufficient number for each participant to receive one copy.

Paul Karasik Associates reserves the right to make available for sale books and learning cassette programs.

No tape recorder, audio or visual, may be used without the expressed, prior written permission of Paul Karasik.

Upon receipt of a 10 percent deposit of _____ and this signed letter, the proposed date will be reserved for you.

The balance of _____ will be given to Paul Karasik prior to the presentation. All expenses will be billed.

Paul Karasik Associates   XYZ Company

By: _____ Pres. By: _____
                          Dated: _____

Figure 7-1. This example shows an agreement used by the author and is for illustrative purposes only. To ensure maximum protection, you should seek professional legal help in drafting an agreement that best covers your specific needs.

www.buyerzone.com will provide you with free quotes from a variety of different vendors.

www.merchantexpress.com will set up low-cost processing for all major credit cards.

www.Internetsecure.com will provide you with the ability to process secure, on-line, real-time credit card orders.

www.paypal.com is the number one on-line payment service for products and services that are sold over the Internet.

You can also check with the following credit card companies directly:

American Express
(800) 528-5200
www.americanexpress.com

Discover Card
(800) 347-6673
www.discovercard.com

Diner's Club & Carte Blanche
(800) 525-7376
www.dinersclub.com

8

How to Create a Winning Brochure

Regardless of the type of program you are marketing, a printed promotional announcement of your program is necessary. This could be anything from a simple flyer or letter format to a multicolor, multipage booklet. For the sake of simplicity, let's refer to your printed marketing piece as your brochure.

The First Step Is Easy

The easiest way to create a winning brochure is to first collect a lot of other brochures. Most successful seminar companies have developed their brochure as a result of many years of trial and error or by spending thousands of dollars on market research studies or both. Why not save your money and reap the benefits of their efforts?

$$$ Saver.   You can refer to the list of public seminar companies in the Yellow Pages in Part 4. Here are a few good companies to start with. Ask to be put on their mailing list.

American Management Association
Phone: (212) 586-8100
www.amanet.org

Career Track
Phone: (800) 944-8503
www.careertrack.com

Franklin Covey Company
Phone: (800) 827-1776
www.franklincovey.com

Skillpath
Phone: (913) 362-1207
www.skillpath.com

Tompeterscompany!
Phone: (513) 683-4702
www.tompeters.com

National Seminars Group
Phone: (800) 258-7246
www.Natsem.com

Using the TADA Strategy

You can put the target audience design approach strategy to work again when creating your brochure. For example, let's say you're marketing a program to lawyers. This is a very conservative profession. Lawyers are in the business of both the written and the spoken word. Much of the material that comes across the desk of a lawyer is in black and white, or perhaps pastel green. The type style is usually Times Roman or Helvetica.

Brochure copy addressed to lawyers must be precise, and any claims must be substantiated with facts or proof. A brochure for lawyers should be written in their language and appropriate to their sensibilities. All creative design decisions should be based on the fact that the target audience is lawyers.

On the other hand, in accordance with the TADA strategy, if you are offering an expensive seminar to a very select group at an exotic location, it would be important to invest in an impressive marketing piece. For example, if you are offering a medical seminar to doctors on a new procedure or technical development at a resort in Hawaii, it might be appropriate to develop an expensive, high-quality, multicolor brochure.

Don't forget to focus on the benefits your target audience will receive when they attend your seminar. Include any and all specific information that will attract your target audience.

Speak the verbal language of your target audience, and visually present the information in a manner that makes them feel comfortable. Your brochure should make the recipient feel that "you are one of them." The target audience should conclude from your brochure that you know them, you know their problems, and you will provide the answers to those problems at your seminar.

Design Your Brochure to Be Electronically Friendly

You will undoubtedly be asked to send your brochure electronically using email and fax. Keep this in mind while you are designing your brochure or you will create unnecessary difficulties when you attempt to send it using these methods.

If your brochure has large sections that are covered with ink creating darkened areas, the fax machines will slow down dramatically. It's OK to use color and design your brochure to look attractive, but be careful not to use too much. If you can't avoid using lots of ink, it is a good idea to create a fax version that is designed with the fax in mind. It will be worth your investment of both time or money. Your fax-friendly version should contain the identical copy but with simplified graphics.

You will also need to offer your brochure in a portable document format, or PDF, version for sending via email. You can even offer your brochure in a variation that can be completed for seminar registration purposes. Your brochure can also refer the prospect to your secure Web site for registration.

The Big-Six Brochure Questions

1. *What kind of paper?*   Glossy or plain? Heavy-weight or standard bond? White or colored? Paper comes in a wide range of thicknesses, colors, and styles. Standard bond (regular typewiter paper) is the least expensive and works well in most cases. On the other hand, if your seminar is a corporate program, glossy paper might be a better choice. If you come across a particular paper you like, bring it to your printer and ask for a quote. Be aware that special paper can add considerably to your printing costs.

$$$ Saver.   You can often get a discount on high-quality paper if you ask the printer to let you know if he or she will be making any big purchases of such paper for other jobs. By tacking your order onto another job, you will get a quantity discount. This strategy for saving money works when you want to use paper of a higher quality than your printer normally stocks.

!!! Resource.   This is a great Web site to learn all about paper as well as design, ink, and lots of other useful information about printing.

www.Book-Printing-Tips.com
Phone: (800) 373-2001

2. *How many colors of ink?*   One color, two colors, or four colors? The addition of each color will increase your overhead costs. If you intend to use one color and have photographs in your brochure, use black ink. Whenever possible, however, use two colors. Two colors add a lot to the overall look of your brochure.

If you will be using your brochure to market to high-level corporate executives or to an upscale audience, or if you want to impress the person who receives the brochure, using lots of color can be very effective.

3. *How big should it be?*   8 by 10 in or 11 by 17 in? Should it be one, six, or eight pages? How will it be folded? Again, economics will play a part in your decision. Each additional page will add to the typesetting, printing, and mailing costs.

4. *What kind of typeface is optimal?*   There are many type styles. Before you choose a printer, make sure he or she has a variety of available type styles from which to choose. Ask for samples.

Choose a typeface that is simple and easy to read. Figure 8-1 shows some typefaces that are excellent for brochure copy.

This is an example of Helvetica typeface.
This is an example of Times Roman typeface.
This is an example of Souvenir typeface.
This is an example of Bookman typeface.
This is an example of Century Old Style typeface.

Figure 8-1. Samples of different styles of typefaces that could be used for brochure copy.

5. *What is the best visual style?* Should you use graphics? Should you use photographs or illustrations? Should there be lots of text or lots of white space?

Graphic design is an art in itself. You have two choices. You can do it yourself or hire a professional. With a little study and a simple straightforward approach based upon professional brochures you have collected, you will be able to design your own brochure. The books listed at the end of this chapter will help you do this.

$$$ Saver. The printing business is fiercely competitive. Many printers have creative design capabilities on-site and will be willing to help you make layout and design decisions for no additional charge.

On the other hand, if you have an adequate budget, your other choice is to hire a professional. Many printers have a design department on-site. If your printer doesn't offer design and layout services, the chances are good you will be referred to a graphic designer. If all else fails, the Yellow Pages of the telephone book provide many choices.

6. *Will you be using an envelope or a self-mailer?* If your brochure is going to be designed as a multipage letter, an envelope is perfect. An envelope gives your mailing a more personal touch.

A self-mailer will save you money. The cost of envelopes can add up quickly when you are mailing thousands of brochures. You will also have to pay your mailing house additional money for stuffing envelopes.

Figure 8-2 illustrates the most common designs for self-mailer brochures.

Principles for Writing Sensational Copy

The basic principles for writing brochure copy are very simple.

1. *Keep your benefits and objectives specific and straightforward.* If you will be teaching 12 ways to save time, say that. If you will be teaching people 17 ways to make money in real estate, say it.

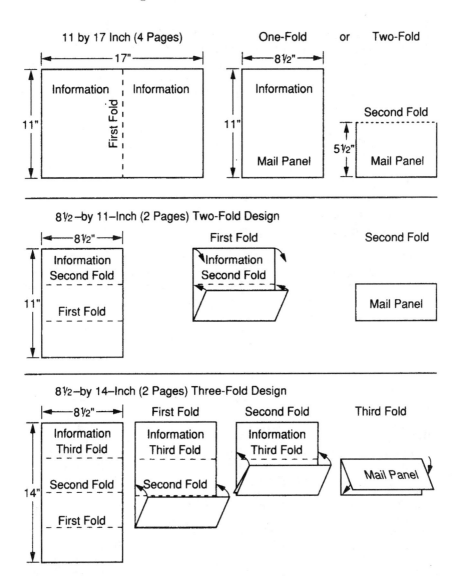

Figure 8-2. Examples of three types of self-mailer brochure designs.

2. *Write copy that is short and snappy.* People do not think or speak in complete sentences. The purpose of your brochure is to persuade people to attend your seminar. For this purpose, a conversational tone works best. The best example of persuasive copy can be found in advertising copy. Study the short, precise style you see in advertisements in newspapers and magazines. Use this style as a model for your brochure.

3. *Repeat your benefits throughout your brochure.* Remember, you are selling information that will help make people's lives better. This is the reason they are willing to pay for your seminar. They are not particularly interested in hearing you speak, no matter how eloquent you are. Put your benefits on the brochure cover, and repeat them as often as possible throughout the brochure.

4. *Use powerful, action-oriented words.* The best words are ones that sell. The Instant Brochure Copy Generator that follows is a gold mine of "power-speak."

How to Use the Instant Brochure Copy Generator]

If you get bogged down trying to describe your seminar, you can consult the following Instant Brochure Copy Generator. The verbs and verb forms in column A are action oriented. The adjectives in column B are benefit oriented. The nouns in column C are implicitly results oriented. You can put together dynamic phrases by combining words from each column, for example, create effective attitudes, achieving competitive quality, and mastering professional relationships.

Instant Brochure Copy Generator

Column A	Column B	Column C
Achieving	Accessible	Abilities
Alert	Administrative	Advances
Answering	Authoritative	Alternatives
Anticipating	Automatic	Attitudes
Assessing	Basic	Awareness
Avoid	Careful	Behavior
Benefiting	Comprehensive	Benchmarks
Building	Competitive	Benefits
Capitalize	Creative	"Bible"
Cash-in	Critical	Blunders
Centering	Definitive	Breakthroughs
Clarify	Dramatic	Challenges
Compare	Dynamic	Change
Confirming	Effective	Climate
Conquering	Executive	Clues
Create	Expansive	Competence
Dealing	Free	Consensus
Demystify	Fresh	Control
Detailing	Full	Culprit
Diagnose	Hands-on	Decisions
Eliminate	Hidden	Development
Evaluating	High-level	Diagnostics
Expanding	Human	Direction

Column A	Column B	Column C
Explode	Immediate	Education
Exploring	Incisive	Effectiveness
Expose	Incremental	Evaluation
Facilitating	Individual	Feedback
Focusing	Individualized	Focus
Gain	In-house	Frontiers
Grasp	Intelligent	Fulfillment
Guarantee	Intensive	Fundamentals
Highlighting	Interpersonal	Gain
Implementing	Key	Goals
Increase	Latest	Growth
Influencing	Lucid	Highlight
Initiate	Mutual	Impact
Integrating	New	Interaction
Investing	No-nonsense	Intervention
Learn	Nuts-and-bolts	Keys
Mastering	Organizational	Kit
Maximize	Original	Landmark
Measuring	Penetrating	Mastery
Monitoring	Personal	Measures
Motivating	Powerful	Mine fields
Negotiating	Practical	Models
Optimize	Professional	Needs
Pinpoint	Proven	Nightmares
Planning	Safe	Objectives
Preclude	Self	Performance
Preempt	Shrewd	Pipeline
Probe	Simple	Planning
Profile	Sophisticated	Potential
Providing	Sound	Power
Receive	Special	Practices
Rethinking	Staff	Prerequisites
Revealing	State-of-the-art	Principles
Sharpen	Step-by-step	Priorities
Shatter	Straight	Problems
Short-circuit	Strategic	Process
Stimulate	Supervisory	Productivity
Strengthening	Targeted	Quality
Survey	Team	Relationships
Tackle	Tested	Research
Tap	Timely	Resources
Target	Tough	Results
Test	Unprecedented	Revelations
Uncover	Vital	Secrets
Understanding	Winning	Skills
Unlocking	Workable	Strategies
Zero in		Styles
		Target
		Techniques
		Theory
		Time

Twenty-Three-Point Brochure Checklist

The easiest way to construct an effective brochure is to break it down into small modules. If you take your time to build each component well, the end result will be a first-class brochure. Here is a list of the necessary components.

- □ *Title.* Choose a title that is clear and direct. A title that starts with "How to..." can work well in a wide variety of situations. Of course, it's always best to convey the benefit of your seminar in the title whenever possible. Some examples of simple and effective titles for business-sector audiences are "Managing Multiple Priorities," "Stress Management Seminar for Secretaries," "How to Handle Difficult People," and "How to Take Control of Your Workday."

- □ *Hook.* Like the title, the hook should focus the reader on the benefits. Here are some examples of titles with hooks.

  Title: "How to Supervise People"
  Hook: Learn techniques to get results through people.
  Title: "Successful Selling Techniques"
  Hook: Learn how to close more sales.
  Title: "How to Manage Your Advertising"
  Hook: Make your advertising really contribute to profits.
  Title: "How to Enter the World of Professional Speaking"
  Hook: Begin a profitable and exciting career now.

- □ *Date, time, and location(s).* Believe it or not, many brochures have been printed without this information.

- □ *Benefits.* The best place to put your benefits is everyplace. Start right on the front page, and continue on throughout the copy. People must be reminded about how much better they'll feel, how much money they'll make, or how their professional or personal life will improve, thanks to your program.

- □ *Who should attend?* Identify the exact audience that will profit from your program. This lets readers know the program will be geared to their particular needs. After a title such as "How to Give Telephone Customer Service," you might include the following:

  Who Should Attend? Receptionists, Administrative Assistants, and Customer Service Representatives

  In some cases, it might even be useful to start the copy of a brochure by targeting the intended audience. For example:

Attention: Separated, Divorced, or Widowed Men and Women
Then continue with the title, "Letting Go of a Relationship."

▫ *What your participants will learn.* In this portion you list the specific top-ics that will be addressed in the program. This section is straightfor-ward. Use action verbs, and list the specific strategies, techniques, skills, and measurable results the participants will receive from your seminar. Use the Instant Brochure Copy Generator to help you write this section.

▫ *Program schedule.* Although it is not essential, you might want to list the complete agenda of what will be covered during the day. For exam-ple:

9:00 a.m.-10:30 a.m.	Personal writing evaluations
10:30 a.m.-10:45 a.m.	Coffee break
10:45 a.m.-12:00 noon	Creative writing techniques
12:00 noon-1:00 p.m.	Lunch
1:00 p.m.-2:30 p.m.	How to overcome writer's block
2:30 p.m.-2:45 p.m.	Afternoon break
2:45 p.m.-4:00 p.m.	How to market your writing
4:00 p.m.-4:10 p.m.	Break
4:10 p.m.-5:15 p.m.	Goal-setting module

▫ *Program methodology.* Are there unique participatory activities or exer-cises that will help fill seats? Will the attendees actually taste wines at your wine lover's workshop? Will the participants of your how-to-make-a-speech program actually deliver a speech? Will they actually write advertising copy at the seminar on success in advertising? This kind of information should be included.

▫ *Client list.* Credibility is important for any marketing effort. Your client list helps to establish credibility. A simple direct approach works best. Here is an example:

Here Is a Partial List of Our Clients:
American Heart Association
American Red Cross
Federal Express
Hallmark Cards
Marriott Corporation
Xerox

Expand and update this list any time you reprint your brochure.

◻ *Endorsements.* An effective endorsement should have four components: name, profession or business, title, and specific benefit the participant received. For example, "Thanks to the sales techniques I learned at Carol Jones's seminar, I was able to earn 20 percent more in commissions for the year." Paul Stuart, Sales Consultant, Atlantic Insurance Company.

If your program is brand-new, you might have to get creative. Ask friends or associates to give you some positive comments you can print. After you have completed a few programs, you will acquire many more endorsements that can be printed in subsequent brochures. See Chapter 18 to find out how to get endorsements the day of your seminar.

Most people who have benefited from your seminar will be more than happy to provide you with endorsements. All you have to do is ask. Be sure to ask for endorsements on the participant's professional letterhead. That way you will have the option of reducing it and including it on future promotional material.

◻ *Seminar leader bio.* A short bio about the seminar leader (you) should be included. Be sure to give your experience with the subject matter. The bio should focus on answering the question, What makes you qualified to present this seminar or workshop?

Other information could include experience as a professional speaker, educational background, honors or recognition you have received pertinent to your topic, and names of associations that you belong to which certify your professionalism. For example, if you belong to the American Seminar Leaders Association or National Speakers Association, be sure to mention them.

Remember, include only information that is relevant to the topic and audience you are addressing. For example, if you are doing a program on stress management, it might be relevant to say you are a certified yoga instructor. If you are doing a program on how to be an entrepreneur, it would be important to include any information on successful businesses you have created.

◻ *Your photograph.* Although it is not essential, in many cases you will want to include your photograph in the brochure. You need a professional quality, black-and-white, promotional head shot.

◻ *Methods of payment.* Who should checks be made out to? List the credit cards you accept. In addition, you might want to use the credit card logos of the cards you accept.

◻ *How to register.* Clearly print this information in one area of the brochure. List your complete fee schedule in this section as well as any group or early-registration discounts. List your registration methods. Most seminars accept registration by telephone, Internet, mail, and fax. Your registration-at-the-door policy should also be stated.

Be sure to print a for-more-information telephone number in this section. (Note: It's a good idea to list this information number a few places in the brochure.)

- *Toll-free number.* A toll-free number is a valuable tool to encourage inquiries and registrations.
- *Web site address.* Put your Web site address and email address in several places on your brochure. Reply to email queries as soon as you can.

$$$ Saver. It is easy to set up your regular telephone number to receive toll-free calls. You can contact your telephone service to set this up. You might also want to check out competitive rates with the following companies.

www.800longdistance.com
www.800today.com
www.mytollfreenumber.com
www.accessline.biz

- *Tear-off registration.* One section of the brochure can be used for a mail-in registration form. Perforate or print a dotted line.
- *What will be included?* Are you giving out a workbook, reference material, CD-ROM, audio or video tapes, email newsletter, samples, and so forth? Are you serving coffee, lunch, and/or dinner? Are you giving out certificates or diplomas? Will participants receive personal evaluations or personal consulting? Any feature that might contribute to your marketing success should be listed and perhaps highlighted in some way. You'd be surprised how important these freebies are to a lot of seminar participants.
- *Act-now motivation.* How about a discount for early registration or a special gift like an audio tape for the first 25 people who register?
- *Guarantee.* Many people feel more secure about taking a chance with a seminar or workshop if there is a money-back guarantee if they are not satisfied. Be sure to say that they must ask for a refund at a break or at some point *before* the seminar is over.
- *Refund policy.* Your refund policy can act as an incentive. People are more likely to register early if you offer a refund policy. You will want to offer a full refund up until a certain date, and then a partial refund after that. A standard unwritten practice in the seminar business is to

offer anyone who can't attend for whatever reason the opportunity to attend a later program. It is a goodwill gesture that will pay dividends at a later time.

▫ *Tax deductible.*   This is a reminder and can encourage additional registrations. "All expenses of continuing education (fees, travel, meals, and lodging) undertaken to maintain and improve professional skills are tax deductible. (Treas. Reg. 1-162-5, Coughlin vs. Commissioner, 203F 2d 307)."

   To be on the safe side, ask participants to consult their accountants. Provide a receipt so your seminar can be claimed as a tax deduction.

▫ *Market other products.*   Upsell. If you have supplementary material or related seminars, say so. Is your program available on audio- or videotape? Do you have an in-house program you would like to mention in your mailing? In this way, you take full advantage of the marketing potential of your brochure.

   Figure 8-3 illustrates many of the brochure design principles that have just been described.

Preliminary Evaluation

Your brochure should be proofread a few times for any errors in spelling, grammar, telephone numbers, names, dates, and so forth.
   After you have completed your brochure, show it to people who might be prospects to attend your program or anyone familiar with the topic. Ask for feedback. Make changes accordingly.

How to Choose the Best Printer

When you are satisfied with your design and copy, you are ready to take your brochure layout and copy to the printer. The best printer is one who will do quality work, at an inexpensive price, and who is located conveniently. Your best source for leads for a good printer is referrals. If you have none, check the phone book Yellow Pages.

Comparison Shop

Make a series of appointments with three or four different printers. Printers rarely give price quotes without seeing the job. If possible, bring a sample of a similar brochure to give the printer some idea of how you want the finished job to look. Prices will often vary greatly among printers.

SPEAK OUT WITH CLOUT

An action-packed one-day communication seminar, with proven strategies and techniques to improve your power to:

- **Deliver Persuasive Presentations**
- **Project Confidence**
- **Gain Respect and Trust**
- **Conquer Nervousness**

Figure 8-3. Sample of a four-page brochure illustrating many of the design principles.

!!! Time Saver. When you telephone a printer to make an appointment, briefly describe the brochure. Almost every printer specializes in specific types of printing. Make sure the printer offers the services you need and is equipped to produce the size, style, and quantity you require.

The Single Most Important Activity of

It's not only __what__ you say, it's __how__ you say it that counts.

What You Say

7%

How You Say It

93%

A research study by Stanford University Graduate School has shown that 93% of our communication effectiveness depends upon <u>HOW</u> we express ourselves.

Let's face it, your success often depends on your ability to influence, motivate and manage others.

Speaking confidently and persuasively can be your greatest asset.

"Speak Out With Clout" offers the practical, hands-on training necessary to your rapidly rising career.

In this program, you'll learn by doing. Our lively, experiential approach will take you step by step through a structured process with self-evaluations, practice sessions and instant video replay. You'll receive the coaching and individual personal attention you'll need to keep you confident in any situation...especially those times when you're not expecting to speak or when you face challenges, arguments or hostility.

SEMINAR CONTENT

Maximize Your Persuasiveness
- The 30 second first impression
- 4 secrets of body language
- Creating instant rapport
- Organizing your presentation
- 5 "hidden persuaders"
- Selling your ideas

Methods To Create Impact
- How to create your power image
- Thinking quickly on your feet
- 3 steps to build a "comfort zone"
- Diffusing anger and challenges
- Influencing with gestures
- Focusing strategies for impact
- Using "leading" and "pacing"

Master Voice Control
- 5 techniques for the "power voice"
- Controlling with pitch and volume
- Projecting energy and inflection
- Applying the "credibility component"
- Establishing your vocal style
- Winning intonation patterns

Expand Your Personal Style
- Projecting your natural self
- 3 methods for overcoming anxiety
- Establishing trust
- Building confidence with eye control
- Making the most of your strengths

✔ Do you want to enhance your professional image?

✔ Do you want to improve your ability to speak under pressure?

✔ Would you like to make the most of every important opportunity?

If you can answer YES to any of these quetions, then this seminar is for you!

SAVE MONEY...REGISTER EARLY... SEATING IS LIMITED.
Call (201) 864-9149.

Figure 8-3. (*Continued*)

$$$ Saver. If the printer is using computer typesetting and you have a compatible computer software program, you can save money on typesetting by bringing in a computer disk with all of your copy on it.

Although price is important, your printer is someone who is a vital member of your marketing team. Therefore, it is important to choose someone you can get along with. Don't forget to take this human factor into consideration when you choose a printer.

Your Life Is Your Ability to Communicate.

HOW YOU'LL BENEFIT

- Create a powerful image
- Project confidence
- Win trust and support
- Take charge immediately
- Gain visibility
- Increase personal influence

ON-SITE TRAINING

Ask About Our **FREE** Intro Program

We can customize this seminar to fit your organization's needs.

It can be presented to your group at a time and location that's convenient. Also available:

- One on one coaching
- Consulting services
- Follow up support
- Special group rates

**For more information call:
(201) 864-9149**

SUPER SAVER REGISTRATION

The regular investment is $195 per participant.

Super Saver Registration: To reserve your seat for only $175, simply call and charge your registration to American Express, MasterCard, or Visa at least 10 days prior to the seminar.

Group Discounts Also Available

CALL: (201) 864-9149.

WHAT YOU'll RECEIVE

VIDEO TRAINING

See yourself the way others do. Thanks to instant video playback and individual coaching, you'll be able to measure your progress and have the opportunity to make immediate improvements in your speaking style.

SPECIALLY DESIGNED SEMINAR HANDBOOK

Every participant will receive a comprehensive handbook for use during the seminar and afterwards.

It contains all the major points covered during the course of the day, as well as specific action steps you will take to achieve your professional goals.

FREE TAKE-HOME BONUS

You will receive your own personal video of your presentations.

You will be able to review what you learned in the seminar and reinforce your achievements.

Your Personal Video

To ensure individual attention and maximum benefit, enrollment is strictly limited. **Reserve your seat now. Call: (201) 864-9149.**

YOUR SEMINAR LEADER

Paul Karasik is a professional speaker who has delivered speeches and conducted seminars for over 18 years. His clients include Citibank, AT&T, Shell Oil, National Association of Accountants and National Council of Savings Institutions.

Paul has earned the reputation as the "Speaker's Speaker." He is founder and president of the American Seminar Leaders Association and an active member of the National Speakers Association and the American Society of Training and Development.

!!! **Resources for Brochure Development and Printing.** The first brochure is always the most difficult. Just remember, it's not carved in stone. It's a creative process. Be prepared to modify it and make improvements. With experience, the process will become quicker, with lots less effort. With time, your printer will know what you like and will help you make creative and economical decisions based on your needs. The following books provide detailed information on how to design the brochure, how to find the right printer, and how to save both money and time getting your job done.

HERE'S WHAT OTHERS ARE SAYING ABOUT "SPEAK OUT WITH CLOUT"

"Your program was by far the most important seminar I've attended in a long time. I can't thank you enough."
-George J. Wilson, District Manager, IBM

"Tremendous learning experience."
-Mary Ann DeCarlo, Training Director, AT&T

"A program whose time has come. Paul Karasik is riveting."
-Richard Zeif, Pres., The Negotiating Institute

"I found the program educational, as well as challenging and practical.
-Carol M. Evans, Criminal Attorney

"Stimulating, provocative, and informative presentation."
-Susan Goldstein, V.P., Citibank

"Paul, you helped me take my career to a new level of success."
-Walter J. Brown Jr., Bell Laboratories

SEMINAR GUARANTEE
If, after attending this seminar, you are not fully satisfied that we have delivered everything promised in this brochure, simply notify the seminar administrator by the lunch break and we will refund the entire registration fee.

TAX DEDUCTIBLE
All expenses of continuing education (fees, travel, meals, lodging) undertaken to maintain and improve professional skills are deductible (Treas. Reg. 1-162-5. Coughlin vs. Commissioner. 203F 2d 307)

CEUs AWARDED
Conforming to the guidelines of the National Task Force on the Continuing Education Unit,this one-day seminar is authorized for 6 CEUs. If you would like to receive a CEU Certificate, please send your written request to the address below.

IT'S EASY TO REGISTER

Regular Tuition: $195 per participant

Super Saver Registration: $175 per participant, when you register 10 days or more in advance.

Group discounts are available.

ALL MAJOR CREDIT CARDS ACCEPTED.

BY PHONE: Call us now at (201) 864-9149
Email: info@paulkarasik.com

BY MAIL: Mail registration form to:
Paul Karasik Associates
899 Boulevard East, Suite 6A
Weehawken, N.J. 07087
Make checks payable to:
Paul Karasik Associates

REGISTERING EARLY SAVES YOU MONEY.

REGISTRATION FORM

www.paulkarasik.com
(Secure Web site)

Paul Karasik Associates
899 Boulevard East, Suite 6A
Weehawken, N.J. 07087

PRESORT MAIL
FIRST CLASS MAIL
U.S. POSTAGE
PAID
FORT LEE NJ 07024
PERMIT NO. 239

Name
Title
Company
Address
City _____ State _____ Zip _____

❑ Visa ❑ Master Card ❑ American Express
My Acct. # _____ Exp. Date _____
Authorized Signature

If undeliverable as addressed, please forward to Training Director.

Figure 8-3. (*Continued*)

Brochure Graphics by John Ziemann (Learning Resources Network)

Better Brochures, Catalogs, and Mailing Pieces: A Practical Guide with 178 Rules for More Effective Sales Pieces That Cost Less, Jane Maas (St. Martin's Griffin, 1984)

Words That Sell, Richard Bayan (McGraw-Hill Trade, 1987)

More Words That Sell, Richard Bayan (McGraw-Hill, 2003)

Phrases That Sell: The Ultimate Phrase Finder to Help You Promote Your Products, Services, and Ideas, Edward W. Werz, Sally Germain (McGraw-Hill Trade, 1998)

Cybertalk That Sells, Herschell Gordon Lewis, Jaime Murphy (McGraw-Hill/Contemporary Books, 1998)

The Copywriter's Handbook: A Step-By-Step Guide to Writing Copy That Sells, Robert W. Bly (Owl Books, 1990)

Teach Yourself Copywriting, J. Jonathan Gabay (McGraw-Hill, 2003)

!!! **Contacts.**   The undisputed master of copywriting is Bob Bly. He has written more than 50 books, countless articles, and his copy has created literally hundreds of millions of dollars of revenues for his clients. Bob is my personal writing coach and mentor and I recommend all of his books, tapes, or services to anyone who is interested in only the best. Be sure to let him know I referred you.

Bob Bly
Phone: (201) 385-1220
www.bly.com

9
Getting Results with Direct Mail

Three Keys to Success

It's no secret. The three keys for success with direct mail are the list, the list, and the list. Seriously, although there are a number of factors that will contribute to your success, the mailing list you use is by far the most important factor.

What Is the Best Mailing List?

The best list you can use is your own house mailing list. When you enter the seminar business, you won't have a list, but if you don't start assembling a list immediately, you never will. Your personal list will include names of qualified people who have expressed interest in or who have already attended a program similar to yours. The return rate from your personal list should be 5 percent or even more. The rate of return from your house list will typically be much higher than any purchased list.

When you do radio or TV interviews, be sure to give your address, an 800 number, or Web site so that people who want more information can respond. Add the names and addresses of anyone who has either purchased or inquired about any products such as books or tapes. These names and addresses all become part of your house list.

Where to Find the Mailing List You Need

The "mother" of all lists, the list of lists, is maintained by:

SRDS Direct Marketing Solutions
1700 Higgins Rd.
Des Plaines, IL 60018
Phone: (800) 851-7737
Fax: (847) 375-5001
www.srds.com

They offer list information in both printed form and online. Most public libraries have copies of the print format available. SRDS Direct Marketing Solutions also offers their database access on a per-project basis with special pricing.

The information revolution has affected the list business in a dramatic fashion. Five years ago there were about 20,000 different lists available, today there are 45,000. SRDS makes on average 3,000 revisions per day to keep these lists absolutely up to date.

SRDS breaks down its lists with the following descriptions:

- Where you can obtain the list.

- The source of the list. Lists are assembled from a variety of sources, including magazines, associations, and companies.

- Rental rates. Rates are listed by cost per thousand. The price can vary from $25 to $100 per thousand names.

- Minimum number of names you must rent.

- How often the list is "cleaned." *Cleaned* means "updated."

- What labeling system is used. Usually labels are available in self-adhesive and chesire styles. Chesire labels cost less and must be applied with a machine. Most big mailing houses use chesire labels.

- Miscellaneous information relevant to the list.

How to Work with List Brokers

List brokers are valuable consultants. They will assist you in choosing the best list for your seminar. List brokers act like travel agents. They make their commission from the original source of the list. The brokers are on *your* side. They want you to have a successful program and come back for more.

You will find names of list brokers in SRDS. List brokers can also be found in the Yellow Pages of the telephone book under the heading "Mailing Lists" and on the Internet.

!!! **Resources.**   Here are a few list brokers you might want to check with regarding availability of the list you are seeking and pricing.

Hugo Dunhill Mailing Lists   Wholesale Lists
www.HDML.com   www.wholesalelists.net

Act One Lists   Buyerzone.com
www.act1lists.com   www.buyerzone.com/
                                  marketing/mailing_lists/

!!! **Caution.**   You are *renting* lists, not buying them. This means you can use the list on a one-time basis only. The control on the system is the inclusion of phony names. If you use the mailing list more than once, the source will know and you will be subject to legal action.

     After someone on the rented mailing list responds to your mailing, he or she is eligible to be placed on your house list.

Test Before You Invest

Although you might feel confident that you have a great mailing list, never initiate a major direct-mail campaign without a test mailing first. Response to a direct-mail campaign can vary tremendously. You can test using a minimum of 1,000 names, but use more if possible. Testing different lists simultaneously will help you determine the best list.

The A/B Split

One variation of the direct-mail test is called the A/B split. The computer is given the command to produce a list made up of every other name. In this way two different offers to the same list can be tested. By doing an A/B split, almost any feature of your offer can be tested to find out what will get the best response rate.

Important Factors to Test

You will be able to refine your direct-mail campaign by testing these 10 factors:

1. Seminar fee

2. Brochure design and copy

3. Location

4. Day and time

5. Length of the seminar

6. Self-mailer versus envelope

7. Bulk mail versus first class

8. Mail permit number versus postal meter versus stamp

9. Multiple mailings

10. Telephone follow-up

Bulk Mail versus First Class

One obvious factor to consider in using bulk mail is its substantial savings. Bulk rates are generally about 45 percent lower than first-class rates. To be eligible for bulk rates, you must get a permit from your local post office. Bulk-mail permits and first-class permits are each $150. You are required to mail a minimum of 200 pieces each time you do a mailing.

When mailing in bulk, you must bundle according to zip codes, and, unless you state "Return postage guaranteed" somewhere on the mailing panel below the label, nondeliverable pieces will be discarded. Bulk mail is slow and unpredictable. First-class mail might take a few days for delivery; bulk mail might take a week or even weeks. Bulk mail is a low priority for the postal service, and it will be delivered when it is convenient for them.

Another important factor is perception. Bulk mail has the connotation of something's being of less importance. If image is vital to the success of your marketing effort, bulk mail might not be desirable.

The postal service offers a discount program to first-class-mail users if items are bundled according to zip code. This rate is worth considering if you want to enjoy the advantages of first-class mail at discount prices.

Results You Can Expect

The return rate from direct mail ranges from $\frac{1}{10}$ of 1 percent to 5 percent. Generally, 1 to $1\frac{1}{2}$ percent is accepted as a good return. The lower the registration fee, the greater the response. Remember that when charging higher fees, you don't need as high a response rate.

When to Use a Mailing House

Mailing houses can take care of the entire mailing procedure for you. They will label, insert, sort, and deliver your mailing to the post office. They will also maintain your house mailing list for you.

The cost for a mailing service is usually reasonable, and prices from one mailing house to the next are competitive. Naturally, the basic costs will be relative to the number of pieces you are mailing. As with any product or service, the quality varies. If you plan to deliver and/or pick up, location might also be a factor to consider.

!!! **Time and $$$ Saver.**   You can save lots of time and money by employing the services of a mailing house. You can locate a mailing house by looking in the Yellow Pages of the telephone book under "Addressing and Mailing Services," "Direct Mail," or "Letter Shop Services."

Another way to save money on a direct-mail campaign is to shop around for a printer who also offers the services of a mailing house.

When Is the Best Time to Mail Brochures?

Your mailing should arrive in the prospects' hands between three and four weeks before the event. If it arrives too early, it is likely to get lost or forgotten. If it arrives too late, the time may not be available to attend the event.

If you are mailing to an audience that will have to travel a considerable distance, your prospect should receive the mailing six to eight weeks before the event.

What Is the Total Cost of Direct-Mail Promotion?

The variables in your direct-mail promotion are

- The cost of the list
- The cost to design and print the brochure
- The postage charge
- Any mailing services charges

The average cost of a direct mailing is between $35 and $75 per thousand.

A realistic cost for a 30,000-piece mailing of an 11- by 17-in four-page brochure would be in the neighborhood of $10,000. This would include all costs.

Once again, your rate of return is your measure of success in direct mail. As a rule of thumb, the return should total a minimum of twice your marketing costs.

!!! **Resources.**   There are two primary resources for direct-mail promotion. These two resources will provide you with a vast array of information and an expansive network of contacts in direct-mail marketing.

Direct Marketing
  Association (DMA)
1120 Avenue of the Americas
New York, NY 10036
Phone: (212) 768-7277
Fax: (212) 302-6714
www.the-dma.org

American Marketing
  Association (AMA)
311 S. Wacker Drive, Suite 5800
Chicago, IL 60606
Phone: (800) AMA-1150
Fax: (312) 542-9001
www.ama.jobcontrolcenter.com

The Direct Marketing Association (DMA) has a huge library of information on the direct-mail industry. It has more than 3,500 company members. The DMA influences government legislation and regulations. It holds 2 major national conventions and 17 specialized conferences each year. Members receive eight publications and have free access to data resources unavailable anywhere else.

Direct Marketing with Email

Email can be harnessed to market your seminar. Many of the same principles in direct-mail marketing apply with a few differences.

The quality of your email list will certainly be a key element in the level of success you will achieve. It is important to understand that quality email lists are difficult to find and must be used carefully. Quality email lists are based upon the same criteria as quality mailing lists: targeted and updated.

The best way to obtain email lists is to use brokers who specialize in email lists. Some list brokers will provide you with the actual addresses, while others will require you to prospect using their service. It is likely one source will not have enough email addresses for you so it is wise to use more than one list broker.

Be sure to continually collect email addresses and create your own email list of individuals who have requested to be notified about your seminars or to be placed on your email list. This list, like your "snail mail" list, will be the best list in terms of response rate.

Be sure to provide an email reply link that will allow prospects to opt out of receiving your emails. If you don't you could be accused of spamming, that is, sending massive numbers of unsolicited emails. Several Internet watchdog groups monitor complaints about spamming and if they believe you are a spammer, you could be blackballed by list brokers or even incur legal problems.

!!! **Contacts.** Here are some organizations that you can investigate to find out if they have a list that is appropriate for your seminar.

BulletMail
www.bulletmail.com

24/7 Media
www.247media.com

PostMasterDirect.com   yesmail.com
www.postmasterdirect.com   www.yesmail.com

The best way to market your seminar using the Internet is to create a "teaser" ad that will entice the prospect to request more information about the seminar. Use headlines like:

"How to Earn a Six Figure Income Working Four Hours a Day" (for a business opportunity seminar)

"Why Some People Almost Always Make Money in the Stock Market" (for an investment seminar)

"How to Cash In on Internet Marketing" (for an Internet seminar directed toward small businesses)

Be sure to keep your teaser ad short. Your goal is to get them to click on your link back to your Web site for more information about the seminar as well as registration instructions.

10

Promoting Your Seminar with Newspaper Ads and Media

Advertising versus Publicity

Whether you choose to go down the path of advertising or publicity, the end result is the same: media coverage. One important difference between the two is that advertising has to be bought. Excluding some incidental costs for phone calls and mailing, publicity is free, although you do have to invest your own time and creativity.

The other major difference is that when you pay to advertise, you have control of what is said or printed. Generally speaking, publicity is controlled by the media. They decide whether your seminar is appropriate to publicize in the print or broadcast media. Their decision is based upon what they think interests their audience.

Since publicity does not require a dollar investment but does generate registrations, it is cost-effective. See Chapter 11 to learn how to take advantage of all of the opportunities to get free publicity in the media.

!!! **Caution.** In theory, an ideal scenario for promoting a seminar would be to run an ad in the newspaper and thereby fill your seminar room with people. That would be wonderful if it could be counted on to work. Although advertising your seminar might generate a few registrations, more often than not it does not work. This chapter provides the guidelines and resources you need to be aware of to advertise, but you should understand that this is a fairly risky marketing vehicle.

Prerequisites for Using
Mass Media

There are a few specific instances when mass media can be utilized. Mass media advertising can be used effectively in five instances:

1. *You are unsure of your target audience.* If you are unable to target your audience, and if locating a direct-mail list is impossible, using mass media becomes a necessary alternative. By taking a detailed survey of the people who answer your advertisement, you should be able to locate the right mailing list for future marketing efforts. For example, if a large number of small-business owners answered your advertisement, in the future you would have the choice to substitute direct-mail marketing, focusing on this target audience.

2. *Your topic is of broad, general interest.* Topics like speed reading, reducing your taxes, investment opportunities, memory improvement, and personal growth appeal to a wide variety of people. Mass media can reach this wide audience.

3. *Your advertisement is being used to generate inquiries for your seminar.* This advertisement is sometimes called the "tickler" ad. The intention here is not to sell the seminar but to create a prospect list from which you can market your seminar. You can follow up the "tickler" ad with a detailed brochure or even a telemarketing campaign. You can also use the names and addresses you collect to market books, tapes, and services on the same topic.

4. *You are advertising a celebrity speaker.* There are a few seminar leaders who have reached celebrity status. They either have written a bestselling book, have hosted a radio or TV talk show, or have had some similar kind of media exposure already. Mass media advertising can work well to advertise this kind of seminar.

5. *Your advertisement is used to get people to a free introductory seminar.* This is probably one of the best ways to take advantage of media advertising. The strategy is very simple. Advertise a free introductory seminar. At this seminar you provide people with the information that you promised, as well as the opportunity to register for a more extensive seminar that will be given a few days later. Of course, there is a charge for the follow-up seminar. This is referred to as the "rollover," because you roll people over from one seminar to another.

This technique is effective for promoting a variety of general-interest seminars, such as real estate investment, and a wide variety of personal-growth seminars. The Dale Carnegie seminars, for example, have been promoted this way for many years.

The free introductory seminar, or "two-step" technique, is discussed in greater detail in Chapter 12.

Mass Media Advertising Categories

There are two advertising categories in the broadcast media: radio and television. In the print media, you can choose between magazines and newspapers. And, of course, there is the Internet.

!!! **Contact.** SRDS Media Solutions has been bringing the media community together for over 82 years. It is the leading provider of media rates and data for magazines, newspapers, television, and radio—as well as today's alternative marketing opportunities, such as online. Information is available by subscription online as well as print form depending on the category.

SRDS Media Solutions
1700 Higgins Rd.
Des Plaines, IL 60018
Phone: (847) 375-5000; (800) 851-7737
Fax: (847) 375-5001
www.srds.com

SRDS breaks down media information into the following groups:

Radio Advertising Source

TV & Cable Source

Newspaper Advertising Source

Community Publication Advertising Source

Business Publication Source

Consumer Magazine Advertising Source

If you are serious about using advertising to promote your seminar, you might want to contact a local advertising agency who can guide you through the process ensuring you make the best choices of media, ad design, and placement.

Radio and Television Advertising

Radio and television can work well for free introductory seminars and those featuring celebrity speakers. Aside from these two applications, radio and TV work better as vehicles for publicity. (As mentioned, see Chapter 11 for information on how to get radio and TV exposure.)

Magazine Advertising

The primary drawback of magazine advertising is the very long lead time necessary. You have to plan your advertisement months in advance.

Another drawback is that, like all mass media advertising, magazine advertising is expensive. Test before you invest too much.

Of course, choosing the right magazine for your target audience also plays a major role in your success. One seminar promoter has found success using four small magazine ads in a weekly magazine to fill her monthly seminar on how to overcome the fear of public speaking. This technique works for her because of the multiday workshop format of her program and the expensive registration fee. She needs only 10 to 15 participants each month to make her seminar profitable.

Specialty magazines, such as trade journals, allow you to target your ad the most. For example, you might use a computer magazine to market a seminar on a computer topic. Although at first glance this would seem to be an effective form of advertising, a number of conditions must exist to make this kind of ad feasible:

- Circulation has to be considerable, since your results will be a small percentage of the total list.

- The audience has to be the type to attend seminars.

- The seminar promotion has to be further supported with other strategies, such as telemarketing.

!!! Contact. SRDS publishes two directories of magazine demographics and advertising rates.

Consumer Magazine and Advertising Source

Business Publication Advertising Source

Newspaper Advertising

Newspapers, by far, are the most effective means of filling seminar seats. Here are 13 guidelines for using newspaper ads efficiently.

1. Don't attempt to reach a pinpointed market. As was already mentioned about mass media as a whole, you will be reaching a broad audience. Your seminar should be geared to topics of general interest. How to make a million dollars and how to achieve peace of mind fall into this category.

2. Don't purchase more space than you actually need. In most cases, a small, well-placed ad will be as effective as a large one. Naturally, the newspaper will try to sell as large a space as they can. The best way to find out optimum size is through testing.

3. Don't be fooled by low rates; they may mean low circulation. Avoid newspapers with low circulation.

4. Design your ad with a catchy headline that is sure to attract attention

and encourage the reader to continue reading. This is a cardinal rule for writing advertising copy. Your first goal is to "grab 'em."

5. Focus your ad on communicating *benefits*. This marketing rule cannot be repeated too many times. *Always focus your marketing efforts on the benefits the participant will receive.*

6. Allow your audience to register at the door. By not demanding advance registration, you are removing one more obstacle to the registration procedure.

7. Advertise in the Sunday edition when possible; it is more widely read. In general, avoid Friday and Saturday editions. They are the least effective.

8. Locate your ad on the right-hand side of the page near the top.

9. Place your ad in the front pages of a section rather than toward the back.

10. Use multiple exposures. This will substantially increase your registrations. However, this is an area where you should proceed cautiously to determine whether your advertising dollars are being spent wisely.

11. For a seminar geared to men, place your ad in the sports section; for affluent men or women, the business section; and for men or women in general, the main section.

12. Always test your advertisement program before making major investments. This applies to test size, multiple insertions, ad design and copy, placement, and newspaper choice.

13. Save money by using regional editions of national newspapers when possible. Newspapers like *The Wall Street Journal* have regional editions and rates.

!!! **Contact.** SRDS also publishes three important directories geared toward newspaper advertising.

Newspaper Advertising Source

Newspaper Circulation Source

Community Publication Advertising Source

Advertising on the Internet

There are lots of choices when advertising on the Internet. There are a number of firms that specialize in Internet advertising placement. There are also a variety of ways to pay for their services. If you are serious about advertising on the Internet, spend some time reviewing options so you can make the best choice for yourself.

!!! **Contacts.**   Here are some firms that can provide you with information regarding options and will provide you with links to firms that can place your ads for you.

Adbility.com   Ad Resource
www.adbility.com   www.adres.internet.com

If you choose, you can contact an ad placement service directly. An excellent resource for placing ads as well as helping you in layout and design is

DoubleClick
www.doubleclick.net

Internet advertising is generally purchased based on a CPM or cost per thousand impression basis. An impression means a visitor visits a target ad page or Web site. In other words, whenever a page is "served" to a computer screen special software counts this as an impression.

If you do decide to advertise on the Internet remember the top half of the page is better than the bottom of the page. And ads that are placed next to the right scroll bar will get a 228 percent better return than ads at the top margin of the page.

!!! **Resources.**   The following books are recommended if you want to develop and refine a mass media advertising campaign for your seminar.

Advertising and Marketing Checklists by Ron Kaatz (McGraw-Hill, 1995)

Advertising Manager's Handbook, Robert W. Big (Prentice Hall, 1998)

How to Write a Good Advertisement, Victor Schwab (Wilshire Books, 1985)

Tested Advertising Methods, John Caples, Fred E. Hann (Prentice Hall, 1998)

Write Great Ads, Eric A. Klein (Wiley, 1990)

11

How to Exploit the Media for Free (or Low-Cost) Publicity

How to Profit from Publicity

The best kind of advertisement is free. The art and science of getting free media coverage is called publicity. Publicity can serve you in three specific ways that are similar to advertising; the big difference is you don't pay a lot for publicity.

First, it will help you fill seats at your seminar without increasing your overhead. Although you will incur minimal postage, copying, and telephone costs, overall they will be negligible. People will have the opportunity to learn about your seminar, and as a result, attend it.

Second, it will get you publicity. As the saying goes, "Any publicity is good publicity." This may not be absolutely true; but generally speaking, it will be to your advantage to have your name in front of the public or your target audience. Becoming a celebrity speaker should be one of your long-term goals if you want to become eligible for the really big money in the seminar business. Each time you get into the media, you move a little closer to that goal.

Third, it will give you a feeling of elation to see your name in print or to know that thousands or perhaps even hundreds of thousands of people are watching or listening to you. Don't underrate the boost in confidence that comes with publicity.

What Is a Media Kit?

You need a media kit. Your media kit is simply a package of all the material you believe will be of interest to the media. You give a media kit to any member of the media who might want to do a story on you or your seminar or to anyone you would like to attend one of your seminars.

You also send out your media kit to anyone who is considering hiring you to be a speaker or to conduct a seminar for their organization. Of course, the materials you include are only those relevant to the particular needs of the client. For example, if you are proposing an in-house seminar for the real estate industry, any materials you can generate related to the real estate industry, such as an article you wrote for a real estate trade magazine or an endorsement from a major real estate author, should certainly be included.

Components of a Media Kit

The contents of a media kit vary according to the situation and the event you are publicizing. However, it will always consist of one or more of the following 12 items:

1. Media release

2. Bio

3. Cover letter

4. Photograph

5. Public service/calendar announcement

6. List of previous appearances (or client list)

7. Copies of any previous publicity

8. Articles or books you have written

9. Your seminar or company brochure

10. Sample question list

11. Testimonials and endorsements

12. Video and audio demonstration tapes

Most of the material can be placed in a folder that has pockets on the inside. It is a good idea to add a little class to your package by buying a high-quality folder. You should put a label on the front to identify the contents. A business card can also be stapled to one of the inner pockets.

Let's look at each element of the media kit in more detail.

The Electronic Media Kit:
Your Web Site

Thanks to the Internet, you can offer your media kit electronically— online using your Web site. This is one of the primary benefits of having your own Web site.

You can offer information about you and your seminars instantly, any time, anywhere, 24 hours a day to anyone who is interested. And best of all you will save lots of money and time.

Every time anyone is interested in your seminars or presentations ask the individual to go to your Web site. If they are interested in "hard copy" you can send it out after they have first reviewed your Web site.

Your Web site will be slightly different than your media kit. Here are the general sections you should consider including when you design your Web site.

1. Brochure of your seminar or presentation descriptions

2. Seminar registration methods

3. Endorsements

4. Client list

5. Books, compact discs, DVDs, and other products for sale

6. Description of other services such as consulting and coaching

7. Your company mission statement

8. Video clips of your presentation

9. Your audiovisual requirements

10. Bio

11. Articles

12. Your seminar schedule

13. Registration for your electronic newsletter

14. Your photo

15. Contact information

Your Web site projects your image to the world. Great Web sites are a marriage of brilliant design and state-of-the-art technology. If you possess expertise in one or both of these areas and you have lots of time to invest, you might consider becoming involved in the construction of your Web site. If not, you need to enlist the help of experts in these areas.

!!! **Contact.** AVALAR is a fantastic Web site development and hosting company that specializes in Web sites and Internet marketing for seminar and workshop leaders. They will provide you with a turn-key Internet solution for your business. The president of AVALAR, Dan Ohlemacher, understands how to connect high-tech to high-touch. Let him know you read about him and his company in this book.

AVALAR
Phone: (760) 751-2235
www.avalar.com

Another creative technique for publicizing and promoting your seminars and business is a CD-ROM. You can transfer your complete Web site or just parts of it to a CD-ROM and make copies that you can send out to anyone requesting information.

!!! **Contacts.**   Here is a great company that will produce promotional CD-ROMs for you that are the size of business cards. You can hand them out to media or prospects for your programs.

JENTEC Interactive
Phone: (800) 522-5051
www.jentec.com

!!! **Resources.**   If you insist on creating your own Web site, there are lots of technical books available. Here are a few to begin with:

Professional Web Site Design from Start to Finish, Anne-Marie Concepcion (How Design Books, 2001)

Designing Websites for Every Audience, Ilise Benun (How Design Books, 2003)

Building a Web Site for Dummies, David A. Crowder and Rhonda Crowder (For Dummies, 2000)

The Media Release and How to Write It

Your media release should attract the attention of the media person who is reading it and then give this person a straightforward presentation about your program. The person to whom you have sent the release is usually under the constant pressure of deadlines and is bombarded with mail and incoming news possibilities. For this reason, if you are going to be given any consideration at all, you must provide your information in an easy-to-read format.

You should write a media release in a form that is ready to go to press. Think of the media release as if it were a final, actual printed story. Your goal is to make it as easy as possible for the news or feature editor to understand the importance of your seminar and to include a story about it in their publication or media.

Components of a Media Release

Let's examine the five parts of a media release.

1. *Source information.*   This includes the name, address, and phone number of the person who should be contacted for more information. If it is written on your own letterhead, the name of the contact person and

telephone number will be enough. Make sure to include your telephone number even if it is on the letterhead.

2. *Release date.* Most media releases are labeled "FOR IMMEDIATE RELEASE." This indicates that the story can be used as soon as it is received. Only in special cases will you use a specific date. This would indicate to the media not to release the story until the date indicated.

3. *Headline.* The headline should summarize the main content of the media release. It should tell what is happening and to whom. The headline should be written to appeal to the audience of the particular media. It should be typed in all capital letters.

4. *Dateline.* This is nothing more than the city of origin of the media release. The dateline might be of importance if the newspaper or magazine covers many different regions.

5. *Body.* The body of the media release should be written in the inverted pyramid style: The most important information up front and the information of lesser importance at the bottom. In this way, if the story needs to be reduced in length, it can be edited quickly without removing the more essential information.

Paragraph 1. The first paragraph should include the who, what, when, where, why, and how. This will include the name of the featured event, speaker, and so forth.

Paragraph 2. Repeat the name of the program and why the event is significant to the target audience. Reinforce the benefits or the importance of the seminar with a quote by the seminar leader or an authority on the topic. This quote should be directed to the target audience of the program.

Paragraph 3. This paragraph gives additional information about the seminar and seminar leader. An additional quote can be used in this paragraph.

Paragraph 4. More information that underscores the importance of the program or its benefits to the targeted population should be included. Another quotation can be added.

Paragraph 5. Include registration information and whom to contact for more information.

Figure 11-1 shows the layout of a typical media release and Fig. 11-2 provides an example of a media release.

Tips for Writing a Winning Media Release

1. Keep your sentences short and to the point.

2. Avoid hype. Provide facts and information that can be substantiated,

Contact: Name

Company

Address

Phone Number

                                                    For Immediate Release

HEADLINE DESIGNED TO GRAB ATTENTION
(TYPED IN CAPS)

Dateline—Paragraph 1: Who, what, when, where, why, how
Paragraph 2: Why program is important to audience
Paragraph 3: Additional important information
Paragraph 4: Good background information
Paragraph 5: Registration or for more information

-End-

Figure 11-1. Sample of a layout for a typical media release.

otherwise you eliminate the possibility of the media's providing an objective story.

3. Proofread it thoroughly. There should be *no* spelling, grammatical, or typing errors.

4. Keep it short. Keep your media release two pages or less in length. People who will be reading your media release are extremely busy. A short press release has a better chance of being read.

5. Always double-space your copy.

6. Use only one side of the paper for your media release.

7. Staple your media release together if it is more than one page.

8. Type the word *more* at the bottom of any page that leads on to a continuing page. The title and page number should appear on each page after the first ("TAX SEMINAR, Page _____").

9. Center the word *end* on the page after your last sentence.

10. Always send a good clean copy.

11. Send your media release to a specific person.

12. Make sure someone is always available to answer the telephone during business hours. There is a good chance the person will not call back if no one answers the first time.

THE BUSINESS INSTITUTE
53 Atwell Lane
Weehawken, NJ 07087

Contact: Lynne Lindahl
          (201) 794-8072

For Immediate Release

PERSUASION SKILLS GIVE BUSINESS PEOPLE
THE COMPETITIVE ADVANTAGE

Weehawken, NJ—"Speak Out with Clout" is the focus of a comprehensive one-day seminar for career-minded businesspeople. It will be held at the Hyatt Hotel in Bayonne, New Jersey, on Tuesday, March 7. This intensive program will begin at 8:30 a.m. and end at 4:30 p.m.

In order to be successful, businesspeople must present a powerful image, project self-confidence, win the trust of others, and "Speak Out with Clout." Dick Zeif, president, The Negotiating Institute, says, "This is a program whose time has come."

This program will provide proven communication strategies and techniques to achieve these objectives. Seminar leader for this program is Paul Karasik, author of the best-selling business book, *Sweet Persuasion*. He is a sales and management consultant to numerous Fortune 500 companies.

In today's marketplace, success often depends upon your ability to persuade, influence, and motivate others. According to a recent research study conducted by Stanford University, communication skills are responsible for up to 85 percent of the success of most people. "Speak Out with Clout" will provide participants with these specific skills.

For registration or information, contact Lynne Lindahl at (201) 794-8072.

-End-

Figure 11-2. Sample of a media release.

Rules for Writing Your Bio

Your bio is an integral part of your brochure, media release, and other promotional materials. Here are the 10 guidelines for you to follow when writing a bio for the media.

1. Write your bio the way you would like to be seen by the media and the public.

2. Make your bio 250 to 400 words in length.

3. Provide interesting, unique, significant, and appealing background information about yourself.

4. Grab the reader's attention with the first paragraph. It should compel the reader to be interested in finding out more about you.

5. Provide the five Ws early in the bio. Your life, like a good story, can be partially described in terms of who, what, where, when, and why.

6. Use quotations freely throughout. They will add color and style.

7. Give the reader a sense of what you are really like personally.

8. Tell the reasons you are important or an expert in your field.

9. Give evidence and facts that clearly demonstrate your competence.

10. Provide interesting or humorous personal information.

Occasions When You Should Use a Cover Letter and What to Say

It is not absolutely necessary to include a cover letter with a media release or a media kit, but it does add a nice personal touch. There are three circumstances in which a cover letter or even a simple cover note is particularly appropriate.

1. When you are sending material to a specific person, remind that person of any previous conversation or of their request for the information.

2. Include a cover letter when you want to provide reasons why your media release would be right for that specific medium. For example, if your seminar is targeted toward women, a TV show aimed at women might be perfect. Your cover letter should point out reasons such as this to the program director or host of the show. In effect, your cover letter becomes a marketing letter.

3. If you see an article or a program in which you believe you could have been included, write a cover letter to explain why. Chances are good the reporter will write a similar article in the future, and in this way you will have a good shot at appearing in it.

Guidelines for Your Media Kit Photograph

You need to include a good photograph of yourself in your professional media kit. Here are some guidelines to follow:

- Use a head shot.
- Use a black-and-white and a color photograph.
- Use a portrait photographer.
- Smile, it is your best look.
- Get 100, 8- by 10-in copies. Copies are cheaper in lots of 100.
- Typeset your name on the bottom when you get your copies.
- Be honest. Have a new photograph made up every couple of years.

Public Service Announcement/Calendar Announcement

Both broadcast and print media announce upcoming events such as seminars. Making such announcements in the broadcast media is called a public service announcement or PSA. In the print media they are called calendar announcements.

Guidelines for a PSA or Calendar Announcement

1. Type and double-space the copy on a letterhead.
2. Give a release date for the announcement.
3. Include the name of the event sponsor, the contact name, and the telephone number.
4. List the who, what, where, when, and why.
5. Include the price for registration.
6. Make it short—50 words for a calendar announcement and a reading length of no more than 30 seconds for a PSA.
7. Send in your announcements at least three weeks in advance.

Figure 11-3 shows a sample PSA.

List of Previous Appearances

Have you ever heard the expression, money breeds money? The same can be said of publicity. The more publicity you get, the easier it becomes to get more publicity. Therefore, list all of the radio and TV shows you have been on. A client list is an acceptable substitute if you have no previous media appearances.

The Business Institute
53 Atwell Lane
Weehawken, NJ 07087

Contact: Lynne Lindahl
       (201) 794-8072

                           PSA for Use Through March 6

ANNOUNCER: Get the competitive advantage in business. Learn how to master the art of persuasion. You will be able to motivate and influence others after you attend the "Speak Out with Clout" seminar.

   This one-day seminar will be held at the Hyatt Hotel in Bayonne, New Jersey, on Tuesday, March 7. Seminar tuition is $195. To register or for more information, call (201) 794-8072.

                                   -End-

Figure 11-3. Sample of a public service announcement.

Copies of Any Print Publicity

The most persuasive previous publicity to include in a media kit is print media, since it can be seen and experienced by the person receiving it.

!!! Caution. Nothing looks worse than illegible photocopies of articles. When you succeed in getting written up in a newspaper or magazine, it is worth it to get good clean copies of the article printed on a high-quality paper stock.

Articles and Books You Have Written

If you have written any articles on the topic of your seminar, be sure to include them in your media kit. As with previous publicity, make sure you invest the extra time and money to get clean, attractive copies of your articles.

   If you have a published book, it will be well worth the investment to mail a copy of it. Nothing adds to your credibility like being an author. It's no accident that the talk show circuit and media are filled with authors.

Your Seminar or Company Brochure

You would like to get some media coverage of your program. Hopefully you can get someone from the media to attend. Therefore, if you are promoting a specific event, you should include the brochure for this event in the media kit.

If you have a company that relates to the topic of your seminar, you will want to include your company brochure as well. For example, if you are giving a seminar on using hypnosis to lose weight, the media would probably like to see your company brochure for general background information.

Sample Question List

When you approach the broadcast media, you should include a list of questions your interviewer can ask you. Talk show producers and hosts are extremely busy. Part of your job is to make their job easier. Do the thinking for the hosts, and they will be more likely to book you on their show.

Here is what a sample question list might look like for a sales seminar:

1. Can everybody be sold?

2. Is there any can't-miss closing technique?

3. How can you overcome an objection?

4. What can a salesperson do to avoid feeling bad about rejection?

5. What kind of person makes the most successful salesperson?

6. Why does the selling profession have a negative connotation?

7. How much money can a good salesperson earn?

Testimonials and Endorsements

Testimonials are statements from people who have attended one of your programs and want to testify to the effectiveness of it. Endorsements are testimonials by recognizable names or celebrities. Both testimonials and endorsements are useful for building credibility for you and your program.

In most cases, endorsements and testimonials will take the form of letters or excerpts from letters. There is a very simple, yet incredibly effective strategy for getting these letters. ASK!

If someone found your program to be exceptional, he or she will likely be more than willing to provide a letter saying so. If the person you are asking is very busy, you have two alternatives to ensure getting the endorsement or testimonial you ask for. First, you can ask for the statement from them orally, write down their words, and read them back. The second method is to ask them if you can write your own testimonial or endorsement. Then, mail or fax it to them for their approval or changes.

Video Demonstration Tapes

Although it is unlikely any of the media will watch a tape of your entire program, they will probably be willing to watch a 5- or 10-minute demo tape. Tapes can be especially helpful for broadcast media or for when you are promoting yourself as a speaker.

A high-quality video demo is an important tool for getting media coverage as well as for promoting your in-house programs. It is the most expensive component of your promotional materials. It is also one of the most valuable for opening doors to opportunities. Your professional-quality video communicates the message that you are not a beginner in the business.

Here are eight guidelines you should follow for creating your demo tape.

1. *Make it short.*   Because people are busy, they won't watch for more than 5 or 10 minutes. Your demo tape should *never* be more than 15 minutes long.

2. *Keep it fast paced.*   Preferably, you should use "bites" with lots of edits. Think MTV.

3. *Start taping your talks and seminars now.*   If you can get a few fantastic minutes from each taping session, you will be able to put together an incredible video demo tape.

4. *Use a professional quality format.*   There are a number of videotape formats. Home videotape formats are VHS and 8MM. The most common professional formats are Betacam, $\frac{3}{4}$ in, and 1 in. Other professional formats include a variety of digital formats. Professional video formats are referred to as broadcast quality.

Your video demo represents you. If the quality is poor, it will reflect poorly on you. It is important to work in a professional format so that the copies maintain their clarity. Copies made from home formats deteriorate very quickly.

The most cost-effective, yet high-quality formats are Betacam and $\frac{3}{4}$ in.

5. *Show some audience shots in your demo.*   It is important to assure the viewer that the audience is reacting favorably to you. Let them see the audience listening attentively, laughing, or participating in your seminar.

6. *Include a few short studio interview clips.*   If you have any footage from other TV shows you have done, review it to see if you can get a few good "bites." If you don't have any clips, you might want to record a few minutes in the studio. You can set it up as an interview type of format, answering any relevant questions about your program or topic.

7. *Be prepared to invest in your video demo.*   Most video demos can be produced for a few thousand dollars. It will cost approximately $500 to have a professional-quality video recording made of your seminar or talk. If you personally take the time to review your tapes, you can save a lot of

money in the editing studio. Editing time can cost from $50 to $200 an hour. Make sure you know exactly what you want to include in your finished product before you begin to edit.

8. *Package your video professionally.* Be sure to create an attractive cover for your video. You can produce a color cover that can slip into a hard plastic video box fairly inexpensively. If you digitize your demo you can make CD-ROM copies also.

$$$ **Saver.** Two inexpensive resources for editing your demo are readily available. Most local cable TV companies and local colleges have video editing available. Although they don't advertise, most will make them available at a very low rate.

Get your seminar recorded for free. If you are doing an in-house seminar for an organization, ask if they would like to make your seminar available on videotape to those who could not attend. Many organizations have professional-quality video recording equipment on the premises. Let them record your seminar, and use the tape to get some clips for your demo. On some occasions the client might ask you if your presentation can be videotaped. If that happens, you can ask for a modest fee, such as $500, to allow the videotaping. You can grant permission with the stipulation that the tape be made available to you for your demo.

Steps for Getting Media Coverage

Your success in getting publicity will be largely determined by your ability to organize and implement your media campaign. Here are the steps you should take to achieve your publicity goals:

1. *Select the appropriate media to approach.* Identify the right media for you, your topic, and your seminar. Who is the target audience for your publicity? If your program is geared toward women, women's magazines such as *Working Woman* and *Woman's Day* might be perfect. If your program is financial, *The Wall Street Journal* or the Financial News Network would be good targets for your publicity efforts.

!!! **Resources.** The following directory will help you identify the appropriate media for you to approach for publicity.

Bacon's Publicity Checker
Bacon's Publishing Company
332 S. Michigan Ave.
Chicago, IL 60604
Phone: (312) 922-2400
www.bacons.com

2. *Send your material to the right person.*   Although directories   are updated on a regular basis, personnel changes are frequent. Make sure you are sending your media material to the correct name.

3. *Prepare or select the proper material.*   If you are approaching a TV show, a demo tape would be great to send. On the other hand, if you are approaching the print media, don't bother to send tapes. They won't watch them.

!!! **Caution.**   Remember that the person who is reviewing your material is seeing it through the eyes of his or her audience. You should always be presenting your material with this fact in mind.

4. *Time your publicity efforts, if possible.*   For example, if you are doing a seminar for secretaries, a media release sent just before National Secretaries Day stands a much better chance of getting used than if it were sent some other time.

Timing is also important in relation to your event. Daily newspapers, radio, and TV want your material approximately one week in advance. Weekly publications need to receive material two to three weeks in advance.

5. *Send out your media kit.*

6. *Follow up with a phone call.*   After you wait an appropriate amount of time, it is good to phone to see if your material has been received. If it has, don't push. Just check. Respect their judgment. Offer some additional information, and develop some rapport. Keep the door open for future publicity efforts.

7. *Prepare thoroughly for the interview or show.*   Interviewers will have questions you have provided and possibly some of their own. Rehearse your answers and offer a few specific points or tips that will interest your audience. Remember, you are the expert!

Short success stories also work well for media coverage. If your seminar is on office organization, tell a humorous story about someone you know and how they solved their problem using your organization methods.

There is no substitute for being totally prepared. The success of your interview or guest appearance on a show will be determined largely by your preparation.

8. *Be sure to say thank you.*   You will have a good chance to get interviewed again if you leave a good impression. Send a thank-you note. Also, this is a small world. It is likely you will get to meet the same person somewhere else further down the road.

How to Get on National Radio and TV Talk Shows

There are three sources for getting on talk shows that you should become familiar with and use. Although it is difficult to coordinate the timing of your appearance with your seminar, if you manage it properly this can turn all publicity into dollars. The next section on how to exploit the media offers more detail.

1. *Radio-TV Interview Report.* This bimonthly magazine opens the door to lots of shows. It is distributed free to more than 4,700 talk show producers and hosts. You pay for an ad, and there is an *excellent* chance someone from the talk shows will contact you. The magazine staff will help design the most effective ad.

Radio-TV Interview Report
Bradley Communications Corp.
135 East Plumstead Ave.
Landsdowne, PA 19050-1206
Phone: (215) 259-1070

2. *Talkers: Directory of Talk Radio.* This is a directory of talk radio shows in America. It contains the names, addresses, fax numbers, email, and Web sites of hundreds of talk stations and individual hosts in the top 350 markets plus the top syndicators and networks. This directory is published by *Talkers Magazine*, the leading trade publication serving talk radio. They also offer a variety of resources for getting on talk radio shows.

Talkers Magazine
Phone: (413) 739-8255
www.Talkers.com

3. *The Yearbook of Experts, Authorities, and Spokespersons.* This directory is sent out to 7000 of the top journalists in America. Listings in this 800-page publication cost $225. The fee includes a 50-word advertisement and multiple listings in the index. The problem is you have to be fairly prominent or famous to get results.

Mitchell Davis
Broadcast Interview Source
2233 Wisconsin Ave., NW
Washington, D.C. 20007
Phone: (202) 333-5000
www.yearbook.com

How to Exploit the Media and Fill Seminar Seats

It's fun and encouraging to appear on talk shows and see your name in print, but what is more important is turning these opportunities into money in your pocket. In order to fully exploit each of your media appearances, you must do the following:

1. *Provide real answers.*   In each interview or article, you must offer some valuable information that will position you as an expert and a resource.

2. *Exploit with permission.*   Arrange with the host or writer for your seminar, book, or tape to be mentioned. This is very simple, ask! Most media people will be glad to offer their audience an opportunity to get more information.

3. *Provide a response mechanism.*   Offer your audience an 800 number, a local number, or your mailing address, or your secure Web site to sign up for your seminar.

4. *Give your audience an incentive to respond.*   Offer an inexpensive gift or bonus for calling or writing you. This can consist of information such as a tip sheet or list of contacts and resources that you can mail out for the price of a stamp. You can also offer a special gift to those who call and register for your program. In either case, the incentive will guarantee valuable benefits to you each and every time you get media exposure.

Each time someone calls, writes, or emails you, you will get invaluable, qualified names for your house mailing list. Remember, the most valuable mailing list you will ever own is your house mailing list that you develop. You will be able to market your books, tapes, and future programs to this list. You will also get registrations for your upcoming program using this proven strategy for exploiting the media.

!!! **Resources.**   These books are excellent sources for the basics of the publicity game.

Professional's Guide to Publicity, Richard Weiner (Public Relations
Publishing Company, Inc., 1975)

Publicity & Media Relations Checklists, David R. Yale, (McGraw-Hill
Trade, 1995)

Streetwise Complete Publicity Plans, Sandra Beckwith (Adams Streetwise
Series, 2003)

*Complete Guide to Internet Publicity: Creating and Launching Successful
Online Campaigns*, Steve O'Keefe (Wiley, 2002)

*Writing Effective News Releases: How to Get Free Publicity for Yourself,
Your Business, or Your Organization*, Catherine V. McIntyre (Piccadilly
Books, 1992)

!!! **Contact.**   The Public Relations Society of America is the major professional association of public relations practitioners in the United States. There are chapters nationwide.

Public Relations Society of America
33 Irving Place
New York, NY 10003
Phone: (212) 995-2230
www.prsa.org

12
Promoting Your Seminar for Less Than $100— The Two-Step Promotion

Would you like to create a profitable seminar business, but are you put off by the prospect of risking thousands of dollars and months of time and energy? Or perhaps you've got the spirit to get into the seminar business but lack the capital for promotion and advertising. In either case, it is important for you to learn and implement the following strategy carefully.

The two-step promotion is a method of marketing your seminar by first presenting a free or inexpensive introductory talk. At this short talk or miniseminar, your audience will have the chance to meet you, to learn more about your topic, and to decide whether they then want to attend a full-length program.

Your goal at the "intro" is to register people for your complete program. You want to sign them up on the spot or a short time later.

Many successful seminars are promoted using this simple technique. It works, but there are some rules to be followed if you want to be successful.

Four Golden Rules for the Two-Step Promotion

1. *Don't rip people off at the intro.* You must provide real information and give people real value at the intro. If you just give a sales pitch, it will

turn people off and they will not trust you. Remember, at the intro your aim is to let people know how much valuable information you have for them.

2. *Don't give them too much.* Conversely, you don't want to spill your guts in the lobby. If you set up your intro with a limited time frame of an hour or less, you will by definition limit how much you can divulge. It's similar to going to an ice-cream store and tasting a spoonful. Chances are you would not have wandered into an ice-cream store unless you were seriously interested in ice cream. At this point you are working percentages. A certain percentage will like the taste you have given them and will be willing to buy the whole ice-cream cone.

3. *Sell the sizzle, and they'll buy the steak.* You will want to create a motivational atmosphere at your intro event. Make it exciting and upbeat. Expose the benefits of your seminar. Point out how others have benefited from your seminar. Avoid the hard sell, though. Make people feel comfortable about you as their seminar leader. Be enthusiastic about your program without being phony. (See Chapter 17 on how to deliver a dynamic seminar.)

4. *Provide act-now motivation.* There are two simple act-now techniques that you should consider applying in order to get registrations at the intro event. The first is the discount. Emphasize the fact that registration on the day of the event will cost 20 to 30 percent more. Buy the ticket now and take advantage of the discount. You might also mention that the ticket is refundable if they change their mind.

The second act-now strategy is the gift. Offer the gift as an incentive for them to sign up at the intro. This gift should be relevant to the seminar itself. For example, if your seminar is on time management, a time organizer would be perfect. Books, audiotapes or videotapes, and nicely printed checklists also make excellent incentive gifts. You could even offer free personal consultations with you.

The idea here is to give your audience reasons to purchase their tickets right then at the intro.

The Two Types of Intro Events

The Public Intro

The public intro is basically promoted as if it were the seminar itself. You will need to rent a room, advertise the event, and prepare the room with a seminar setup.

Although you will be able to convert a good percentage of the audience to the full event, you will have to spend money on promoting the intro.

The big advantage to promoting your seminar with the two-step method is that you will be able to register many people for your seminar who would not otherwise have signed up for it.

The public intro works best for seminars that have mass appeal—topics such as stress control, weight loss, real estate, financial investment, or personal growth. The advantage of these seminars is that, in most cases, advertising in newspapers or radio works well to fill the intro event with people.

The most successful example of the public intro is the legendary Dale Carnegie seminars. The Dale Carnegie intro is free and offers to teach the audience a specific skill, such as memory training. Those who attend receive a rather entertaining program by a motivational speaker. At the intro, those present are invited to sign up for the longer, tuition-based programs on public speaking and the like.

The In-House Intro

The premise for the two-step promotion remains the same with an in-house intro, except the logistics for the intro are different. The intro is presented at an event that is sponsored by a specific group.

For example, let's say you are invited to speak at a meeting or conference of some kind. Although the event is not billed as an intro event for your seminar, at the end of your talk you can distribute flyers announcing an upcoming seminar. Basically, you will follow the same four golden rules described for the two-step promotion.

The mathematics for promoting a seminar with the in-house intro remain the same. That is, in order to sell X number of seminar seats, you have to speak to Y number of people at the intro.

The opportunities to speak at in-house events are endless and are described more fully in Chapter 13. Many trade and professional associations, nonprofit organizations, and church and civic groups are more than willing to let you promote your upcoming seminar in exchange for a free program to their group.

The one big advantage here is that the cost of promotion is negligible. A simple letter or phone call can often land you the speaking engagement for the intro. If you are hoping to attract 40 people to your full seminar, you should plan to speak to 200 or more people at the intro. The only additional expense, then, is the seminar flyer or brochure you will hand out at the intro. The following real-life case study illustrates how effectively this can work.

Case Study

Successful Seminar Promotion for Less Than $100 Using the In-House Intro

Goal: To sell out 20–25 seats to full seminar
Seminar topic: Selling skills

Target audience: Real estate salespeople
Place: Northern New Jersey
Procedure:

1. Telephone local real estate companies with 10 or more salespeople and speak with the sales manager.

2. Offer the sales manager a free mini sales training program for his or her sales staff. This program will be approximately 30 minutes in length and will be a part of their regularly scheduled weekly sales meetings.

3. Deliver a quality intro program and ask for sign-ups for your seminar at the end of each intro.

Total revenue (23 participants @ $99 each)		$2,277.00
Promotion expense (typesetting and printing)	$ 92.50	
Room rental expense	125.00	
Total expenses		−217.50
Total profit		$2,059.50

As you can see from this actual case study, the profit margin on the two-step promotion using in-house intros is enormous. Promotion costs were kept to less than $100. The only additional expense is the room rental. This will vary according to your location and group size.

The two-step requires initiative, but if you follow the four golden rules of two-step promotion, it is practically impossible to lose. The two-step method is not theory; it is a promotional strategy that works.

$$$ Saver. When you print the flyers that you will distribute at your intro, leave off the date, time, and place. Instead, leave a space where you can rubber-stamp or write in this information. Using this technique, you can extend your print run and save up to 50 percent in printing expenses.

The Rollover Principle

The success of the two-step promotion is dependent on your ability to roll people over from one program to another. If you are sincere and straightforward with your intentions, you will have no problem with the rollover principle. Let people know that you have information that will improve their lives, and they will be more than willing to roll over from the free program to the paid one.

13
How to Tap a Hidden Gold Mine—The In-House Market

Most newcomers seem to have a one-track mind when it comes to the seminar business. They immediately imagine the hotel meeting room filled to capacity with hundreds of participants who have paid a handsome fee to attend their program.

While it is true that there is lots of money to be made in the public seminar business, the same can be said of the in-house market. The big advantage of the in-house seminar market is that you do not have to sell the individual seats. You do have to market your program to the organizations that will utilize your program. But it is much simpler and requires much less investment and risk. The organization that sponsors your seminar will provide the people and take care of all of the detail work. This frees you to concentrate on delivering a great seminar.

If you don't like the sales and marketing game and the financial risk that accompanies it, you should seriously consider approaching the in-house market with your seminar. The sponsoring group offers a fixed fee for programs. The fees range usually from $500 to $5,000 or more per day.

Let's look at the range of opportunities in the in-house market.

What Are the Three Major In-House Seminar Markets?

1. *Corporate.* The largest in-house seminar market is the corporate seminar market. It has been reported that corporations spend more on education than the entire budget for all of the high schools and colleges in

America combined. Corporations depend on a variety of outside sources for their programs. Although credibility helps, your success in marketing to corporations depends less on who you are than on how much you can deliver. Helping them to improve productivity and profitability is the name of the game. Seminar companies that specialize in delivering programs to corporations are known as training companies.

!!! **Contacts.** In the Yellow Pages in Part 4 of this book, under the section titled "Corporate Training Companies," you will find a directory of more than 250 of the largest corporate training companies. In addition to the list of corporate training companies, there are thousands of individual consultants who deliver training programs to corporate America.

!!! **Resources.** There are two excellent resources if you are interested in the corporate seminar market.

Training
800 S. Ninth St.
Minneapolis, MN 55402
Phone: (800) 328-4329
www.trainingmag.com

Corporate Meeting and Event Planners Directory
Douglas Publications
2807 N. Parham Rd., Suite 200
Richmond, VA 23294
Phone: (804) 762-9600
Fax: (804) 217-8999
www.douglaspublications.com

Training magazine is full of information on corporate training. It also sponsors a conference and trade show each year in the winter. The trade show offers an opportunity for you to meet representatives from many training companies. Many of the seminars offered there will help to tune you into the corporate training field as a whole. In both cases, your attending will help you get an overview of corporate training. Call or write and ask to be put on the mailing list.

If your program is appropriate for the corporate market, *Corporate Meeting and Event Planners* is a directory listing 18,494 corporate meeting planners with information on how to locate them. What is particularly helpful is that the directory identifies which ones use professional speakers. They will customize a list for you. Lists are available on labels or computer disk. Call or write for more information.

!!! **Contact.** If you are serious about targeting the corporate market, you should join the Instructional Systems Association. There are some requirements for membership into ISA and you might not be eligible right away, but as soon as you qualify you must join.

ISA will provide you with the information and network of colleagues you need to succeed in the corporate training market. They collect and disseminate industry data, conduct a variety of conferences and meetings, and share insights that are not available anywhere else. Their membership roster reads like a *Who's Who* in the training industry.

Instructional Systems Association
12427 Hedges Run Dr., Suite 120
Lake Ridge, VA 21112
Phone: (877) 533-4914
www.isaconnection.org

2. *Trade and professional associations.* America is association crazy. Practically everyone belongs to some kind of professional association. Taken together, associations hold many thousands of meetings each year in which seminar leaders and speakers are employed. They have meetings on the local, state, regional, and national levels, and they continually look for new speakers and seminar leaders to work at their various functions.

!!! **Resources.** There are three excellent references for organizations and contacts in the vast and lucrative association market.

National Trade and Professional
  Associations of America
Columbia Books
1825 Connecticut Ave., NW
Suite 625
Washington, D.C. 20009
Phone: (888) 265-0600
www.columbiabooks.com

Association of Meeting and Event
  Planners Directory
Douglas Publications
2807 N. Parham Rd., Suite 200
Richmond, VA 23294
Phone: (804) 762-9600
Fax: (804) 217-8999
www.douglaspublications.com

Encyclopedia of Associations
Gale Research Company
362 Lakeside Dr.
Foster City, CA 94404
Phone: (800) 877-4253
www.library.dialog.com

National Trade and Professional Associations of America is a book that lists more than 6,300 trade and professional associations. It also offers such other valuable information as when and where these associations hold their meetings and conventions.

The *Encyclopedia of Associations* is a three-volume reference source that lists associations and members as well as the names of individuals in charge of educational programs for their association.

The *Association of Meeting and Event Planners* is one of the best directories for contacting 8,000 national associations that hold conventions, meetings, and seminars. It notes which ones hire professional speakers. Customized lists are available on mailing labels and computer disk.

!!! Contact. The association business is a multimillion-dollar business. In fact, there is even a national association that consists of people who are the leaders of associations.

American Society of Association Executives
1575 I St., NW
Washington, D.C. 20005
Phone: (202) 626-ASAE
www.asaenet.org

The American Society of Association Executives (ASAE) publishes an annual directory entitled *Who's Who in Association Management*. The directory lists the individual in charge of the educational programs for each association. ASAE holds three major conventions each year.

ASAE has regional societies of association executives. Many of these local chapters hold monthly meetings and annual conferences for which they need the services of seminar leaders and speakers. You might want to attend some of their regional meetings or conferences and explore the possibility of speaking at one of them. You will be networking and speaking to the people who hire you or recommend you to speak at their association programs.

To learn more about ASAE and how it works, write or email your regional chapter, listed below.

National and State Societies of Association Executives (alphabetized by state)

National Headquarters
1575 I St., NW
Washington, D.C. 20005
Phone: (202) 626-2723
www.asaenet.org

Alabama Chapter of Association Executives
P.O. Box 11594
Montgomery, AL 36111
Phone: (334) 260-7970
www.acae.org

Arizona Society of Association Executives
2302 N. Third St.
Suite D
Phoenix, AZ 85004
Phone: (602) 266-0133
www.azsae.com

Arkansas Society of Association Executives
P.O. Box 23034
Little Rock, AR 72221
Phone: (501) 223-9188
www.arksae.org

California Society of Association Executives
P.O. Box 188100
Sacramento, CA 95818
Phone: (916) 443-8998
www.calsae.org

Northern California Society of Association Executives
74 New Montgomery, Suite 230
San Francisco, CA 94105
Phone: (415) 927-5735
www.ncsae.org

Colorado Society of Association Executives
2170 S. Parker Rd., Suite 265
Denver, CO 80231
Phone: (303) 368-9090
www.csaenet.org

Connecticut Society of Association Executives
214 Warrenton Ave.
West Hartford, CT 06119
Phone: (860) 519-1843
www.csae.net

Greater Washington Society of Association Executives
1300 Pennsylvania Ave., NW
Washington, D.C. 20004
Phone: (202) 326-9500
www.gwsae.org

Central Florida Society of Association Executives
526 Simpson Rd.
Kissimmee, FL 34744
Phone: (407) 933-7879
www.cfsae.org

Florida Society of Association Executives
P.O. Box 11119
Tallahassee, FL 32302
Phone: (850) 222-7994
www.fsae.org

Tallahassee Society of Association Executives
P.O. Box 1139
Tallahassee, FL 32302
Phone: (850) 222–7994
www.tallysae.org

Georgia Society of Association Executives
2175 Northlake Pkwy.
Suite 128
Tucker, GA 30084
Phone: (770) 934-6210
www.gsae.org

Idaho Society of Association Executives
P.O. Box 6239
Boise, ID 83707
Phone: (208) 863-0391
www.isaeonline.org

Association Forum of Chicagoland
20 N. Wacker Dr.
Suite 3000
Chicago, IL 60606
Phone: (312) 236-2288
www.associationforum.org

Illinois Society of Association Executives
P.O. Box 7513
Springfield, IL 62791
Phone: (217) 793-5420
www.isae.com

Indiana Society of Association Executives
9202 N. Meridian St., Suite 200
Indianapolis, IN 46260
Phone: (317) 571-5614
www.isae.org

Iowa Society of Association Executives
431 E. Locust St., Suite 300
Des Moines, IA 50309
Phone: (515) 243-1558
www.iowasae.org

Kansas Society of Association Executives
4301 SW Huntoon #9
Topeka, KS 66604
Phone: (785) 272-0083
www.accesskansas.org

Kansas City Society of Association Executives
P.O. Box 23728
Shawnee Mission, KS 66283
www.kcsae.org

Kentucky Society of Association Executives
1501 Twilight Trail
Frankfort, KY 40601
Phone: (502) 223-5322
www.ksae.com

Louisiana Society of Association Executives
1914 S. Carrollton Ave.
New Orleans, LA 70118
Phone: (504) 866-3855
www.lsae.org

Maryland Society of Association Executives
1305 Huntsman Court
Bel Air, MD 21015
Phone: (410) 569-3425
www.mdsae.org

Michigan Society of Association Executives
300 E. Michigan Ave.
Suite 350
Lansing, MI 48933
Phone: (517) 702-9011
www.msae.org

Midwest Society of Association Executives
1885 University Ave., Suite 222
St. Paul, MN 55104
Phone: (651) 647-6388
www.msae.com

Mississippi Society of Association Executives
319 S. Main St.
Yazoo City, MS 39194
Phone: (662) 751-4626
www.msassociations.com

Missouri Society of Association Executives
722 E. Capitol Ave.
Jefferson City, MO 65102
Phone: (573) 659-8898
www.msae.net

St. Louis Society of Association Executives
8000 Bonhomme
Suite 412
St. Louis, MO 63105
Phone: (314) 863-2258
www.slsae.org

Nevada Society of Association Executives
PMB 106
8665 W. Flamingo Rd.
Las Vegas, NV 89147
Phone: (702) 889-1673
Fax: (702) 889-1674
www.nsae.net

New England Society of Association Executives
305 Second Ave.
Suite 200
Waltham, MA 02451
Phone: (781) 895-9078
www.nesae.org

New Jersey Society of Association Executives
215 Amherst St., Suite 1
Highland Park, NJ 08904
Phone: (732) 339-9095
www.njsae.org

New Mexico Society of Association Executives
P.O. Box 9284
Santa Fe, NM 87504
Phone: (505) 989-8473
www.nmsae.org

Empire State Society of Association Executives
275 ½ Lark St.
Albany, NY 12210
Phone: (518) 463-1755
www.essae.org

New York Society of Association Executives
322 Eighth Ave., Suite 1400
New York, NY 10001
Phone: (212) 206-8230
www.nysaenet.org

Association Executives of North Carolina
P.O. Box 10828
Raleigh, NC 27605
Phone: (919) 821-1648
www.aencnet.org

Greater Cleveland Society of Association Executives
3487 Center Rd., Suite 6C
Brunswick, OH 44212
Phone: (330) 273-5756
www.gcsae.com

Ohio Society of Association Executives
500 W. Wilson Bridge Rd.
Suite 80
Worthington, OH 43085
Phone: (614) 846-0998
www.osae.org

Oklahoma Society of Association Executives
601 NW Grand Blvd.
Suite C
Oklahoma City, OK 73118
Phone: (405) 879–0027
www.ok.osae.org

Oregon Society of Association Executives
147 SE 102nd Ave.
Portland, OR 97216
Phone: (503) 253-9026
www.osam.org

Delaware Valley Society of Association Executives
P.O. Box 187
Montgomeryville, PA 18936
Phone: (215) 393-3144
www.dvsae.net

Pennsylvania Alliance for Association Executives
800 Corporate Circle, Suite 201
Harrisburg, PA 17110
Phone: (717) 232-4500
www.pa3.biz

Pittsburgh Society of Association Executives
5004 Holly Court
Murrysville, PA 15668
Phone: (724) 733-4751
www.psae.org

Tennessee Society of Association Executives
644 W. Iris Dr.
Nashville, TN 37204
Phone: (615) 298-5944
www.tnsae.org

Dallas/Fort Worth Society of Association Executives
P.O. Box 71076
Dallas, TX 75371
Phone: (214) 827-4425
www.dfwae.org

Houston Society of Association Executives
P.O. Box 22111
Houston, TX 77227
www.hsaenet.org

San Antonio Society of Association Executives
14602 Huebner Rd. M116
PMB 149
San Antonio, TX 78230
Phone: (210) 408-1699
www.sasae.org

Texas Society of Association Executives
3724 Executive Center Dr.
Suite 150
Austin, TX 78731
Phone: (512) 444-1974
www.tsae.org

**Vermont Society of Association
Executives**
P.O. Box 1013
Montpelier, VT 05601
www.vsae.net

**Virginia Society of Association
Executives**
10231 Telegraph Rd., Suite A
Glen Allen, VA 23059
Phone: (804) 747-4971
www.vsae.org

**Washington Society of
Association Executives**
P.O. Box 2016
Edmonds, WA 98020
Phone: (425) 778-6162
www.wsaenet.org

**Wisconsin Society of Association
Executives**
1123 N. Water St.
Milwaukee, WI 53202
Phone: (414) 277-9723
www.wssae.org

3. *Continuing education.* There are more than 2,000 colleges and universities offering a variety of seminars or short multiday educational programs. This is an extremely accessible market. It is an ideal market in which to begin making money in the seminar business very quickly. In fact, if you follow the simple seven-step plan described in Chapter 14, you may be able to jump-start your career in the seminar business.

How to Market to Corporations and Associations

Whether you are marketing to corporations or associations, the steps are very simple.

1. *Locate organizations that would profit from your seminar, and identify the decision maker.* Some of the directories that have been mentioned in this chapter are a good place to start.

Direct-mail companies might also be a source of lists of people who could bring you in to speak to their group. For example, if you have a seminar for salespeople, a list of corporate sales managers would be a good list. List brokers can also provide you with the telephone numbers of the people on their list.

2. *Contact your prospects.* There are a few variations on this step. You can use direct mail followed by a phone call, or you can phone first to further qualify the prospect before mailing. The purpose of your direct-mail campaign or phone calls is to generate inquiries for more detailed information about your program and to find out exactly what you must do to get the job.

3. *Mail out detailed information to qualified prospects.* They will probably want a detailed outline of your program, background information on you,

and various items from your media kit. These items are described in more detail in Chapter 11.

4. *Follow up.*   A follow-up call or letter is needed to make sure the information was received and to answer any questions the prospect might have.

5. *Don't give up.*   They might not be immediately ready for your program, and they may ask you to call back at a later date. In most cases, they really do want you to call back. It is your responsibility to use a tickler file to give them a call or send a letter at a later date.

Corporations and associations take a considerable amount of time from contact to contract. You must be patient. Sometimes an association will be planning for a conference or meeting a year or more away. It is not unusual for it to take six months from contact to contract, but the wait is well worth it. If you do a good job, you have a very good chance of getting referral business within the same organization. Your time and investment marketing to the in-house market could easily result in tens of thousands of dollars of seminar programs.

$$$ Saver.   Remember, as a general rule all expenses are billed back to the client. See Chapter 7 for a sample contract you can use when you have been accepted for an in-house program.

!!! Contact and Resource.   One of the easiest ways to market to the corporate and association market is to get listed in the online directory of training companies: Training Registry. The Training Registry Web site attracts visitors who are looking for training and training-related resources and a quick, easy way to find them. If you are interested in marketing to this market, Training Registry will get you on the map with a flow of qualified leads. Let them know you heard about them from this book.

Richard Borgen
Training Registry
Phone: (919) 847-0331
www.trainingregistry.com

How to Use Speakers Bureaus to Get Booked for In-House Seminars

There are hundreds of speakers bureaus that focus their attention on the in-house market. These bureaus market speakers and seminar leaders to the corporate and association market. Although some of these organizations focus their efforts on celebrity speakers such as former presidents and popular entertainment personalities, many book experts on a wide variety of topics.

Speakers bureaus will be willing to book you if you can provide information to the audiences of their clients. Of course, they will examine your experience and credentials closely.

There are a few basic steps you must take in order to get booked by speakers bureaus. First, you must contact them and find out what the bureau wants you to send them. Although it will vary slightly from bureau to bureau, initially they will want your media kit, and, in particular, most will want a videotape.

Speakers bureaus get a lot of inquiries, therefore you will need to niche market yourself. You can niche market by target industry or by topic. For example, you can say your focus is high-tech industries or your topic is humor in business.

In addition to niche marketing yourself, you must be persistent. Most bureaus need to get to know you to some degree. They will want to feel confident about you, your presentation, and your promotability. Some will want to come see you before they will book you. If you concentrate on developing rapport with the bureau, you will increase your chances of getting booked.

Financial arrangements vary from bureau to bureau, but you can count on paying a commission of somewhere between 20 and 30 percent. Most bureaus will also want a commission of spin-off engagements that result from the initial booking.

!!! **Contacts.**   The Yellow Pages in Part 4 of this book has a list of speakers bureaus you can contact.

If you decide you would like to start your own bureau or you would like to seriously pursue speakers bureaus for building your business, you should be aware of the International Association of Speakers Bureaus (IASB).

The International Association of Speakers Bureaus is a worldwide trade association of speakers agencies and bureaus. They offer an assortment of valuable books, tapes, and other materials.

IASB also offers a service called eSpeakers. eSpeakers can help you electronically market yourself and your programs to both the speakers bureau community as well as prospective clients.

International Association of Speakers Bureaus
2780 Waterfront Pkwy., East
Suite 120
Indianapolis, IN 46214
Phone: (317) 297-0872
Fax: (317) 387-3387
www.iasbweb.org

14
How to Start Making Money Right Now

If you've got an idea for a seminar and want to get started right away, you can! The college and adult continuing education market is wide open and relatively simple to enter. Best of all, you'll make money while you're learning the ropes.

Besides making money and getting great experience, you can test your seminar and tune it up before rolling it out for a larger audience, possibly even on a national level.

Practically every college and university in America offers a variety of noncredit courses. In addition, most high schools and athletic clubs, such as your local YMCA and YWCA, offer adult education programs. Many parks and recreation facilities also offer similar programs. Check the bulletin board section of your local newspaper for groups or organizations that run adult education programs.

These groups are always looking for new programs and are open to trying new ideas. Program directors rely on outside suggestions to provide innovative programs. Because the fees paid are not exceedingly high, the requirements for getting the opportunity to present your program are not exceedingly high either.

Most of these adult continuing education programs are offered in the evening or on the weekend. The big advantage to you is that you can begin to make money in the seminar business while you maintain your regular job or profession.

All you have to do is adhere to the following seven-step system.

$$$ One seminar leader who followed this system booked 13 seminars within the first 30 days he applied this system.

Ways to Start Making Money Right Now

1. Identify your prospective local continuing education market. Investigate two-year and four-year colleges and universities. Most telephone books list educational facilities. If not, your local library will have a complete list in the *Educational Directory of Colleges and Universities*. Also, check with any Ys in your area, and ask if they offer adult education programs.

2. Call or write to them and ask for their continuing education catalog.

3. Study these catalogs to determine what kinds of programs they currently offer. Ideally, your seminar will not exist in their catalog. If it does, perhaps you can focus on a slightly different aspect of the topic. For example, if the school is offering a program on leadership, perhaps you could offer a program on leadership skills for women. Or if your specialty is writing and they already offer a program on creative writing, you could tailor a program on business writing.

4. Call the facility, and find out who the program director is. In order to prevent getting bounced around, it's best to ask specifically, "I'd like to speak to whoever is in charge of choosing your programs." When you speak to that person, simply ask, "What do I have to do to be considered for your next seminar catalog listing?"

5. Mail out whatever the program planner requests from you. More than likely you will be asked for one or more of the following: a description of your program; your bio, including credentials *and the experience that makes you an expert on the topic*; and endorsements or reference letters. It is also helpful to the program director to include reasons why you think your seminar would be popular and timely.

6. Follow up with another phone call about 10 days later. Find out what else is needed in order to make a decision. Set up another contact date if no decision has been made.

7. Follow up. Be persistent without being a pest. Don't be upset if you don't get into the catalog the first time. There is a good chance you will get into a later one if you stay in touch.

The two best times of the year to pursue seminar opportunities at colleges and universities are September for programs beginning in February, and March for programs beginning in September. The other adult education programs are not as predictable when it comes to accepting proposals for new programs.

Additional Techniques for Getting Booked Quickly

There are two additional techniques for increasing your chances of getting booked quickly. First, offer to assist the program director in marketing your program. Perhaps you have friends or associates who would be interested in attending your program and could be used to prime the pump. Or maybe you can pull strings to get some publicity in the newspaper or on local radio talk shows.

Second, you might try a direct-mail marketing program to all of the potential continuing education programs throughout the country. Although the costs of the mailing can run into the hundreds of dollars, you would only need to book one or two programs to recover your investment and break even. Anything beyond that is profit.

The fees paid for these programs usually vary from about $50 an hour to a couple of hundred dollars a day. Some programs pay you according to the number of participants.

$$$ You can match, double, or triple your profits by offering additional services or products such as books and tapes. Remember, you don't need to have your own books and tapes. You can make substantial profits by selling products you get at wholesale prices. See Chapter 16 for more strategies and techniques you can use to produce substantial income.

*!!! * **Contacts.**   There are three excellent organizations you will probably want to contact if you are going to deliver your seminars to the continuing education market.

American Association for Adult
  and Continuing Education
4380 Forbes Blvd.
Lanham, MD 20706
Phone: (301) 918-1913
Fax: (301) 918-1846
E-Mail: aaace10@aol.com
www.aaace.org

National University Continuing
  Education Association
One Dupont Plaza Circle, Suite 420
Washington, D.C. 20036
Phone: (202) 659-3130
www.ucea.edu

Learning Resources Network (LERN)
P.O. Box 9
River Falls, WI 54022
Phone: (715) 426-9777
www.lern.com

15

How to Get a Job with a Seminar Company

Help Wanted: Seminar Leader

You may never have seen an ad for a seminar leader in the want ad section of your local paper. Nevertheless, there are hundreds of companies that hire seminar leaders to deliver the company's seminar program. These seminar leaders travel all around the country making really good money, and so can you.

Getting a job as a seminar leader is much like a job search in any particular industry. The biggest problem is finding the industry. Who do you call? Where are they located? Which are the best seminar companies for you to apply to?

Do you Fit the Job Description? Fill Out This Questionnaire

	Yes	No
1. Are you highly motivated?	☐	☐
2. Are you able to travel?	☐	☐
3. Do you love to be in front of an audience?	☐	☐
4. Do you enjoy helping others?	☐	☐
5. Do you like to teach?	☐	☐
6. Do you love to learn?	☐	☐

If you can't answer yes to *all* the above questions, you probably aren't suited to pursue a career working for a seminar company. You might succeed in promoting your own seminars, but it's not likely you would enjoy working with a seminar company.

Unlike many other professions, there is no career development track in the seminar business. You can't major at the university in seminar leading.

Expertise and experience as they relate to the seminar topic are always helpful. But in most cases, if you are teachable and highly motivated, you'll be seriously considered and have a reasonable chance of getting hired.

Advantages and Disadvantages of Working for a Seminar Company

Advantages:

- No investment necessary
- Excellent financial rewards
- Great experience
- No seminar marketing necessary
- No need to develop your own seminar

Disadvantages:

- Limited control of seminar content
- Less autonomy (You're not your own boss.)
- Definite ceiling on earnings

In brief, if you are ready to make money presenting seminars but lack marketing expertise and money, working for a seminar company might be perfect for you. In addition, the professional experience you will get is invaluable. Many of the most famous speakers and seminar leaders in America started by delivering seminars for national companies.

Who Hires Seminar Leaders?

Organizations that hire seminar leaders come in three varieties: public seminar companies, training companies, and corporations that have in-house training departments. They all rely on talented leaders to present programs.

How Much Do Seminar Leaders Get Paid?

In order to understand *how much* seminar leaders get paid, you must first understand *how* seminar leaders get paid.

Per Diem

Per diem means literally "by the day." Public seminar companies and corporate training companies pay their speakers a daily rate. This does not include expenses. Rates vary considerably—from $300 to $1,500 per day. Per diem rates will vary according to your expertise, experience, type of seminar, company, and length of time with the company. Your pay scale can also be affected by the amount of product (books and tapes) or consulting services sold as a result of the seminar.

The number of days you work on a per diem basis will vary according to the needs of the company with which you are affiliated. As a contract or per diem employee, you will be on call. On many occasions these companies are very busy and utilize the services of many seminar leaders. Likewise, when the company's business is slow, you are affected too.

Hiring seminar leaders on a per diem basis is standard for the seminar business. It is the most economical and efficient hiring system for public seminar companies and training companies to use. By hiring you as an outside consultant, they have the freedom to use you on an as-needed basis.

Standard Weekly Salary

Many established corporate training companies and public seminar companies offer full-time staff positions for seminar leaders. Because of their steady number of programs, both of these types of companies find it economical to hire full-time speakers. The Yellow Pages in Part 4 of this book will help you identify, target, and pursue these prospective employers.

In the Yellow Pages you will find a section titled, "Corporate Training Companies." All of these companies provide high-quality business seminars on a wide variety of topics. To get an idea of the variety of topics offered by these companies, refer back to Fig. 1-2, the professional development topic list.

Also in the Yellow Pages of this book, you will find a list titled "Public Seminar Companies." This list notes which public seminar companies utilize staff seminar leaders, which ones utilize outside consultants who work on a per diem basis, and which ones use both. All depend on qualified seminar leaders to deliver their programs. As in any business, there is turnover and openings occur on a regular basis.

The third opportunity for anyone seeking a full-time salaried position as a seminar leader is to work as a trainer within a corporation or a large nonprofit organization. Because of the constant need to train employees, all large organizations, and even most medium-sized ones, have a training department. Many of these training departments consist of 10 to 20 full-time seminar leaders. Along with the opportunity to deliver programs on a regular basis, you get the job security and benefits that come with a salaried position of this kind.

!!! Contact. If you are seeking a full-time salaried position within a training department, the best place to start networking is with members of the American Society for Training and Development (ASTD). ASTD has more than 50,000 members nationally. This organization provides job postings for in-house trainers. To find out about meetings in your local area, contact the national office:

American Society for Training and Development
1630 Duke St., P.O. Box 1443
Alexandria, VA 22313
Phone: (703) 683-8100
www.astd.org

How to Conduct a Job Search

The strategies for finding a position as a seminar leader are similar to the ones you would use for any position. The big difference is that, except for a position as an in-house trainer, there are very few help-wanted listings.

!!! Contact. As any career counselor will tell you, networking is one of the most effective techniques you can use. Check the Yellow Pages in Part 4 of this book under "Professional Associations for Networking and Education." By speaking with other seminar leaders, speakers, and trainers, you will learn about topics and about the seminar companies themselves. You will also get some idea of salaries and benefits.

Besides networking, you can phone and write specific seminar companies to get more information. You might want to start with some located nearby if possible. Find out what kinds of programs they specialize in and where they market their programs.

After you have targeted some companies that you feel are compatible with your interests, area of expertise, and experience, you should make inquiries to learn what steps you must take to apply for a position as a program leader.

The application procedure will vary according to the company. Some companies will ask for a videotape of you in action. Others will ask you to come in and deliver a few minutes of a program in their office.

Sometimes you will be accepted for a position, but there will not be a job opening. In that situation, your challenge is to remind the company subtly that you are ready to begin as soon as an opening arises. In other cases, the company will only interview when it needs seminar leaders. If you are accepted, you will start immediately.

Once you have been accepted as a program leader, the company will teach you how to deliver its seminar. There is usually some form of payment for this learning period. In the final step, you are evaluated as you deliver the program. If the quality of your work is satisfactory, you will be offered either a staff or per diem position.

Many companies allow some leeway in how you present the material. This offers you some creative input into the seminar itself and allows you to control the program to some degree.

Getting a job as a seminar leader can be an important first step for anyone seriously considering a career in the seminar business. Don't eliminate this possibility as a strategic step in your professional growth. Many giants in the business started this way.

16
Double Your Profits with Back-of-the-Room Sales

It's no secret that book, compact disc, and video product sales at seminars result in millions of dollars in additional revenues for the seminar business as a whole. In many cases the profits from the sale of products and services far outweigh those produced by seminar tuition. The advent of the electronic age has opened the door to even more opportunities to multiply your seminar profits. Let's first examine the various products and services that lend themselves to back-of-the-room or post-seminar sales, and then the best strategies and techniques to market them.

$$$ Regardless of the product or service, it is important to understand why products and services are so enormously profitable. It is not the actual cost of the product your seminar participants are buying, it is the *value* of the information that it contains. In fact when viewed in terms of value, the price of your books, tapes, CDs, coaching, or whatever is probably insignificant in terms of how it will affect the people who actually apply the information. This is why a CD that costs you $1.50 to reproduce can easily be sold for five or ten times this amount, providing you with an extremely lucrative business opportunity.

It is important when pricing your products and services to remember that the information you are selling can change lives and significantly benefit those who purchase them. When pricing your products and services you should always first consider the value of the information you are providing and not the cost of producing or distributing it.

Profitable Products

Printed Materials

Although not everybody is a writer, it is safe to say that anyone who is in the seminar business is capable of producing some form of printed material that can generate extra income.

The Resource Guide. The most simple and quickly printed document you can produce is the resource guide. A resource guide can be as short as 5 pages or as long as 50. The essential component is the value of the information contained within it. For example, if your seminar is on investing in real estate, you might want to include sample contracts, letters of agreement, and lists of various banks and mortgage companies. Similarly, if your seminar is on some aspect of personal growth, a complete list of all books and tapes that relate to your topic would be worthwhile.

Names, addresses, and phone numbers that provide important contacts make excellent information for a resource guide. The type of information found in the Yellow Pages in Part 4 of this book is a good example of resource information you can make available for sale.

There is no limit to the types of information you can include in a resource guide. Checklists, tips, dos and don'ts, sample forms, and so forth, are the kinds of resources for which people are willing to pay good money to take home with them.

The price you will be able to charge for your resource guide depends upon its size and value. A minimum price for a resource guide is probably about $10. In most cases, it should be a minimum length of 10 to 20 pages.

The beauty of the resource guide is that it is assembled rather than written. This means you don't need highly refined writing skills to make this idea work. Anyone who has a grasp of his or her topic can quickly assemble a valuable resource guide.

The Monograph. The monograph, or minireport, is a short booklet that summarizes or expands the material discussed at the seminar. It is a short treatise on your topic, *written by you*. Ideally, a monograph should focus on a specific area. In general, it should be a minimum of 10 to 20 pages. By definition, your monograph graduates to the status of a book when it exceeds about 50 pages.

Besides the obvious advantage of being an additional source of income, a monograph or a series of monographs has another important benefit. It provides you with an added level of credibility as an authority. There is no doubt our society places tremendous importance on the printed word. You further your image, enhance your reputation, and ultimately increase your value in the marketplace as a result of producing these short written expositions.

$$$ It's also easy to see how a series of monographs could become chapters for a subsequent book. Keep this possibility in mind as you develop your monographs.

How to Self-Publish Resource Guides and Monographs. It is important to mention here how *easy* and *inexpensive* it is to produce print- ed products once they are written. You don't need to find a literary agent or a publisher. Your local copy center will do. After you have written your resource guide or monograph, print it out on a word processor or your printer. Then simply copy it for a few cents a page, and staple it together.

If you are more exacting or ambitious, there are a number of ways you can jazz up your resource guide or monograph.

- Typeset your material using desktop publishing technology, and have it printed on a laser printer.

- Typeset your front cover.

- Use a colored card stock for the front and back covers.

- Instead of using one staple in the corner, use two or three staples along the left edge to give it more of the appearance of a book.

- Insert your resource guide or monograph into fancy colored folders with a clear-plastic cover.

- If your resource guide or monograph is 25 pages or more, use a plastic spiral binding.

- Use a color cover. It will add only a few cents to the cost but consider- ably to the perceived value. This works especially well if you use a clear-plastic cover and a spiral binding.

The creative possibilities are endless. All of the above features can be provided by any good quick-copy shop.

!!! Caution. The costs of all of these improvements add up quickly and can reduce your profits substantially. Your material has the potential of being a gold mine of revenue for you, but you must keep your production costs to a minimum.

After you have completed your prototype product, bring the actual product with you and shop around for prices.

The Book. The ultimate in printed products is, of course, the book. The book has immense financial value as a product. It is also your passport to big money in the seminar business. A book establishes you as an expert. Your value as a speaker and seminar leader increases significantly when you're the person who literally wrote the book.

View it as a building process. You may not feel capable of sitting down and writing a book right now, but you can begin to write down and organize your thoughts, ideas, and words of wisdom.

Slowly but surely you will begin to assemble a collection of writings. Your monographs, articles, resource material, seminar workbooks, and notes will take shape as a longer treatise. You can also get lots of great material for your book from the people who attend your seminars.

Also, as you continue to speak at your seminars and market them, your knowledge of the needs of your audience will increase and you will develop a better idea of the direction your book should take. There are two ways to publish your book.

1. *Sell it to a publisher.* This is a long-term process. First you must write a proposal, then submit it to publishing companies that might handle your type of book. An alternative to speaking directly to the publisher is to find an agent who will send it out to the appropriate prospective publishers.

!!! **Resources.** One of the best all-around sources for information on becoming a published author is *Writer's Digest* magazine. It is a cornucopia of information on all aspects of the book business. The monthly issues of this magazine have great in-depth how-to articles on both the creative process and the marketing of your book idea. *Writer's Digest* is also one of the best sources for books on how to succeed as a writer. Books advertised in the magazine include such topics as how to get published, how to write a nonfiction book, how to write a proposal, and how to find a literary agent. Write, call, or go online for a complete book catalog.

Writer's Digest
P.O. Box 2123
Harlan, IA 51593
Phone: (800) 333-0133
www.writersdigest.com

If you want more information on the services literary agents provide, how they work and how to make contact with them, the following resources are recommended.

Association of Author's Representatives
P.O. Box 23701
Ansonia Station
New York, NY 10003
www.aar-online.com

Here are online resources that will provide you with everything you need to know to secure an agent for your book.

www.writers.net
www.writelinks.com
www.literaryagents.org
www.authorlink.com

All agents require a query letter before submission of a manuscript. Not all agents will handle your type of book, nor will they necessarily be willing to take on new clients. Remember the cardinal rule in any form of promotion and marketing: Persistence is the key to success.

2. *Self-publish your book.*   Although prestige is a primary factor in selling your book to a mainstream publisher, your profits are greater if you self-publish your book.

You can self-publish in two different ways. The first is the low-budget route. Create your book using word-processing software and print it out on regular $8\frac{1}{2}$- by 11-in paper, quick copy at your local copy center, and have it spiral bound. You can spruce it up with some of the same suggestions made above regarding resource guides and monographs.

The second way to self-publish is with a perfect binding. Perfect binding makes the book look "real." There are countless choices to make when you choose to publish your book with a perfect binding; hard cover or soft cover, size of the book, type of paper, and number of copies to print are just a few of the most obvious ones.

Although self-publishing might seem like a tall order, it is a relatively simple thing to do. In addition, the financial reward is outstanding. The average royalty on a book published by a mainstream publisher usually isn't more than 10 percent of the selling price. The same book self-published will return an average of 40 percent of the selling price.

Naturally the biggest advantage of selling your book to a publisher is that the publisher has a distribution network in place. As a self-publisher, you have to design your own avenues of distribution.

!!! Resources.   If you choose to investigate the self-publishing route, there are several excellent resources available.

Dan Poynter
Para Publishing
P.O. Box 4232-P
Santa Barbara, CA 93140-4232
Phone: (805) 968-7277
www.parapub.com

Communication Creativity
P.O. Box 909
Buena Vista, CO 81211
Phone: (800) 331-8355
www.communicationcreativity.
com

The Editorial Freelancers
  Association
71 W. 23rd St., Suite 1910
New York, NY 10010
Phone: (212) 929-5400
www.the-efa.org

Publishers Marketing
  Association
627 Aviation Way
Manhattan Beach, CA 90266
Phone: (310) 372-2732
www.pma-online.org

The foremost authority and one-stop resource on the subject of self-publishing is Para Publishing. For a complete list of the products and services offered, write or call for their complete catalog. Communication Creativity is a good source as well. The Editorial Free-Lancers Association is a good contact if you are interested in hiring a free-lance editor to review your manuscript before self-publishing.

Publishers Marketing Association provides a wide variety of educational resources as well as actual marketing services to help you market your book successfully. This association is a must for any self-publisher.

!!! Resources. Here are some excellent printers that specialize in printing books. Their prices are competitive and their quality is excellent. Many of them will also provide valuable advice and direction to assist you in producing a quality book.

Vaughan Printing
www.vaughanprinting.com

Bang Printing
www.bangprinting.com

Sheridan Books
www.sheridanbooks.com

Whitehall Printing Company
www.whitehallprinting.com

Thompson-Shore, Inc.
www.tshore.com

Malloy Press
www.malloy.com

Compact Discs

The most popular audio product is the compact disc. Although some people still prefer to listen to spoken word recordings on audiotape, it is now obsolete technology. Many people prefer to listen in their cars and most cars have CD players rather than cassette players.

Compact discs are a popular and profitable product to consider for creating additional income streams. After initial recording and setup costs, compact discs cost $.50 to $2 to produce depending on the quantity. Even with the additional costs of packaging the CD, the profit margin is substantial.

Figure 16-1 represents an expense and profit sheet for a six–compact disc package. These prices are based upon producing an initial run of 100 units. In the case of the color covers, the cost to produce 1,000 covers is about the same as it is for 200, so the price is based upon a quantity of 1,000.

A Quick Way to Estimate the Cost of Producing a CD Album

The basic rule of thumb for producing an album is:

Number of compact discs in album × $2 + cost of printing album cover + printed materials + cost of album + cost of recording and editing master = total cost.

Gross receipts (for 100 albums at $69.95)		$6,995
Expenses		
One-time expenses		
Setup		
Film output for labels	$150	
Cover design	$200	$350
Recording and editing		
14 hours for studio recording		
@ $40 per hour	$560	
Packaging and duplicating expenses		
Compact discs	$1,200	
20-page workbook	$100	
Albums	$500	
Total packaging and duplicating expenses		$1,800
Total expense for the first 100 albums		$3,160
Total profit for the first 100 albums		$3,875
To figure the total profit on the next 100 albums, add $1,800 in one-time costs to the total profit. Therefore:		
Total profit for the next 100 albums		$5,195

Figure 16-1. Example of an expense and profit sheet for a six–compact disc package.

Should You Record Your Seminar Live or in the Studio?
Recording your audio album will be one of your one-time overhead costs and probably the first consideration you will face once you have decided to produce an audio product. There are three methods of recording an audio album. Let's look at each method so that you can make the best decision for your product.

Method 1. Recording Your Seminar Live

  Advantages:

- Live conversational feeling
- Interaction with the audience
- No need to write a script

  Disadvantages:

- Audience distraction
- Logistical problems of microphones and equipment
- More expensive editing

Although you can invest in the equipment to record your seminar, unless you intend to produce lots of audio programs, it is a lot simpler and probably cheaper to hire a professional to set up a high-quality microphone and recorder.

With someone else recording you, you can focus your attention on speaking and not on recording. A professional recording company oversees the myriad details that must be attended to in order to create a quality product.

The easiest way to find a professional recording company is to check the Yellow Pages of your local telephone book. Look under the heading "Recording Service." More than likely, you will find a number of companies to choose from, although not all of them will have the capability of remote recording.

The charge for a professional recording company to record your seminar live will generally run a couple of hundred dollars for a full-day seminar.

Method 2. Recording Your Seminar in the Studio

Advantages:

- High-quality recording
- No distractions
- Opportunity to retake when necessary
- Less editing time

Disadvantages:

- No live spontaneous feeling
- Time required to write a script
- No audience interaction

Again, the easiest way to find a studio is the Yellow Pages of your telephone book. Shop around. Prices for voice recording in the studio can vary from $25 to $150 an hour. Check your local radio station. In many cases radio stations offer excellent recording and editing services to outside clients.

Method 3. Combine Live Segments with Studio Segments

Advantages:

- Audio variety
- Best of both worlds, live and studio

Disadvantages:

- Planning time
- Extensive editing

Even though this method requires even more planning and design, many popular cassette programs are now being produced this way.

!!! Contacts.   If you would like to save both time and money producing your audio album, contact Tony Tyler at Play-It Productions. Tony has vast experience producing spoken-word albums with her state-of-the-art production facilities for recording, editing, and duplication.

Ms. Tony Tyler
Play-It Productions
259 West 30th Street
New York, NY 10001
Phone: (212) 695-6530
Fax: (212) 695-4304
www.play-itproductions.net

Add Value to Your Audio Album to Increase Sales.   Perceived value will always increase sales. The best way to add value is to include a workbook or booklet with your audiocassette album. The written material should reinforce the material on the cassettes.

!!! Resources.   Here is a list of compact disc duplication companies that are equipped to produce quantities of 1,000 or more CDs. Digital Media Reproductions is a cut above the rest in service and the best price for many types of jobs. Check with Rick Needles first.

Digital Media Reproductions
Phone: (877) 387-5428
www.dmrepro.com

Other excellent companies you might want to check out are the following:

World Media Group   Novus Media Services, Inc.
Phone: (800) 400-4964   Phone: (877) 726-6887
www.worldmediagroup.com   www.novusmedia.com

Triple Disc
Phone: (800) 414-7564
www.tripledisc.com

There are an almost endless variety of ways to package your compact disc product depending on how many disks and other material you are including such as a workbook, etc. Here's a great contact for the albums. If they don't have exactly what you want they will create it for you.

They offer a wide variety of stock albums and also create custom albums based on your needs. In addition to excellent service, their prices are extremely good.

Polyline Corporation
1401 Estes Ave.
Elk Grove Village, IL 60007
Phone: (800) 701-5865
www.polylinecorp.com

DVD/Video Products

The video world has digitized. The video product that will rule in the future is the DVD. It offers the highest-quality image and is inexpensive to reproduce, package, and ship.

If you are creating a video product, you might want to offer it in both DVD and VHS videotape format, depending on your audience and how they will likely be viewing it.

You should consider producing a video product. Video products are relatively inexpensive to produce and the profit margin is huge. Video products are especially viable if your information lends itself to a training film or if it will be viewed by groups.

Guidelines for Producing and Marketing a Video Product

1. *Increase the value of your video using TADA.* Generic videos tend to sell for much less than targeted products. The difference between the titles "Stress Management" and "Stress Management for Nurses" could mean a 100 percent increase in profits for you.

2. *Keep your video less than an hour in length.* In general, videotape programs are less than an hour long. Many programs are just 20 to 30 minutes. There are two good reasons for this. First, many people have limited viewing time. Second, people are already mentally conditioned to viewing half-hour and one-hour TV shows (including commercial breaks).

3. *Script your program, and record in the studio.* Videotaping live is much more complicated than audio taping. Lighting, room design, and the presence of an audience create a multitude of technical problems. Unless you absolutely require a live audience, avoid taping live. Live recordings are necessary, however, when you are creating a demo to promote your program to the in-house market.

4. *Do not record on VHS or other home-video formats.* The quality of home-video formats is not suitable for professional use. Tape formats that are acceptable are 3/4 inch, Betacam, 1 inch, and digital tape.

5. *Plan to add video effects when you edit your tape.* The eyes of the TV generation are very sophisticated. A cheap production will get you poor reviews and, in some cases, returned product. Some added cost for video effects is worth it.

6. *Do your marketing homework.* Check your trade and professional associations. See what the market for your video product is like. Determine whether you can produce a video product that is not currently available or is unique in some way.

7. *Price your tape competitively.* The selling price of video products varies widely, from $50 to $500. Some go even higher, especially if the information is hard to find.

!!! **Contact.** Producing a video product is much more complicated than producing an audio album. Before you proceed, discuss your project with the Video Wizard, Bob Chesney. He specializes in video products for seminar leaders and speakers. He will save you money and help you produce the most economical and profitable video products. Call or write:

Mr. Bob Chesney
Chesney Communications
2302 Martin St.
Irvine, CA 92715
Phone: (800) 223-8878, Ext. 126
www.speakersdemos.com

Secrets for Selling Your Consulting Services

Books, audio albums, and video products are not the only source of additional income your seminar can produce for you. Chances are, if you present a quality seminar, your participants will want to tap you for more information. You are in a perfect position to sell your services as a consultant. Consultants, like doctors and lawyers, usually sell their services by the hour. And, like doctors and lawyers, you have the opportunity to earn big money. Here are some tips for marketing consulting services:

1. Avoid the hard sell. The hard sell gives people the wrong message. You will appear hungry, and that impression will turn off your audience.

2. Make yourself accessible. Let participants know they can call you. Follow up with a letter reminding them of your availability. Freely answer any quick question they have, but politely suggest that for more detailed discussions your time is billable.

3. Be sure to refer to your consulting service in your materials.

4. Indirectly refer to your consulting services in case studies.

5. Don't forget to put *everyone* on your mailing list.

6. Do a fantastic job! If you do, you will be the first person people call when they need more help. Everyone should be totally convinced you are a gold mine of information in your field of expertise.

!!! **Contacts.**   Here are two excellent contacts for information on how to develop and market consulting services:

Institute of Management
  Consultants USA, Inc.
2025 M Street NW, Suite 800
Washington, D.C. 20036
Phone: (202) 367-1134
www.imcusa.org

American Consultants League
245 NE 4th Ave., Suite 102
Delray Beach, FL 33483
Phone: (866) 344-7201
www.acl@agora-inc.com

Coaching

Another service that has become very popular in recent years is one-on-one coaching. Coaching is essentially personal consulting service. If you enjoy the mentoring process, coaching can produce a considerable income stream.

It is important to be clear about how your coaching process works and what the participant can expect in terms of both the process and the results. After you have succeeded helping a few people, you will have more work than you will know what to do with.

!!! **Resource.**   If you are interested in learning more about coaching, getting trained, and even getting certified as a coach, you should explore the International Coach Federation Web site.

International Coach Federation
Phone: (888) 423-3131
www.coachfederation.org

Secrets for Closing the Back-of-the-Room Sale

Your success selling products and services from the back of the room will depend largely on following a few simple strategies and techniques. Follow these guidelines, and your products and services will practically sell themselves.

1. Display your products near the door where people will see them when they arrive.

2. Sell products in the morning.

3. Sell products just before the break.

4. Bring enough products to sell to at least 10 percent of your audience. If your products truly fill the needs of your audience, you can sell up to 40 percent.

5. Avoid the hard sell. It is appropriate to refer to your products during appropriate times, in reference to additional information.

6. Increase your sales by 10 to 20 percent by accepting credit cards. (See Chapter 7 for information on how to open up a merchant's account.)

7. Increase sales by creating product packages or combining your products. For example, attendees who buy the DVD, get the compact disc for free.

8. Increase sales by offering discounts for purchasing on the spot. Take advantage of the fact that people are most motivated the day of the program.

9. Always have a drawing for one or more of your products. The best time to do this is just before the break. You will create goodwill as well as the perfect opportunity to introduce your products and describe some of the benefits.

10. Hire temporary help to facilitate fast sales transactions.

11. Include information on how to order other products in your handouts, workbooks, or other take-home materials.

12. Always remember, if you are providing people with valuable information, they will *want* to buy. This means you don't have to sell; you simply have to make your products and services available.

Using Your Web Site to Sell Products and Services

Besides being a valuable tool for promoting your seminars as described in Chapter 10, your Web site can be a storefront for your products and services 24 hours a day, 7 days a week.

The most important strategy to focus on for creating post-seminar sales is to create traffic to your Web site. Similar to a retail store of brick and mortar, the more traffic you can create the more likely you are to sell your products and services.

The most obvious technique for promoting your Web site is to display it everywhere possible: on your cards, letterheads, brochures, slides, workbooks, seminar materials, etc.

It is an excellent idea to make sure your Web site is listed on the major search engines but you are most likely to sell your products and services on your own Web site to those who are familiar with you or who have attended one of your programs.

Therefore it is important to focus your energies on driving your seminar participants to your Web site. Most of the techniques for doing this involve adding value to their experience in the form of additional information and free offerings. Here are a few to consider:

1. Offer a free e-zine (e-mail newsletter).   The e-zine will create an ongoing communication after the seminar and will provide you with the opportunity to feature various products or services in each installment of your e-zine.

One of the most efficient strategies for getting subscribers to your e-zine is to collect business cards and have a drawing for a few of your products. Most of the participants will have their email address on their cards. Send them the e-zine automatically after your program. Be sure to provide them with instructions on how to unsubscribe if they choose to.

!!! Resource.   If you are going to manage the emailing of your e-zine yourself, you will need software. Mailloop is excellent software for this purpose. It also is capable of other processes such as autoresponding.

The Internet Marketing Center
Phone: (888) 462-7006
www.mailloop.com

2. Offer handouts or copies of your slide presentation. This works especially well if you deliver shorter in-house presentations. Let your audience know right at the beginning they will not have to take notes because they can download a handout from your Web site.

3. Offer additional in-depth articles on various topics that relate to your seminar. Let them know they can download and print out free articles of interest from your Web site and encourage them to do so.

4. Offer checklists, lists of tips, and resources that will add value to your information.

5. Provide an assessment that Web site visitors can take free of charge on your Web site such as a skills-based assessment or a personality-style assessment.

6. Create special discounts that are only available by ordering from your Web site. If you offer specials, it is best to display the offer on your home page.

7. Provide links to other sites that will be of interest to your seminar audience but do not offer products and services that will compete with yours. It is easy to find others you can exchange Web site links with and both of you can profit.

!!! Resource. There are a number of books out that will provide you with additional strategies and techniques for driving your seminar participants to your Web site. Here's one that will provide you with a wealth of information.

101 Ways to Promote Your Website, Susan Sweeney (Maximum Press, 2004)

!!! Resource. There is a great one-stop service available to provide your Web site everything you need to take and confirm orders online. They will also set you up so you can deliver digital products such as e-books and audio. It's easy to use, requires no software, and is inexpensive. They make selling on your Web site easy to manage.

www.webmarketingmagic.com
Phone: (888) 255-6230

E-Products for Creating Additional Post-Seminar Profits

The availability of new inexpensive technology has opened the door to new products you can offer and create that can literally double your profits after your seminar. Here are a few you will want to consider. All of them should be promoted on your Web site.

Tele-Seminars

You can create an ongoing profit stream by offering one-hour tele-seminars. The biggest advantage to you is that you can conduct your tele-seminar in the comfort and convenience of your own office.

The technology is very accessible, easy to use, and inexpensive. The profit margin is enormous. Tele-seminars can be offered at $20 to $50 per person. Your cost for each participant is less than a dollar. You can speak to hundreds of participants at a time via "bridge lines." It's as easy as one, two, three.

Step 1. Promote your program to past seminar participants via email. Write a short compelling email describing the benefits of your tele-seminar and email it approximately two weeks before your program. Make it easy for them to register by providing them with a link to register online. As always, offer multiple ways for them to register including phone and fax.

Step 2. When you receive their registration, send them an email with the telephone number to call and the code they will need.

Step 3. Send out an email one or two days prior to the program reminding them of the day, date, and time of the program and the contact information.

Here are some additional ways you can increase your success with tele-seminars.

1. Offer a money-back guarantee. If you do a good job and offer real value, very few people will ask for their money back anyway.

2. If your target market is located in offices with three or more possible participants, offer a group price at a substantial discount. For example, if you are offering customer service tele-seminars, there is a great likelihood that there is more than one person at the call center.

3. Create a tele-seminar subscription series. Create a series of "modules" that your target market will be interested in and sell a one-year subscription to your tele-seminars.

4. Post endorsements on your Web site of people who have participated in your tele-seminars in the past.

5. Add value to your program by making it an interactive program. Solicit questions from participants by email before the program and open up your program to live questions at the end of your presentation.

Webinars

It's easy to transform your tele-seminar into a full-scale multimedia event. There are a variety of elements you can add to deliver additional impact.

Webinars include an online slide presentation. Participants can follow your presentation on their computer with a live PowerPoint slide presentation.

Webinars offer your participants the capability of instant massaging during the program. This feature provides an additional interactive element so participants can respond in "real time" to your presentation via email.

Another feature webinars offer is the ability to appear "live" on-screen. Using a video camera in your office you can appear on the computer screen in addition to your slide presentation.

!!! Resource.   There is one company that is by far the technology leader in tele-seminars and webinars. They offer state-of-the-art technology that is user-friendly and very inexpensive. They are the number-one technology provider for electronic seminars of any kind.

IM Conferencing
Phone: (800) 251-3863
www.imconferencing.com

E-Books and Special Reports

You can offer your written products in digital form on your Web site. Participants can purchase any written product from your Web site and download it.

You can also offer your e-books on a CD as an incentive for registering for one of your programs or for an early-bird registration special. Be sure to include your logo and/or Web site on every page of your e-book.

You can't go wrong using the Amazon.com model for promoting e-books, or any books for that matter, online. Include a picture of the cover, excerpts from your book, table of contents, and endorsements from industry leaders.

Outsourcing Your Back-of-the-Room Sales

If you are more interested in presenting your programs and selling your products and services than handling the production and administration end of the business, you might want to consider outsourcing.

Outsourcing is a very practical way to avoid the overhead and headaches associated with product sales. There are a variety of activities you can outsource including product production, fulfillment, billing, customer service, etc.

!!! **Contact.** Product Distribution Center is the top of the line. They specialize in the seminar market. In many cases they can manage and expedite product sales less expensively than if you did it yourself. Call them for a quote.

Pat Shinners
Seminar Product Distribution Center
186 Mantoloking Rd.
Brick, NJ 08723
Phone: (201) 865-1152

PART 3

How to Hold Your Audience in the Palm of Your Hand

17

How to Deliver a Dynamic Seminar

The Building Blocks of a Dynamic Delivery

Like a great broadway show, a hit song, or an Academy Award–winning film, all top-rated seminars have a few consistent elements. Here are the four cornerstones of a dynamic seminar: content, participation, visual aids, and presentation skills.

Content

It goes without saying that to enjoy success as a seminar leader, you have to do your homework. That means identifying the needs of the participants and researching your topic thoroughly. There are three primary sources of information. First, your own experience and expertise provide the best credibility. Second, you should speak with experts on the topic to get other first-hand perspectives. Third, you can supplement experience and interview-based material by doing research in books, articles, and reports.

Tactics to Make Your Content More Solid and More Interesting. In order to make your content substantial and mentally stimulating, utilize the following devices:

1. *Figures and statistics.* These help quantify statements and demonstrate preciseness. Many audiences, such as engineers, accountants, and doctors, not only appreciate but also demand exactness of information.

2. *Research reports.* These give your content credibility.

3. *Facts.* Facts provide pivotal support material. They can also be fascinating. The popularity of publications such as the *World Almanac* and

the *Guinness Book of World Records* underscore the universal interest almost everybody has with concise tidbits of information.

4. *Definitions.*   Definitions help to clarify meaning. Definitions can be used to open a seminar or a module of a seminar and thereby help to focus the content more effectively.

5. *Anecdotes.*   These provide you with the opportunity to make your content engaging. Everybody loves a good story. Be on the lookout for stories related to your topic.

6. *Examples.*   Examples serve as models that your participants can refer to as they apply the content of your seminar to their own situation.

7. *Case studies.*   Case studies combine the personal touch of the anecdote with the specificity of the example. They make the transference of information to your participants' own story easier.

8. *Authoritative sources.*   These work best when they are named. (Don't just say, "An expert told… .") Authoritative sources allow you to reinforce the credibility of your information. Remember to choose your sources with care to make sure they really are perceived as a higher authority.

!!! Resource.   If you want to research a particular topic to add value to your content, go to eLibrary.com. This Web site provides access to full text periodicals, newswires, maps, photographs, and reference books of all kinds.

www.eLibrary.com

Participation

Adults need to be involved in order to have a motivational learning environment. More important, research has proven that adults also retain more when they are actively involved. The wisdom of Confucius is still true today.

> What I hear, I forget;
> What I see, I remember;
> What I do, I understand.

Techniques for Generating Audience Participation.   The only limit to making your seminar participatory is your own imagination. Each one of these 15 techniques is a door to an infinite number of effective, exciting, and fun ways to keep your seminar lively. For example, under the first technique, tests and quizzes, you could include riddles or even brainteasers that open a door to further discussion. Or under the fourteenth technique, right before a break you could ask your participants to join in on a funny chorus to a song.

1. *Tests and quizzes.* These are especially effective when they allow the participants to evaluate their knowledge or skill level in a specific area related to the seminar topic.

2. *Group questions.* Posing open-ended questions provides the participants an opportunity to respond with their opinions and personal experiences. This works best with groups of fewer than 30 people, but can work with virtually any size group.
One of the most simple yet highly effective questioning techniques to use is asking for a show of hands. You can say something like, "How many people...?" or "Can I see a show of hands of anyone who...?"

3. *Brainstorming.* Ask participants to contribute quickly and spontaneously to an issue or problem. Record all responses on a flipchart or chalkboard. Then lead the group through a discussion and evaluation of each item on the list.

4. *Pairs.* Break your group into pairs, and give them an activity to do. This is good for breaking the ice and for a large group.

5. *Triads.* Break up your audience into groups of three. Triads are excellent when two members are engaged in a role-playing activity and the third is providing feedback.

6. *Small groups.* Breaking up into small groups of four or more people is very effective when you have broken down a problem or an issue into smaller topics and you want each group to work on a specific area and report back to the whole group.

7. *Role playing.* Two or more of your participants can act out a real or hypothetical situation. The advantage of this technique is that it allows your audience to examine a situation from another perspective. This technique can be further enhanced with videotape replay, if you can arrange the technology.

8. *Show and do.* This technique requires the seminar leader to demonstrate a particular skill. The participants are then asked to perform the skill.

9. *Games.* There are a lot of games that can be created to allow full participation while teaching a lesson. Awarding simple, inexpensive prizes, such as T-shirts or coffee mugs, adds excitement and interest.

!!! **Resource.** There is a series of books with an assortment of great games for seminars. The games included in these three books are proven winners.

Games Trainers Play, More Games Trainers Play, and *Still More Games Trainers Play* by Edward E. Scannell and John W. Newstrom (McGraw-Hill, Inc., 2 Penn Plaza, New York, NY 10121)

10. *Props.* Giving your participants something they can touch helps keep them involved. Props like Playdoh, peanuts, potatoes, and paper hats can add fun to your presentation and be used to make important points.

11. *Staging of a debate.* If you set up a debate on an emotionally charged issue, your audience will automatically become involved. The challenge here is to channel the participation in a constructive direction.

12. *Questions and answers (Q&A sessions).* When possible, it is best to allow questions throughout your seminar. If this is not possible, at least allow time for questions at appropriate intervals within each module you are presenting.

13. *Food.* Eating always helps to get your participants involved. Even if your group is fairly large, you can easily distribute inexpensive, yet welcome snacks, such as peanuts or candy. Use the food to reinforce a point. For example, you can say, "You're bound to go nuts if you don't manage your time effectively." Then hand out nuts to everybody.

14. *Music.* Another technique for getting the participants involved is to have them listen to a musical "bite" or song that makes a point.

15. *Movement.* Getting participants involved in any kind of movement works well to create interaction and participation. For example, it's extremely easy to get a group to take a one-minute stretch or make movement a component of a game or role-playing exercise.

Visual Aids

Hotels and conference centers can usually provide or rent you any visual aid you might need. Traveling with your own equipment is more of an inconvenience than it is worth. Nevertheless, always check with your facility beforehand to make sure it has everything you need.

There are seven reasons why you *must* use visuals in your seminar.

1. To increase retention of material

2. To teach more in less time

3. To keep and maintain the attention of your audience

4. To provide a picture of something you have described in words

5. To minimize misunderstanding or to clarify your information

6. To add some drama and variety by creating a multimedia effect

7. To add a level of professionalism to your presentation

Among the visuals available to you are

1. *Flipcharts.* The flipchart is one of the most inexpensive, easy to use, and versatile teaching aids available. It is usually a 24- by 36-in pad of

fairly heavy-weight paper mounted on an easel. The advantage of the flipchart is that you can write quickly using colored markers. You can write spontaneously or prepare your pad beforehand. The flipchart is most effective with groups of fewer than 30 people, since it becomes difficult for larger groups to read flipcharts from a distance.

2. *Chalkboards and marker boards.* Remember elementary school? Well, the chalkboard is still an effective teaching aid, although the more modern marker board has largely replaced it. The marker board uses colored markers and is erasable. The biggest drawback to both of these is that it requires time to erase. As with the flipcharts, these are most useful with groups of fewer than 30 people.

3. *LCD projector.* The advent of the LCD projector has for all intents and purposes eliminated the use of the overhead projector and the slide projector in the seminar business. The LCD projector is the first choice of presenters moving into the future. It is light, bright, and easy to use. If you plan to use it for lots of seminars, it is a wise investment to buy one rather than rent one.

$$$ Savers. If you intend to purchase an LCD, check out these Web sites for steep discounts.

www.projectorpress.com www.projectorsforsale.com
(800) 847-8577 (888) 318-0500

A good site for discounted projectors and just about anything else is Bizrate.

www.shop.bizrate.com

PowerPoint™ is a component of the Microsoft Office suite. It is easy to use and you can create or customize a presentation in a matter of minutes. It offers you an immense range of visual possibilities such as adding sound, animation, etc. PowerPoint is the universal first choice in presentation software.

!!! Resources. There are a number of books on how to use PowerPoint. Here are two of the best. Be aware new editions of these books are released practically every year when PowerPoint updates their software.

PowerPoint for Dummies, Doug Lowe (Wiley, 2003)

How to Do Everything with Microsoft Office PowerPoint, Ellen Finklestein (Sagebrush Education Resources, 2003)

Here are some incredible Web sites that offer a wide array of resources for improving your PowerPoint presentation. Many of the resources such as terrific templates are free. These Web sites also offer lots of other information on presentation design and delivery.

PresentationPro   Presenters Online
www.presentationpro.com   www.presentersonline.com

Presenters University   Website Estates
www.presentersuniversity.com   www.websiteestates.com

Digital Studio by Sonia Coleman
www.soniacoleman.com

If you really want to go wild with your PowerPoint presentation, adding all kinds of incredible visual effects, add-on software is available. Some of the most powerful software is produced by Crystal Graphics.

Crystal Graphics, Inc.
Phone: (408) 496-6175
www.crystalgraphics.com

***!!!* Contact.**   If you don't feel like spending any time at all designing or working on your slides but you want them to be incredible, outsource the process to Marilyn Snyder. She is a professional graphics designer who specializes in PowerPoint presentations for presenters. She will create a PowerPoint image that will reflect your unique brand and elevate your professional image. Tell her you heard about her work here.

Marilyn Snyder
Interactive Concepts
Phone: (877) 307-9009
www.InteractiveConceptsOnline.com

4. *Overhead projector.*   With the advent of the LCD projector, the overhead projector is almost extinct. But there are some presenters who still use them because of familiarity, and there are some applications they do lend themselves to.

If your group is over 100 people or more and you want the flexibility and spontaneity of a flipchart, an overhead might be a good choice. You can write or draw on a transparency while you are speaking.

Anything on a printed page can be transferred to an overhead transparency using a standard printer and you can add flair by using color markers or colored transparencies.

5. *Slide projectors.*   Like the overhead projector, technology has rendered the slide projector almost obsolete. PowerPoint slides can be revised in a matter of seconds at no cost whereas traditional film slide must be ordered, usually requiring at least a day, and can cost up to $20 a slide to produce.

Slides are cumbersome to rearrange and are prone to a variety of technical problems such as jamming, blown projector bulbs, and are often placed in the carousel upside down or backwards.

It's easy to understand why the LCD/PowerPoint combination has become the presentation standard. Perhaps the only time slides must seriously be considered is when clarity is the primary criterion. For example, if your visuals are showing detailed art, the LCD projector could never match the clarity of film slides.

6. *Videotapes.*   Showing a DVD or videotape at some point in your seminar can be a wonderful addition. Videos are most effective when they are used to emphasize a point, to serve as an icebreaker, or to open the group to discussion.

The disadvantage of the DVD or videotape is that it requires a video projector or multiple monitors if the group numbers more than 15. This can add expense and inconvenience to your seminar.

!!! **Caution.**   Showing a video is not the same as presenting a seminar. Use it as a tool, not as a crutch. The best use of video is in small doses. Try to keep videos less than 10 minutes in length.

!!! **Resources.**   There are quite a few good sources for training videos on a full range of topics. They can be previewed and either rented or purchased. If you are interested in using videos, call or write for a catalog. Here are some of the most notable sources:

Advanced Training Sources
Phone: (800) 525-3368
www.atsmedia.com

Business Training Media
Phone: (888) 337-2121
www.business-media.com

Training ABC
Phone: (888) 281-8038
www.TrainingABC.com

7. *Objects.*   Using tangible objects—similar to the grade school show-and-tell—is still an effective teaching technique. Objects are wonderful to use in games and puzzles. Adults, like children, enjoy the fun of touching and holding things. Seminar leaders can use everything from rubber bands and paper clips to potatoes and paper planes to add dimension to their seminars. The possibilities are endless.

Presentation Skills

Your appeal as a seminar leader is largely determined by your personal delivery style and the presentation techniques you use during the seminar.

Components of Your Personal Style

1. *Clothing and accessories.*   It is important to dress appropriately for your audience. If you have a formal business audience, dress formally. If

your seminar is at a resort and people are dressed in a more informal manner, you should dress informally also.

2. *Grooming.* This goes without saying. Your own image aside, good grooming shows your audience you think they are important.

3. *Facial expression.* Your face should communicate your message. Of course, one of the best facial expressions is the smile. Use it liberally throughout your seminar as you see performers do on TV. This is, after all, a form of show biz.

4. *Gestures.* Using your arms and hands tends to keep people's interest. It is rare that anyone uses gestures too much.

5. *Body movement.* Get out from behind the lectern. Your participants will react positively to movement. Move around the room freely. You will be able to focus your audience's attention. Be careful though that you don't pace. Pacing is usually an expression of nervous energy and can be distracting to your audience. Try not to be too predictable in your body movement.

6. *Posture.* Stand tall but avoid appearing stiff or nervous.

7. *Enthusiasm.* You can use both your voice and your body to express enthusiasm.

8. *Tone of voice.* How you say your words is important. Your tone of voice should be expressive, not a monotone.

9. *Clarity.* Speak clearly. Make sure your pronunciation is correct and that you enunciate your words well, but without exaggeration or affection.

10. *Rate of delivery.* As a general rule, it is better to speak at as quick a pace as possible without forfeiting clarity. This works best to keep the attention of your audience, and you can cover more ground. But since variety is the spice of a seminar delivery, slowing down and speeding up at different times makes any presentation more dynamic.

11. *Eye contact.* Always maintain good eye contact with your audience—all of them, not just the closest, best looking, or most attentive.

12. *Audience contact.* Greet the people at the beginning, roam the aisles, and chat at breaks. Props are great, but physical obstructions between you and your audience should be removed.

13. *Personal information.* Your audience will respond better to you if you reveal something about yourself. They will see you more as a person and become more engaged in the seminar.

14. *Simple language.* Don't speak above an audience's level of understanding. Don't use unfamiliar words.

15. *Listening.* Listen when your participants share. By doing so, you are telling them that they are important.

*!!! * **Contacts.**   There are two very important organizations that can provide you with presentation skill education and training. Regardless of your presentation skill level, these organizations will enable you to increase the value of your seminars.

Toastmasters International
P.O. Box 9052
Mission Viejo, CA 92690
Phone: (949) 858-8255
www.toastmasters.org

Toastmasters International will help you develop your public speaking skills. The organization holds literally thousands of meetings each month nationwide. Everyone gets a chance to speak in a supportive environment, which is great for learning how to overcome nervousness and get public speaking experience. Contact them to find out about meetings near you.

National Speakers Association
1500 S. Priest Dr.
Tempe, AZ 85281
Phone: (480) 968-2552
www.nsaspeaker.org

The National Speakers Association (NSA) is the leading organization for individuals who speak professionally. NSA's 3500 members include experts in a variety of industries and disciplines including trainers, seminar leaders, educators, consultants, authors, and motivators.

In addition to helping you to improve your professional communication skills, NSA is a valuable contact for networking with other professionals and learning how to market your programs, products, and services more successfully.

Contact them or go to their Web site and locate one of the 38 local chapters nearest you.

How to Hold an Audience in the Palm of Your Hand

In order to get excellent evaluations, every seminar leader should master the basics of the craft of leading seminars: substantive and interesting content, audience participation, proper use of audiovisuals, and personal presentation skills. At the top of the profession are presenters who incorporate the following additional techniques that allow them to rise above the rest.

1. *Tell stories.*   People love to hear stories. Your stories should have relevance to your topic or to a specific point you are making. The best source for stories is your own personal experience. Review your own experiences, and identify good stories that are relevant to your topic. Be on the lookout for new ones. The other good source for stories is the people who attend your seminar. Many people will share with you personal experiences that make great "war stories" for future seminars.

!!! **Resource.**   The best resource for wonderful stories is the journal that you keep. You can begin immediately by writing down personal experiences you've had that make good stories. Keep your eyes and ears open for new ones, and write them down.

2. *Use humor.*   You can tell jokes and use prepared one-liners. You don't have to be funny to get laughs. Find cartoons and use them to make transparencies or slides. Always make sure your humor does not put any one down, except possibly yourself.

!!! **Resource.**   The following Web site is a great source for books, jokes, cartoons, stories, etc., to help you to add humor to your programs. This site is of particular value because much of the humor is appropriate for the seminar setting.

www.kushnergroup.com

3. *Use quotes.*   Quotes are a wonderful way to state a truth, motivate, or elicit a response. When you hear or read an excellent quote that you might want to use, put it in your journal, in a file labeled "quotes," or on your computer.

!!! **Resources.**   More than 50,000 quotes as well as jokes, poems, famous statements, and funny anecdotes can be found on the Quotemaster CD. It's a great resource for seminar leaders. It's got a fast search engine to help you find quotes quickly.

Quote Master
(888) 765-0335
www.acrllc.com (Go to Education)

Here are some excellent Web sites for quotations of all kinds.

www.quotationspage.com
www.bartleby.com
www.theotherpages.com
www.quoteland.com

4. *Recite a poem.*   A poem is a wonderful tool for creating an emotional response to your presentation. As with stories and quotes, begin to collect special poems that you can use in a moment when you want to inspire your audience.

5. *Motivate with benefits.* Since most seminars are designed to solve problems, you must continuously relate what you are talking about to the benefits your audience will receive.

As you begin each new module, open with a reminder of the benefits they can expect to receive. For example, use statements such as, "Next we're going to be talking about.... This is very important because it will...." Reminding your audience of benefits will keep their attention on you and on what you are saying.

Be sure to amend that old speaker's adage, "Tell 'em what you're gonna tell 'em, then tell 'em, then tell 'em what you told 'em," with the *benefits* of what you're tellin 'em.

!!! Contacts and Resources. Without a doubt, the best source for tips, exercises, methodology, and content is networking with your peers. The adage, if you want to learn how to climb the mountain, speak to someone who has done it is especially true for your development as a professional seminar leader. See the Yellow Pages in Part 4 of this book under "Professional Associations for Networking and Education" for the addresses and phone numbers of organizations that will provide this opportunity.

18
How to Create Valuable Handout Material

Generally, any material which is included in the price of the seminar is referred to as a handout. The handout material is free to the participants.

Why You Need Handouts

Remember you are an "information entrepreneur." Although people are attending your seminar to hear you speak, the printed word is a critical element to the success of your seminar.

1. *Handouts add value.* You are more likely to get good evaluations and referral business if you give out good handouts that supplement your spoken presentation.

2. *People expect handouts.* Most participants probably have already attended one or more seminars at which they received handouts. If you don't give them anything, they will be disappointed. Really.

3. *Handouts create flexibility.* If your handouts are somewhat comprehensive and cover your major points, you will be able to refer your participants to them if you run short on time or if you want to skip a particular module of your seminar.

4. *Handouts provide take-home information.* You will provide your audience with the opportunity to continue learning after the seminar is over.

5. *Handouts are good, inexpensive advertising.* Your name, address, phone number, email address, and Web site should be on all your handouts. People usually save them, and you will very likely get inquiries at a later date.

Types of Handout Material You Can Use

There is a variety of material you can include as handouts. The best handouts often include combinations from the following list:

1. *Outline.* The outline summarizes the major points of your presentation. It usually follows the flow of the seminar. It is best to leave space on the outline sheet or sheets for note taking.

2. *Fill-in-the-blank.* The fill-in-the-blank handout creates instant audience participation. It also gives the audience a certain kind of satisfaction. In most cases, participants will try to guess the correct words in advance, so this format becomes a kind of game.

3. *Quizzes, tests, and self-evaluations.* This type of handout also creates participation and gives the participant nonthreatening feedback.

4. *Resource lists.* You can include names, addresses, phone numbers, local contacts, organizations, Web sites, and anything else that will give your participants sources they can draw upon later.

5. *Reprints.* Articles you have written that are relevant to your seminar make good handout material. Also, articles others have written are good for handouts. Always be sure to get copyright permission.

6. *Roster of participants.* In most seminars that last a half a day or longer, people network and get to know each other. They may also want to contact each other at a later date. Your participants will appreciate having a complete list of participants, including company affiliations, addresses, phone numbers, email addresses, and Web sites when they leave.

7. *Bibliography.* If you have been successful as a seminar leader, your audience will be motivated to reinforce what they have learned by consulting other books and articles. A complete bibliography on the topic presented at the seminar is always welcome.

8. *Books.* Many types of high-priced seminars will include one or more books in the handout materials. Ideally, these books are written by you. If not, you can distribute a book you consider to be the best on the given topic. You may be able to get books at a discount by simply calling the publisher and telling him or her what you are doing. These books are distinguished from the ones you sell at the back of the room because the handout books are free of charge.

9. *Extra paper.* If you give your participants exercises and lots of information that they will want to write down, you might want to include blank unlined or lined sheets of paper with the handouts.

Handout Formats from Which to Choose

In most cases, the length and price of your seminar are the most critical elements affecting the number of handouts you distribute and the format. Naturally the three-day seminar will probably require more handouts and a more elaborate format than the one-day seminar.

Bound

You can assemble your material to correspond with the order in which you will be presenting it in the seminar and bind it together. The simplest and least expensive way to bind it is to staple the sheets together. Binding with staples works best when your handout materials have fewer than 20 pages.

Another way to bind your pages is with a spiral plastic-comb binding. This usually costs between $3 and $5 per workbook. Most quick-copy printers offer a comb-binding service.

The third method you can use to bind your workbook is with a perfect binding. This is a soft-cover book style, and it gives your workbook a more professional appearance. If you are printing more than a couple of hundred copies, a perfect binding can become cost-effective. It costs around $2 to $5 a copy in large quantities, depending on paper stock, cover, and number of pages.

!!! Contacts. A complete list of printing companies that print short runs (100 or more) of perfect-bound workbooks can be found in Dan Poynter's book, *The Self-Publishing Manual.* See Chapter 16, in a list of contacts for self-publishing, for the information on where to write or call to get this book.

Loose-leaf

Using a three-ring loose-leaf binder allows a lot of flexibility.

Double-number your pages according to the module. For example, pages in the first module would be numbered 1-1, 1-2, 1-3, 1-4, and so forth. Pages in the second module would be numbered 2-1, 2-2, 2-3, 2-4, and so forth. In this way you can revise, add, or delete material easily and inexpensively.

$$$ and Contacts. Use the binders that have a clear overlay on the front cover. By printing a page with the title of your seminar on a colored paper stock and inserting it beneath the clear overlay, you can create an extremely inexpensive and yet totally professional-looking workbook.

Here are four great sources for binders for seminars. These companies can customize and imprint your binders and their prices are excellent. Visit their Web sites, then call them and ask for samples of what interests you.

Folder Factory
Phone: (800) 296-4321
www.folders.com

LooseLeaf.com
Phone: (800) 621-0493
www.looseleaf.com

Custom Craft Binders
Phone: (800) 428-0934
www.customcraftbinders.com

Three Ring Systems
Phone: (800) 223-3022
www.threeringsystems.com

If you will be ordering small quantities of stock binders, you might want to contact one of the national office goods suppliers. They often run specials on binders.

Quill Corporation
Phone: (800) 789-0041
www.quill.com

Office Depot
Phone: (800) 463-3768
www.officedepot.com

Viking Office Products
Phone: (800) 421-1222
www.vikingoffice.com

Office Max
Phone: (800) 283-7674
www.officemax.com

Staples
Phone: (800) 3STAPLE
www.staples.com

Loose Pages

If you deliver a variety of shorter programs, it is convenient to have handouts that consist of loose pages. If you develop a library of one- and two-page handouts, you can instantly pull together effective handout material in various configurations. Then just clip them together with a paper clip.

Another big advantage of loose pages is that you can control the flow of the seminar and the attention of the participants by handing out a page at a time. They will not be able to read ahead or get distracted by the handout material.

One problem with loose pages is that you will have to organize the flow and distribution of the material carefully to make sure the correct material is handed out at the proper time.

In addition, there is the logistical challenge of getting the various loose pages handed out quickly and efficiently. You can usually solve this problem in two ways. The first way involves precounting your handouts and putting them into piles according to the number of people at each table, the number of people in each row, and so forth. Then, before you begin, ask your assistants or a few participants if they would help you pass out the materials. With this technique you will be able to pass out hundreds of loose pages in a minute or two. The second way you can distribute a set of loose pages quickly is to preassemble them in folders. The folders give your material a professional look and still allow for a lot of flexibility.

The Most Important Handout: The Seminar Evaluation Form

The evaluation is the last handout you will be giving your audience. Because it needs to be returned to you, it *must be* a loose page. The completed evaluation forms can give you the exact information you need to make improvements on your seminar. Look for patterns in the comments.

For example, if you consistently receive comments on the readability of your handouts or your overhead transparencies, you know this is an area in which you should make adjustments.

Besides giving you valuable feedback, the evaluation allows participants to share any strong feelings they might have. It serves as a release for both positive and negative emotions.

It is helpful to get the name of the participant on the completed evaluation because comments make more sense if you know who made them. For example, if the evaluation is very negative and if the individual was very negative even before the seminar began, you will be able to evaluate the comments in the proper light. So, ask for signed evaluations, but don't demand them. Participants are usually less forthright if they are signing the form.

Remember, your seminar participants will be asked to fill out the evaluation at the end of the seminar. Since many of them will be rushing off to something else, it is best to keep it simple and brief. Schedule a few minutes at the very end for completing evaluations. This will maximize your response rate.

Figure 18-1 shows a sample of a basic evaluation that works.

$$$ The completed evaluation forms can be a source of valuable endorsements. With initialed approvals, you can use any positive comments on future promotional material.

The completed evaluations can also be a source of valuable referrals for future programs. If your participants filled out the last question, you have valuable leads for your mailing list and prospects for future programs.

Additional Evaluation Questions

If you want more refined feedback, the questions in Fig. 18-2 can be added. Respondents should be instructed to award each question a numerical rating on a scale of 1 to 5, with 1 being the lowest and 5 being the highest.

Name _____

Date _____

Location _____

Please circle the appropriate number.

1. How valuable were the ideas, concepts, and program content?
10   9   8   7   6   5   4   3   2   1
Highly   Mostly   Fairly   Slightly

2. How effective was the presentation of the material?
10   9   8   7   6   5   4   3   2   1
Highly   Mostly   Fairly   Slightly

3. How do you rate the program overall?
Excellent   Good   OK   Fair   Poor

4. What did you like most about this seminar?
_____
_____

5. What did you like least about this seminar?
_____
_____

6. May we use your comments for our promotional material? If yes, please initial for your approval. Yes   No

7. Who do you know that might be interested in attending this type of program?

Name _____

Title _____

Company _____

Address _____

City _____   State _____

Zip _____

Telephone _____

Figure 18-1. Sample of an effective evaluation form.

Seminar Leader

    1. How extensive was the presenter's
       knowledge of the subject matter?   1   2   3   4   5

    2. How effective was the presenter's
       style?   1   2   3   4   5

    3. Was the presenter successful in
       achieving group participation?   1   2   3   4   5

    4. Did the presenter maintain control?   1   2   3   4   5

    5. What was the quality of the visual
       aids?   1   2   3   4   5

Seminar Content

    6. How well was the content
       organized?   1   2   3   4   5

    7. How was the quality of the
       workbook or handout material?   1   2   3   4   5

    8. Do you think you will be able
       to apply the content?   1   2   3   4   5

    9. Did you find the exercises
       beneficial?   1   2   3   4   5

Program Overall

    10. Did the program address
        your particular needs?   1   2   3   4   5

    11. Did you feel challenged by
        the program?   1   2   3   4   5

    12. How would you rate the facility
        where the seminar was held?   1   2   3   4   5

Figure 18-2. Additional evaluation questions that can be added to the evaluation form for more refined feedback.

19

How to Set Up Your Seminar Room

Factors You Must Consider When You Set Up Your Room

The setup of your seminar room is critical to the success of your seminar. Although the four factors discussed here may seem to be simple and you might take them for granted, the comfort of your audience is at stake. Part of your job is to create as ideal a learning environment as possible.

1. *Temperature.* The ideal temperature of your room should be between 66 and 72°F. If it is warmer, your participants will get drowsy. If it is cooler, they will turn blue. It is always preferable, however, to err on the cooler side.

No matter what the temperature is when you begin, there always seems to be some difficulty with the temperature of the room at some point during the seminar. The best way to deal with a temperature problem is to make plans for handling it when you first arrive. Find out who is in charge of controlling the temperature of your room. Contact this individual and, if possible, arrange in advance for someone to make adjustments as necessary during the presentation.

2. *Lighting.* Become acquainted with the lighting controls. Set up the room with enough lights to facilitate note taking and alertness. Make sure, however, that your lights do not interfere with any projectors you might be using. If necessary, you can unscrew a few bulbs if they are shining directly on your screens.

3. *Logistics.* The ideal setup for your registration area is to the right and left of the door to the seminar room. Set up enough tables to allow for a quick signing in or registration process. If you set up your registration tables outside the seminar room, latecomers will not disturb the people who arrived on time. If you cannot set up registration tables outside the room, set them up just inside the door.

An additional table should be set up at the back of the room for books and tapes and any materials you want to put out for sale or display. Food and refreshments should also be put on a table in the back.

Always make a detailed diagram of your particular setup. Send this to the banquet department of the hotel or facility before you arrive. Include the table locations, where you want the refreshments, seating layout, and any other details you would like to have attended to.

Figure 19-1 illustrates a sample layout.

4. *Seating.*   There are a number of ways to set up the seating in your seminar room. In many cases you will have little control over how your seating is arranged. For example, if your seminar is part of a luncheon program, it might already be set up banquet style. Similarly, if you are using a conference center facility and have a large group, you might be in an auditorium with theater- style seating.

Figures 19-2 through 19-7 suggest various seating arrangements from which you can choose. There are advantages and disadvantages to each arrangement.

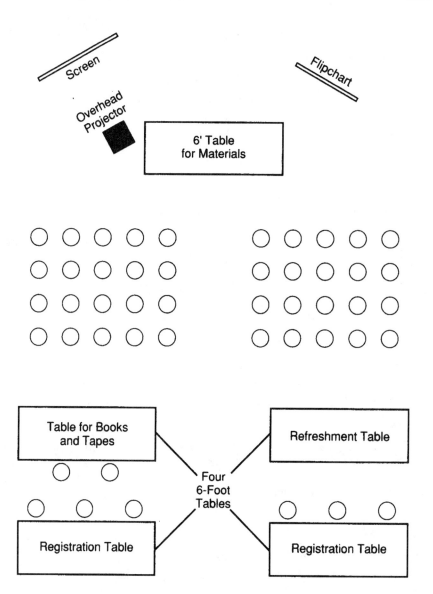

Figure 19-1. Sample layout of seminar room.

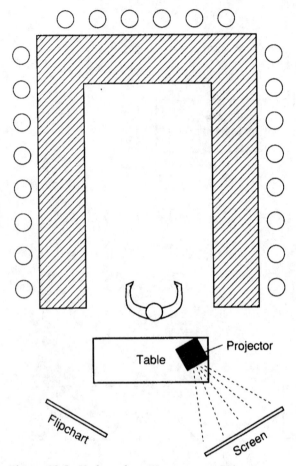

Figure 19-2. U-shaped seating arrangement.

Advantages:

- Interaction and participation encouraged
- Good available writing surfaces

Disadvantage:

- Limited space (10–25 participants)

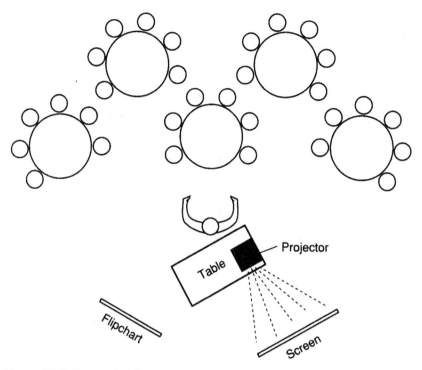

Figure 19-3. Banquet-style seating arrangement.

Advantages:

- Space for group exercises
- Convivial atmosphere encouraged

Disadvantages:

- Poor viewing
- Distractions from food and drink service
- Considerable floor space required

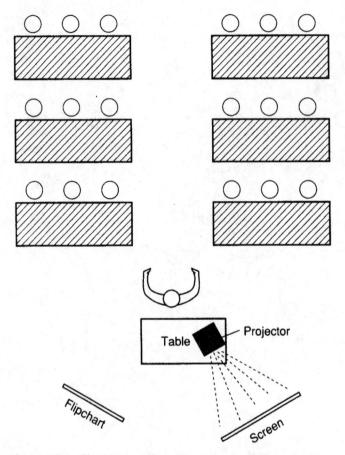

Figure 19-4. Classroom-style seating arrangement.

Advantages:

- Easy setup
- Good available writing surfaces
- Good format for lectures

Disadvantages:

- Bad for interactive exercises
- Considerable floor space required

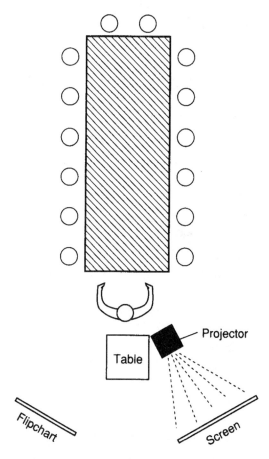

Figure 19-5. Conference table seating arrangement.

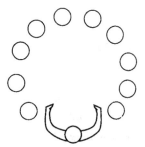

Figure 19-6. Circle seating arrangement.

Advantages:

- Good available writing surfaces
- Interaction encouraged

Disadvantage:

- Limited space (10–15 participants)

Advantage:

- Interaction and participation encouraged

Disadvantages:

- Difficult use of visual aids
- Limited space (10–20 participants)

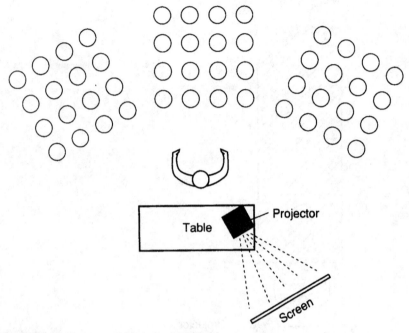

Figure 19-7. Theater-style seating arrangement.

Advantages:

■ Large audiences accommodated
■ Good viewing

Disadvantages:

■ No writing surfaces
■ Interactive exercises discouraged

20

Show Time! You're On!

What to Do the Night Before

If possible, it is best to arrive at the site of the seminar the day before so you can check it out. If there are any problems, you still have an opportunity to correct them. By arriving the night before, you also have a chance to relax a bit and get a good night's rest. This is especially important if you have traveled across a few time zones.

Why You Must Arrive at the Seminar Room Early

Arriving early means getting into the room a minimum of one hour before your program is scheduled to begin. Whenever possible, you should arrive closer to two hours in advance. The reasons for this are

1. To make sure the signs in the lobby are properly displayed and are correct

2. To test all the audiovisual equipment

3. To locate the rest rooms, telephones, and other points of interest to which you will want to orient your participants

4. To correct the temperature so that your audience will be neither too hot nor too cold

5. To arrange the furniture appropriately

6. To help set up the registration or sign-in table

7. To place the handouts on the chairs

8. To meet with support staff and review the agenda

9. To make sure coffee or food will be delivered on time

10. To set up your products table at the back of the room

11. To allow time for you to relax before anyone arrives

12. To make sure you arrive before your first participant

The Seminar Leader's Tool Kit

Although every seminar leader has specific unique tools of the trade, the following items are the most common. In the beginning, it is a good idea to include them all. After a while, you can personalize your checklist.

Name tags

Felt-tipped pens

Chalk

Masking tape

Sign-in sheets

Clock or watch

Change for your product sales

Cash receipt book

Credit card machine

Stapler and staples

Scissors

Blank pads of paper

Pushpins and thumbtacks

List of participants

Handout materials

Leader's guide and notes

Props

Overhead transparencies

Tape recorder

Blank and recorded tapes

DVD/video training tapes

List of contact names and telephone numbers

Books, tapes, and CDs for sale

Brochures of future programs

Your introduction

Duplicate PowerPoint disk

See Fig. 20-1 for a last-minute checklist of important items to review before you begin the seminar.

What to Do as People Start to Arrive

1. Check people in and give them their name tags and any materials they will need for the seminar.

2. Play some soft, easy-listening music (classical is good) to create a pleasant, relaxed atmosphere. Baroque chamber music works very well.

3. Introduce yourself to people who arrive early. Find out why they signed up for the program and what their specific needs are. Show them that you care. Speaking with the participants at this point will help both you and your participants to relax.

4. Introduce people to one another. Many people are too shy to introduce themselves to others but will speak freely if you introduce them to

□ Personal grooming and clothes

□ Microphone (if needed)

□ LCD projector or audiovisual equipment (including spare bulbs)

□ PowerPoint disk, overhead transparencies or slides (slides checked)

□ Spare pens for flipcharts

□ Water pitcher and glass at front

□ Handouts or workbooks ready for distribution

□ Props (for activities)

□ Room temperature

□ Stopwatch or clock

□ Introduction (if needed)

□ Extra pencils, pens, and paper

□ Your leader's guide

□ Prearranged meal and breaks

□ A few deep breaths to relax before stepping up to speak

Figure 20-1. Last-minute checklist.

each other. Identify some nonthreatening areas for them to discuss, such as where they come from or their business affiliations.

5. Encourage your participants to have coffee and whatever refreshments you have available.

Rules for Beginning Your Presentation

1. *Begin on time.* Don't penalize the people who arrive on time by waiting for latecomers. You will antagonize the punctual ones, and the others will fail to appreciate your kindness. Sometimes there are legitimate excuses for lateness, such as traffic problems. If you want to buy a few minutes, you could say, "We're going to start on time with a short networking opportunity. Please introduce yourself to someone you do not know and find out a little about each other."

This technique turns a negative into a positive. People need to feel comfortable and relaxed. This little technique will help you create the most favorable climate for the success of your seminar, and it buys four or five minutes for latecomers.

2. *Start out with lots of energy.*   Show a lot of enthusiasm for your audience in your delivery style. Your opening remarks and attitudes in general will set the tone for the whole day.

3. *Thoroughly prepare your opening.*   In order for you to gain the confidence of your participants, you should know exactly what you are going to say and do when you begin.

A Winning Agenda for Your Seminar

Using the modular design approach to the actual content of your seminar, here is a proven agenda that works. You can amend this format to meet the specific needs of your seminar length and content.

1. *Introduction.*   Whether you are introduced by someone else or you introduce yourself, make your introduction brief. But make sure you provide information that lets the audience know you are qualified to speak on the topic at hand.

2. *Opening remarks.*   Once again, keep it brief. Also, keep it light. A joke or humorous remark works wonderfully here. You might want to refer to the city or locale the seminar is in or remark on some of the comments you have heard from the participants. This helps connect you to the audience.

There are three points you will want to communicate to your audience in some way:

- Let them know you're glad to be there.

- Let them know you're happy *they* are there.

- Let them know that you care. Your audience will always respond favorably to you when they know you really care about them.

3. *Introductions.*   If the group numbers fewer than 25, each person can introduce himself or herself to the whole group. If the group is larger, you can break up into groups of four or five.

!!! **Remember.**   The sweetest sound to anyone's ear is his or her own name. Name tags or name cards are one of the most valuable tools a seminar leader has for creating a relaxed atmosphere that is conducive for adults to learn. Call people by their names as much as possible throughout the program, but be sensitive to sounding phony.

4. *Needs and concerns.*   By asking the audience about their needs and concerns, you are accomplishing two very important objectives. First, you are letting the audience know that you care about them. Second, you will be able to modify your presentation to address the needs of that specific audience.

There are two ways to elicit the audience's needs and concerns. If the group is small, ask participants to voice their needs and concerns when they introduce themselves. Make sure you list each concern on a flipchart. If people mention areas they want to cover but you know you will not cover them, stop and tell that to them.

If the group is large, the second way to do this exercise is first to have the members of the group write down their personal needs and concerns. Then break them up into groups of four or five and have them come to a group decision about what they specifically want discussed. Ask each group what they have decided, and list the information on a flipchart.

If you have done your homework or have had even minimal experience delivering the seminar, you will have a very good idea in advance of what they want to know.

5. *Details.*   Most people are concerned about the flow of the day and logistics. Although they are important, it is best to delay discussing these mundane details until you've broken the ice. You can deal with the details anytime before you begin discussing specific subject matter.

Details include the location of bathrooms, rules about smoking, location of telephones, break times, lunch information, and any other logistical information that you need to announce.

6. *Lecture.*   The very word *lecture* makes many people uncomfortable. Most people identify it with a negative experience from childhood. Nevertheless, you will have to spend a portion of each seminar providing specific information to the participants.

The best way to keep the energy alive and everyone awake and engaged is to encourage questions to be asked throughout. Just be careful about getting sidetracked with questions. If necessary, say, "I can talk to you more about that at the break," or, when appropriate, "I think we'll be addressing that problem a little later."

7. *Participatory exercises.*   You can choose from any of the exercises discussed in Chapter 17. Your audience will come alive each time you give them the opportunity to get actively involved in the learning process. Be sure to use a variety of participatory exercises throughout the seminar.

8. *Breaks.*   You should schedule breaks every hour to hour and a half. You can ask everyone to join in a stretch with you.

When you take a break, it is important to announce exactly how many minutes the break will be. Say, "We will begin again in exactly 14 minutes." Keep your word. Regardless of how many people have made it back, start speaking to whoever is present. If you do not keep your word, you will quickly find that the members of your audience will not keep theirs. Likewise, if they find out you mean what you say, they will be seated and ready to go when you are.

A valuable tool for timing breaks, seminar exercises, and maintaining your schedule in general, is a digital stopwatch. A digital wristwatch that has this feature works well and is convenient as you move around the room.

Sample Agenda for a Seminar on Stress Management

Here is a script for a half-day seminar on stress management.

8:30 a.m.–8:40 a.m.	Introduction of seminar leader and goals of the program
8:40 a.m.–8:50 a.m.	Introduction—participants' names, company affiliations, and job functions
8:50 a.m.–9:00 a.m.	Sources of stress for participants
9:00 a.m.–9:15 a.m.	Needs and concerns
9:15 a.m.–9:20 a.m.	Details
9:20 a.m.–9:45 a.m.	Stress theory lecture
9:45 a.m.–10:00 a.m.	Break
10:00 a.m.–10:30 a.m.	Self-scoring self-evaluation stress test
10:30 a.m.–11:00 a.m.	Overview of stress-management techniques
11:00 a.m.–11:10 a.m.	Break
11:10 a.m.–11:30 a.m.	Relaxation exercise
11:30 a.m.–12:00 noon	Personal stress management goal setting
12:00 noon–12:20 p.m.	Open question-and-answer period
12:20 p.m.–12:30 p.m.	Closing remarks and participants' evaluations

Rules for Ending Your Seminar

1. *Summarize your key points.* Tell 'em what you told 'em is an old adage. Review the most important things you covered.

2. *Acknowledge sponsors or assistants.* If your program was sponsored by an organization, thank them. If anyone helped you with administration, express your gratitude.

3. *Thank your participants for coming.* Without an audience there is no seminar. Let them know they are important to you. Every audience appreciates hearing this.

4. *Call for action.*   Provide your participants with a challenge to apply the information they received at your seminar, to continue their research, or to take any step that might be appropriate.

5. *Close with a motivational flair.*   You want to leave everyone feeling positive about the seminar experience, the material they learned, and you. You can use humor, wit, quotes, a success story about a former seminar participant, music, or anything else that will make everyone feel good. See Chapter 17 for some creative ideas.

Leave them with the feeling they have what it takes to put the information or skills they learned to work.

6. *Plan and rehearse your closing.*   Your closing should be well thought out and specially designed. Don't try to wing it. Very often what stands out in people's minds is the last feeling they had. A big finish is the best policy.

7. *End on time.*   A professional seminar leader starts on time and ends on time. Your participants have arranged their schedules according to the announced completion time. Finishing late is discourteous and breaks a cardinal rule—avoid breaking late at all costs.

When possible, you can offer to stay around for a short while after the completion of the program. This will show goodwill, help anyone who still has a few quick questions, and allow anyone who wants to talk to you about further professional assistance to make arrangements.

Don't Forget! Leading Seminars Is a Calling and an Art

At the end of your seminar you will experience an incredible feeling of deep satisfaction. You have made a positive contribution to the lives of others. Winston Churchill said, "We make a living by what we get, but we make a life by what we give."

Besides providing you with the opportunity to make both a living and a life, the seminar business is an incredible vehicle for your own creativity. No matter how successful you become, you will find new inspiration and information to share with your audience. From the creative point of view, your possibilities are endless.

Like any artist you will continually want to experiment, modify, and improve your skills. And like any artist you will enjoy the immense rewards that result from continually investing your energy in maximizing your professional skills.

PART 4

The Seminar Business Yellow Pages

National Seminar Sites

ALABAMA

Auburn

Auburn University Hotel & Dixon
Conference Center
241 South College Street
Auburn, AL 36830
(334) 821-8200

Birmingham

Convention Halls

Birmingham/Jefferson Convention
Complex
2100 Richard Arrington Jr. Blvd. N
Birmingham, AL 35203
(205) 458-2522

Best Western Civic Center
2230 Richard Arrington Jr. Blvd. N
Birmingham, AL 35203
(205) 328-6320

Radisson Hotel Birmingham
808 S. 20th Street
Birmingham, AL 35205
(205) 933-0920

Sheraton Birmingham
2101 Richard Arrington Jr. Blvd. N
Birmingham, AL 35203
(205) 324-5000

Embassy Suites
2300 Woodcrest Place
Birmingham, AL 35209
(205) 879-7400

Sheraton Birmingham South
8 Perimeter Drive
Birmingham, AL 35243
(205) 967-2700

Wynfrey Hotel
1000 Riverchase Galleria
Birmingham, AL 35244
(205) 444-5730

Holiday Inn Airport
5000 10th Avenue N
Birmingham, AL 35212
(205) 591-2093

Ramada Inn Airport
5216 Airport Highway
Birmingham, AL 35212
(800) 767-2426

Gulf Shores

Resorts

Gulf State Park Resort
P.O. Box 437
Gulf Shores, AL 36547
(800) 544-4853

Huntsville

Convention Halls

Von Braun Center
700 Monroe Street
Huntsville, AL 35801
(256) 551-2377

Hilton Huntsville
401 Williams Avenue
Huntsville, AL 35801
(256) 533-1400

Holiday Inn Research Park
5903 University Drive
Huntsville, AL 35806
(800) 845-7275

Huntsville Marriott
5 Tranquility Base
Huntsville, AL 35805
(256) 830-2222

Mobile

Convention Halls

Arthur R. Outlaw Mobile Convention
  Center
One S. Water Street
Mobile, AL 36602
(251) 208-2100

Mobil Civic Center
401 Civic Center Drive
Mobile, AL 36602
(251) 208-7261

Adam's Mark Mobile
64 S. Water Street
Mobile, AL 36602
(251) 438-4000

Radisson Admiral Semmes
251 Government Street
Mobile, AL 36602
(251) 432-8000

The Lafayette Plaza Hotel
301 Government Street
Mobile, AL 36602
(251) 694-0100

Airport Plaza Hotel & Conference
Center
600 S. Beltline Highway
Mobile, AL 36608
(251) 344-8030

Mobile Marriott
3101 Airport Blvd.
Mobile, AL 36606
(251) 476-6400

Montgomery

Convention Halls

Montgomery Civic Center
300 Bibb Street
Montgomery, AL 36104
(334) 241-2100

Embassy Suites
300 Tallapoosa Street
Montgomery, AL 36104
(334) 269-5055

Governors House Hotel &
Conference Center
2705 E. South Boulevard
Montgomery, AL 36116
(334) 288-2800

Holiday Inn East
1185 Eastern Bypass
Montgomery, AL 36117
(334) 272-0370

The Legends at Capitol Hill
2500 Legends Circle
Prattville, AL 36066
(334) 290-1235

Orange Beach

Perdido Beach Resort
27200 Perdido Beach Blvd.
Orange Beach, AL 36561
(251) 981-9811

Point Clear

Marriott Grand Hotel Resort
Golf Club & Spa
One Grand Blvd.
Point Clear, AL 36564
(251) 990-6322

ALASKA

Anchorage

Convention Halls

Sullivan Arena
1600 Gambell Street
Anchorage, AK 99501
(907) 279-0618

William A. Egan Civic & Convention Center
555 W. 5th Avenue
Anchorage, AK 99501
(907) 263-2800

Anchorage Marriott Downtown
820 W. 7th Avenue
Anchorage, AK 99501
(907) 279-8005

Hilton Anchorage
500 W. 3rd Avenue
Anchorage, AK 99501
(907) 265-7155

Holiday Inn Anchorage—Downtown
239 W. 4th Avenue
Anchorage, AK 99501
(907) 793-5500

Hotel Captain Cook
P.O. Box 102280
Anchorage, AK 99510
(907) 276-6000

Sheraton Anchorage
401 E. 6th Avenue
Anchorage, AK 99501
(907) 343-3118

Millennium Alaskan Hotel Anchorage
4800 Spenard Road
Anchorage, AK 99517
(907) 266-2235

Fairbanks

Westmark Fairbanks Hotel &
Conference Center
813 Noble Street
Fairbanks, AK 99701
(907) 459-7706

Fairbanks Princess Riverside Lodge
4477 Pikes Landing Road
Fairbanks, AK 99709
(907) 455-5022

Girwood

Alyeska Prince Hotel
P.O. Box 249
Girwood, AK 99587
(907) 754-2213

Juneau

Convention Halls

Centennial Hall Convention Center
One Sealaska Plaza #305
Juneau, AK 99801
(907) 586-1737

ARIZONA
Flagstaff

Little America Hotel
P.O. Box 3900
Flagstaff, AZ 86003
(928) 779-7920

Phoenix/Scottsdale Metro Area

(Includes Carefree, Chandler, Litchfield Park, Mesa & Temple)

Mesa

Convention Centers

Mesa Centennial Center
P.O. Box 1466
Mesa, AZ 85211
(480) 644-3311

Sheraton Phoenix East
200 N. Centennial Way
Mesa, AZ 85201
(480) 464-5026

Best Western Dobson Ranch Inn & Resort
1666 S. Dobson Road
Mesa, AZ 85202
(480) 831-7000

Holiday Inn Hotel & Suites
1600 S. Country Club Drive
Mesa, AZ 85210
(480) 964-7000

Arizona Golf Resort & Conference Center
425 S. Power Road
Mesa, AZ 85206
(480) 832-3202

Hilton Phoenix East/Mesa
1011 W. Holmes Avenue
Mesa, AZ 85210
(480) 833-5555

Phoenix

Convention Halls

America West Arena
201 E. Jefferson Street
Phoenix, AZ 85004
(602) 379-2000

Arizona State Fair Park & Exposition
1826 W. McDowell Road
Phoenix, AZ 85007
(602) 252-6771

Phoenix Civic Plaza
111 N. 3rd Street
Phoenix, AZ 85004
(602) 262-6225

Crown Plaza Phoenix—Downtown
100 N. 1st Street
Phoenix, AZ 85004
(602) 333-4360

Hilton Suites Phoenix
101 E. Thomas Road
Phoenix, AZ 85012
(602) 222-1111

Hyatt Regency Phoenix
122 N. 2nd Street
Phoenix, AZ 85004
(602) 252-1234

Ritz Carlton Phoenix
2401 E. Camelback Road
Phoenix, AZ 85016
(602) 468-0700

Villager Premier
3710 NW Grand Avenue
Phoenix, AZ 85017
(602) 279-3211

Crown Plaza North Phoenix
2532 W. Peoria Avenue
Phoenix, AZ 85029
(602) 943-2341

Embassy Suites Biltmore
2630 E. Camelback Road
Phoenix, AZ 85016
(602) 955-3992

Embassy Suites Phoenix North
2577 W. Greenway Road
Phoenix, AZ 85023
(602) 375-4015

Four Points By Sheraton
Phoenix/Metro Center
10220 N. Metro Parkway East
Phoenix, AZ 85051
(602) 997-5900

Residence Inn by Phoenix
Marriott North
8242 N. Black Canyon Hwy.
Phoenix, AZ 85051
(602) 864-1900

Sheraton Crescent
2620 W. Dunlap Avenue
Phoenix, AZ 85021
(602) 371-2822

Airport Hotels

Doubletree Guest Suites
Phoenix Gateway Center
320 N. 44th Street
Phoenix, AZ 85008
(602) 683-9488

Embassy Suites Phoenix
Airport at 44th Street
1515 N. 44th Street
Phoenix, AZ 85008
(602) 244-8800

Hilton Phoenix Airport
2435 S. 47th Street
Phoenix, AZ 85034
(480) 894-1600

Holiday Inn Select Phoenix Airport
4300 E. Washington Street
Phoenix, AZ 85034
(602) 286-1120

Wyndham Garden Chandler
7475 W. Chandler Blvd.
Chandler, AZ 85226
(480) 961-4444

Wyndham Phoenix Airport Hotel
427 N. 44th Street
Phoenix, AZ 85008
(602) 220-4400

Arizona Biltmore Resort & Spa
24th Street & Missouri
Phoenix, AZ 85016
(602) 954-2527

Pointe Hilton Squaw Peak Resort
7677 N. 16th Street
Phoenix, AZ 85020
(602) 870-8188

Pointe Hilton Taxation Cliffs
Resort
1111 N. 7th Street
Phoenix, AZ 85020
(602) 870-8188

Pointe South Mountain Resort
7777 S. Pointe Parkway
Phoenix, AZ 85044
(602) 438-9000

Royal Palms Resort & Spa
5200 E. Camelback Road
Phoenix, AZ 85018
(602) 840-3610

Sheraton San Marcos Golf Resort
& Conference Center
One San Marcos Place
Chandler, AZ 85225
(480) 812-0900

Sheraton Wild Horse Pass
Resort & Spa
5594 W. Wild Horse Pass Blvd.
Phoenix, AZ 85070
(602) 225-0100

Sunshine Hotel & Resort
3600 N. 2nd Avenue
Phoenix, AZ 85013
(602) 248-0222

The Boulders Resort & Golden
Door Spa
34631 N. Tom Darlington Drive
Carefree, AZ 85377
(480) 488-9009

The Legacy Golf Resort
6808 S. 32nd Street
Phoenix, AZ 85042
(602) 305-5500

Wigwam Resort
300 Wigwam Blvd.
Litchfield Park, AZ 85340
(632) 856-1088

Scottsdale

Old Town Hotel & Conference Center
7353 E. Indian School Road
Scottsdale, AZ 85251
(480) 994-9203

Renaissance Scottsdale Resort
6160 N. Scottsdale Road
Scottsdale, AZ 85253
(480) 991-1414

Scottsdale Marriott Suites Old Town
7325 E. 3rd Avenue
Scottsdale, AZ 85251
(480) 945-1550

Carefree Conference Resort & Villas
37220 Mule Train Road
Carefree, AZ 85377
(480) 488-5300

Doubletree Paradise Valley Resort
Scottsdale
5401 N. Scottsdale Road
Scottsdale, AZ 85250
(480) 947-5400

Fairmont Scottsdale Princess
7575 E. Princess Drive
Scottsdale, AZ 85255
(480) 585-4848

Chaparral Suites Resort
5001 N. Scottsdale Road
Scottsdale, AZ 85250
(800) 648-4020

Four Seasons Resort Scottsdale
at Trion North
10600 E. Crescent Moon Drive
Scottsdale, AZ 85262
(480) 515-5700

Holiday Inn Sun Spree Resort
7601 E. Indian Bend Road
Scottsdale, AZ 85250
(800) 364-9145

Hyatt Regency Scottsdale at
Gainer Ranch
7500 E. Doubletree Ranch Road
Scottsdale, AZ 85258
(480) 991-3388

Doubletree La Posada Resort
4949 E. Lincoln Drive
Scottsdale, AZ 85253
(602) 952-0420

JW Marriott Desert Ridge Resort
& Spa
5350 East Marriott Drive
Phoenix, AZ 85054
(480) 905-0004

Marriott's Camelback Inn & Resort
5402 E. Lincoln Drive
Scottsdale, AZ 85253
(480) 948-1700

Marriott's Mountain Shadows
Resort & Golf Club
5641 E. Lincoln Drive
Scottsdale, AZ 85253
(480) 948-7111

Merv Griffin's Hilton Scottsdale
Resort & Villas
6333 N. Scottsdale Road
Scottsdale, AZ 85250
(480) 315-2032

Millennium Resort Scottsdale-
McCormick Ranch
7401 N. Scottsdale Road
Scottsdale, AZ 85253
(480) 948-5050

Orange Tree Golf Resort
10601 N. 56th Street
Scottsdale, AZ 85254
(480) 443-2130

Radisson Resort & Spa Scottsdale
7171 N. Scottsdale Road
Scottsdale, AZ 85253
(480) 991-3800

Ramada Valley Ho Resort &
Conference Center
6850 Main Street
Scottsdale, AZ 85251
(800) 231-5223

Resort Suites of Scottsdale
7677 E. Princess Blvd.
Scottsdale, AZ 85255
(480) 585-1488

Sanctuary on Camelback Mountain
5700 E. McDonald Drive
Paradise Valley, AZ 85253
(840) 948-2100

Scottsdale Conference Resort
7700 E. McCormick Parkway
Scottsdale, AZ 85258
(800) 528-0293

Scottsdale Marriott at McDowell
Mountains
16700 N. Perimeter Drive
Scottsdale, AZ 85260
(480) 502-3836

The Phoenician
6000 E. Camelback Road
Scottsdale, AZ 85251
(480) 941-8200

The Scottsdale Plaza Resort
7200 N. Scottsdale Road
Scottsdale, AZ 85253
(480) 922-3300

Westin Kierland Resort & Spa
6902 E. Greenway Parkway
Scottsdale, AZ 85254
(480) 624-1000

Tempe

Tempe Mission Palms Hotel
& Conference Center
60 E. 5th Street
Tempe, AZ 85281
(480) 894-1400

Embassy Suites Phoenix—Tempe
4400 S. Rural Road
Tempe, AZ 85282
(480) 897-7444

Fiesta Inn Resort
2100 S. Priest Drive
Tempe, AZ 85282
(480) 967-1441

Sheraton Phoenix Airport Hotel
1600 S. 52nd Street
Tempe, AZ 85281
(480) 967-6600

Wyndham Buttes Resort
2000 Westcourt Way
Tempe, AZ 85282
(602) 225-9000

Rio Rico

Rio Rico Resort & Country Club
1069 Camino Caralampi
Rio Rico, AZ 85648
(520) 377-8888

Sedona

Enchantment Resort
525 Boynton Canyon Road
Sedona, AZ 86336
(928) 204-6024

Hilton Sedona Resort & Spa
90 Ridge Trail Drive
Sedona, AZ 86351
(928) 284-6928

L'Auberge De Sedona
301 L'Auberge Lane
Sedona, AZ 86336
(928) 282-1661

Los Abrigodos Resort
160 Portal Lane
Sedona, AZ 86336
(928) 282-1777

Tucson

Convention Halls

Tucson Convention Center
260 S. Church Street
Tucson, AZ 85701
(520) 791-4101

Marriott University Park Hotel
880 E. Second Street
Tucson, AZ 85719
(520) 792-4100

Radisson City Center
181 W. Broadway
Tucson, AZ 85701
(520) 624-8711

Doubletree Guest Suites Tucson
6555 E. Speedway Blvd.
Tucson, AZ 85710
(520) 721-7100

Hilton Tucson East
7600 E. Broadway
Tucson, AZ 85710
(520) 721-5600

Airport Hotels

Embassy Suites
Tucson International Airport
7051 S. Tucson Blvd.
Tucson, AZ 85706
(520) 573-0700

Loews Ventana Canyon Resort
7000 N. Resort Drive
Tucson, AZ 85750
(520) 299-2020

Omni Tucson National Golf
Resort & Spa
2727 W. Club Drive
Tucson, AZ 85742
(520) 877-2350

Sheraton El Conquistador Resort
& Country Club
10000 N. Oracle Road
Tucson, AZ 85757
(520) 544-5000

The Westin La Paloma Resort
& Spa
3800 E. Sunrise Drive
Tucson, AZ 85718
(520) 742-6000

Westward Look Resort
245 E. Ina Road
Tucson, AZ 85704
(520) 297-1151

Yuma

Convention Halls

Yuma Civic & Convention Center
1440 Desert Hills Drive
Yuma, AZ 85365
(928) 344-3800

ARKANSAS
Eureka Springs

Best Western Inn of the Ozarks
P.O. Box 431
Eureka Springs, AR 72632
(800) 552-3785

Fairfield Bay

Shadow Ridge Villas & Conference
  Center
P.O. Box 1030
Fairfield Bay, AR 72088
(501) 884-6060

Fayetteville

UA Center for Continuing Education
2 E. Center Street
Fayetteville, AR 72701
(800) 952-1165

Radisson Hotel Fayetteville
70 N. East Avenue
Fayetteville, AR 72701
(501) 479-5555

Ft. Smith

Fort Smith Convention Center
55 South 7th Street
Fort Smith, AR 72901
(479) 788-8932

Holiday Inn City Center
700 Rogers Avenue
Fort Smith, AR 72901
(479) 783-1000

Ramada Inn
5711 Rogers Avenue
Fort Smith, AR 72903
(479) 452-4119

Hot Springs

Hot Springs Civic & Convention
Center
134 Convention Blvd.
Hot Springs, AR 71901
(501) 321-2835

Majestic Resort & Spa
101 Park Avenue
Hot Springs, AR 71901
(501) 623-5511

Royal Vista Inn
2204 Central Avenue
Hot Springs, AR 71901
(501) 624-5551

The Austin Hotel & Convention
Center
305 Malvern Avenue
Hot Springs, AR 71901
(501) 623-6600

Arlington Resort Hotel
239 Central Avenue
Hot Springs, AR 71901
(501) 623-7771

Bay Point Resort
2803 Albert Pike Road
Hot Springs, AR 71913
(501) 767-3606

Velda Rose Resort Hotel
217 Park Avenue
Hot Springs, AR 71901
(501) 623-3311

Little Rock

Convention Halls

Robinson Center
P.O. Box 3232
Little Rock, AR 72203
(501) 370-3232

Statehouse Convention Center
1 Statehouse Plaza
Little Rock, AR 72201
(501) 370-3232

Doubletree Hotel
424 W. Markham Road
Little Rock, AR 72201
(501) 372-4371

Peabody Little Rock
3 Statehouse Plaza
Little Rock, AR 72201
(501) 399-8050

Radisson City Center
617 S. Broadway
Little Rock, AR 72201
(501) 374-9000

Riverfront Hilton North Little Rock
2 Riverfront Place
North Little Rock, AR 72114
(501) 371-9000

The Capital Hotel
Markham & Louisiana
Little Rock, AR 72201
(501) 374-7474

Howard Johnson's
111 W. Pershing Blvd.
North Little Rock, AR 72114
(501) 758-1440

Pine Bluff

Pine Bluff Convention Center
One Convention Center Plaza
Pine Bluff, AR 71601
(870) 535-4867

Ramada Inn & Suites Convention Hotel
2 Convention Center Plaza
Pine Bluff, AR 71601
(870) 535-3111

Springdale

Holiday Inn & NWA Convention Center
1500 S. 48th Street
Springdale, AR 72762
(479) 751-8300

West Little Rock

Embassy Suites
11301 Financial Center Parkway
Little Rock, AR 72211
(501) 312-9000

Hilton Little Rock
925 S. University Avenue
Little Rock, AR 72204
(501) 664-5020

CALIFORNIA

Anaheim/Orange County Area

Anaheim Convention Center
800 W. Katella Avenue
Anaheim, CA 92802
(714) 765-8950

Anaheim Ramada
1331 E. Katella Avenue
Anaheim, CA 92805
(714) 978-8088

Embassy Suites Hotel
Anaheim South
11767 Harbor Blvd.
Garden Grove, CA 92840
(714) 539-3300

Hyatt Regency Orange County
11999 Harbor Blvd.
Garden Grove, CA 92840
(714) 740-6009

Radisson Hotel Maingate
1850 S. Harbor Blvd.
Anaheim, CA 92802
(714) 750-2801

Anaheim Marriott
700 W. Convention Way
Anaheim, CA 92802
(714) 750-8000

Suburban Hotels

Anaheim Plaza Hotel
1700 S. Harbor Blvd.
Anaheim, CA 92802
(714) 782-0205

Disney's Paradise Pier Hotel
1717 S. Disneyland Drive
Anaheim, CA 92802
(714) 999-0990

Embassy Suites Hotel
Anaheim-North
3100 E. Frontera
Anaheim, CA 92806
(714) 666-8954

Hilton Anaheim
777 Convention Way
Anaheim, CA 92802
(714) 740-4234

Sheraton Anaheim Hotel
900 S. Disneyland Drive
Anaheim, CA 92802
(714) 234-2452

Westcoast Anaheim Hotel
1855 S. Harbor Blvd.
Anaheim, CA 92802
(714) 750-1811

Resorts

Anaheim Fairfield Inn
1460 S. Harbor Blvd.
Anaheim, CA 92802
(714) 772-6777

Crown Plaza Resort
Anaheim/Garden Grove
12021 Harbor Blvd.
Garden Grove, 92840
(714) 867-5123

Disney's Grand Californian Hotel
1600 S. Disneyland Drive
Anaheim, CA 92802
(714) 959-6510

Disneyland Hotel
1150 W. Magic Way
Magic Way, CA 92802
(714) 956-6510

Holiday Inn at the Park
1221 S. Harbor Blvd.
Anaheim, CA 92805
(714) 758-0900

Quality Hotel Maingate
616 Convention Way
Anaheim, CA 92802
(714) 750-3131

Buena Park

Buena Park Sequoia Convention
Center
7530 Orangethorpe Avenue
Buena Park, CA 90621
(714) 670-9252

Holiday Inn Buena Park
Hotel & Convention Center
7000 Beach Blvd.
Buena Park, CA 90620
(714) 522-7000

Radisson Resort
Knott's Berry Farm
7675 Crescent Avenue
Buena Park, CA 90620
(714) 220-5411

Embassy Suites Buena Park
7762 Beach Blvd.
Buena Park, CA 90620
(714) 739-5600

Costa Mesa

Orange County Fair & Expo Center
88 Fair Drive
Costa Mesa, CA 92626
(714) 708-1572

Costa Mesa Marriott Suites
500 Anton Blvd.
Costa Mesa, CA 92626
(949) 798-3335

Holiday Inn—Costa Mesa
3131 S. Bristol Street
Costa Mesa, CA 92626
(714) 557-3000

Hilton Costa Mesa
3050 Bristol Street
Costa Mesa, CA 92626
(714) 540-7000

Weston South Coast Plaza
686 Anton Blvd.
Costa Mesa, CA 92626
(714) 662-6619

Wyndham Hotel
Orange County Airport
3350 Avenue of the Arts
Costa Mesa, CA 92626
(714) 751-5100

Dana Point

Laguna Cliffs Marriott
Resort at Dana Point
25135 Park Lantern
Dana Point, CA 92629
(800) 545-7483

Ritz-Carlton Laguna Niguel
One Ritz Carlton Drive
Dana Point, CA 92629
(949) 240-2000

St. Regis Monarch Beach
One Monarch Beach Resort
Dana Point, CA 92629
(800) 722-1534

Fullerton

Radisson Hotel Fullerton
222 W. Houston Avenue
Fullerton, CA 92832
(714) 992-1700

Four Points Sheraton
Fullerton/Anaheim
1500 S. Raymond Avenue
Fullerton, CA 92831
(714) 635-9000

Fullerton Marriott
2701 E. Nutwood Avenue
Fullerton, CA 92831
(714) 738-7800

Huntington Beach

Hotel Huntington Beach
7667 Center Avenue
Huntington Beach, CA 92647
(877) 891-0123

Hilton Waterfront Beach Resort
21100 Pacific Coast Highway
Huntington Beach, CA 92648
(714) 845-8000

Hyatt Regency Huntington
Beach Resort & Spa
21500 Pacific Coast Highway
Huntington Beach, CA 92648
(714) 698-1234

The Ritz-Carlton Half Moon Bay
One Miramontes Point Road
Huntington Beach, CA 94019
(800) 241-3333

Irvine

Hilton Irvine/Orange County Airport
18800 MacArthur Blvd.
Irvine, CA 92715
(949) 833-9999

Hyatt Regency Irvine
17900 Jamboree Road
Irvine, CA 92614
(949) 225-6760

Irvine Marriott
18000 von Karman Avenue
Irvine, CA 92612
(949) 724-3650

Newport Beach

Hyatt Newporter
1107 Jamboree Road
Newport Beach, CA 92660
(800) 233-1234

Marriott Hotel & Tennis Club
Newport Beach
900 Newport Center Drive
Newport Beach, CA 92660
(949) 640-4000

Marriott Suites Newport Beach
500 Bayview Drive
Newport Beach, CA 92660
(949) 509-6095

Radisson Newport Beach
4545 MacArthur Blvd.
Newport Beach, CA 92660
(949) 833-0570

The Sutton Place Hotel
4500 MacArthur Blvd.
Newport Beach, CA 92660
(949) 476-2001

Balboa Bay Club Resort & Spa
1221 W. Coast Highway
Newport Beach, CA 92663
(949) 645-5000

Four Seasons Newport Beach
690 Newport Center Drive
Newport Beach, CA 92660
(949) 759-0808

Orange

Doubletree Hotel
100 The City Drive
Orange, CA 92868
(714) 634-4500

Santa Ana

Embassy Suites
1325 E. Dyer Road
Santa Ana, CA 92705
(714) 241-3800

Bakersfield

Best Western Inn at Crystal Palace
2620 Buck Owens Blvd.
Bakersfield, CA 93308
(661) 327-9651

Holiday Inn Select Conference Center
801 Truxtun Avenue
Bakersfield, CA 93301
(661) 323-1500

Four Points Hotel by Sheraton
5101 California Avenue
Bakersfield, CA 93309
(800) 500-5399

Red Lion Hotel
2400 Camino del Rio Court
Bakersfield, CA 93308
(661) 327-0681

Carmel

La Lyaya Hotel
8th at Camino Real
Carmel, CA 93921
(831) 624-6476

Highland Inn, Park Hyatt Carmel
120 Highlands Drive
Carmel, CA 93923
(800) 682-4811

Quail Lodge Resort & Golf Club
8205 Valley Greens Drive
Carmel, CA 93923
(831) 620-8876

Concord

Hilton Concord
1970 Diamond Blvd.
Concord, CA 94520
(800) 826-2644

Sheraton Hotel & Conference Center
45 John Glenn Drive
Concord, CA 94520
(925) 825-7000

Fremont

Fremont Marriott Hotel
46100 Landing Parkway
Fremont, CA 94538
(877) 373-2229

Fresno

Fresno Convention Center
848 M Street
Fresno, CA 93721
(559) 498-4711

Radisson Hotel & Convention Center
2233 Ventura Street
Fresno, CA 93721
(559) 268-1000

Holiday Inn Fresno Airport
5090 E. Clinton
Fresno, CA 93727
(559) 252-3611

Kelseyville

Konocti Harbor Resort
8727 Soda Bay Road
Kelseyville, CA 95451
(707) 279-4281

Lake Arrowhead

Lake Arrowhead Resort
27984 Highway 189
Lake Arrowhead, CA 92352
(800) 800-6791

*Lake Tahoe Area (Includes North Lake
Tahoe, Olympic Valley & South Lake Tahoe.
See also Nevada)*

North Lake Tahoe

Northstar at Tahoe
P.O. Box 129
Truckee, CA 96160
(530) 562-2265

Olympic Valley

Resort at Squaw Creek
400 Squaw Creek Road
Olympic Valley, CA 96146
(530) 583-6300

South Lake Tahoe

Embassy Suites Hotel
Lake Tahoe Resort
4130 Lake Tahoe Blvd.
South Lake Tahoe, CA 96150
(530) 544-4900

Lakeland Village Beach & Mountain
Resort
3535 Lake Tahoe Blvd.
South Lake Tahoe, CA 96150
(530) 544-1685

Los Angeles/Long Beach Metro Area Beverly Hills

In-Town Hotels

Crown Plaza Beverly Hills
1150 S. Beverly Drive
Beverly Hills, CA 90035
(310) 553-6561

Le Meridian at Beverly Hills
465 S. La Cienega Blvd.
Los Angeles, CA 90048
(310) 247-0400

Regent Beverly Wilshire
9500 Wilshire Blvd.
Beverly Hills, CA 90212
(310) 275-5200

Beverly Hills Hotel
9641 Sunset Blvd.
Beverly Hills, CA 90210
(800) 283-8885

Beverly Hilton
9876 Wilshire Blvd.
Beverly Hills, CA 90210
(310) 285-1344

Four Seasons at Beverly Hills
300 S. Doheny Drive
Los Angeles, CA 90048
(310) 273-2222

Raffles L'Ermitage Beverly Hills
9291 Burton Way
Beverly Hills, CA 90210
(310) 278-3344

Sofitel Los Angeles
8555 Beverly Blvd.
Los Angeles, CA 90048
(310) 358-3906

Culver City

Radisson Los Angeles Westside
6161 W. Centinela Avenue
Culver City, CA 90231
(310) 348-4517

Ramada Plaza Hotel LAX North
6333 Bristol Parkway
Culver City, CA 90230
(800) 321-5575

El Segundo

Doubletree Club Hotel—LAX
1985 E. Grand Avenue
El Segundo, CA 90245
(310) 744-2044

Embassy Suites LAX South
1440 E. Imperial Avenue
El Segundo, CA 90245
(310) 640-3600

Hacienda Hotel at LAX
525 N. Sepulveda Blvd.
El Segundo, CA 90245
(310) 615-0015

Hollywood

Hollywood Palladium
6215 Sunrise Blvd.
Hollywood, CA 90028
(323) 962-7600

Hollywood Roosevelt
7000 Hollywood Blvd.
Hollywood, CA 90028
(323) 466-7000

Renaissance Hollywood Hotel
1755 N. Highland Avenue
Hollywood, CA 90028
(323) 856-1200

Long Beach

Long Beach Convention
& Entertainment Center
300 E. Ocean Blvd.
Long Beach, CA 90802
(562) 436-3636

Hilton Long Beach
701 W. Ocean Blvd.
Long Beach, CA 90831
(562) 983-3400

Hotel Queen Mary
1126 Queens Highway
Long Beach, CA 90802
(562) 499-1749

Hyatt Regency Long Beach
200 S. Pine Avenue
Long Beach, CA 90802
(562) 624-6100

Renaissance Long Beach
111 E. Ocean Blvd.
Long Beach, CA 90802
(562) 437-5900

Westin Long Beach
333 E. Ocean Blvd.
Long Beach, CA 90802
(562) 436-3000

Marriott Long Beach Airport
4700 Airport Plaza Drive
Long Beach, CA 90815
(562) 421-1075

Los Angeles

Convention Halls

Californiamart
110 E. 9th Street
Los Angeles, CA 90079
(213) 630-3631

Los Angeles Convention Center
1201 S. Figueroa Street
Los Angeles, CA 90015
(213) 741-1151

Shrine Auditorium & Expo Center
649 W. Jefferson Blvd.
Los Angeles, CA 90007
(213) 748-5116

USC Davidson Executive Conference
Center
3415 S. Figueroa Street
Los Angeles, CA 90038
(213) 740-5956

In-Town Hotels

Airtel Plaza Hotel & Conf. Center
7277 Vajean Avenue
Van Nuys, CA 91406
(818) 997-7676

Best Western Mayfair Hotel
1256 W. 7th Street
Los Angeles, CA 90017
(213) 483-1313

Holiday Inn Los Angeles Downtown
750 Garland Avenue
Los Angeles, CA 90017
(213) 628-9900

Hyatt Regency Los Angeles
711 S. Hope Street
Los Angeles, CA 90017
(213) 683-1234

Los Angeles Marriott Downtown
333 S. Figueroa Street
Los Angeles, CA 90071
(213) 617-1133

Millennium Biltmore Hotel Los
Angeles
506 S. Grand Avenue
Los Angeles, CA 90071
(213) 612-1500

Omni Los Angeles Hotel
251 S. Olive Street
Los Angeles, CA 90012
(213) 356-4099

Radisson Hotel Midtown Los
Angeles
3540 S. Figueroa Street
Los Angeles, CA 90007
(213) 748-4141

Radisson Wilshire Plaza Hotel Los
Angeles
3515 Wilshire Blvd.
Los Angeles, CA 90010
(213) 385-2653

The New Otani Hotel & Garden
120 S. Los Angeles Street
Los Angeles, CA 90012
(213) 253-9213

UCLA Conference & Event
Management
330 DeNeve Drive
Los Angeles, CA 90095
(310) 825-5305

Westin Bonaventure Hotel & Suites
404 S. Figueroa Street
Los Angeles, CA 90071
(213) 612-4837

Wyndham Checkers Los Angeles
535 S. Grand Avenue
Los Angeles, CA 90071
(213) 891-0563

Wilshire Grand Los Angeles
930 Wilshire Blvd.
Los Angeles, CA 90017
(213) 688-7777

Crown Plaza Redondo Beach
& Marina Hotel
300 N. Harbor Drive
Redondo Beach, CA 90277
(310) 318-8888

Doubletree Hotel Los Angeles—
Westwood
10740 Wilshire Blvd.
Los Angeles, CA 90024
(310) 475-8711

Embassy Suites Los Angeles—Covina
1211 E. Garvey Street
Covina, CA 91724
(626) 915-3441

Hilton Carson Civic Plaza
2 Civic Plaza
Carson, CA 90745
(310) 830-9200

Hilton Los Angeles North/Glendale
100 W. Glenoaks Blvd.
Glendale, CA 91202
(818) 956-5466

Holiday Inn Brentood/Bel-Air
170 N. Church Lane
Brentwood, CA 90049
(310) 476-6411

Hyatt Westlake Plaza
880 S. Westlake Blvd.
Westlake Village, CA 91361
(805) 557-4620

Park Hyatt Los Angeles at Century City
2151 Avenue of the Stars
Century City, CA 90067
(800) 233-1234

Sheraton Cerritos
12725 Center Court Drive
Cerritos, CA 90703
(562) 403-2002

Marina Del Rey

The Ritz-Carlton Marina Del Rey
4375 Admiralty Way
Los Angeles, CA 90292
(310) 823-1700

Courtyard by Marriott Marina Del Rey
13480 Maxella Avenue
Los Angeles, CA 90292
(310) 577-6065

Marina Beach Marriott
4100 Admiralty Way
Los Angeles, CA 90292
(310) 448-4890

Resorts

Marina International Hotel
4200 Admiralty Way
Los Angeles, CA 90292
(310) 301-2000

Pasadena

Pasadena Center
300 East Green Street
Pasadena, CA 91101
(626) 793-2122

In-Town Hotels

Hilton Pasadena
168 South Los Robles Avenue
Pasadena, CA 91101
(626) 577-1000

Westin Hotel Pasadena
191 North Los Robles Avenue
Pasadena, CA 91101
(626) 792-2727

Sheraton Pasadena Hotel
303 East Cordova Street
Pasadena, CA 91101
(626) 449-4000

The Ritz-Carlton Huntington Hotel
& SPA
141 South Oak Knoll Avenue
Pasadena, CA 91101
(626) 568-3900

Santa Monica

Convention Halls

Santa Monica Civic Auditorium
1855 Main Street
Santa Monica, CA 90401
(310) 458-8551

In-Town Hotels

Doubletree Guest Suites
1707 4th Street
Santa Monica, CA 90401
(310) 395-3332

Four Points Hotel Santa Monica
530 West Pico Blvd.
Santa Monica, CA 90401
(310) 399-9344

Radisson Huntley Hotel
1111 2nd Street
Santa Monica, CA 90401
(310) 394-5454

Loews Santa Monica Beach Hotel
1700 Ocean Avenue
Santa Monica, CA 90401
(310) 458-6700

Fairmont Miramar Hotel Santa Monica
101 Wilshire Blvd.
Santa Monica, CA 90401
(310) 576-7777

Torrance

Hilton Torrance/South Bay
21333 Hawthorne Blvd.
Torrance, CA 90503
(310) 540-5000

Holiday Inn Torrance
19800 South Vermont Avenue
Torrance, CA 90503
(310) 781-9100

Marriott Torrance
3635 Fashion Way
Torrance, CA 90503
(310) 316-3636

Universal City

Hilton Los Angeles/ Universal City
555 Universal Hollywood Drive
Universal City, CA 91608
(818) 506-2500

Sheraton Universal
333 Universal Terrace Parkway
Universal City, CA 91608
(818) 980-1212

Millbrae

Clarion Hotel San Francisco Airport
401 East Millbrae Avenue
Millbrae, CA 94030
(650) 777-7783

Westin San Francisco Airport
One Old Bayshore Highway
Millbrae, CA 94030
(650) 872-8147

Milpitas

Embassy Suites Milpitas
901 East Calaveras Blvd.
Milpita, CA 95035
(408) 942-0400

Sheraton San Jose
1801 Barber Lane
Milpita, CA 95035
(408) 473-8163

Modesto

Convention Hall

Modesto Center Plaza Convention
   Center
1000 L Street
Modesto, CA 95354
(209) 571-6480

Doubletree Hotel Modesto
1150 9th Street
Modesto, CA 95354
(209) 525-3037

Monterey

Convention Halls

Monterey Convention Authority
380 Alvarado Street
Monterey, CA 93940
(831) 646-3388

In-Town Hotels

Hilton Monterey
1000 Aguajito Road
Monterey, CA 93940
(831) 373-6141

Marriott Monterey
350 Calle Principal Street
Monterey, CA 93940
(831) 647-4005

Doubletree Monterey
2 Portola Plaza
Monterey, CA 93940
(831) 649-4511

Hyatt Regency Resort & Conference
Center
One Old Golf Course Drive
Monterey, CA 93940
(831) 647-2000

Monterey Plaza Hotel & Spa
400 Cannery Row
Monterey, CA 93940
(831) 646-1700

Pebble Beach

Inn at Spanish Bay
2700 17 Mile Drive
Pebble Beach, CA 93953
(831) 647-7500

Lodge at Pebble Beach
17 Mile Drive
Pebble Beach, CA 93953
(831) 647-7500

Napa

Embassy Suites Napa Valley
1075 California Blvd.
Napa, CA 94559
(707) 253-9540

Napa Valley Marriott Hotel & Spa
3425 Solano Avenue
Napa, CA 94558
(707) 253-3350

Silverado Resort
1600 Atlas Peak Road
Napa, CA 94558
(707) 257-5400

Ontario

Doubletree Hotel Ontario Airport
222 North Vineyard Avenue
Ontario, CA 91764
(909) 417-4156

Hilton Ontario Airport
700 North Haven Avenue
Ontario, CA 91764
(909) 980-0400

Ontario Airport Marriott
2200 East Holt Blvd
Ontario, CA 91761
(909) 975-5000

Pleasanton

Crowne Plaza Pleasanton
11950 Dublin Canyon Road
Pleasanton, CA 94588
(925) 847-6000

Hilton Pleasanton at the Club
7050 Johnson Drive
Pleasanton, CA 94588
(925) 737-5612

Indian Wells

Hyatt Grand Champions Resort
44-600 Indian Wells Lane
Indian Wells, CA 92210
(760) 341-1000

Indian Wells Resort Hotel
76-661 Highway 111
Indian Wells, CA 92210
(760) 345-6466

Miramonte Resort
45-000 Indian Wells Lane
Indian Wells, CA 92210
(760) 341-2200

Renaissance Esmeralda Resort & Spa
44-400 Indian Wells Lane
Indian Wells, CA 92210
(760) 773-4444

La Quinta

La Quinta Resort & Club
49-499 Eisenhower Drive
La Quinta, CA 92253
(760) 564-7602

Palm Desert

Embassy Suites
74-700 Highway 111
Palm Desert, CA 92260
(760) 340-6600

Marriott's Desert Springs Resort
& SPA
74855 Country Club Drive
Palm Desert, CA 92260
(760) 341-2211

Palm Springs

In-Town Hotels

Hyatt Regency Suites Palm Springs
285 North Palm Canyon Drive
Palm Springs, CA 92262
(760) 322-9000

Spa Resort Casino
100 North Indian Canyon Drive
Palm Springs, CA 92262
(760) 778-1500

Palm Springs Hilton
400 East Acquits Canyon Way
Palm Springs, CA 92262
(760) 320-6868

Doral Palm Springs Resort
67-967 Vista Chino
Palm Springs, CA 92234
(760) 322-7000

Palm Springs Marquis Conference
Resort
150 South Indian Canyon Drive
Palm Springs, CA 92262
(760) 322-2121

Palm Springs Riviera Resort
1600 North Indian Canyon Drive
Palm Springs, CA 92262
(760) 778-6603

Wyndham Palm Springs Hotel
888 Acquits Canyon Way
Palm Springs, CA 92262
(760) 322-6000

Rancho Mirage

Marriott's Rancho Las Palmas Resort
& Spa
41000 Bob Hope Drive
Rancho Mirage, CA 92270
(760) 862-4520

The Lodge at Rancho Mirage
68-900 Frank Sinatra Drive
Rancho Mirage, CA 92270
(760) 321-8282

Westin Mission Hills Resort
Dinah Shore & Bob Hope Drives
Rancho Mirage, CA 92270
(760) 328-5955

Riverside

Convention Halls

Riverside Convention Center
3443 Orange Street
Riverside, CA 92501
(909) 222-4700

Mission Inn
3649 Mission Inn Avenue
Riverside, CA 92501
(909) 341-6798

Riverside Marriott
3400 Market Street
Riverside, CA 92501
(909) 784-8000

Sacramento

Sacramento Convention Center
1030 15th Street
Sacramento, CA 95814
(916) 264-5291

In-Town Hotels

Clarion Hotel Mansion Inn
700 16th Street
Sacramento, CA 95814
(916) 444-8000

Holiday Inn Capitol Plaza
300 J Street
Sacramento, CA 95814
(916) 446-0100

Hyatt Regency Sacramento
1209 L Street
Sacramento, CA 95814
(916) 321-3540

Sheraton Grand Sacramento
1230 J Street
Sacramento, CA 95814
(916) 447-1700

Doubletree Hotel Sacramento
2001 Point West Way
Sacramento, CA 95815
(916) 929-8855

Hilton Sacramento Arden West
2200 Harvard Street
Sacramento, CA 95815
(916) 922-4700

Holiday Inn Sacramento Northeast
5321 Date Avenue
Sacramento, CA 95841
(916) 338-5800

Radisson Sacramento
500 Leisure Lane
Sacramento, CA 95815
(916) 922-2020

San Bernardino

Radisson San Bernardino
295 North East Street
San Bernardino, CA 92401
(909) 381-6181

Hilton San Bernardino
285 East Hospitality Lane
San Bernardino, CA 92408
(909) 388-7910

San Jose

San Jose Scenery Convention Center
408 Aladdin Blvd.
San Jose, CA 95110
(408) 277-5277

Crowne Plaza San Jose
282 Alma den Blvd.
San Jose, CA 95113
(408) 998-0400

Fairmont San Jose
170 South Market Street
San Jose, CA 95113
(408) 998-3909

Hilton Newark/Fremont
39900 Valentine Drive
Newark, CA 94560
(510) 490-8390

Holiday Inn Silicon Valley
399 Silicon Valley Blvd.
San Jose, CA 95138
(408) 972-7800

Hyatt San Jose
1740 North 1st Street
San Jose, CA 95112
(408) 793-3977

Radisson Plaza Hotel San Jose Airport
1471 North 4th Street
San Jose, CA 95112
(408) 452-0200

Wyndham Hotel San Jose
1350 North 1st Street
San Jose, CA 95112
(408) 998-6219

Santa Barbara

Montecito Inn
1295 Coast Village Road
Montecito, CA 93108
(805) 969-7854

Baccarat Resort & Spa, Santa Barbara
8301 Hollister Avenue
San Jose, CA 95117
(408) 571-3100

Fess Parker's Doubletree Resort
633 East Carrillo Blvd
San Jose, CA 95103
(408) 564-4333

Four Seasons Resort Santa Barbara
1260 Channel Drive
San Jose, CA 95108
(408) 969-2261

Radisson Santa Barbara
1111 East Carrillo Blvd
San Jose, CA 95103
(408) 963-0744

Santa Barbara Miramar Resort
1555 South Jameson Lane
San Jose, CA 95108
(408) 969-2203

Santa Clara

Convention Halls

Network Meeting Center at Tec Mart
5201 Great America Parkway
Santa Clara, CA 95054
(408) 562-6111

Santa Clara Convention Center
5001 Great America Parkway
Santa Clara, CA 95054
(408) 748-7047

Hilton Santa Clara
4949 Great America Parkway
Santa Clara, CA 95054
(408) 562-6717

Marriott Santa Clara
2700 Mission College Blvd.
Santa Clara, CA 95054
(408) 988-1500

The Plaza Suites Silicon Valley
3100 Lakeside Drive
Santa Clara, CA 95054
(408) 748-9800

Westin Santa Clara
5101 Great America Parkway
Santa Clara, CA 95054
(408) 980-3909

Biltmore Hotel & Suites
2151 Laurel Wood Road
Santa Clara, CA 95054
(408) 988-8411

Embassy Suites Hotel Santa Clara
2885 Lakeside Drive
Santa Clara, CA 95054
(408) 845-7205

Stockton

Holiday Inn Stockton
111 East March Lane
Stockton, CA 95207
(209) 474-3301

Radisson Hotel Stockton
2323 Grand Canal Blvd
Stockton, CA 95207
(209) 957-9090

Sunnyvale

Four Points By Sheraton Sunnyvale
1250 Lakeside Drive
Sunnyvale, CA 94085
(408) 328-8130

Wyndham Sunnyvale Hotel
1300 Chesapeake Terrace
Sunnyvale, CA 94089
(408) 747-0999

Carlsbad

Four Season Resort Aviary
7100 Four Seasons Point
Carlsbad, CA 92009
(760) 603-6800

La Costa Resort & Spa
2100 Costa del Mar Road
Carlsbad, CA 92009
(760) 438-9111

Coronado

Coronado Island Marriott Resort
2000 2nd Street
Coronado, CA 92118
(619) 435-3000

Hotel Del Coronado
1500 Orange Avenue
Coronado, CA 92118
(619) 522-8265

Loews Coronado Bay Resort
4000 Coronado Bay Road
Coronado, CA 92118
(619) 424-4000

La Jolla

Embassy Suites Hotel San Diego–
La Jolla
4550 La Jolla Village Drive
San Diego, CA 92122
(858) 453-0400

Hyatt Regency La Jolla
3777 La Jolla Village Drive
San Diego, CA 92122
(858) 552-6024

Marriott La Jolla
4240 La Jolla Village Drive
La Jolla, CA 92037
(858) 587-1414

Hilton La Jolla Torrez Pines
10950 North Torrez Pines Road
La Jolla, CA 92037
(858) 558-1500

Mission Bay

Holiday Inn Mission Bay Sea World
3737 Sports Arena Blvd
San Diego, CA 92110
(619) 881-6106

Catamaran Resort Hotel
3999 Mission Blvd
San Diego, CA 92110
(858) 539-8700

Hilton San Diego Resort
1775 East Mission Bay Drive
San Diego, CA 92109
(619) 275-8950

Hyatt Regency Islander Hotel & Marina
1441 Quiver Road
San Diego, CA 92109
(619) 224-1234

Mission Valley

Doubletree Hotel San Diego Mission
Valley
7450 Hazard Center Drive
San Diego, CA 92108
(619) 688-4017

Hilton San Diego Mission Valley
901 Camino del Rio South
San Diego, CA 92108
(619) 682-3947

Holiday Inn Select
595 Hotel Circle South
San Diego, CA 92108
(619) 291-5720

Red Lion Hanalei Hotel
2270 Hotel Circle North
San Diego, CA 92108
(619) 293-7302

San Diego

San Diego Convention Center
111 West Harbor Drive
San Diego, CA 92101
(619) 615-4111

Clarion Hotel Bay View
660 K Street
San Diego, CA 92101
(619) 696-0234

Courtyard by Marriott San Diego
Downtown/Gaslamp
530 Broadway
San Diego, CA 92101
(619) 446-3005

Doubletree Golf Resort San Diego
14455 Penasquitos Drive
San Diego, CA 92129
(858) 672-9100

Embassy Suites San Diego Bay
601 Pacific Highway
San Diego, CA 92101
(619) 233-9922

Hilton San Diego Gaslamp Quarter
401 K Street
San Diego, CA 92101
(619) 702-8262

Holiday Inn on the Bay
1355 North Harbor Drive
San Diego, CA 92101
(619) 232-2000

Hyatt Regency San Diego
One Market Place
San Diego, CA 92101
(619) 232-1234

Radisson Hotel Harbor View
1646 Front Street
San Diego, CA 92101
(619) 819-4650

San Diego Marriott Hotel & Marina
333 West Harbor Drive
San Diego, CA 92101
(619) 234-1500

U.S. Grant–A Wyndham Historic Hotel
326 Broadway
San Diego, CA 92101
(619) 232-3121

Westin Horton Plaza
910 Broadway Circle
San Diego, CA 92101
(619) 239-2200

Wyndham San Diego at Emerald Plaza
400 West Broadway
San Diego, CA 92101
(619) 239-4500

Holiday Inn San Diego Bayside
4875 North Harbor Drive
San Diego, CA 92106
(800) 650-6660

Sheraton San Diego Hotel & Marina
1380 Harbor Island Drive
San Diego, CA 92101
(619) 692-2266

Bahia Resort Hotel
998 West Mission Bay Drive
San Diego, CA 92109
(858) 539-7700

Paradise Point Resort & Spa
1404 Vacation Road
San Diego, CA 92100
(858) 581-5900

Town & Country Resort & Convention
Center
500 Hotel Circle North
San Diego, CA 92108
(619) 297-6006

Burlingame

Crowne Plaza San Francisco
International Airport
1177 Airport Blvd.
San Diego, CA 94010
(650) 373-7028

Embassy Suites San Francisco Airport
150 Anza Blvd.
San Diego, CA 94010
(650) 342-4600

Hyatt Regency San Francisco Airport
1333 Old Bayshore Highway
San Diego, CA 94010
(650) 347-1234

Marriott San Francisco Airport
1800 Old Bayshore Highway
San Diego, CA 94010
(650) 692-9100

Sheraton Gateway Hotel
600 Airport Blvd.
San Diego, CA 94010
(650) 340-8500

Oakland

Oakland Convention Center
1001 Broadway
San Diego, CA 94607
(510) 455-6416

Oakland Marriott City Center
1001 Broadway
San Diego, CA 94607
(510) 451-4000

Hilton Oakland Airport
1 Hegenberger Road
San Diego, CA 94621
(510) 635-5000

Claremont Resort & Spa
41 Tunnel Road
Berkeley, CA 94705
(510) 843-3000

San Francisco

Cow Palace
2600 Geneva Avenue
Daly City, CA 94014
(415) 404-4100

San Francisco Design Center
2 Henry Adams Street
San Francisco, CA 94103
(415) 490-5860

The Miscode Center
747 Howard Street
San Francisco, CA 94103
(415) 974-4023

Cathedral Hill Hotel
1101 Van Ness
San Francisco, CA 94109
(415) 776-8200

Clift Hotel
495 Geary Street
San Francisco, CA 94102
(415) 929-2301

Crowne Plaza San Francisco Union
Square
480 Sutter Street
San Francisco, CA 94108
(415) 398-8900

Fairmont Hotel San Francisco
950 Mason Street
San Francisco, CA 94108
(415) 772-5000

Grand Hyatt San Francisco
345 Stockton Street
San Francisco, CA 94108
(415) 403-4827

Handlery Union Square
351 Geary Street
San Francisco, CA 94102
(415) 781-7800

Hilton San Francisco
333 O'Farrell Street
San Francisco, CA 94102
(415) 771-1400

Hilton San Francisco Fisherman's Wharf
2620 Jones Street
San Francisco, CA 94102
(415) 885-4700

Holliday Inn Civic Center
50 Eighth Street
San Francisco, CA 94103
(415) 626-6103

Holiday Inn Financial District
750 Kearny Street
San Francisco, CA 94108
(415) 273-4000

Holiday Inn Fisherman's Wharf
1300 Columbus Avenue
San Francisco, CA 94133
(415) 273-4000

Holiday Inn Golden Gateway
1500 Van Ness Avenue
San Francisco, CA 94109
(415) 441-4000

Hotel Monaco San Francisco
501 Geary Street
San Francisco, CA 94102
(415) 292-8130

Hotel Nikon San Francisco
222 Mason Street
San Francisco, CA 94102
(415) 394-1111

Huntington Hotel & Knob Hill Spa
1075 California Street
San Francisco, CA 94108
(415) 345-2820

Hyatt Fisherman's Wharf San Francisco
555 North Point Street
San Francisco, CA 94133
(415) 563-1234

Hyatt Regency Hotel
5 Embarcadero Center
San Francisco, CA 94111
(415) 788-1234

Intercontinental Mark Hopkins San
Francisco
999 California Street
San Francisco, CA 94108
(415) 392-3434

Mandarin Oriental San Francisco
222 Ransomed Street
San Francisco, CA 94104
(415) 276-9615

Marriott Fisherman's Wharf
1250 Columbus Avenue
San Francisco, CA 94133
(415) 775-7555

Palace Hotel San Francisco
2 New Montgomery Street
San Francisco, CA 94105
(415) 546-5012

Park Hyatt San Francisco
333 Battery Street
San Francisco, CA 94111
(415) 392-1234

Radisson Myakka Hotel
1625 Post Street
San Francisco, CA 94115
(415) 922-3200

Renaissance Parc 55 Hotel
55 Cyril Magnin Street
San Francisco, CA 94102
(415) 392-8000

Ramada Plaza San Francisco—
Downtown
1231 Market Street
San Francisco, CA 94103
(415) 626-4400

San Francisco Marriott
55 4th Street
San Francisco, CA 94103
(415) 442-6029

Serrano Hotel
405 Taylor Street
San Francisco, CA 94102
(415) 351-76703

Sheraton at Fisherman's Wharf
2500 Mason Street
San Francisco, CA 94133
(415) 627-6505

Sir Francis Drake Hotel
450 Powell Street
San Francisco, CA 94102
(415) 677-9341

The Argent Hotel
50 3rd Street
San Francisco, CA 94103
(415) 974-7556

The Pan Pacific Hotel San Francisco
500 Post Street
San Francisco, CA 94102
(415) 771-8600

The Ritz-Carlton San Francisco
600 Stockton Street at California Street
San Francisco, CA 94108
(415) 296-7465

The Stanford Court, Renaissance Hotel
905 California Street
San Francisco, CA 94108
(415) 989-3500

Tuscan Inn
425 North Point Street
San Francisco, CA 94133
(415) 292-4545

Warwick Regis Hotel
490 Geary Street
San Francisco, CA 94102
(415) 928-7900

Westin St. Francis
335 Powell Street
San Francisco, CA 94102
(415) 774-0112

Holiday Inn San Francisco—Oakland
Bay Bridge
1800 Powell Street
Emeryville, CA 94608
(510) 658-9300

Best Western Grosvenor
380 South Airport Blvd.
South San Francisco, CA 94080
(650) 873-3200

Embassy Suites San Francisco—Airport
North
250 Gateway Blvd.
South San Francisco, CA 94080
(650) 589-3400

Holiday Inn San Francisco—
International Airport North
275 South Airport Blvd.
South San Francisco, CA 94080
(650) 873-3550

Ramada Inn San Francisco—
International Airport North
245 South Airport Blvd.
South San Francisco, CA 94080
(650) 873-3560

COLORADO

Aspen

Hotel Jerome
330 East Main Street
Aspen, CO 81611
(970) 920-1000

Inn at Aspen Resort & Conference Hotel
38750 Highway 82
Aspen, CO 81611
(970) 925-1500

The Little Nell
675 East Durant Avenue
Aspen, CO 81611
(970) 920-6332

The St. Regis Aspen
315 East Dean Street
Aspen, CO 81611
(970) 920-3300

Aspen Meadows Resort Hotel
& Conf. Ctr.
845 Meadows Road
Aspen, CO 81611
(970) 544-7850

Beaver Creek

Christie Lodge
47 East Beaver Creek Blvd.
Avon, CO 81620
(970) 845-4554

Park Hyatt Beaver Creek Resort
and Spa
P.O. Box 1595
Avon, CO 81620
(970) 949-1234

The Beaver Creek Lodge
26 Avondale
Avon, CO 81620
(970) 845-1712

The Charter at Beaver Creek
120 Offerson Road
Avon, CO 81620
(970) 949-6660

Boulder

Convention Halls

University of Colorado Coors Events
　　Conference Center
University of Colorado, Campus
　　Box 410
Boulder, CO 80309
(303) 492-5316

Boulder Broker Inn
555 30th Street
Boulder, CO 80303
(303) 444-3330

Hotel Boulderado
2115 13th Street
Boulder, CO 80302
(303) 440-2580

Millennium Hotel Boulder
1345 28th Street
Boulder, CO 80302
(303) 443-3850

Beaver Run Resort & Conference
Center
620 Village Road
Boulder, CO 80324
(970) 453-6000

The Great Divide Lodge
P.O. Box 8329
Boulder, CO 80324
(970) 453-3150

The Village at Breckenridge Resort
P.O. Box 8329
Boulder, CO 80324
(970) 453-3150

OMNI Interlocked Resort
500 Interlocked Blvd.
Boulder, CO 80321
(303) 438-6600

Colorado Springs

Pikes Peak Center
190 South Cascade
Colorado Springs, CO 80903
(719) 520-7453

Antlers Adam's Mark
4 South Cascade Avenue
Colorado Springs, CO 80903
(719) 630-6209

Red Loin Colorado Springs Hotel
314 West Bijou Street
Colorado Springs, CO 80905
(719) 329-7457

Doubletree Hotel Colorado Springs
World Arena
1775 East Cheyenne Mountain Blvd.
Colorado Springs, CO 80905
(719) 527-4661

Radisson Inn Colorado Springs North
8110 North Academy Blvd.
Colorado Springs, CO 80920
(719) 598-5770

Sheraton Colorado Springs
2886 South Circle Drive
Colorado Springs, CO 80906
(719) 576-5900

Wyndham Colorado Springs
5580 Tech Center Drive
Colorado Springs, CO 80919
(719) 260-1800

Radisson Inn & Suites Colorado Springs
Airport
1645 North Newport Road
Colorado Springs, CO 80916
(719) 597-7000

The Broadmoor
1 Lake Avenue
Colorado Springs, CO 80906
(719) 577-5777

Durango

Doubletree Hotel Durango
501 Camino Del Rio
Durango, CO 81301
(970) 259-6580

Tall Timber Resort
No 1 Silverton Star
Durango, CO 81301
(970) 259-4813

Tamarron Resort
40292 US Highway, 550 North
Durango, CO 81301
(970) 259-2000

Aurora

Doubletree Denver Southeast
13696 East Iliff Place
Aurora, CO 80014
(303) 337-2800

Radisson Hotel Denver Southeast
3200 South Parker Road
Aurora, CO 80014
(303) 695-1700

Denver Airport Marriott Hotel
16455 East 40th Circle
Aurora, CO 80014
(303) 371-4333

Denver

Colorado Convention Center
700 14th Street
Denver, CO 80202
(303) 228-8022

Adam's Mark Denver
1550 Court Place
Denver, CO 80202
(303) 626-2500

Brown Palace
321 17th Street
Denver, CO 80202
(303) 297-3111

Embassy Suites—Downtown Denver
1881 Curtis Street
Denver, CO 80202
(303) 297-8888

Executive Tower
1405 Curtis Street
Denver, CO 80202
(303) 571-0300

Holiday Inn Denver—Downtown
1450 Glenarm Place
Denver, CO 80202
(303) 573-1450

Holiday Inn Select Denver—Cherry
Creek
455 South Colorado Blvd.
Denver, CO 80246
(303) 388-5561

Hotel Monaco Denver
1717 Champa Street at 17th Street
Denver, CO 80202
(303) 294-3021

Hyatt Regency Denver
1750 Welton Street
Denver, CO 80202
(303) 295-5801

Marriott City Center Denver
1701 California Street
Denver, CO 80202
(303) 297-1300

Regency Hotel & Convention Center
3900 Elati Street
Denver, CO 80216
(303) 458-0808

Warwick Hotel Denver
1776 Grant Street
Denver, CO 80203
(303) 861-2000

Westin Tabor Center Denver
1672 Lawrence Street
Denver, CO 80202
(303) 572-9100

Denver Marriott Tech Center
4900 South Syracuse
Denver, CO 80237
(303) 779-1100

Doubletree Denver
3203 Quebec Street
Denver, CO 80207
(303) 321-3333

Embassy Suites Denver Southeast
7525 East Hampden Avenue
Denver, CO 80231
(303) 696-6644

Four Points by Sheraton Denver
Southeast
1475 South Colorado Blvd.
Denver, CO 80222
(303) 757-8797

Four Points Sheraton Cherry Creek
600 South Colorado Blvd.
Denver, CO 80246
(303) 757-3341

Hyatt Regency Tech Center
7800 East Tufts Avenue
Denver, CO 80237
(303) 714-4615

Marriott Southeast Denver
6363 East Hampden Avenue
Denver, CO 80222
(303) 758-7000

Radisson Hotel Denver, Stapleton Plaza
3333 Quebec Street
Denver, CO 80207
(303) 329-2701

Red Lion Hotel Denver Central
4040 Quebec Street
Denver, CO 80216
(303) 321-6666

Renaissance Denver Hotel
3801 Quebec Street
Denver, CO 80207
(303) 399-7500

Sheraton Denver West
360 Union Blvd.
Lakewood, CO 80228
(303) 987-2000

Embassy Suites Denver Airport
Gateway South
4444 North Havana Street
Denver, CO 80239
(303) 375-0400

Englewood

Embassy Suites Denver Tech Center
1025 East Costilla Avenue
Englewood, CO 80112
(303) 792-0433

Sheraton Denver Tech Center
7007 South Clinton Street
Englewood, CO 80112
(303) 799-6200

Inverness Hotel & Conference Center
200 Inverness Drive West
Englewood, CO 80112
(303) 799-5800

Ft. Collins

Ft. Collins Marriott
350 East Horsetooth Road
Fort Collins, CO 80525
(970) 226-5200

University Park Holiday Inn
425 West Prospect Road
Fort Collins, CO 80526
(970) 482-2626

Grand Junction

Adam's Mark Grand Junction
743 Horizon Drive
Grand Junction, CO 81506
(970) 241-8888

Holiday Inn Grand Junction
755 Horizon Drive
Grand Junction, CO 81506
(970) 243-6790

Steamboat Springs

Sheraton Steamboat Resort &
Conference Center
P.O. Box 774808
Steamboat Springs, CO 80477
(970) 879-7980

Steamboat Grand Resort Hotel &
Conference Center
2300 Mt. Werner Circle
Steamboat Springs, CO 80487
(970) 871-5540

Vail

Lion Square Lodge & Conference
Center
660 West Lionshead Place
Vail, CO 81657
(970) 476-2281

Lodge at Vail
174 East Gore Creek Drive
Vail, CO 81657
(970) 476-5011

Montaneros Condos
641 West Lionshead Circle
Vail, CO 81657
(970) 476-2491

Sonnenalp Resort of Vail
20 Vail Road
Vail, CO 81657
(970) 479-5534

Vail Cascade Resort & Spa
1300 Westhaven Drive
Vail, CO 81657
(970) 476-7111

Vail Marriott Mountain Resort & Spa
715 West Lionshead Circle
Vail, CO 81657
(970) 479-6997

Vail's Mountain Haus
292 East Meadow Drive
Vail, CO 81657
(970) 476-2434

CONNECTICUT
Bridgeport

Holiday Inn & Conference Center
1070 Main Street
Bridgeport, CT 06604
(203) 334-1234

Fairfield

Trumbull Marriott Merritt Parkway
180 Hawley Lane
Trumbull, CT 06611
(203) 378-1400

Hartford

Hartford Civic Center
One Civic Center plaza
Hartford, CT 06103
(860) 246-7825

Crowne Plaza Hartford—Downtown
50 Morgan Street
Hartford, CT 06120
(860) 549-2400

Hilton Hartford Hotel
315 Trumbull Street
Hartford, CT 06103
(860) 240-7272

Hartford Marriott Rocky Hill
100 Capital Blvd.
Rocky Hill, CT 060676
(860) 257-6000

Marriott Farmington
15 Farm Springs Road
Farmington, CT 06032
(860) 678-1000

New Haven

OMNI New Haven Hotel at Yale
155 Temple Street
New Haven, CT 06510
(203) 772-6664

Old Greenwich

Hyatt Regency Greenwich
1800 East Putnam Avenue
Old Greenwich, CT 06870
(203) 637-1234

Stamford

Holiday Inn Select Stamford
700 Main Street
Stamford, CT 06901
(203) 358-8400

Marriott Stamford
2 Stamford Forum
Stamford, CT 06901
(203) 357-9555

Westin Stamford Hotel
One First Stamford Place
Stamford, CT 06902
(203) 351-1868

Sheraton Stamford Hotel
2701 Summer Street
Stamford, CT 06905
(203) 359-1300

Delaware
Dover

Sheraton Dover
1570 North Dupont Highway
Dover, DE 19901
(302) 678-8500

Newark

Christiana Hilton
100 Continental Drive
Newark, DE 19713
(302) 454-1500

Wilmington

Hotel Du Pont
11th & Market Streets
Wilmington, DE 19801
(302) 594-3107

Sheraton Suites Wilmington
422 Delaware Avenue
Wilmington, DE 19801
(302) 576-8009

The Wyndham Hotel
700 King Street
Wilmington, DE 19801
(302) 655-0400

Doubletree Hotel Wilmington
4727 Concord Pike, US Rte. 202
Wilmington, DE 19803
(302) 478-6000

Holiday Inn Select Wilmington
I-95 and Names Road
Claymont, DE 19703
(302) 792-2700

Washington, D.C.

Washington Convention Center
900 9th Street NW
Washington, D.C. 20001
(202) 371-3021

Capital Hilton
16th and K Streets NW
Washington, D.C. 20036
(202) 797-5771

Embassy Suites Washington D.C.
1250 22nd Street NW
Washington, D.C. 20037
(202) 857-3388

Four Seasons Washington D.C.
2800 Pennsylvania Avenue NW
Washington, D.C. 20007
(202) 342-1673

Georgetown Suites
1111 30th Street NW
Washington, D.C. 20007
(202) 298-7800

Georgetown University Conference
Center
3800 Reservoir Road NW
Washington, D.C. 20057
(202) 687-3242

Grand Hyatt Washington
1000 H Street NW
Washington, D.C. 20001
(202) 637-4700

Henley Park Hotel
926 Massachusetts Avenue NW
Washington, D.C. 20001
(202) 414-0515

Hilton Washington & Towers
1919 Connecticut Avenue NW
Washington, D.C. 20009
(202) 797-5827

Hilton Washington Embassy Row
2015 Massachusetts Avenue NW
Washington, D.C. 20036
(202) 265-1600

Holiday Inn Capitol
550 C Street SW
Washington, D.C. 20024
(202) 554-2780

Holiday Inn—Downtown
1155 14th Street NW
Washington, D.C. 20005
(202) 737-1200

Holiday Inn on the Hill
415 New Jersey Avenue NW
Washington, D.C. 20001
(202) 434-0113

Hotel Washington
515 15th Street NW
Washington, D.C. 20004
(202) 628-9764

Hyatt Regency Washington on
Capitol Hill
400 New Jersey Avenue NW
Washington, D.C. 20001
(202) 383-1300

JW Marriott Hotel on Pennsylvania
Avenue
1331 Pennsylvania Avenue NW
Washington, D.C. 20004
(202) 393-2000

Loews L'enfant Plaza Hotel
480 L'Enfant Plaza
Washington, D.C. 20024
(202) 646-04418

Madison Hotel
1177 15th Street NW
Washington, D.C. 20005
(202) 862-1600

Marriott at Metro Center
775 12th Street NW
Washington, D.C. 20005
(202) 824-6150

Marriott Wardman Park
2660 Woodley Road NW
Washington, D.C. 20008
(202) 328-2950

Monarch Hotel
2401 M Street NW
Washington, D.C. 20037
(202) 429-2400

OMNI Shoreham
2500 Calvert Street NW
Washington, D.C. 20008
(202) 756-5110

Park Hyatt Washington D.C.
1201 24th Street NW
Washington, D.C. 20037
(202) 789-1234

Radisson Barcelo
2121 P Street NW
Washington, D.C. 20037
(202) 293-3100

Renaissance Mayflower
1127 Connecticut Avenue NW
Washington, D.C. 20036
(202) 347-3000

Renaissance Washington D.C.
999 Ninth Street NW
Washington, D.C. 20001
(202) 898-9000

Swissotel the Watergate
2650 Virginia Avenue NW
Washington, D.C. 20037
(202) 965-2300

The Hamilton Crowne Plaza
14th and K Street NW
Washington, D.C. 20005
(202) 218-7527

The Jefferson Hotel—A Loews
Hotel
1200 16th Street NW
Washington, D.C. 20036
(202) 347-2200

The St. Regis Washington D.C.
923 16th Street NW
Washington, D.C. 20006
(202) 879-6935

Washington Court Hotel on
Capitol Hill
525 New Jersey Avenue NW
Washington, D.C. 20001
(202) 628-2100

Washington Marriott
1221 22nd Street NW
Washington, D.C. 20037
(202) 872-1500

Washington Plaza
10 Thomas Circle NW
Washington, D.C. 20005
(202) 842-1300

Washington Terrace Hotel
1515 Rhode Island Avenue NW
Washington, D.C. 20005
(202) 232-7000

Wyndham City Center
1143 New Hampshire
   Avenue NW
Washington, D.C. 20037
(202) 775-0800

Wyndham Washington D.C.
1400 M Street NW
Washington, D.C. 20005
(202) 429-1700

FLORIDA

Boca Raton

Embassy Suites Boca Raton
661 NW 53rd Street
Boca Raton, FL 33487
(561) 994-8200

Radisson Suite Hotel Boca Raton
7920 Glades Road
661 NW 53rd Street
Boca Raton, FL 33434
(561) 852-4023

Marriott Boca Raton
5150 Town Center Circle
661 NW 53rd Street
Boca Raton, FL 33486
(561) 392-4600

Boca Raton Resort & Club
501 East Camino Real
Boca Raton, FL 33432
(561) 447-3656

Clearwater

Harborview Center
300 Cleveland Street
Clearwater, FL 33755
(727) 462-6778

Belleview Biltmore Resort & SPA
25 Belleview Blvd.
Clearwater, FL 33756
(727) 442-6171

Clearwater Beach

Sheraton Sand Key Resort
1160 Gulf Blvd.
Clearwater, FL 33767
(727) 593-6001

Adam's Mark Clearwater Beach Resort
430 South Gulfview Blvd.
Clearwater Beach, FL 33767
(727) 443-5714

Hilton Clearwater Beach Resort
400 Mandalay Avenue
Clearwater Beach, FL 33767
(727) 461-3222

Holiday Inn Sunspree Resort
& Conference Center
715 South Gulfview Blvd.
Clearwater Beach, FL 33767
(727) 447-9566

Radisson Suite Resort on
Sand Key
1201 Gulf Blvd.
Clearwater Beach, FL 33767
(727) 593-6103

Ramada Inn Gulfview
521 South Gulfview Blvd.
Clearwater Beach, FL 33767
(727) 447-6461

Daytona Beach

Adam's Mark Daytona Beach
Resort
100 North Atlantic Avenue
Daytona Beach, FL 32118
(386) 947-8004

Best Western La Playa Resort
2500 North Atlantic Avenue
Daytona Beach, FL 32118
(386) 672-0990

Daytona Beach Hilton Oceanfront
Resort
2637 South Atlantic Avenue
Daytona Beach, FL 32118
(386) 767-7350

Daytona Beach Resort and
Conference Center
2700 North Atlantic Avenue
Daytona Beach, FL 32118
(386) 672-3770

Plaza Resort & SPA
600 North Atlantic Avenue
Daytona Beach, FL 32118
(386) 267-1630

Treasure Island Resort
2025 South Atlantic Avenue
Daytona Beach, FL 32118
(386) 255-8371

Florida Keys

Doubletree Grand Key Resort
3990 South Roosevelt Blvd.
Key West, FL 33040
(305) 293-1818

Hawk's Cay Resort
61 Hawk's Cay Blvd.
Duck Key, FL 33050
(305) 743-7000

Hilton Key West Resort & Marina
245 Front Street
Key West, FL 33040
(305) 292-4367

Holiday Inn Beachside
3841 North Roosevelt Blvd.
Key West, FL 33040
(305) 294-2571

Holiday Inn Resort & Marina
99701 Overseas Highway
Key Largo, FL 33037
(305) 451-2121

Marriott Key Largo Bay Beach Resort
103800 Overseas Highway
Key Largo, FL 33037
(305) 453-0582

Pier House Resort & Caribbean Spa
One Duval Street
Key West, FL 33040
(305) 296-4600

Westin Beach Resort Key Largo
97000 South Overseas Highway Mile
    Marker 97
Key Largo, FL 33037
(305) 852-5553

Wyndham Casa Marina Resort
1500 Reynolds Street
Key West, FL 33040
(305) 293-6205

Wyndham Reach Resort
1435 Simonton Street
Key West, FL 33040
(305) 293-6217

Ocean Reef Club
31 Ocean Reef Drive
Key Largo, FL 33037
(305) 367-5814

Fort Meyers

Lee Civic Center
11831 Bayshore Road
North Fort Myers, FL 33917
(941) 543-8368

Ramada Inn & Suites at Amtel Marina
2500 Edwards Drive
Fort Meyers, FL 33901
(239) 337-0300

Best Western Pink Shell Beach Resort
275 Estero Blvd.
Fort Meyers, FL 33931
(239) 463-6181

Diamondhead all Suite Beach Resort
2000 Estero Blvd.
Fort Myers, FL 33931
(239) 765-9400

Sanibel Harbour Resort & SPA
17260 Harbour Pointe Drive
Fort Meyers, FL 33908
(239) 466-2150

Gainesville

Doubletree Hotel & Conference Center,
University of Florida
1714 Southwest 34th Street
Gainesville, FL 32607
(352) 371-3600

Sheraton Gainesville Hotel
2900 Southwest 13th Street
Gainesville, FL 32608
(352) 377-6721

Fort Lauderdale

Fort Lauderdale Marriott Marina
1881 Southeast 17th Street
Fort Lauderdale, FL 33316
(954) 463-4000

Renaissance Ft. Lauderdale
1617 Southeast 17th Street
Fort Lauderdale, FL 33316
(954) 626-1708

Fort Lauderdale Marriott North
6650 North Andrews Avenue
Fort Lauderdale, FL 33309
(954) 771-0440

The Westin Fort Lauderdale
400 Corporate Drive
Fort Lauderdale, FL 33334
(954) 772-6867

Hyatt Regency Pier 66
2301 Southeast 17th Street
Fort Lauderdale, FL 33316
(954) 334-5774

Marriott Hotel Coral Springs
11775 Heron Bay Blvd.
Fort Lauderdale, FL 33376
(954) 227-4115

Marriott's Harbor Beach Resort & Spa
3030 Holiday Drive
Fort Lauderdale, FL 33316
(954) 766-6133

Radisson Bahia Mar Beach
801 Seabreeze Blvd.
Fort Lauderdale, FL 33316
(954) 764-2233

Sheraton Yankee Clipper Beach Hotel
1140 Seabreeze Blvd.
Fort Lauderdale, FL 33316
(954) 467-1110

Sheraton Yankee Trader Beach Hotel
321 North Fort Lauderdale Beach
  Blvd.
Fort Lauderdale, FL 33304
(954) 467-1110

Wyndham Bonaventure Resort
and Spa
250 Racquet Club Road
Fort Lauderdale, FL 33326
(954) 389-3300

Hollywood

Ambassador Resort & Corporate
Center
4000 South Ocean Drive
Hollywood, FL 33019
(954) 458-1900

The Westin Diplomat Hotel Resort
& Spa
3555 South Ocean Drive
Hollywood, FL 33019
(954) 602-6000

Jacksonville

Adam's Mark Hotel Jacksonville
225 East Coastline Drive
Jacksonville, FL 32202
(904) 633-9095

Hilton Jacksonville Riverfront
1201 Riverplace Blvd.
Jacksonville, FL 32207
(904) 398-8800

OMNI Jacksonville Hotel
245 Water Street
Jacksonville, FL 32202
(904) 355-6664

Radisson Riverwalk Hotel
1515 Prudential Drive
Jacksonville, FL 32207
(904) 396-5100

Ramada Inn & Conference Center
Downtown
5865 Arlington Expressway
Jacksonville, FL 32211
(904) 724-3410

Embassy Suites
9300 Baymeadows Road
Jacksonville, FL 32256
(904) 731-3555

Holiday Inn Baymeadows
9150 Baymeadows Road
Jacksonville, FL 32256
(904) 737-1700

Jacksonville Marriott
4670 Salisbury Road
Jacksonville, FL 32256
(904) 296-2222

Clarion Hotel Airport Conference
Center
2102 Dixie Clipper Drive
Jacksonville, FL 32218
(904) 741-1997

Marco Island

Hilton Marco Island Beach Resort
560 South Collier Blvd.
Marco Island, FL 34145
(941) 394-5000

Marco Island Marriott Resort & Golf
Club
400 South Collier Blvd.
Marco Island, FL 34145
(941) 642-2794

Radisson Suite Beach Resort on Marco
Island
600 South Collier Blvd.
Marco Island, FL 34145
(239) 394-4100

Marco Beach Ocean Resort
480 South Collier Blvd.
Marco Island, FL 34145
(239) 393-1400

Coral Gables

Biltmore Hotel
1200 Anastasia Avenue
Coral Gables, FL 33134
(305) 445-1926

Hyatt Regency Coral Gables
50 Alhambra Plaza
Coral Gables, FL 33134
(305) 441-1234

OMNI Colonnade Hotel
180 Aragon Avenue
Coral Gables, FL 33134
(305) 441-2600

Miami

Best Western Marina Park Hotel
340 Biscayne Blvd.
Miami, FL 33132
(305) 371-4400

Clarion Hotel & Suites/Downtown
Convention Center
100 Southeast 4th Street
Miami, FL 33131
(305) 374-5100

Dupont Plaza Hotel
300 Biscayne Blvd. Way
Miami, FL 33131
(305) 358-2541

Everglades Hotel
244 Biscayne Blvd.
Miami, FL 33132
(305) 358-0983

Hyatt Regency Miami
400 Southeast 2nd Avenue
Miami, FL 33131
(305) 679-3045

Intercontinental Miami
100 Chopin Plaza
Miami, FL 33131
(305) 577-10000

Mandarin Oriental Miami
500 Bricell Key Drive
Miami, FL 33131
(305) 913-8288

Renaissance Miami Biscayne Bay
1601 Biscayne Blvd.
Miami, FL 33132
(305) 714-3795

Sheraton Biscayne Bay Hotel
495 Brickell Avenue
Miami, FL 33131
(305) 373-6000

Miami Dadeland Marriott
9090 South Dadeland Blvd.
Miami, FL 33156
(305) 671-5022

Airport Regency
1000 Northwest Le Jeune Road
Miami, FL 33126
(305) 441-1600

Crowne Plaza Miami International
Airport
950 Northwest Lejeune Road
Miami, FL 33126
(305) 446-9000

Embassy Suites Miami Airport
3974 Northwest South River Drive
Miami, FL 33142
(305) 634-5000

Hilton Miami Airport
5101 Blue Lagoon Drive
Miami, FL 33126
(305) 265-3800

Radisson Mart Plaza Hotel &
Convention Center
711 Northwest 72nd Avenue
Miami, FL 33126
(305) 261-3800

Sofitel Miami
5800 Blue Lagoon Drive
Miami, FL 33136
(305) 264-4888

Wyndham Miami Airport
3900 Northwest 21st Street
Miami, FL 33142
(305) 870-8150

Doral Golf Resort and Spa
4400 Northwest 87th Avenue
Miami, FL 33178
(305) 591-6453

Grove Isle Club & Resort
4 Grove Isle Drive
Miami, FL 33133
(305) 860-4301

Miami Beach

Miami Beach Marriott at South Beach
161 Ocean Drive
Miami Beach, FL 33139
(305) 536-7700

Best Western Beach Resort
4333 Collins Avenue
Miami Beach, FL 33140
(305) 532-3311

Delano
1685 Collins Avenue
Miami Beach, FL 33139
(305) 674-5769

Eden Roc Renaissance Resort & Spa
4525 Collins Avenue
Miami Beach, FL 33140
(305) 531-0000

Fontainebleau Hilton Resort
4441 Collins Avenue
Miami Beach, FL 33140
(305) 538-2000

Loews Miami Beach Hotel
1601 Collins Avenue
Miami Beach, FL 33139
(305) 604-1601

Marco Polo Ramada Plaza Beach Resort
19201 Collins Avenue
North Miami Beach, FL 33139
(305) 932-2233

Radisson Deauville Resort
6701 Collins Avenue
Miami Beach, FL 33141
(305) 865-8511

Ramada Resort Miami Beach
4041 Collins Avenue
Miami Beach, FL 33140
(305) 531-5771

Roney Palace Beach Resort
2399 Collins Avenue
Miami Beach, FL 33139
(305) 604-1000

The Ritz-Carlton South Beach
2901 Collins Avenue
Miami Beach, FL 33140
(786) 276-4000

Wyndham Miami Beach Resort
4833 Collins Avenue
Miami Beach, FL 33140
(305) 535-2035

Naples

The Inn of Fifth
699 Fifth Avenue South
Naples, FL 34102
(239) 403-8777

Bellasera Resort
221 9th Street South
Naples, FL 34102
(239) 280-1790

La Playa Beach & Golf Resort
9891 Gulf Shore Drive
Naples, FL 34108
(239) 597-3123

Edgewater Beach Hotel
1901 Gulf Shore Blvd. North
Naples, FL 34102
(941) 403-2155

Naples Beach Hotel & Golf Club
851 Gulf Shore Blvd. North
Naples, FL 34102
(941) 261-2222

Registry Resort Naples
475 Seagate Drive
Naples, FL 34103
(941) 597-3232

Ritz-Carlton Naples Golf Resort
2600 Tiburon Drive
Naples, FL 34109
(239) 593-2000

Kissimmee

Holiday Inn Kissimmee—Downtown
2009 West Vine Street
Kissimmee, FL 34471
(407) 846-2713

Radisson Resort Parkway
2900 Parkway Blvd.
Kissimmee, FL 34747
(407) 396-7000

La Quinta Inn Lakeside
7769 West Irio Bronson Memorial
    Highway
Kissimmee, FL 34747
(407) 396-2222

Ramada Inn Resort Maingate
2950 Reedy Creek Blvd.
Kissimmee, FL 34747
(407) 390-9124

Gaylord Palms Resort & Convention
Center
6000 Oseceola Parkway
Kissimmee, FL 34746
(407) 586-1234

Hyatt Orlando
6375 West Irio Bronson Memorial
    Highway
Kissimmee, FL 34747
(407) 396-1234

Orange Lake Resort & Country Club
8505 West Irio Bronson Memorial
    Highway
Kissimmee, FL 34747
(407) 239-5119

Ramada Plaza Hotel & Inn Gateway
7470 Highway 192 West
Kissimmee, FL 34747
(407) 396-4000

Renaissance Worldgate Hotel
3011 Maingate Lane
Kissimmee, FL 34747
(407) 396-1400

Travelodge Hotel Maingate East
5711 West US Highway 293
Kissimmee, FL 34746
(407) 396-4222

Orlando

Orange County Convention Center
9800 International Drive
Orlando, FL 32819
(407) 685-5650

Radisson Plaza Orlando
60 South Ivanhoe Blvd.
Orlando, FL 32804
(407) 425-4455

Rosen Plaza Hotel
9700 International Drive
Orlando, FL 32819
(407) 352-9700

Embassy Suites International
Drive/Jamaican Court
8250 Jamaican Court
Orlando, FL 32819
(407) 345-8250

Orlando Marriott—Downtown
400 West Livingston Street
Orlando, FL 32801
(407) 843-6664

Marriott Village at Little Lake Bryan
8623 Vineland Avenue
Orlando, FL 32821
(407) 938-9001

The Peabody Orland
9801 International Drive
Orlando, FL 32819
(407) 352-4500

Wyndham Orlando Resort
8001 International Drive
Orlando, FL 32819
(407) 351-2420

Hyatt Regency Orlando International
Airport
9300 Airport Blvd.
Orlando, FL 32827
(407) 825-1234

Adam's Mark Orlando
1500 Sand Lake Road
Orlando, FL 32809
(407) 859-1500

Orlando Airport Marriott
7499 Augusta National Drive
Orlando, FL 32822
(407) 851-9000

Delta Orlando Resort Maingate at
Universal Studios
5715 Major Blvd.
Orlando, FL 32819
(407) 248-1100

Orlando World Center Marriott Resort
& Convention Center
8701 World Center Drive
Orlando, FL 32821
(407) 239-4200

Rosen Centre Hotel
9840 International Drive
Orlando, FL 32819
(407) 996-2301

Royal Pacific Resort at Universal
Studios Escape
6300 Hollywood Way
Orlando, FL 32819
(407) 224-6222

The Hard Rock Hotel
5800 Universal Blvd.
Orlando, FL 32819
(407) 503-ROCK

Sheraton World Resort
10100 International Drive
Orlando, FL 32821
(407) 354-5025

The Ritz-Carlton Orlando, Grande
Lakes
6649 Westwood Blvd., #100
Orlando, FL 32821
(407) 529-2255

Hyatt Regency Grand Cypress
One Grand Cypress Blvd.
Lake Buena Vista, FL 32836
(407) 239-3921

Panama City Beach

Edgewater Beach Resort & Conference
Center
11212 Front Beach Road
Panama City Beach, FL 32407
(850) 235-4044

Howard Johnson at Boardwalk Beach
Resort & Convention Center
9600 South Thomas Drive
Panama City Beach, FL 32408
(850) 234-3484

Howard Johnson Resort—Boardwalk
9400 South Thomas Drive
Panama City Beach, FL 32408
(850) 230-4630

Marriott's Bay Point Resort Village
4200 Marriott Drive
Panama City Beach, FL 32408
(850) 236-6000

Pensacola

Crowne Plaza Pensacola Grand Hotel
200 East Gregory Street
Pensacola, FL 32501
(850) 433-3336

Holiday Inn Express Pensacola
6501 North Pensacola Blvd
Highway 29
Pensacola, FL 32505
(850) 476-7200

Palm Beach

Four Seasons Resort Palm Beach
2800 South Ocean Blvd.
Palm Beach, FL 33480
(561) 582-2800

The Breakers
One South County Road
Palm Beach, FL 33480
(561) 659-8404

Palm Beach Gardens

Doubletree Hotel Palm Beach
Gardens
4431 PGA Blvd.
Palm Beach Gardens, FL 33410
(561) 776-2928

Embassy Suites Palm Beach Gardens
4350 PGA Blvd.
Palm Beach Gardens, FL 33410
(561) 622-1000

Palm Beach Gardens Marriott
4000 RCA Blvd.
Palm Beach Gardens, FL 33410
(561) 622-8888

PGA National Resort & Spa
400 Avenue of the Champions
Palm Beach Gardens, FL 33418
(561) 627-2000

Palm Beach Shore

Crowne Plaza West Palm Beach Hotel
1601 Belvedere Road
Palm Beach Shore, FL 33406
(561) 689-6400

Hilton Palm Beach Airport
150 Australian Avenue
Palm Beach Shore, FL 33406
(561) 684-9400

Holiday Inn Palm Beach Airport Hotel
& Conference Center
1301 Belvedere Road
Palm Beach Shore, FL 33405
(561) 659-3880

Sarasota

Hyatt Sarasota
1000 Blvd. of the Arts
Sarasota, FL 34236
(941) 953-1234

Ritz-Carlton Sarasota
1111 Ritz-Carlton Drive
Sarasota, FL 34236
(941) 309-2000

Radisson Lido Beach Resort
700 Ben Franklin Drive
Sarasota, FL 34236
(941) 388-2161

The Helmsley Sandcastle Hotel
1540 Ben Franklin Drive
Sarasota, FL 34236
(941) 388-2181

St. Augustine

Casa Monica Hotel
95 Cordova Street
St. Augustine, FL 32084
(904) 648-1888

Ponce De Leon Golf & Conference
Resort
4000 US 1 North
St. Augustine, FL 32096
(904) 824-2821

World Golf Village Renaissance
Resort
500 South Legacy Trail
St. Augustine, FL 32092
(904) 940-8000

St. Pete Beach

The Don Cesar Beach Resort & Spa
3400 Gulf Blvd.
St. Pete Beach, FL 33706
(727) 360-1881

Holiday Inn Hotel & Suites Beachfront
Resort & Conference Center
5250 Gulf Blvd.
St. Pete Beach, FL 33706
(727) 360-1811

Tradewinds Island Grand Beach Resort
& Conference Center
5500 Gulf Blvd.
St. Pete Beach, FL 33706
(727) 363-2240

Tradewinds Sandpiper Hotel & Suites
6000 Gulf Blvd.
St. Pete Beach, FL 33706
(727) 562-1240

Tradewinds Sirata Beach Resort &
Conference Center
5300 Gulf Blvd.
St. Pete Beach, FL 33706
(727) 363-2240

St. Petersburg

Hilton St. Petersburg
333 First Street South
St. Petersburg, FL 33701
(727) 894-5000

Tropicana Field
One Tropicana Drive
St. Petersburg, FL 33705
(727) 825-3413

Radisson Hotel & Conference Center
12600 Roosevelt Blvd.
St. Petersburg, FL 33705
(727) 825-3167

Renaissance Vinoy Resort & Golf Club
501 5th Avenue, Northwest
St. Petersburg, FL 33701
(727) 894-1000

Tallahassee

Turnbull Conference Center
Florida State University
Tallahassee, FL 32306
(850) 644-7549

Doubletree Hotel Tallahassee
101 South Adams Street
Tallahassee, FL 32301
(850) 224-5000

Ramada Inn & Conference Center
2900 North Monroe Street
Tallahassee, FL 32303
(850) 386-1027

Tampa

Tampa Convention Center
333 South Franklin Street
Tampa, FL 33602
(813) 274-8422

Hyatt Regency Tampa
211 North Tampa Street
Tampa, FL 33602
(813) 225-1234

Radisson Riverwalk Hotel Tampa
200 North Ashley Drive
Tampa, FL 33602
(813) 221-5292

Tampa Marriott Waterside
700 South Florida Avenue
Tampa, FL 33602
(813) 221-4900

Wyndham Harbour Island Hotel
725 South Harbour Island Blvd.
Tampa, FL 33602
(813) 229-5000

Crowne Plaza Hotel Tampa at Sabal
Park
10221 Princess Palm Avenue
Tampa, FL 33610
(813) 623-6363

Holiday Inn Busch Gardens
2701 East Fowler Avenue
Tampa, FL 33612
(813) 971-4710

Best Western, The Westshore Hotel
1200 North Westshore Blvd.
Tampa, FL 33607
(813) 282-3636

Crowne Plaza Tampa Westshore
1200 North Westshore Blvd.
Tampa, FL 33609
(813) 289-8200

Doubletree Hotel Tampa
Airport/Westshore
4500 West Cypress Street
Tampa, FL 33607
(813) 998-2201

Grand Hyatt Tampa Bay
6200 Courtney Campbell Causeway
Tampa, FL 33607
(813) 874-1234

Hilton Westshore Tampa Airport
2225 North Lois Avenue
Tampa, FL 33607
(813) 874-5003

Tampa Airport Marriott
Tampa International Airport
Tampa, FL 33607
(813) 879-5151

Wyndham Westshore
4860 West Kennedy Blvd.
Tampa, FL 33609
(813) 286-4050

Saddlebrook Resort Tampa
5700 Saddlebrook Way
Tampa, FL 33543
(813) 973-1111

GEORGIA

Augusta

Holiday Inn Augusta West
1075 Stevens Creek Road
Augusta, GA 30907
(706) 737-3600

Radisson Riverfront Hotel Augusta
Two Tenth Street
Augusta, GA 30901
(706) 823-6505

Ramada Plaza Hotel & Convention
Center
640 Broad Street
Augusta, GA 30901
(706) 722-5541

Atlanta

Atlanta CVB
233 Peachtree Street, Northwest
Atlanta, GA 30303
(404) 521-6600

Atlanta Marriott Marquis
265 Peachtree Center Avenue
Atlanta, GA 30303
(404) 521-0000

Atlanta Marriott Suites Midtown
35 14th Street
Atlanta, GA 30309
(404) 876-8888

Courtyard By Marriott—Downtown
Atlanta
175 Piedmont Avenue Northwest
Atlanta, GA 30303
(404) 659-7777

Crowne Plaza Atlanta—Buckhead
3377 Peachtree Road North
Atlanta, GA 30326
(404) 264-1111

Crowne Plaza Atlanta—Perimeter
Northwest
6345 Powers Ferry Road, Northwest
Atlanta, GA 30339
(770) 790-1007

Embassy Suites at Centennial
Olympic Park
267 Manetta Street
Atlanta, GA 30313
(404) 223-2300

Four Seasons Hotel Atlanta
75 14th Street
Atlanta, GA 30309
(404) 881-9898

Georgian Terrace Hotel
659 Peachtree Street
Atlanta, GA 30308
(404) 898-8300

Hilton Atlanta
225 Courtland Street, Northeast
Atlanta, GA 30303
(404) 222-2860

Hyatt Regency Atlanta
265 Peachtree Street, Northeast
Atlanta, GA 30303
(404) 588-4110

OMNI at CNN Center
100 CNN Center
Atlanta, GA 30335
(800) 843-6664

Ramada Downtown
70 John Wesley Dobbs Avenue,
   Northeast
Atlanta, GA 30303
(404) 659-2660

Ramada Inn Six Flags
4225 Fulton Industrial Blvd., Southwest
Atlanta, GA 30336
(404) 659-2660

Renaissance Atlanta Hotel—Downtown
590 West Peachtree Street, Northwest
Atlanta, GA 30308
(404) 881-6000

Sheraton Atlanta
165 Courtland Street
Atlanta, GA 30303
(404) 659-6500

Sheraton Colony Square
Peachtree & 14th Street, Northeast
Atlanta, GA 30361
(404) 892-6000

The Ritz-Carlton Atlanta (Downtown)
181 Peachtree Street, Northeast
Atlanta, GA 30303
(404) 659-0400

Westin Peachtree Plaza
210 Peachtree Street, Northwest
Atlanta, GA 30303
(404) 589-7463

Wyndham Atlanta
160 Spring Street, Northwest
Atlanta, GA 30303
(678) 686-3335

Wyndham Midtown Atlanta
125 10th Street, Northeast
Atlanta, GA 30309
(404) 873-4800

Atlanta Century Center Marriott
2000 Century Blvd., Northeast
Atlanta, GA 30345
(404) 262-8687

Atlanta Marriott Norcross
475 Technology Parkway
Norcross, GA 30092
(770) 263-8558

Atlanta Marriott Northwest
200 Interstate North Parkway
Atlanta, GA 30339
(770) 952-7900

Crowne Plaza Ravinia
4355 Ashford-Dunwoody
Atlanta, GA 30346
(770) 395-7700

Doubletree Guest Suites Perimeter
6120 Peachtree-Dunwoody Road
Atlanta, GA 30328
(770) 668-0808

Embassy Suites Atlanta Galleria
2815 Akers Mill Road
Atlanta, GA 30326
(770) 984-9300

Embassy Suites in Buckhead
3285 Peachtree Road, Northeast
Atlanta, GA 30305
(404) 261-7733

Embassy Suites Perimeter Center
1030 Crown Pointe Parkway
Atlanta, GA 30338
(770) 394-5454

Grand Hyatt Buckhead
3300 Peachtree Road, Northeast
Atlanta, GA 30305
(404) 365-8100

Hawthorn Suites Atlanta
Northwest
1500 Parkwood Circle
Atlanta, GA 30339
(770) 952-9595

Hilton Atlanta Northeast
5993 Peachtree Industrial Blvd.
Norcross, GA 30092
(770) 447-4747

Hilton Atlanta Northwest Windy
Hill Road
2055 South Park Place
Atlanta, GA 30339
(770) 953-9300

Holiday Inn Select Atlanta Peachtree
Corners
6050 Peachtree Industrial Blvd.
Norcross, GA 30071
(678) 533-2966

Hyatt Regency Suites Perimeter
Northwest Atlanta
2999 Windy Hill Road
Marietta, GA 30067
(770) 956-1234

JW Marriott Hotel Lenox
3300 Lenox Road, Northeast
Atlanta, GA 30326
(404) 262-8674

Marriott Perimeter Center Atlanta
246 Perimeter Center Parkway
Atlanta, GA 30346
(770) 394-6500

Radisson Inn Buckhead/Emory Area
Atlanta
2061 North Druid Hills Road, Northeast
Atlanta, GA 30329
(404) 321-4174

Ramada Inn & Conference Center
418 Armour Drive, Northeast
Atlanta, GA 30324
(404) 253-2637

Renaissance Waverly
2450 Galleria Parkway
Atlanta, GA 30339
(770) 953-4500

Ritz-Carlton Buckhead
3434 Peachtree Road, Northeast
Atlanta, GA 30326
(404) 237-2700

Sheraton Buckhead Hotel Atlanta
3405 Lenox Road, Northeast
Atlanta, GA 30326
(404) 261-9250

Sheraton Suites Galleria
2844 Cobb Parkway, Southeast
Atlanta, GA 30339
(770) 916-3193

Swissotel Atlanta
3391 Peachtree Road, Northeast
Atlanta, GA 30326
(404) 365-0065

W Atlanta at Perimeter Center
111 Perimeter Center West
Atlanta, GA 30346
(770) 396-6800

Westin Atlanta North
7 Concourse Parkway
Atlanta, GA 30328
(770) 395-3900

Hilton Atlanta Airport
1031 Virginia Avenue
Atlanta, GA 30354
(404) 559-6888

Holiday Inn Atlanta Airport North
1380 Virginia Avenue
Atlanta, GA 30344
(404) 762-8411

Ramada Plaza Atlanta Airport North
1419 Virginia Avenue
Atlanta, GA 30337
(404) 768-7800

Renaissance Concourse Hotel
One Hartsfield Center Parkway
Atlanta, GA 30354
(404) 209-9999

Jekyll Island

Holiday Inn Beach Resort
200 South Beachview Drive
Jekyll Island, GA 31527
(912) 635-2531

Jekyll Island Club Resort
371 Riverview Drive
Jekyll Island, GA 31527
(912) 635-2600

Wyndham Garden Atlanta Northwest
1775 Parkway Place, Northwest
Marietta, GA 30067
(770) 354-5244

Savannah

Hilton Savannah Desoto
15 East Liberty Street
Savannah, GA 31401
(912) 443-2003

Hyatt Regency Savannah
2 West Bay Street
Savannah, GA 31401
(912) 944-3680

Savannah Marriott Riverfront
100 Gen. McIntosh Blvd.
Savannah, GA 31401
(912) 233-7722

Westin Savannah Harbor Resort
One Resort Drive
Savannah, GA 31401
(912) 201-2000

Hawaii
Hilo

Hawaii Naniloa
93 Banyan Drive
Hilo, HI 96720
(808) 969-3333

Hilo Hawaiian Hotel
71 Banyan Drive
Hilo, HI 96720
(808) 935-9361

Kohala Coast

Hapuna Beach Prince Hotel
62-100 Kauna'oa Drive
Kohala Coast, HI 96743
(808) 880-1111

Hilton Waikoloa Village
425 Waikoloa Beach Drive
Waikoloa, HI 96738
(808) 886-1234

Mauna Kea Beach Hotel
62-100 Mauna Kea Beach Drive
Kohala Coast, HI 96743
(808) 882-7222

Mauna Lani Bay Hotel & Bungalows
68-1400 Mauna Lani Drive
Kohala Coast, HI 96743
(808) 885-6622

Outrigger Waikola Beach Resort
69-275 Waikoloa Beach Drive
Waikoloa, HI 96738
(808) 886-6789

The Fairmont Orchid
One North Kaniku Drive
Kohala Coast, HI 96743
(808) 885-2000

Koloa

Hyatt Regency Kauai Resort & Spa
1571 Poipu Road
Kohala Coast, HI 96756
(808) 742-1234

Outrigger Kiahuna Plantation
2253 Poipu Road
Kohala Coast, HI 96756
(808) 742-6411

Sheraton Kauai Resort
2440 Hoonani Road
Kohala Coast, HI 96756
(808) 742-4018

Kona

King Kamehameha Kona
Beach Hotel
75-5660 Palani Road
Kailua Kona, HI 96740
(808) 921-6198

Kona Village Resort
PO Box 1299
Kailua Kona, HI 96745
(808) 325-5555

Royal Kona Resort
75-5852 Alii Drive
Kailua Kona, HI 96740
(808) 329-3111

Maui Island
Kaanapali

Royal Lahaina Resort
2780 Kekaa Drive
Kaanapali, HI 96761
(808) 661-3611

Kapalua

The Ritz-Carlton Kapalua
One Ritz Carlton Drive
Kapalua, HI 96761
(808) 669-6200

Lahaina

Embassy Vacation Resort
104 Kaanapali Shores Place
Lahaina, HI 96761
(808) 661-2000

Hyatt Regency Maui
200 Nohea Kai Drive
Lahaina, HI 96761
(808) 667-4440

Westin Maui
2365 Kaanapali Parkway
Lahaina, HI 96761
(808) 667-2525

Wailea

Four Seasons Resort Maui at Wailea
3900 Wailea Alanui
Wailea, HI 96753
(808) 874-8000

Grand Wailea Resort Hotel & Spa
3850 Wailea Alanui
Wailea, HI 96753
(808) 874-2411

Wailea Marriott An Outrigger Resort
3700 Wailea Alanui
Wailea, HI 96753
(808) 874-7800

Oahu Island

Honolulu

Ala Moana Hotel
410 Atkinson Drive
Honolulu, HI 96814
(808) 955-4811

Doubletree Alana Hotel Waikiki
1956 Ala Moana Blvd.
Honolulu, HI 96815
(808) 941-7275

Hawaii Prince Hotel Waikiki
100 Holomoana Street
Honolulu, HI 96815
(808) 956-1111

Hilton Hawaiian Village
2005 Kalia Road
Honolulu, HI 96815
(808) 947-7843

Outrigger Waikiki
2335 Kalakaua Avenue
Honolulu, HI 96815
(808) 921-6711

Sheraton Moana Surfrider
2365 Kalakaua Avenue
Honolulu, HI 96815
(808) 922-3111

Sheraton Princess Kaiulani
120 Kaiulani Avenue
Honolulu, HI 96815
(808) 931-4525

Sheraton Waikiki
2255 Kalakaua Avenue
Honolulu, HI 96815
(808) 939-2239

Waikiki Beach Marriott Resort
2552 Kalakaua Avenue
Honolulu, HI 96815
(808) 921-5116

IDAHO

Boise

Doubletree Hotel Boise Riverside
2900 Chinden Blvd.
Boise, ID 83714
(208) 331-4937

Grove Hotel
245 South Capitol Blvd.
Boise, ID 83702
(208) 472-35702

West Coast Hotel Boise—Downtown
1800 Fairview Avenue
Boise, ID 83702
(208) 386-4912

Holiday Inn Boise Airport
3300 Vista Avenue
Boise, ID 83705
(208) 344-8365

Sun Valley

Sun Valley Lodge Inn & Condominiums
1 Sun Valley Road
Sun Valley, ID 83353-0010
(208) 622-2183

ILLINOIS

Bloomington

Indian Lakes Resort
250 West Schick Road
Bloomington, IL 60108
(603) 529-0200

Arlington Heights

Radisson Arlington Heights
75 West Algonquin Road
Arlington Heights, IL 60005
(847) 427-4220

Sheraton Chicago Northwest
3400 West Euclid Avenue
Arlington Heights, IL 60005
(847) 394-2000

Chicago

McCormick Place Complex
2301 South Lake Drive
Chicago, IL 60616
(312) 791-6430

Navy Pier
600 East Grand Avenue
Chicago, IL 60611
(312) 595-5300

Allerton Crowne Plaza
701 North Michigan Avenue
Chicago, IL 60611
(800) 621-8311

Best Western Inn Chicago
162 East Ohio Street
Chicago, IL 60611
(312) 573-3105

Blackstone Hotel
636 South Michigan Avenue
Chicago, IL 60605
(312) 427-4300

Chicago Downtown Marriott
540 North Michigan Avenue
Chicago, IL 60611
(312) 836-0100

Chicago's Essex Inn
800 South Michigan Avenue
Chicago, IL 60605
(312) 542-5115

Clarion Executive Plaza
71 East Wacker Drive
Chicago, IL 60601
(312) 346-7100

Congress Plaza Hotel & Convention
Center
520 South Michigan Avenue
Chicago, IL 60605
(312) 427-3800

Courtyard By Marriott Chicago
Downtown
30 East Hubbard Street
Chicago, IL 60611
(847) 318-1295

Doubletree Guest Suites Chicago
198 East Delaware Place
Chicago, IL 60611
(312) 664-1100

Drake Chicago
140 East Walton Street
Chicago, IL 60611
(312) 943-6678

Embassy Suites Hotel Chicago
Downtown
600 North State Street
Chicago, IL 60610
(312) 943-3800

Fairmont Chicago Hotel
200 North Columbus Drive
Chicago, IL 60601
(312) 565-8000

Four Seasons Chicago
120 East Delaware Place
Chicago, IL 60611
(312) 280-8800

Hilton Chicago
720 South Michigan Avenue
Chicago, IL 60605
(312) 922-4400

Holiday Inn Chicago Mart Plaza
350 North Orleans Street
Chicago, IL 60654
(312) 836-5000

Holiday Inn City Center Chicago
300 East Ohio Street
Chicago, IL 60611
(312) 787-6100

Hotel Allegro Chicago
171 West Randolph Street
Chicago, IL 60601
(312) 696-2421

Hotel Monaco Chicago
225 North Wabash at Wacker
Chicago, IL 60601
(312) 960-8500

House of Blues Hotel, A Loews Hotel
333 North Dearborn Street
Chicago, IL 60610
(312) 923-2460

Hyatt On Printers Row
500 South Dearborn Street
Chicago, IL 60605
(312) 986-1234

Hyatt Regency Chicago
151 East Wacker Drive
Chicago, IL 60601
(312) 565-1234

Intercontinental Chicago
505 North Michigan Avenue
Chicago, IL 60611
(312) 944-4100

Le Meridien Chicago
520 North Michigan Avenue
Chicago, IL 60611
(312) 645-1500

Lenox Suites
616 North Rush Street
Chicago, IL 60611
(312) 337-1000

Hyatt Regency McCormick Place
2233 South Martin Luther King Drive
Chicago, IL 60616
(312) 567-1234

Millennium Knickerbocker Hotel
163 East Walton Place
Chicago, IL 60611
(312) 751-8100

OMNI Chicago
676 North Michigan Avenue
Chicago, IL 60611
(312) 944-6664

Palmer House Hilton
17 East Monroe Street
Chicago, IL 60603
(312) 726-7500

Park Hyatt Chicago
800 North Michigan
Chicago, IL 60611
(312) 239-4011

Quality Inn Downtown Chicago
One Mid City Plaza
Chicago, IL 60661
(312) 829-5000

Renaissance Chicago Hotel
One West Wacker Drive
Chicago, IL 60601
(312) 372-7200

Sheraton Chicago Hotel & Towers
301 East North Water Street
Chicago, IL 60611
(312) 329-7001

Sofitel Chicago Water Tower
20 East Chestnut Street
Chicago, IL 60611
(312) 324-4000

The Ritz-Carlton Chicago
160 East Pearson Street
Chicago, IL 60611
(312) 266-1000

The Westin Michigan Avenue
909 North Michigan Avenue
Chicago, IL 60611
(312) 943-7200

Tremont Hotel
100 East Chestnut Street
Chicago, IL 60611
(312) 751-1900

Westin River North Chicago
320 North Dearborn
Chicago, IL 60610
(312) 744-1900

Whitehall Hotel
105 East Delaware Place
Chicago, IL 60611
(312) 944-6300

Hilton Chicago O'Hare Airport
O'Hare International Airport
Chicago, IL 60677
(773) 686-8000

Holiday Inn Select Chicago/Midway
Airport
6520 South Cicero Avenue
Chicago, IL 60638
(708) 728-2840

Marriott O'Hare Airport
8535 West Higgins Road
Chicago, IL 60631
(773) 693-4444

Lisle

Hilton Lisle/Naperville
3003 Corporate West Drive
Lisle, IL 60532
(630) 505-0900

Hyatt Lisle Corporetum
1400 Corporetum Drive
Lisle, IL 60532
(630) 852-1234

Wyndham Lisle
3000 Warrenville Road
Lisle, IL 60532
(630) 577-6003

Northbrook

Adam's Mark Chicago—Northbrook
2875 North Milwaukee Avenue
Northbrook, IL 60062
(847) 298-2525

Renaissance Chicago North Shore
933 Skokie Blvd.
Northbrook, IL 60062
(847) 498-6500

Oak Brook

Hyatt Lodge at McDonald's Campus
2815 Jorie Blvd.
Oak Brook, IL 60523
(630) 990-5800

Hyatt Regency Oak Brook
1909 Spring Road
Oak Brook, IL 60523
(630) 573-1234

Marriott Oak Brook
1401 West 22nd Street
Oak Brook, IL 60523
(630) 573-8555

Rosemont

Doubletree Hotel O'Hare—Rosemont
5460 North River Road
Rosemont, IL 60018
(847) 292-3273

Embassy Suites Hotel O'Hare—
Rosemont
5500 North River Road
Rosemont, IL 60018
(847) 678-4000

Embassy Suites Schaumburg
1939 North Meacham Road
Rosemont, IL 60018
(847) 397-1313

Hyatt Regency Woodfield
1800 East Golf Road
Rosemont, IL 60018
(847) 517-6910

Holiday Inn O'Hare International
5440 North River Road
Rosemont, IL 60018
(847) 671-6350

Holiday Inn Select Hotel & Suites
10233 West Higgins Road
Rosemont, IL 60018
(847) 954-8600

Hyatt Regency O'Hare Airport
9300 West Bryn Mawr Avenue
Rosemont, IL 60018
(847) 696-1234

Hyatt Rosemont
6350 North River Road
Rosemont, IL 60018
(847) 518-1234

Marriott Schaumburg
50 North Martingale Road
Rosemont, IL 60018
(847) 240-0100

Marriott Suites O'Hare Airport
6155 North River Road
Rosemont, IL 60018
(847) 696-4400

Radisson Hotel O'Hare
6810 North Mannheim Road
Rosemont, IL 60018
(847) 297-1234

Radisson Hotel Schaumburg
1725 East Algonguin Road
Rosemont, IL 60018
(847) 397-1500

Ramada Plaza O'Hare Airport
6600 North Mannheim Road
Rosemont, IL 60018
(847) 827-5131

Sheraton Gateway Suites—
O'Hare
6501 North Mannheim Road
Rosemont, IL 60018
(847) 699-6300

Sofitel Chicago O'Hare
5550 North River Road
Rosemont, IL 60018
(847) 928-6924

Westin O'Hare Airport
6100 River Road
Rosemont, IL 60018
(847) 698-6000

Schaumburg

Greater Woodfield CVB
1430 North Meacham Road
Schaumburg, IL 60173
(847) 490-1010

Peoria

Holiday Inn City Centre
500 Hamilton Blvd
Peoria, IL 60602
(309) 674-2500

Hotel Pere Marquette
501 Main Street
Peoria, IL 61602
(309) 637-6555

Springfield

Hilton Springfield
700 East Adams Street
Springfield, IL 62701
(217) 789-1530

Crowne Plaza Hotel
3000 South Dirksen Parkway
Springfield, IL 62703
(217) 529-7777

INDIANA
Bloomington

Fourwinds Resort & Marina
9301 South Fairfax Road
Bloomington, IL 47401
(812) 824-2628

Evansville

Casino Aztar Hotel
421 Northwest Riverside Drive
Evansville, IL 47708
(812) 433-4352

Executive Inn Evansville Hotel &
Conference Center
600 Walnut Street
Evansville, IL 47708
(812) 424-8000

Evansville Airport Marriott
7101 US Highway 41 North
Evansville, IL 47725
(812) 867-7999

Holiday Inn Conference Center
4101 US Highway 41 North
Evansville, IL 47711
(812) 424-6400

Fort Wayne

Grand Wayne Convention Center
120 West Jefferson Blvd.
Fort Wayne, IL 46802
(260) 426-4100

Hilton at the Convention Center
1020 South Calhoun Street
Fort Wayne, IL 46802
(260) 422-4002

Holiday Inn Hotel & Suites
300 East Washington Blvd.
Fort Wayne, IL 46802
(260) 422-4002

Fort Wayne Marriott
305 East Washington Center Road
Fort Wayne, IL 46825
(260) 484-0411

Holiday Inn Northwest
3330 West Coliseum Blvd.
Fort Wayne, IL 46808
(574) 484-7711

Indianapolis

Adam's Mark Hotel & Suites
Indianapolis
120 West Market Street
Indianapolis, IL 46204
(317) 972-0600

Courtyard By Marriott—Downtown
501 West Washington Street
Indianapolis, IL 46802
(317) 635-4443

Crowne Plaza Hotel & Conf. Center
at Historic Union Station
123 West Louisiana Street
Indianapolis, IL 46825
(317) 631-2221

Embassy Suites—Downtown
110 West Washington Street
Indianapolis, IL 46802
(317) 236-1819

Hyatt Regency Indianapolis
One South Capitol Avenue
Indianapolis, IL 46802
(317) 616-6060

Indianapolis Marriott—Downtown
350 West Marland Street
Indianapolis, IL 46825
(317) 822-3500

OMNI Severin
40 West Jackson Place
Indianapolis, IL 46825
(317) 634-6664

Radisson Hotel City Centre
Indianapolis
31 West Ohio Street
Indianapolis, IL 46802
(317) 236-2539

Westin Indianapolis
50 South Capitol Avenue
Indianapolis, IL 46802
(317) 262-8100

Embassy Suites North
3912 Vincennes Road
Indianapolis, IL 46868
(317) 876-6625

Holiday Inn East
6990 East 21st Street
Indianapolis, IL 46219
(317) 359-5341

Holiday Inn Select North
3850 De Pauw Blvd.
Indianapolis, IL 46268
(317) 872-9790

Indianapolis Marriot
7202 East 21st Street
Indianapolis, IL 46219
(317) 352-1231

OMNI Hotel Indianapolis North
8181 North Shadeland Avenue
Indianapolis, IL 46250
(317) 847-6668

Sheraton Indianapolis Hotel & Suites
8787 Keystone Crossing
Indianapolis, IL 46240
(317) 846-2700

Adam's Mark Hotel Indianapolis
Airport
2544 Executive Drive
Indianapolis, IL 46241
(317) 381-6168

Days Inn Airport
5860 Fortune Circle West
Indianapolis, IL 46241
(317) 248-0621

Holiday Inn Select Airport
2501 South High School Road
Indianapolis, IL 46241
(317) 244-6861

Radisson Hotel Indianapolis Airport
2500 South High School Road
Indianapolis, IL 46241
(317) 243-1408

South Bend

Marriott South Bend
123 North Saint Joseph Street
South Bend, IL 46601
(574) 234-2000

Ramada Inn South Bend
52890 SR933 North
South Bend, IL 46637
(574) 272-5220

IOWA

Cedar Rapids

Crowne Plaza Five Seasons Hotel
350 1st Avenue Northeast
Cedar Rapids, IA 52401
(319) 363-8161

Davenport

Holiday Inn Davenport
5202 Brady Street
Davenport, IA 52806
(563) 391-1230

Des Moines

Veterans Memorial Auditorium
833 5th Avenue
Des Moines, IA 50309
(515) 323-5400

Marriott Des Moines—Downtown
700 Grand Avenue
Des Moines, IA 50309
(515) 245-5530

Holiday Inn Airport Conference Center
6111 Fleur Drive
Des Moines, IA 50321
(515) 287-2400

Sioux City

Hilton Sioux City
707 4th Street
Sioux City, IA 51101
(712) 277-4101

KANSAS

Overland Park

Sheraton Overland Park Hotel
6406 College Blvd.
Overland Park, KS 66211
(913) 234-2100

Doubletree Hotel Overland Park—
Corporate Woods
10100 College Blvd.
Overland Park, KS 66210
(913) 323-1902

Overland Park Marriott
10800 Metcalf Avenue
Overland Park, KS 66210
(913) 451-8000

Topeka

Capital Center Inn
914 Southeast Madison
Topeka, KS 66607
(785) 232-7721

Capitol Plaza Hotel
1717 Southwest Topeka Blvd.
Topeka, KS 66612
(785) 431-7200

Ramada Inn & Tower
420 East 6th Street
Topeka, KS 66607
(785) 234-5400

Wichita

Holiday Inn Select Wichita
549 South Rock Road
Wichita, KS 67207
(316) 686-7131

Hyatt Regency Wichita
400 West Waterman Street
Wichita, KS 67202
(316) 293-1234

Radisson Broadview Hotel
400 West Douglas Avenue
Wichita, KS 67202
(316) 262-5000

Marriott Wichita
9100 Corp Hills Drive
Wichita, KS 67207
(316) 651-0333

KENTUCKY

Bowling Green

Holiday Inn University Plaza
1021 Wilkinson Trace
Bowling Green, KY 42103
(270) 745-0088

Covington

Cincinnati Marriott at Rivercenter
10 West Rivercenter Blvd.
Covington, KY 41011
(859) 392-3720

Embassy Suites Cincinnati Rivercenter
10 East River Center Blvd.
Covington, KY 41011
(859) 261-8400

Radisson Hotel Cincinnati
Riverview/Covington
668 West 5th Street
Covington, KY 41011
(859) 491-1200

Frankfort

Holiday Inn Capital Plaza
405 Wilkinson Blvd.
Frankfort, KY 40601
(502) 227-5100

Lexington

Hyatt Regency Lexington
401 West High Street
Lexington, KY 40507
(859) 253-1234

Radisson Plaza Lexington
369 West Vine Street
Lexington, KY 40507
(859) 281-3708

Continental Inn Villager Lodge
801 Northeast New Circle Road
Lexington, KY 40505
(859) 299-5281

Marriott's Griffin Gate Resort
Lexington
1800 Newtown Pike
Lexington, KY 40511
(859) 231-5100

Louisville

Holiday Inn—Downtown
120 West Broadway
Louisville, KY 40202
(502) 582-2241

Hyatt Regency Louisville
320 West Jefferson Street
Louisville, KY 40202
(502) 540-3120

The Camberley Brown
335 West Broadway
Louisville, KY 40202
(502) 583-1234

Kentucky Fair & Exposition Center
P.O. Box 37130
Louisville, KY 40233
(502) 367-5150

The Galt House
140 North 4th Street
Louisville, KY 40202
(502) 589-5200

The Seelbach Hilton
500 4th Avenue
Louisville, KY 40202
(502) 585-3200

Louisville Marriott East
1903 Embassy Square Blvd.
Louisville, KY 40299
(502) 499-6220

Executive West
830 Phillips Lane
Louisville, KY 40209
(502) 367-2251

LOUISIANA

Alexandria

Hampton Inn Alexandria
2301 North MacArthur Drive
Alexandria, LA 71301
(318) 445-6996

Holiday Inn Convention Center
701 4th Street
Alexandria, LA 71301
(318) 442-9000

Baton Rouge

Embassy Suites Baton Rough
4914 Constitution
Baton Rouge, LA 70808
(225) 924-6566

Baton Rouge Marriott
5500 Hilton Avenue
Baton Rouge, LA 70808
(225) 924-5000

Radisson Hotel & Conference Center
4728 Constitution Avenue
Baton Rouge, LA 70808
(225) 925-2244

Bossier City

Holiday Inn Bossier
2015 Old Minden Road
Bossier City, LA 71111
(318) 742-9700

Horseshoe Casino Hotel & Tower
711 Horseshoe Blvd.
Bossier City, LA 71111
(318) 741-7794

Isle of Capri Inn
3033 Hilton Drive
Bossier City, LA 71111
(318) 678-7646

Lake Charles

Harrah's Casino Lake Charles
505 North Lakeshore Drive
Lake Charles, LA 70601
(337) 437-1510

New Orleans

Avenue Plaza Hotel
2111 Street Charles Avenue
New Orleans, LA 70116
(504) 523-2222

Bourbon Orleans
717 Orleans Street
New Orleans, LA 70116
(504) 523-2222

Chateau Soonest New Orleans
800 Iberville Street
New Orleans, LA 70112
(504) 586-0800

Days Inn Canal Street
1630 Canal Street
New Orleans, LA 70112
(504) 522-1906

Doubletree Hotel New Orleans
300 Canal Street
New Orleans, LA 70130
(504) 581-1300

Embassy Suites Hotel New Orleans
315 Julia Street
New Orleans, LA 70130
(504) 525-1993

Hilton New Orleans Riverside
2 Poydras at Mississippi River
New Orleans, LA 70140
(504) 556-3700

Holiday Inn—Downtown Superdome
330 Loyola Avenue
New Orleans, LA 70112
(504) 581-1600

Hotel Intercontinental New Orleans
444 St. Charles Avenue
New Orleans, LA 70130
(504) 525-5566

Hyatt Regency New Orleans
500 Poydras Plaza
New Orleans, LA 70113
(504) 561-1234

Marriott New Orleans
555 Canal Street
New Orleans, LA 70130
(504) 553-5520

New Orleans Grande Hotel
614 Canal Street
New Orleans, LA 70130
(504) 525-6500

Radisson New Orleans
1500 Canal Street
New Orleans, LA 70112
(504) 522-4500

Hotel Monteleone
214 Royal Street
New Orleans, LA 70130
(504) 523-3341

Royal Sonesta
300 Bourbon Street
New Orleans, LA 70130
(504) 586-0300

Sheraton New Orleans
500 Canal Street
New Orleans, LA 70130
(504) 595-5527

The Fairmont New Orleans
123 Baronne Street
New Orleans, LA 70112
(504) 529-7111

The Ritz-Carlton New Orleans
921 Canal Street
New Orleans, LA 70112
(504) 524-1331

W. New Orleans
333 Poydras Street
New Orleans, LA 70130
(504) 525-9444

Shreveport

Holiday Inn Downtown/Riverfront
102 Lake Street
Shreveport, LA 71101
(318) 222-8381

MAINE

Portland

Eastland Park Hotel
157 High Street
Portland, ME 04101
(207) 775-5418

Holiday Inn By The Bay
88 Spring Street
Portland, ME 04101
(207) 775-2311

Holiday Inn West
81 Riverside Street
Portland, ME 04103
(207) 774-5601

South Portland

Marriott Hotel
200 Sable Oaks Drive
South Portland, ME 04106
(207) 871-8000

Sheraton South Portland
363 Maine Mall Road
South Portland, ME 04106
(207) 775-6161

MARYLAND

Annapolis

Governor Calvert House
58 State Circle
Annapolis, MD 20401
(410) 280-9404

Loews Annapolis Hotel
126 West Street
Annapolis, MD 21401
(410) 263-7777

Radisson Hotel Annapolis
210 Holiday Court
Annapolis, MD 21401
(410) 224-3150

Sheraton Barcelo Annapolis
173 Jennifer Road
Annapolis, MD 21401
(410) 266-3131

Annapolis Marriott Waterfront
80 Compromise Street
Annapolis, MD 21401
(410) 268-7555

Bethesda

Bethesda Suites Marriott
6711 Democracy Blvd.
Bethesda, MD 20817
(301) 571-2218

Holiday Inn Select Bethesda
8120 Wisconsin Avenue
Bethesda, MD 20814
(301) 652-2000

Hyatt Regency Bethesda
One Bethesda Metro Center
Bethesda, MD 20814
(301) 657-6400

Marriott Bethesda
5151 Pooks Hill Road
Bethesda, MD 20814
(301) 897-9400

Baltimore Metro Area

Baltimore Marriott Inner Harbor
110 South Eutaw Street
Baltimore, MD 21201
(410) 962-0202

Baltimore Marriott Waterfront
700 Aliceanna Street
Baltimore, MD 20202
(410) 385-3000

Harbor Court
550 Light Street
Baltimore, MD 20202
(410) 347-9702

Holiday Inn Inner Harbor
301 West Lombard Street
Baltimore, MD 20201
(410) 685-3500

Hyatt Regency Baltimore
300 Light Street
Baltimore, MD 21202
(410) 528-1234

Pier 5 Hotel
711 Eastern Avenue
Baltimore, MD 21202
(410) 539-2000

Radisson Plaza Lord Baltimore
20 West Baltimore Street
Baltimore, MD 20201
(410) 539-8400

Renaissance Harborplace
202 East Pratt Street
Baltimore, MD 21202
(410) 547-1200

Sheraton Inner Harbor
300 South Charles Street
Baltimore, MD 20201
(410) 962-8300

Tremont Plaza Suites
222 Street Paul Place
Baltimore, MD 20202
(410) 685-7777

Wyndham Inner Harbor
101 West Fayette Street
Baltimore, MD 20201
(410) 385-6500

College Park

Sheraton College Park
4095 Powder Mill Road
Beltsville, MD 20705
(301) 937-4422

Flintstone

Rocky Gap Lodge & Golf Resort
16701 Lakeview Road Northeast
Flintstone, MD 21530
301-784-8420

Ocean City

Carousel Beachfront Hotel & Suites
11700 Coastal Highway
Ocean City, MD 21842
(410) 524-1000

Holiday Inn Oceanfront and Conference
Center
67th Street and Oceanfront
Ocean City, MD 21842
(410) 524-1600

Clarion Resort Fontainebleau Hotel
10100 Coastal Highway
Ocean City, MD 21842
(410) 524-3535

Princess Royale Oceanfront Hotel
& Conference Center
9100 Coastal Highway
Ocean City, MD 21842
(410) 524-8292

Rockville

Doubletree Hotel & Executive Meeting
Center Rockville
1750 Rockville Pike
Rockville, MD 20852
(301) 468-1100

Silver Spring

Hilton Silver Spring
8727 Colesville Road
Silver Spring, MD 20910
(301) 589-5200

MASSACHUSETTS

Boston

Boston Harbor Hotel
Rowes Wharf
Boston, MA 02110
(617) 439-7000

Boston Marriott Copley Place
110 Huntington Avenue
Boston, MA 02116
(617) 236-5800

Boston Marriott Long Wharf
296 State Street
Boston, MA 02109
(617) 227-0800

Boston OMNI Parker House Hotel
60 School Street
Boston, MA 02108
(617) 227-8600

Boston Park Plaza Hotel & Towers
64 Arlington Street
Boston, MA 02116
(617) 457-2241

Colonnade Hotel
120 Huntington Avenue
Boston, MA 02116
(617) 424-7000

Four Seasons Boston
200 Boylston Street
Boston, MA 02116
(617) 351-2011

Hilton Boston Back Bay
40 Dalton Street
Boston, MA 02115
(617) 236-1100

Fairmont Copley Plaza
138 Saint James Avenue
Boston, MA 02116
(617) 867-8527

Holiday Inn Select Government
Center
5 Blossom Street
Boston, MA 02114
(617) 742-7630

Le Meridien Boston
250 Franklin Street
Boston, MA 02110
(617) 451-1900

Millennium Bostonian Hotel
Faneuil Hall Marketplace
Boston, MA 02109
(617) 523-3600

Radisson Hotel Boston
200 Stuart Street
Boston, MA 02116
(617) 457-2626

Ritz-Carlton Boston
15 Arlington Street
Boston, MA 02117
(617) 536-5700

Seaport Hotel at the World Trade Center
200 Seaport Blvd.
Boston, MA 02110
(617) 385-4212

Sheraton Boston Hotel
39 Dalton Street
Boston, MA 02199
(617) 236-6033

The Lenox Hotel
710 Boylston Street
Boston, MA 02116
(617) 536-5300

The Ritz Carlton Boston Common
10 Avery Street
Boston, MA 02111
(617) 574-7100

Swissotel Boston
One Avenue de Lafayette
Boston, MA 02111
(617) 451-0054

The Tremont Boston/A Wyndham
Historic Hotel
275 Tremont Street
Boston, MA 02116
(617) 426-1400

Westin Copley Place Boston
10 Huntington Avenue
Boston, MA 02116
(617) 262-9600

Wyndham Boston Hotel
89 Broad Street
Boston, MA 02110
(617) 556-0006

Hilton Boston Logan Airport
85 Terminal Road
Boston, MA 02108
(617) 568-6811

Holiday Inn Logan Airport
225 McClellan Highway
East Boston, MA 02128
(617) 569-5250

Hyatt Harborside
101 Harborside Drive
Boston, MA 02128
(617) 568-1234

Cambridge

The Charles Hotel Harvard Square
One Bennett Street
Cambridge, MA 02138
(617) 864-1200

Hyatt Regency Cambridge,
Overlooking Boston
575 Memorial Drive
Cambridge, MA 02139
(617) 492-1234

Marriott Cambridge
2 Cambridge Center
Cambridge, MA 02142
(617) 494-6600

Royal Sonesta Hotel Boston
5 Cambridge Parkway
Cambridge, MA 02142
(617) 806-4200

University Park Hotel at MIT
20 Sidney Street
Cambridge, MA 02139
(617) 577-0200

Dedham

Hilton Boston/Dedham Hotel
25 Allied Drive
Dedham, MA 02026
(781) 407-1636

Newton

Boston Marriott Newton
Commonwealth Avenue at Route
  128 & Mass. Turnpike
Newton, MA 02466
(617) 969-8464

Norwood

Four Points Norwood Hotel &
Conference Center
1125 Boston-Providence Highway
Norwood, MA 02062
(781) 255-3159

Waltham

Doubletree Guest Suites Waltham
550 Winter Street
Waltham, MA 02154
(781) 487-4217

Westin Waltham
70 3rd Avenue
Waltham, MA 02451
(800) 423-7846

Brewster

Ocean Edge Resort & Golf Club
207 Main Street
Brewster, MA 02631
(508) 896-9000

Hyannis

Sheraton Hyannis Resort
West End Circle
Hyannis, MA 02601
(508) 775-7775

New Seabury

New Seabury Cape Cod
P.O. Box 549
New Seabury, MA 02649
(508) 539-8263

North Falmouth

Sea Crest Oceanfront Resort &
Conference Center
350 Quaker Road
North Falmouth, MA 02556
(508) 540-5300

Danvers

Sheraton Ferncroft Conference Resort
50 Ferncroft Road
Danvers, MA 01923
(978) 777-2500

Framingham

Sheraton Framingham Hotel
1657 Worcester Road
Framingham, MA 01701
(508) 879-7200

Lenox

Cranwell Resort Spa & Golf Club
55 Lee Road
Lenox, MA 01240
(413) 637-1662

Marlborough

Best Western Royal Plaza Hotel
& Trade Center
181 Boston Post Road West
Marlborough, MA 01752
(508) 460-0700

Radisson Hotel Marlborough
73 Felton Street
Marlborough, MA 01752
(508) 480-0015

The Learning Center at Marlborough
280 Locke Drive
Marlborough, MA 01752
(508) 263-5700

Nantucket

Harbor House
South Beach Street
Nantucket, MA 02554
(860) 528-5858

White Elephant
Easton Street
Nantucket, MA 02554
(860) 528-5858

Needham

Sheraton Needham Hotel
100 Cabot Street
Needham, MA 02494
(781) 444-1110

Martha's Vineyard

Harbor View Hotel of Martha's
Vineyard
131 North Water Street
Edgartown, MA 02539
(508) 627-7000

Springfield

Holiday Inn Springfield
711 Dwight Street
Springfield, MA 01104
(413) 750-3107

Sheraton Monarch Place Springfield
One Monarch Place
Springfield, MA 01144
(413) 263-2077

MICHIGAN

Ann Arbor

Best Western Executive Plaza
2900 Jackson Avenue
Ann Arbor, MI 48103
(734) 665-4444

Campus Inn
615 East Huron Street
Ann Arbor, MI 48104
(734) 769-2224

Courtyard Ann Arbor
3205 Boardwalk
Ann Arbor, MI 48108
(734) 995-5900

Dearborn

Hyatt Regency Dearborn
Fairlane Town Center
Dearborn, MI 48126
(313) 382-6898

The Dearborn Inn, A Marriott Hotel
20301 Oakwood Blvd.
Dearborn, MI 48124
(313) 271-3899

Detroit

Courtyard by Marriott Detroit
Downtown
333 East Jefferson Avenue
Detroit, MI 48226
(313) 568-8287

Detroit Marriott Renaissance Center
Renaissance Center
Detroit, MI 48243
(313) 568-8300

Hotel Pontchartrain
2 Washington Blvd.
Detroit, MI 48226
(313) 965-0200

The Westin Detroit Metropolitan
Airport
2501 Worldgateway Place
Detroit, MI 48242
(734) 942-6500

Southfield

Ambassador Hotel & Conference Center
16400 J. L. Hudson Drive
Southfield, MI 48075
(248) 552-8833

Embassy Suites Hotel Detroit—
Southfield
28100 Franklin Road
Southfield, MI 48034
(248) 350-2000

Holiday Inn Detroit— Southfield
26555 Telegraph Road
Southfield, MI 48034
(248) 353-7700

Marriott Southfield
27033 Northwest Highway
Southfield, MI 48034
(248) 356-7400

Westin Southfield Detroit
1500 Town Center
Southfield, MI 48075
(248) 827-4000

Grand Rapids

Grand Rapids/Kent County CVB
140 Monroe Center
Grand Rapids, MI 49503
(616) 459-8287

Amway Grand Plaza
187 Monroe Street Northwest
Grand Rapids, MI 49503
(616) 776-6400

Courtyard By Marriott
11 Monroe Avenue, Northwest
Grand Rapids, MI 49503
(616) 242-6600

Lansing

Radisson Hotel Lansing
111 North Grand Avenue
Lansing, MI 48933
(517) 482-0188

Sheraton Lansing Hotel
925 South Creyts Road
Lansing, MI 48917
(517) 323-7100

Holiday Inn Lansing West Conference
Center
7501 West Saginaw Highway
Lansing, MI 48917
(517) 627-3211

MINNESOTA

Duluth

Holiday Inn Hotel & Suites
200 West 1st Street
Duluth, MN 55802
(218) 727-7492

Radisson Hotel Duluth Harborview
505 West Superior Street
Duluth, MN 55802
(218) 727-1490

Grand Rapids

Sugar Lake Lodge
P.O. Box 847
Grand Rapids, MN 55744
(218) 327-1462

Minneapolis/St. Paul Metro Area

Bloomington

Bloomington CVB
7900 International Drive
Bloomington, MN 55425
(952) 858-8500

Radisson Hotel South & Plaza Tower
7800 Normandale Blvd.
Bloomington, MN 55439
(952) 835-7800

Doubletree Hotel—Minneapolis Airport
at the Mall
7901 24th Avenue South
Bloomington, MN 55425
(952) 851-6325

Embassy Suites Bloomington
2800 West 80th Street
Bloomington, MN 55431
(952) 884-4811

Holiday Inn Select International
Airport
3 Appletree Square
Bloomington, MN 55425
(952) 854-9000

Howard Johnson Hotel—Bloomington
Thunderbird
2201 East 78th Street
Bloomington, MN 55425
(952) 854-3411

Minneapolis Airport Marriott
2020 East 79th Street
Bloomington, MN 55425
(952) 854-7441

Sofitel Minneapolis
5601 West 78th Street
Bloomington, MN 55439
(952) 656-5921

Wyndham Minneapolis Airport
4460 West 78th Street Circle
Bloomington, MN 55435
(952) 831-3131

Minneapolis

Best Western—Downtown
405 South 8th Street
Minneapolis, MN 55404
(612) 370-1400

Crowne Plaza Northstar
618 2nd Avenue South
Minneapolis, MN 55402
(612) 338-2288

Embassy Suites Minneapolis
Downtown
425 South 7th Street
Minneapolis, MN 55415
(612) 333-3111

Holiday Inn Metrodome
1500 Washington Avenue South
Minneapolis, MN 55454
(612) 334-1310

Hyatt Regency Minneapolis
1300 Nicollet Mall
Minneapolis, MN 55403
(612) 370-1450

Millennium Hotel Minneapolis
1313 Nicollet Mall
Minneapolis, MN 55403
(612) 359-2227

Hilton Minneapolis
1001 Marquette Avenue South
Minneapolis, MN 55403
(612) 376-1000

Minneapolis Marriott City Center
30 South 7th Street
Minneapolis, MN 55402
(612) 349-4030

Radisson Hotel Metrodome
615 Washington Avenue Southeast
Minneapolis, MN 55414
(612) 362-6625

The Marquette Hotel
710 Marquette Avenue
Minneapolis, MN 55402
(612) 333-4545

Doubletree Park Place Hotel
1500 Park Place Blvd.
Minneapolis, MN 55416
(952) 582-5305

Sheraton Minneapolis West
Hotel
12201 Ridgedale Drive
Minnetonka, MN 55305
(52) 593-0000

St. Paul

Four Points By Sheraton St.
Paul/Capitol
400 Hamline Avenue North
St. Paul, MN 55104
(651) 642-1234

Holiday Inn Rivercentre
175 West 7th Street
St. Paul, MN 55102
(651) 556-1419

Radisson Riverfront Hotel St. Paul
11 East Kellogg Blvd.
St. Paul, MN 55101
(651) 292-1900

The Saint Paul Hotel
350 Market Street
St. Paul, MN 55102
(651) 292-9292

Red Lion Hotel & Conference Center
1870 Old Hudson Road
St. Paul, MN 55119
(651) 735-2333

Rochester

Holiday Inn City Centre
220 South Broadway Avenue
Rochester, MN 55904
(507) 252-8200

Rochester Marriott
101 Southwest 1st Avenue
Rochester, MN 55901
(507) 285-2776

The Kahler Grand Hotel
20 Southwest 2nd Avenue
Rochester, MN 55902
(507) 280-6200

MISSISSIPPI

Biloxi

President Casino Broadwater Resort
2110 Beach Blvd.
Biloxi, MS 39531
(228) 385-3500

Casino Magic Biloxi
195 Beach Blvd.
Biloxi, MS 39530
(228) 386-3019

Beau Rivage
875 Beach Blvd.
Biloxi, MS 39530
(228) 386-7171

Grand Casino Biloxi Hotel
265 Beach Blvd.
Biloxi, MS 39530
(228) 386-1908

Holiday Inn Biloxi Beachfront
(Coliseum)
2400 Beach Blvd.
Biloxi, MS 39531
(228) 388-3551

Imperial Palace Biloxi
850 Bayview Avenue
Biloxi, MS 39530
(228) 436-3000

Isle of Capri Casino
151 Beach Blvd.
Biloxi, MS 39530
(228) 436-7814

Jackson

Cabot Lodge Millsaps
2375 North State Street
Jackson, MS 39202
(601) 948-6161

Edison Walthall Hotel
225 East Capitol Street
Jackson, MS 39201
(601) 948-6161

Hilton Jackson
1001 East County Line Road
Jackson, MS 39211
(601) 957-2800

Natchez

Isle of Capri Casino
645 South Canal Street
Natchez, MS 39120
(601) 445-0605

Natchez Eola Hotel
110 North Pearl Street
Natchez, MS 39120
(601) 445-6000

Tupelo

Ramada Inn & Convention Center
854 North Gloster Street
Tupelo, MS 38804
(662) 844-4111

MISSOURI
Columbia

Ramada Columbia Conference Center
1100 Vandiver Drive
Columbia, MO 65202
(573) 442-1557

Holiday Inn Select Executive Center
2200 I-70 Drive Southwest
Columbia, MO 65203
(573) 445-3940

Jefferson City

Jefferson City CVB
PO Box 2227
Jefferson City, MO 65102
(573) 632-2820

Capitol Plaza
415 West McCarty Street
Jefferson City, MO 65101
(573) 635-1234

Ramada Inn & Conference Center
1510 Jefferson Street
Jefferson City, MO 65110
(573) 635-7171

Kansas City

Doubletree Hotel Kansas City
1301 Wyandotte
Kansas City, MO 64105
(816) 460-6622

Fairmont Hotel at the Plaza
401 Ward Parkway
Kansas City, MO 64112
(816) 303-2916

Four Points by Sheraton Country
Club Plaza
One East 45th Street
Kansas City, MO 64111
(816) 216-8006

Hotel Phillips
106 West 12th Street
Kansas City, MO 64105
(816) 221-7000

Hyatt Regency Crown Center
2345 McGee Street
Kansas City, MO 64108
(816) 421-1234

Kansas City Marriott Country Club
Plaza
4445 Main Street
Kansas City, MO 64111
(816) 531-3000

Kansas City Marriott—Downtown
200 West 12th Street
Kansas City, MO 64105
(816) 421-6800

Sheraton Suites Country Club Plaza
770 West 47th Street
Kansas City, MO 64112
(816) 931-4400

Westin Crown Center
One Pershing Road
Kansas City, MO 64108
(816) 474-4400

Adam's Mark Kansas City
9103 East 39th Street
Kansas City, MO 64133
(816) 737-4705

Embassy Suites City Plaza
220 West 43rd Street
Kansas City, MO 64111
(816) 756-1720

Lake Ozark

Holiday Inn Sunspree Resort &
Conference Center
Bus Route 54
Lake Ozark, MO 65049
(314) 365-2334

The Lodge of the Four Seasons
Horseshoe Bend Parkway
Lake Ozark, MO 65049
(573) 365-3000

Springfield

Days Inn & Conference Center
3050 North Kenwood
Springfield, MO 65803
(417) 883-3108

Holiday Inn University Plaza
333 John Q. Hammons Parkway
Springfield, MO 65806
(417) 864-7333

Sheraton Hawthorn Park
2431 North Glenstone Avenue
Springfield, MO 65803
(417) 831-3131

Clarion Springfield
3333 South Glenstone
Springfield, MO 65804
(417) 883-6550

Bridgeton

Crowne Plaza St. Louis Airport
11228 Lone Eagle Drive
Bridgeton, MO 63044
(314) 291-6700

Chesterfield

Doubletree Hotel & Conference
Center, St. Louis
16625 Swingley Ridge Road
Chesterfield, MO 63017
(636) 532-5000

St. Louis Marriott West
660 Marville Centre Drive
Chesterfield, MO 63141
(314) 878-2747

Clayton

Radisson Clayton
7750 Carondelet Avenue
Clayton, MO 63105
(314) 726-5400

Ritz-Carlton St. Louis
100 Carondelet Plaza
Clayton, MO 63105
(314) 863-6300

Sheraton Clayton Plaza Hotel
St Louis
7730 Bonhomme Avenue
Clayton, MO 63105
(314) 719-4304

St. Louis

Adam's Mark St. Louis
4th & Chestnut Streets
St. Louis, MO 63102
(314) 241-7400

Embassy Suites Hotel— St. Louis
Down
901 North 1st Street
St. Louis, MO 63102
(314) 241-4200

Hampton Inn By the Arch
333 Washington Avenue
St. Louis, MO 63102
(314) 621-7900

Holiday Inn Select Downtown/
Convention Center
811 North Ninth Street
St. Louis, MO 63101
(314) 421-4000

Hyatt Regency St. Louis
One St. Louis Union Station
St. Louis, MO 63103
(314) 231-1234

Marriott Pavilion
One South Broadway
St. Louis, MO 63102
(314) 421-1776

Millennium Hotel St. Louis
200 South 4th Street
St. Louis, MO 63102
(314) 241-9500

OMNI Majestic Hotel
1019 Pine Street
St. Louis, MO 63101
(314) 436-4155

Radisson Hotel & Suites— St. Louis
Downtown
200 North 4th Street
St. Louis, MO 63102
(314) 621-8200

Renaissance Grand Hotel St. Louis
505 North 7th Street
St. Louis, MO 63101
(314) 241-9100

The Mayfair, A Wyndham Historic
Hotel
806 St. Charles Street
St. Louis, MO 63101
(314) 421-2500

The Westin St. Louis
811 Spruce Street
St. Louis, MO 63102
(314) 621-2000

Hilton Frontenac St. Louis
1335 South Lindbergh Blvd.
St. Louis, MO 63131
(314) 824-6035

Holiday Inn Southwest— Viking
10709 Watson Road
St. Louis, MO 63127
(314) 821-6600

Holiday Inn Westport
1973 Craigshire Drive
St. Louis, MO 63146
(314) 434-0100

Holiday Inn St. Louis Airport North
4545 North Lindbergh Blvd.
St. Louis, MO 63144
(314) 731-2100

Renaissance St. Louis Hotel Airport
9801 Natural Bridge Road
St. Louis, MO 63134
(314) 429-1100

St. Louis Airport Hilton
10330 Natural Bridge Road
St. Louis, MO 63134
(314) 426-5500

Sheraton West Port Hotel Lakeside
Chalet
191 West Port Plaza
St. Louis, MO 63146
(314) 878-1500

MONTANA

Billings

Sheraton Billings
27 North 27th Street
Billings, MT 59101
(406) 252-7400

The Northern Hotel
19 North Broadway
Billings, MT 59101
(406) 245-5121

Billings Hotel & Convention Center
1223 Mullowney Lane
Billings, MT 59101
(406) 248-7151

Holiday Inn Grand Montana
5500 Midland Road
Billings, MT 59101
(406) 248-7701

Great Falls

Townhouse Inn of Great Falls
1411 10th Avenue South
Great Falls, MT 59405
(406) 761-4600

Best Western Heritage Inn
1700 Fox Farm Road
Great Falls, MT 59404
(406) 761-1900

Helena

Westcoast Colonial Hotel
2301 Colonial Drive
Helena, MT 59601
(406) 443-2100

Kalispell

Best Western Outlaw Hotel
1701 Highway 93
Kalispell, MT 59901
(406) 755-6859

Westcoast Kalispell Center Hotel
20 North Main
Kalispell, MT 59901
(406) 751-5050

Missoula

Holiday Inn Parkside Missoula
200 South Pattee Street
Missoula, MT 59802
(406) 728-3565

NEBRASKA

Lincoln

Embassy Suites Lincoln
1040 "P" Street
Lincoln, NE 68508
(402) 474-1111

Holiday Inn—Downtown
141 North 9th Street
Lincoln, NE 68508
(402) 435-2837

The Cornhusker
333 South 13th Street
Lincoln, NE 68508
(402) 479-8206

Omaha

Doubletree Hotel—Downtown
1616 Dodge Street
Omaha, NE 68102
(402) 636-4905

Embassy Suites Downtown Old
Market Omaha
555 South 10th Street
Omaha, NE 68102
(402) 346-9000

Red Lion Hotel Omaha
7007 Grover Street
Omaha, NE 68106
(402) 397-7030

Clarion Hotel Executive Center
3650 South 72nd Street
Omaha, NE 68124
(402) 397-3700

Crowne Plaza Omaha Old Mill
655 North 108th Avenue
Omaha, NE 68154
(402) 516-1263

Doubletree Guest Suites
7270 Cedar Street
Omaha, NE 68124
(402) 397-5141

Holiday Inn Central Hotel
3321 South 72nd Street
Omaha, NE 68124
(402) 393-3950

Omaha Marriott
10220 Regency Circle
Omaha, NE 68114
(402) 399-9000

NEVADA

Carson City

Ormsby House Hotel & Casino
600 S. Carson Street
Carson City, NV 89701
(775) 882-1890

Henderson

Green Valley Ranch Resort & Spa
2300 Paseo Verdo
Henderson, NV 89052
(702) 617-7717

Hyatt Regency Lake Las Vegas Resort
101 Montelago Blvd.
Henderson, NV 89011
(702) 567-1234

The Ritz-Carlton Lake Las Vegas
29 Grand Mediterra Blvd.
Henderson, NV 89011
(702) 568-6858

Las Vegas

Las Vegas Convention Center
3150 Paradise Road
Las Vegas, NV 89109
(702) 892-0711

Aladdin Resort & Casino
3667 Las Vegas Blvd. South
Las Vegas, NV 89109
(702) 785-5066

Bally's Las Vegas
3645 Las Vegas Blvd. South
Las Vegas, NV 89109
(702) 946-4401

Bellagio
3600 Las Vegas Blvd. South
Las Vegas, NV 89109
(702) 693-7171

Boardwalk Hotel & Casino
3750 Las Vegas Blvd. South
Las Vegas, NV 89109
(702) 730-3104

Castaways Hotel & Casino
2800 Fremont Street
Las Vegas, NV 89104
(702) 385-9123

Embassy Suites Hotel Convention Center
3600 Paradise Road
Las Vegas, NV 89109
(702) 893-8000

Embassy Suites Las Vegas
4315 Swenson Street
Las Vegas, NV 89119
(702) 795-2800

Excalibur Hotel & Casino
3850 Las Vegas Blvd. South
Las Vegas, NV 89109
(702) 597-7100

Flamingo Las Vegas
3555 Las Vegas Blvd. South
Las Vegas, NV 89109
(702) 733-3211

Four Seasons Hotel Las Vegas
3960 Las Vegas Blvd. South
Las Vegas, NV 89119
(702) 632-5000

New York-New York Hotel & Casino
3790 Las Vegas Blvd. South
Las Vegas, NV 89109
(702) 740-6800

Gold Nugget Hotel & Casino
129 East Fremont Street
Las Vegas, NV 89101
(702) 386-8302

Las Vegas Hilton
3000 Paradise Road
Las Vegas, NV 89109
(702) 732-5631

Riviera Hotel & Casino
2901 Las Vegas Blvd. South
Las Vegas, NV 89109
(702) 794-9561

Stardust Resort & Casino
3000 Las Vegas Blvd. South
Las Vegas, NV 89109
(702) 732-6312

Crowne Plaza Las Vegas
4255 South Paradise Road
Las Vegas, NV 89109
(702) 369-4400

Alexis Park Resort
375 East Harmon Avenue
Las Vegas, NV 89109
(702) 796-3300

Caesars Palace
3570 Las Vegas Blvd. South
Las Vegas, NV 89109
(702) 731-7110

Hard Rock Hotel & Casino
4455 Paradise Road
Las Vegas, NV 89109
(702) 693-5000

MGM Grand Hotel/Casino
3799 Las Vegas Blvd. South
Las Vegas, NV 89109
(702) 891-1200

Harrah's Hotel & Casino
3475 Las Vegas Blvd. South
Las Vegas, NV 89109
(702) 369-4147

Monte Carlo Resort & Casino
3770 Las Vegas Blvd. South
Las Vegas, NV 89109
(702) 730-7300

The Palms Casino Resort
4321 West Flamingo Road
Las Vegas, NV 89103
(702) 942-7024

The Mirage
3400 Las Vegas Blvd. South
Las Vegas, NV 89109
(702) 791-7171

Tropicana Resort & Casino
3801 Las Vegas Blvd. South
Las Vegas, NV 89109
(702) 739-2581

The Venetian Resort Hotel Casino
3355 Las Vegas Blvd. South
Las Vegas, NV 89109
(702) 414-1000

Laughlin

Edgewater Hotel & Casino
2020 South Casino Drive
Laughlin, NV 89028
(702) 298-2453

Flamingo Laughlin
1900 South Casino Drive
Las Vegas, NV 89109
(702) 298-5111

Harrah's Laughlin
2900 South Casino Drive
Las Vegas, NV 89109
(702) 298-4600

River Palms Resort & Casino
2700 South Casino Drive
Las Vegas, NV 89029
(702) 298-2244

Lake Tahoe

Harrah's Lake Tahoe
PO Box 128 Highway 50 at Stateline
Lake Tahoe, NV 89449
(775) 588-6611

Harveys Resort & Casino
PO Box 128 Highway 50 at Stateline
Lake Tahoe, NV 89449
(775) 558-2411

Cal-Nava Resort Hotel Spa & Casino
2 Stateline Road, P.O. Box 368
Crystal Bay, NV 89402
(775) 832-4000

Lake Tahoe Horizon Casino Resort
P.O. Box C
Lake Tahoe, NV 89449
(775) 588-6211

Reno

Circus Circus Hotel & Casino Reno
500 North Sierra Street
Reno, NV 89503
(775) 328-9502

Eldorado Hotel Casino
345 North Virginia Street
Reno, NV 89501
(775) 348-9250

Harrah's Reno
219 North Center Street
Reno, NV 89501
(775) 348-9250

Holiday Inn & Diamond's Casino
1000 East 6th Street
Reno, NV 89512
(775) 786-5151

Ramada Inn & Speakeasy Casino
200 East 6th Street
Reno, NV 89501
(775) 329-7400

Sands Regency Hotel & Casino
345 North Arlington Avenue
Reno, NV 89501
(775) 348-2242

Airport Plaza
1981 Terminal Way
Reno, NV 89502
(775) 348-6370

Peppermill Hotel & Casino
2707 South Virginia Street
Reno, NV 89502
(775) 689-7161

NEW HAMPSHIRE

Manchester

Holiday Inn Center of New Hampshire
700 Elm Street
Manchester, NH 03101
(603) 625-1000

Mountain Club on Loon
Route 112, Kancamagus Highway
Lincoln, NH 03251
(603) 745-2244

Nashua

Crowne Plaza Nashua
2 Somerset Parkway
Nashua, NH 06063
(603) 886-1200

Sheraton Nashua
11 Tara Blvd.
Nashua, NH 03062
(603) 579-3273

NEW JERSEY

Atlantic City

The Atlantic City Convention Center
2314 Pacific Avenue
Atlantic City, NJ 08401
(609) 449-7110

Bally's Atlantic City
Park Place & Boardwalk
Atlantic City, NJ 08401
(609) 340-2150

Caesars Atlantic City Hotel/Casino
2100 Pacific Avenue
Atlantic City, NJ 08401
(609) 343-2789

Claridge Casino & Hotel
Boardwalk & Park Place
Atlantic City, NJ 08401
(609) 340-3500

Holiday Inn Boardwalk
Chelsea Avenue & Boardwalk
Atlantic City, NJ 08401
(609) 348-8821

Sands Casino Hotel
Indiana Avenue & Brighton Park
Atlantic City, NJ 08401
(609) 441-4600

Sheraton Atlantic City Convention
Center Hotel
2 Miss America Way
Atlantic City, NJ 08401
(609) 441-2911

Showboat Casino & Hotel
801 Boardwalk
Atlantic City, NJ 08401
(609) 343-4000

The Borgata
8025 Black Horse Pike
West Atlantic City, NJ 08232
(800) 845-0711

Tropicana Casino & Resort
Brighton Avenue & Boardwalk
Atlantic City, NJ 08401
(609) 340-4398

Trump Plaza Hotel & Casino
Boardwalk at Mississippi
Atlantic City, NJ 08401
(609) 441-2729

Atlantic City Hilton at Boston & Pacific
Boston & The Boardwalk
Atlantic City, NJ 08401
(800) 231-8687

Trump Marina Hotel Casino
Huron Avenue & Brigantine Blvd.
Atlantic City, NJ 08401
(609) 441-8600

Cherry Hill

Hilton At Cherry Hill
2349 West Marlton Pike
Cherry Hill, NJ 08002
(856) 665-6666

Eatontown

Sheraton Hotel & Conference Center
Eatontown
6 Industrial Way East
Eatontown, NJ 07724
(732) 542-6500

Elizabeth

Hilton Newark Airport
1170 Spring Street
Elizabeth, NJ 07201
(908) 351-3900

Wyndham Newark Airport
1000 Spring Street
Elizabeth, NJ 07201
(908) 351-3900

Fort Lee

Hilton Fort Lee
2117 Route, 4 East
Fort Lee, NJ 07024
(201) 461-9000

Morristown

The Westin Hotel—Morristown
2 Whippany Road
Morristown, NJ 07960
(793) 539-7300

Secaucus

Meadowlands Exposition Center
355 Plaza Drive
Secaucus, NJ 07094
(201) 330-7773

Crowne Plaza Meadowlands
2 Harmon Plaza
Secaucus, NJ 07094
(201) 210-7216

Embassy Suites Meadowlands
455 Plaza Drive
Secaucus, NJ 07094
(201) 864-7300

Newark

Hilton Gateway
Gateway Center at Raymond Blvd.
Newark, NJ 07102
(973) 622-5000

Marriott Newark Airport
Newark International Airport
Newark, NJ 07114
(973) 623-0006

Sheraton Newark Airport
128 Frontage Road
Newark, NJ 07114
(973) 690-5500

Princeton

Nassau Inn
10 Palmer Square
Princeton, NJ 08542
(609) 921-7500

Hyatt Regency Princeton
102 Carnegie Center
Princeton, NJ 08540
(609) 987-1820

Chauncey Conference Center
P.O. Box 6652
Princeton, NJ 08541
(609) 921-3600

Doral Forrestal Hotel & Spa
100 College Road East
Princeton, NJ 08540
(609) 452-7800

Short Hills

Hilton Short Hills
41 JFK Parkway
Short Hills, NJ 07078
(973) 379-0100

NEW MEXICO

Albuquerque

Hilton Albuquerque
1901 University Blvd. Northeast
Albuquerque, NM 87102
(505) 884-2500

Holiday Inn Mountain View
2020 Menaul Blvd. Northeast
Albuquerque, NM 87102
(505) 884-2500

Hyatt Regency Albuquerque
330 Tijeras Northwest
Albuquerque, NM 87102
(505) 842-1234

Marriott Albuquerque
2101 Louisiana Blvd. Northeast
Albuquerque, NM 87110
(505) 881-6800

Crowne Plaza Pyramid
5151 San Francisco Road, Northeast
Albuquerque, NM 87109
(505) 821-3333

Sheraton Uptown Albuquerque
2600 Louisiana Blvd. Northeast
Albuquerque, NM 87110
(505) 881-0000

Santa Fe

Hilton Santa Fe
100 Sandoval Street
Santa Fe, NM 87501
(505) 989-5309

Taos

Holiday Inn Don Fernando
1005 Paseo del Pueblo Sur, P.O. Drawer
Taos, NM 87571
(505) 758-4444

NEW YORK

Albany

Crowne Plaza Albany
State & Lodge Street
Albany, NY 12207
(518) 462-6611

Albany Marriott
189 Wolf Road
Albany, NY 12205
(518) 458-8444

Holiday Inn Turf
205 Wolf Road
Albany, NY 12205
(518) 458-7250

Buffalo

Adam's Mark Buffalo
120 Church Street
Buffalo, NY 14202
(716) 845-5116

Hyatt Regency Buffalo
Two Fountain Plaza
Buffalo, NY 14221
(716) 689-6900

Four Points By Sheraton Buffalo
Airport
2040 Walden Avenue
Buffalo, NY 14225
(716) 681-5489

Radisson Hotel & Suites
4243 Genesee Street
Buffalo, NY 14225
(716) 634-2300

Catskill Mountains

Holiday Inn Kingston
503 Washington Avenue
Kingston, NY 12401
(845) 338-0400

Concord Resort
P.O. Box 137
Kiamesha Lake, NY 12751
(845) 794-4000

Friar Tuck Spa Resort & Convention
Center
4858 Route 32
Catskill, NY 12414
(518) 678-2271

Kutshers Country Club
Kutshers Road
Monticello, NY 12701
(845) 744-6000

Mohonk Mountain House
1000 Mountain Rest Road
New Paltz, NY 12561
(845) 256-2125

Nevele Grande Resort & Country Club
US Highway 209 Nevele Road
Ellenville, NY 12428
(845) 647-6000

Raleigh Hotel
Thompsonville Road
South Fallsburg, NY 12779
(845) 434-7000

Villa Roma
356 Villa Roma Road
Callicoon, NY 12723
(845) 887-4880

Lake Placid

Lake Placid Resort Hotel & Golf Club
One Olympic Drive
Lake Placid, NY 12946
(518) 523-2556

Mirror Lake Inn Resort and Spa
5 Mirror Lake Drive
Lake Placid, NY 12946
(518) 523-2544

Long Island

Danfords Inn Marina Conference
Center
25 East Broadway
Port Jefferson, NY 11777
(631) 928-5200

Harrison Conference Center Glen
Cove
Dosoris Lane
Glen Cove, NY 11542
(914) 631-8100

Hilton Huntington
598 Broad Hollow Road
Melville, NY 11747
(631) 845-1000

Eslandia Marriott Long Island
3635 Express Drive North
Islandia, NY 11749
(631) 232-3000

Marriott Hotel & Conference Center
Long Island
101 James Doolittle Blvd.
Uniondale, NY 11553
(516) 794-3800

Melville Marriott Long Island
1350 Old Walt Whitman Road
Melville, NY 11747
(631) 423-1600

Quality Hotel & Convention Center
80 Clinton Street
Hempstead, NY 11550
(516) 486-4100

Sheraton Long Island Hotel, Smithtown
110 Vanderbilt Motor Parkway
Smithtown, NY 11788
(631) 233-4321

The Garden City Hotel
45 Seventh Street
Garden City, NY 11530
(516) 747-3000

Wyndham Wind Watch Hotel
1717 Motor Parkway
Hauppauge, NY 11788
(631) 232-9815

Gurney's Inn Resort Spa & Conference
Center
290 Old Montauk Highway
Montauk, NY 11954
(631) 668-3365

Montauk Yacht Club Resort Marina
32 Star Island Road, P.O. Box 5048
Montauk, NY 11954
(631) 668-3100

New Rochelle

Ramada Plaza
One Ramada Plaza
New Rochelle, NY 10801
(914) 576-3700

Brooklyn

Brooklyn Marriott
333 Adams Street
Brooklyn, NY 11201
(718) 222-6520

Manhattan

Crowne Plaza at the United Nations
304 East 42nd Street
New York, NY 10017
(212) 986-8800

Crowne Plaza Times Square
Manhattan
1605 Broadway
New York, NY 10017
(212) 986-8800

Doubletree Guest Suites
1568 Broadway
New York, NY 10036
(212) 403-6318

Embassy Suites Hotel New York City
102 North End Avenue
New York, NY 10281
(212) 945-0100

Four Seasons New York
57 East 57th Street
New York, NY 10022
(212) 758-5700

Grand Hyatt New York
Park Avenue at Grand Central Station
New York, NY 10017
(646) 213-6830

Hilton New York
1335 Avenue of the Americas
New York, NY 10019
(212) 261-5227

Hotel Sofitel New York
45 West 44th Street
New York, NY 10036
(212) 782-3013

Intercontinental Central Park South
New York
112 Central Park South
New York, NY 10019
(212) 237-1605

Mandarin Oriental
509 Madison Avenue
New York, NY 10022
(212) 207-8880

Marriott Marquis New York
1535 Broadway
New York, NY 10036
(212) 704-8748

Millennium UN Plaza Hotel, New York
One United Nations Plaza
First Avenue at 44th Street
New York, NY 10017
(212) 758-1234

New York Helmsley
212 East 42nd Street
New York, NY 10017
(212) 490-8900

New York Marriott East Side
525 Lexington Avenue
New York, NY 10017
(212) 755-4000

New York Marriott Financial Center
85 West Street
New York, NY 10006
(212) 385-4900

New Yorker Hotel, A Ramada Inn
& Plaza
481 8th Avenue
New York, NY 10001
(212) 244-0719

Ritz-Carlton New York Battery Park
Two West Street
New York, NY 10004
(212) 930-7400

The Mark Hotel
Madison Avenue at East 77th Street
New York, NY 10021
(212) 744-4300

The Plaza
5th Avenue and 59th Street
New York, NY 10019
(212) 546-5410

The Ritz-Carlton New York, Central
Park
50 Central Park South
New York, NY 10019
(212) 308-9100

Waldorf-Astoria
301 Park Avenue
New York, NY 10022
(212) 872-4800

Queens

Crowne Plaza Laguardia
104-04 Ditmars Blvd.
East Elmhurst, NY 11369
(718) 457-6300

Marriott La Guardia Airport
102-05 Ditmars Blvd.
East Elmhurst, NY 11369
(718) 533-3005

Rochester Metro Area

Four Points Sheraton Rochester
Riverside
120 East Main Street
Rochester, NY 14604
(585) 546-6400

Hyatt Regency Rochester
125 East Main Street
Rochester, NY 14604
(585) 546-1234

Rit Inn & Conference Center
5257 West Henrietta Road
Rochester, NY 14602
(585) 359-7746

Holiday Inn Rochester South
1111 Jefferson Road
Rochester, NY 14623
(716) 475-1510

Syracuse

Syracuse Convention and Visitors
Center
572 South Salina Street
Syracuse, NY 13202
(315) 470-1825

Hotel Syracuse
500 South Warren Street
Syracuse, NY 13202
(315) 422-5121

The Marx Hotel & Conference Center
701 East Genesee
Syracuse, NY 13210
(315) 479-7000

NORTH CAROLINA

Asheville

Renaissance Asheville Hotel
One Thomas Wolfe Plaza
Asheville, NC 28801
(828) 252-8211

Great Smokies Holiday Inn Sunspree
Resort
One Holiday Inn Drive
Asheville, NC 28806
(828) 254-3211

Inn On Biltmore Estate
One Antler Hill Road
Asheville, NC 28803
(828) 225-1613

The Grove Park Inn Resort & Spa
290 Macon Avenue
Asheville, NC 28804
(828) 252-2711

Chapel Hill

Sheraton Chapel Hill Hotel
One Europa Drive
Chapel Hill, NC 27517
(919) 968-4900

Charlotte

Adam's Mark Hotel Charlotte
555 South McDowell Street
Charlotte, NC 28204
(704) 348-4119

Charlotte Marriott City Center
100 West Trade Street
Charlotte, NC 28202
(704) 333-9000

Hilton Charlotte & Towers
222 East 3rd Street
Charlotte, NC 28202
(704) 377-1500

Westin Charlotte
601 South College Street
Charlotte, NC 28202
(704) 375-2600

Charlotte Hilton University Place
8629 J. M. Keynes Drive
Charlotte, NC 28262
(704) 547-7444

Doubletree Guest Suites
Charlotte/Southpark
6300 Morrison Blvd.
Charlotte, NC 28211
(704) 364-2400

Hyatt Charlotte at Southpark
5501 Carnegie Blvd.
Charlotte, NC 28209
(704) 554-1234

Durham

Durham Marriott at the Civic Center
201 Foster Street
Durham, NC 27701
(919) 768-6020

Millennium Hotel Durham
2800 Campus Walk Avenue
Durham, NC 27705
(919) 383-8575

Washington Duke Inn & Golf Club
3001 Cameron Blvd.
Durham, NC 27705
(919) 490-0999

Sheraton Imperial Hotel & Convention
Center
4700 Emperor Blvd.
Durham, NC 27703
(919) 941-5050

Greensboro

Sheraton Greensboro Hotel at Four
Seasons
3121 High Point Road at I-40
Greensboro, NC 27407
(336) 292-9161

Grandover Resort & Conference Center
1000 Club Road
Greensboro, NC 27407
(336) 294-1800

Winston-Salem

Adam's Mark Winston Plaza Hotel
425 North Cherry Street
Winston-Salem, NC 27101
(336) 728-4020

Pinehurst

Pinehurst Resort
1 Carolina Vista Drive
Pinehurst, NC 28374
(10) 235-8500

Raleigh

Holiday Inn-Brownstone
1707 Hillsborough Street
Raleigh, NC 27605
(919) 828-0811

Sheraton Capital Center Hotel
421 South Salisbury Street
Raleigh, NC 27601
(919) 834-9900

Hilton North Raleigh
3415 Wake Forest Road
Raleigh, NC 27609
(919) 872-2323

NORTH DAKOTA
Bismarck

Best Western Ramkota Hotel
800 South 3rd Street
Bismarck, ND 58504
(701) 258-7700

Radisson Hotel Bismarck
605 East Broadway
Bismarck, ND 58501
(701) 255-6000

Fargo

Radisson Hotel Fargo
201 5th Street North
Fargo, ND 58102
(701) 232-7363

Holiday Inn Fargo
3803 13th Avenue South
Fargo, ND 58103
(701) 282-2700

OHIO
Akron

Radisson Hotel Akron City Centre
20 West Mill Street
Akron, OH 44308
(330) 384-1500

Sheraton Suites Akron/ Cuyahoga
Falls
1989 Front Street
Cuyahoga Falls, OH 44221
(330) 929-3000

Columbus

Adam's Mark Columbus
50 North 3rd Street
Columbus, OH 43215
(614) 228-5050

Crowne Plaza Columbus
33 Nationwide Blvd.
Columbus, OH 43215
(614) 461-4100

Holiday Inn Columbus City
Center
175 East Town Street
Columbus, OH 43215
(614) 221-3281

Hyatt on Capitol Square
75 East State Street
Columbus, OH 43215
(614) 228-1234

Hyatt Regency Columbus City
Center
175 East Town Street
Columbus, OH 43215
(614) 221-3281

Hyatt on Capitol Square
75 East State Street
Columbus, OH 43215
(614) 228-1234

Hyatt Regency Columbus
350 North High Street
Columbus, OH 43215
(614) 280-3035

The Westin Great Southern
310 South High Street
Columbus, OH 43215
(614) 220-7042

Embassy Suites
2700 Corp. Exchange Drive
Columbus, OH 43231
(614) 890-8600

Hilton Columbus
3900 Chargrin Drive
Columbus, OH 43219
(614) 414-5000

Holiday Inn East
4560 Hilton Corp Drive
Columbus, OH 43232
(614) 868-1380

Ramada Plaza Hotel & Conference
Center
4900 Sinclair Road
Columbus, OH 43229
(614) 846-0300

Radisson Airport Hotel & Conference
Center
1375 North Cassady Avenue
Columbus, OH 43219
(614) 475-7551

Cincinnati

Crowne Plaza Cincinnati
15 West 6th Street
Cincinnati, OH 45202
(513) 562-2611

Hilton Cincinnati Netherland Plaza
35 West 5th Street
Cincinnati, OH 45202
(513) 421-9100

Hyatt Regency Cincinnati
151 West 5th Street
Cincinnati, OH 45202
(513) 579-1234

Millennium Hotel Cincinnati
141 West Sixth Street
Cincinnati, OH 45202
(513) 352-2100

Westin Cincinnati
21 East 5th Street
Cincinnati, OH 45202
(513) 852-2722

Holiday Inn Cincinnati
3855 Hauck Road
Cincinnati, OH 45241
(513) 563-8330

Holiday Inn Eastgate Conference Center
4501 Eastgate Blvd.
Cincinnati, OH 45245
(513) 943-5819

Radisson Hotel Cincinnati
11320 Chester Road
Cincinnati, OH 45246
(513) 772-1720

Cleveland

Cleveland Intercontinental Hotel &
Conference Center
8800 Euclid Avenue
Cleveland, OH 44106
(216) 707-4300

Cleveland Marriott Downtown
at Key Center
127 Public Square
Cleveland, OH 44114
(216) 696-9200

Embassy Suites Cleveland
Downtown
1701 East 12th Street
Cleveland, OH 44114
(216) 523-8000

Hilton Garden Inn Cleveland
Gateway & Conference Center
1100 Carnegie Avenue
Cleveland, OH 44115
(216) 658-6400

Holiday Inn Select
1111 Lakeside Avenue
Cleveland, OH 44114
(216) 241-5100

Hyatt Regency Cleveland at
The Arcade
420 Superior Avenue
Cleveland, OH 44114
(216) 575-1234

Renaissance Cleveland Hotel
24 Public Square
Cleveland, OH 44113
(216) 696-5600

Ritz-Carlton, Cleveland
1515 West 3rd Street
Cleveland, OH 44113
(216) 623-1300

Sheraton Cleveland City Center
777 St. Clair Avenue
Cleveland, OH 44114
(216) 771-7600

Wyndham Cleveland Hotel at
Playhouse Square
1260 Euclid Avenue
Cleveland, OH 44115
(216) 615-7500

Ramada Inn Cleveland Airport
13930 Brookpark Road
Cleveland, OH 44135
(216) 267-5700

Sheraton Cleveland Airport Hotel
5300 Riverside Drive
Cleveland, OH 44135
(216) 267-1500

Dayton

Crowne Plaza Dayton
33 East 5th Street
Dayton, OH 45402
(937) 224-0800

Dayton Marriott
1414 South Patterson Blvd.
Dayton, OH 45400
(937) 223-1000

Holiday Inn Dayton North
2301 Wagner Ford Road
Dayton, OH 45414
(937) 278-4871

Toledo

Radisson Toledo
101 North Summit Street
Toledo, OH 43604
(419) 241-3000

Wyndham Toledo Hotel
2 Seagate
Toledo, OH 43604
(419) 241-1411

Clarion Hotel Westgate
3536 Secor Road
Toledo, OH 43606
(419) 535-7070

Hilton Toledo and Dana Conference
Center
3100 Glendale Avenue
Toledo, OH 43614
(419) 381-6800

OKLAHOMA

Oklahoma City

Renaissance Oklahoma City
10 North Broadway
Oklahoma City, OK 73102
(405) 228-8000

The Westin Oklahoma City
One North Broadway
Oklahoma City, OK 73102
(405) 235-2780

Ramada Inn & Conference Center
4345 North Lincoln Blvd.
Oklahoma City, OK 73105
(405) 528-2741

Waterford Marriott Hotel
6300 Waterford Blvd.
Oklahoma City, OK 73118
(405) 848-4782

Biltmore Hotel
401 South Meridian Avenue
Oklahoma City, OK 73108
(405) 947-7681

Clarion Meridian Hotel & Convention
Center
737 South Meridian Avenue
Oklahoma City, OK 73108
(405) 942-8511

Tulsa

Adam's Mark Tulsa
100 East 2nd Street
Tulsa, OK 74103
(918) 582-9000

Holiday Inn Select
5000 East Skelly Drive
Tulsa, OK 74135
(918) 622-7000

Doubletree Warren Place
6110 South Yale Avenue
Tulsa, OK 74136
(918) 495-1000

Sheraton Tulsa Hotel
10918 East 41st Street
Tulsa, OK 74146
(918) 627-5000

Tulsa Marriott Southern Hills
1902 East 71st Street South
Tulsa, OK 74136
(918) 493-7000

OREGON

Eugene

Hilton Eugene & Conference Center
66 East 6th Avenue
Eugene, OR 97401
(541) 342-6651

Valley River Inn
1000 Valley River Way
Eugene, OR 97401
(541) 341-3472

Portland

Doubletree Lloyd Center
1000 Northeast Multnomah
Portland, OR 97232
(503) 249-3129

Embassy Suites Portland Downtown
319 Southwest Pine Street
Portland, OR 97204
(503) 279-9000

Hilton Portland & Executive Tower
921 Southwest 6th Avenue
Portland, OR 97204
(503) 226-1611

Holiday Inn Portland Convention
Center
1021 Northeast Grand Avenue
Portland, OR 97232
(503) 820-4156

PENNSYLVANIA

Harrisburg

Clarion Hotel & Convention Center
1700 Harrisburg Park
Carlisle, PA 17013
(717) 243-1717

Harrisburg-Hershey Marriott
4650 Lindle Road
Harrisburg, PA 17111
(717) 564-5511

Holiday Inn Harrisburg East
4751 Lindle Road
Harrisburg, PA 17111
(717) 564-5511

Holiday Inn Harrisburg East
4751 Lindle Road
Harrisburg, PA 17111
(717) 939-7841

Radisson Penn Harris Hotel &
Convention Center
1150 Camp Hill ByPass
Camp Hill, PA 17011
(717) 763-7117

Hershey

Hershey Lodge & Convention Center
West Chocolate Avenue &
   University Drive
Hershey, PA 17033
(866) PA MEETS

The Hotel Hershey
100 Hotel Road
Hershey, PA 17033
(800) HERSHEY

Philadelphia

Adam's Mark Philadelphia
City Avenue & Monument Road
Philadelphia, PA 19131
(215) 581-5033

Crowne Plaza
1800 Market Street
Philadelphia, PA 19103
(215) 561-7500

Doubletree Philadelphia
Broad & Locust Streets
Philadelphia, PA 19107
(215) 893-1600

Four Seasons Philadelphia
One Logan Square
Philadelphia, PA 19103
(215) 963-1500

Holiday Inn Independence Mall
400 Arch Street
Philadelphia, PA 19106
(215) 923-8660

Hyatt Regency Philadelphia at Penn's
Landing
201 South Columbus Blvd.
Philadelphia, PA 19106
(215) 928-1234

Loews Philadelphia Hotel
1200 Market Street
Philadelphia, PA 19107
(215) 627-1200

Park Hyatt Philadelphia at the
Bellevue
Broad & Walnut Street
Philadelphia, PA 19102
(215) 790-2891

Philadelphia Marriott
1201 Market Street
Philadelphia, PA 19107
(215) 625-2900

Radisson Plaza Warwick Hotel
Philadelphia
1701 Locust Street
Philadelphia, PA 19103
(215) 735-6000

Ritz-Carlton Philadelphia
Ten Avenue of the Arts
Philadelphia, PA 19102
(215) 523-8000

Embassy Suites Philadelphia Airport
9000 Bartram Avenue
Philadelphia, PA 19153
(215) 365-4500

Holiday Inn Philadelphia Stadium
900 Packer Avenue
Philadelphia, PA 19148
(800) 424-0291

Renaissance Philadelphia Hotel
Airport
500 Stevens Drive
Philadelphia, PA 19113
(610) 521-5900

Pittsburgh

Hilton & Towers Pittsburgh
Gateway Center
600 Commonwealth Avenue
Pittsburgh, PA 15222
(412) 391-4600

OMNI William Penn
530 William Penn Place
Pittsburgh, PA 15219
(412) 553-5000

Pittsburgh Marriott City Center
Hotel
112 Washington Place
Pittsburgh, PA 15219
(412) 471-4000

Sheraton Station Square
7 Station Square Drive
Pittsburgh, PA 15219
(412) 261-2000

Radisson Hotel Greentree
101 Radisson Drive
Pittsburgh, PA 15205
(412) 922-8400

Ramada Inn Pittsburgh South
164 Fort Couch Road
Pittsburgh, PA 15241
(412) 833-5300

Hyatt Regency Pittsburgh
International Airport
1111 Airport Blvd.
Clinton, PA 15231
(724) 899-6070

State College

Nittany Lion Inn
200 West Park Avenue
State College, PA 16803
(814) 863-5084

The Penn State Conference Center
Hotel
215 Innovation Blvd.
State College, PA 16803
(814) 863-5084

RHODE ISLAND

Newport

Marriott Newport
25 America's Cup Avenue
Newport, RI 02840
(401) 849-1000

Hotel Viking
One Bellevue Avenue
Newport, RI 02840
(401) 848-4800

Hyatt Regency Newport
1 Goat Island
Newport, RI 02840
(401) 851-1234

Newport Harbor Hotel & Marina
49 America's Cup Avenue
Newport, RI 02840
(401) 847-9000

Providence

Holiday Inn Downtown Providence
21 Atwells Avenue
Providence, RI 02903
(401) 831-3900

Marriott Providence
One Orms Street
Providence, RI 02904
(401) 272-2400

Providence Biltmore
Kennedy Plaza
Providence, RI 02903
(401) 455-3020

The Westin Providence
One West Exchange Street
Providence, RI 02903
(401) 598-8004

Sheraton Providence Airport Hotel
1850 Post Road
Warwick, RI 02886
(401) 738-4000

SOUTH CAROLINA

Columbia

Adam's Mark Columbia
1200 Hampton Street
Columbia, SC 29201
(803) 771-7000

Embassy Suites
200 Stoneridge Drive
Columbia, SC 29210
(803) 252-8700

Holiday Inn Northeast
7510 Two Notch Road
Columbia, SC 29223
(800) EMBASSY

Charleston

Charleston Place
205 Meeting Street
Charleston, SC 29401
(843) 722-4900

Charleston Riverview
170 Lockwood Drive
Charleston, SC 29403
(843) 723-3000

Doubletree Guest Suites Historic
Charleston
181 Church Street
Charleston, SC 29401
(843) 577-2644

Wild Dunes Resort
5757 Palm Blvd.
Isle of Palms, SC 29451
(843) 886-2269

Greenville

Hyatt Regency Greenville
220 North Main Street
Greenville, SC 29601
(864) 235-1234

Westin Poinsett Hotel
120 South Main Street
Greenville, SC 29601
(864) 421-9700

Crowne Plaza Greenville
851 Congaree Road
Greenville, SC 29607
(864) 297-6300

Embassy Suites Golf Resort
670 Verdae Blvd.
Greenville, SC 29607
(864) 676-9090

Greenville Hilton & Towers
45 West Orchard Park Drive
Greenville, SC 29615
(864) 232-4747

Hilton Head Island

Crowne Plaza Hilton Head
Island Beach Resort
130 Shipyard Drive
Hilton Head Island, SC 29928
(843) 842-2400

Holiday Inn Oceanfront Resort
One South Forest Beach Drive
Hilton Head Island, SC 29928
(843) 785-5126

Sea Pines Resort
32 Greenwood Drive
Hilton Head Island, SC 29928
(843) 363-4372

The Westin Resort Hilton Head
Island
Two Grasslawn Avenue
Hilton Head Island, SC 29928
(843) 681-4000

Kiawah Island

Kiawah Island Golf Resort
12 Kiawah Beach Drive
Kiawah Island, SC 29455
(843) 768-6040

The Sanctuary At Kiawah Island
12 Kiawah Beach Drive
Kiawah Island, SC 29455
(843) 768-2121

Myrtle Beach

Beach Colony Resort
5308 North Ocean Blvd.
Myrtle Beach, SC 29577
(843) 448-9441

Caravelle Resort/St Johns Inn
6900 North Ocean Blvd.
Myrtle Beach, SC 29572
(843) 918-7013

Four Points Sheraton Hotel Myrtle
Beach Oceanfront
2701 South Ocean Blvd.
Myrtle Beach, SC 29572
(843) 448-2518

Hilton Myrtle Beach Resort
10000 Beach Club Drive
Myrtle Beach, SC 29572
(843) 449-5000

Holiday Inn Oceanfront
415 South Ocean Blvd.
Myrtle Beach, SC 29577
(843) 448-4481

Legends Resorts
P.O. Box 2038
Myrtle Beach, SC 29578
(888) 246-9797

Ocean Dunes
Resort & Conference Center
201 75th Avenue North
Myrtle Beach, SC 29572
(843) 692-5269

Sands Ocean Club Resort
9550 Shore Drive
Myrtle Beach, SC 29572
(843) 692-5269

SOUTH DAKOTA

Rapid City

Ramkota Hotel & Conference
Center
2111 LaCrossee
Rapid City, SD 57701
(605) 343-8550

Sioux Falls

Holiday Inn City Centre
100 West 8th Street
Sioux Falls, SD 57104
(605) 339-2000

Sheraton Sioux Falls Hotel
& Convention Center
1211 North West
Sioux Falls, SD 57104
(605) 331-0100

Best Western Ramkota Hotel
3200 West Maple
Sioux Falls, SD 57107
(605) 336-0650

Ramada Inn Airport at Convention
Center
1301 West Russell Street
Sioux Falls, SD 57104
(605) 336-1020

TENNESSEE

Chattanooga

Chattanooga Clarion Hotel
407 Chestnut Street
Chattanooga, TN 37402
(423) 756-5150

Chattanooga Marriott
2 Carter Plaza
Chattanooga, TN 37402
(423) 756-0002

Holiday Inn Chattanooga Choo Choo
1400 Market Street
Chattanooga, TN 37402
(423) 266-5000

The Chattanoogan
1201 S. Broad Street
Chattanooga, TN 37415
(423) 756-3400

The Read House Hotel & Suites
827 Broad Street
Chattanooga, TN 37402
(423) 266-4121

Gatlinburg

Edgewater Hotel
P.O. Box 170
Gatlinburg, TN 37738
(865) 436-4151

Glenstone Lodge
504 Historic Nature Trail Road
Gatlinburg, TN 37738
(865) 436-9361

River Terrace Resort & Convention
Center
240 River Road
Gatlinburg, TN 37738
(865) 436-5161

Holiday Inn Sunspree Resort
520 Historic Nature Trail
Gatlinburg, TN 37738
(865) 436-9201

Park Vista Resort
P.O. Box 30
Gatlinburg, TN 37738
(865) 436-9211

Knoxville

Hilton Knoxville
501 Church Avenue S.W.
Knoxville, TN 37902
(865) 523-2300

Holiday Inn Knoxville Central at
Papermill
1315 Kirby Road
Knoxville, TN 37909
(865) 584-3911

Holiday Inn Select Downtown at
Convention Center
525 Henley Street
Knoxville, TN 37902
(865) 522-2800

Hyatt Regency Knoxville
500 Hill Avenue Southeast
Knoxville, TN 37915
(865) 594-4330

Holiday Inn Select Cedar Bluff
304 North Cedar Bluff Road
Knoxville, TN 37923
(865) 342-3421

Howard Johnson-North
118 Merchant Drive
Knoxville, TN 37923
(865) 342-3421

Memphis

Peabody Memphis
149 Union Avenue
Memphis, TN 38103
(901) 529-4000

Marriott Downtown Memphis
250 North Main Street
Memphis, TN 38103
(901) 527-7300

Radisson Memphis
185 Union Avenue
Memphis, TN 38103
(901) 528-1800

Adam's Mark Memphis
939 Ridgelake Blvd.
Memphis, TN 38120
(901) 684-6664

Hilton East Memphis
5069 Sanderlin Avenue
Memphis, TN 38117
(901) 767-6666

Holiday Inn Select Memphis East
5795 Poplar Avenue
Memphis, TN 38119
(901) 682-7881

Holiday Inn Select Memphis
Airport
2240 Democrat Road
Memphis, TN 38132
(901) 332-1130

Radisson Memphis Airport
2411 Winchester Road
Memphis, TN 38116
(901) 332-2370

Nashville

Doubletree Nashville
315 4th Avenue North
Nashville, TN 37219
(615) 244-8200

Holiday Inn Select Vanderbilt
2613 West End Avenue
Nashville, TN 37203
(615) 327-4707

Loews Vanderbilt Plaza
2100 West End Avenue
Nashville, TN 37203
(615) 320-1700

Hilton Suites Nashville Downtown
121 Fourth Avenue
Nashville, TN 37201
(615) 620-1000

Renaissance Nashville
611 Commerce Street
Nashville, TN 37203
(615) 255-8400

Sheraton Nashville Downtown
Hotel
623 Union Street
Nashville, TN 37219
(615) 742-6030

Maxwell House Hotel Nashville
2025 MetroCenter Blvd.
Nashville, TN 37228
(615) 259-4343

Holiday Inn Select
2200 Elm Hill Pike
Nashville, TN 37214
(615) 883-9770

Nashville Airport Marriott
600 Marriott Drive
Nashville, TN 37214
(615) 889-9300

Sheraton Music City
777 McGavock Pike
Nashville, TN 37214
(615) 885-2200

TEXAS

Amarillo

Ambassador Hotel
3100 I-40 West
Amarillo, TX 79102
(806) 358-6161

Fifth Season Inn
6801 Interstate 40 West
Amarillo, TX 79106
(806) 358-7881

Clarion Hotel Amarillo Airport
7909 Interstate 40 East
Amarillo, TX 79118
(806) 373-3303

Austin

Austin Marriott at the Capitol
701 East 11th Street
Austin, TX 78701
(512) 478-1111

Driskill Hotel
604 Brazos Street
Austin, TX 78701
(512) 474-5911

Embassy Suites Downtown
300 South Congress Avenue
Austin, TX 78704
(512) 469-9000

Four Seasons Hotel Austin
98 San Jacinto Blvd.
Austin, TX 78701
(512) 478-4500

Hilton Austin
500 East 4th Street
Austin, TX 78701
(512) 482-8000

OMNI Austin Hotel—Downtown
700 San Jacinto & 8th Street
Austin, TX 78701
(512) 476-3700

Embassy Suites Austin North
5901 North IH-35
Austin, TX 78723
(512) 454-8004

Hilton Austin North
6000 Middle Fiskville Road
Austin, TX 78752
(512) 451-5757

OMNI Austin Hotel Southpark
4140 Governors Row
Austin, TX 78744
(512) 448-2222

Renaissance Austin
9721 Arboretum Blvd.
Austin, TX 78759
(512) 343-2626

Corpus Christi

Holiday Inn Emerald Beach
1102 South Shoreline
Corpus Christi, TX 78401
(361) 883-5731

OMNI Corpus Christi Hotel
  Bayfront & Marina Towers
900 North Shoreline Blvd.
Corpus Christi, TX 78401
(361) 886-3535

Ramada Hotel Bayfront
601 North Water Street
Corpus Christi, TX 78401
(361) 882-8100

Port Royal
6317 State Highway 361
Port Aransas, TX 78373
(316) 749-5011

Radisson Beach Hotel
3200 Surfside Blvd.
Corpus Christi, TX 78403
(361) 883-9700

Dallas

Adam's Mark Dallas
400 North Olive Street
Dallas, TX 75201
(214) 922-0392

Embassy Suites Market Center
2727 Stemmons Freeway
Dallas, TX 75207
(214) 630-5332

Holiday Inn Market Center
1955 Market Center Blvd.
Dallas, TX 75207
(214) 747-9551

Hotel Adolphus
1321 Commerce Street
Dallas, TX 75202
(214) 742-8200

Hyatt Regency Dallas at Reunion
300 Reunion Blvd.
Dallas, TX 75207
(214) 712-7265

Le Meridian Dallas
650 North Pearl Street
Dallas, TX 75201
(214) 979-9000

Renaissance Dallas Hotel
2222 Stemmons Freeway
Dallas, TX 75207
(214) 631-2222

The Fairmont Hotel Dallas
1717 North Akard Street
Dallas, TX 75201
(214) 720-5293

Westin Park Central
12720 Merit Drive
Dallas, TX 75251
(972) 385-3000

Wyndham Anatole
2201 Stemmons Freeway
Dallas, TX 75207
(214) 761-7209

Crowne Plaza North Dallas
14315 Midway Road
Addison, TX 75001
(972) 980-8877

Dallas Addison Marriott Quorum by the Galleria
14901 Dallas Parkway
Dallas, TX 75254
(972) 687-7490

Doubletree at Lincoln Center
5410 LBJ Freeway
Dallas, TX 75240
(972) 934-8400

Hilton Dallas Parkway
4801 LBJ Freeway
Dallas, TX 75244
(972) 661-3600

Hotel Intercontinental Dallas
15201 Dallas Parkway
Addison, TX 75001
(972) 789-3040

Sheraton Park Central Dallas Hotel
7750 LBJ Freeway
Dallas, TX 75251
(972) 233-4421

Crowne Plaza Dallas Market Center
7050 North Stemmons Parkway
Dallas, TX 75247
(214) 630-8500

Hyatt Regency DFW Airport
P.O. Box 619014, International Parkway
Dallas, TX 75261
(972) 453-1234

Radisson Hotel Dallas
1893 West Mockingbird Lane
Dallas, TX 75235
(214) 630-2523

Ramada Inn Texas Stadium/ Love Field
1055 Regal Row
Dallas, TX 75247
(214) 634-8550

Fort Worth

Radisson Plaza Fort Worth
815 Main Street
Fort Worth, TX 76102
(817) 870-2100

Renaissance Worthington Hotel
200 Main Street
Fort Worth, TX 76102
(817) 870-1000

Green Oaks Hotel
6901 West Freeway
Fort Worth, TX 76116
(817) 738-7311

Holiday Inn Fort Worth North
2540 Meacham Blvd.
Fort Worth, TX 76106
(817) 625-9911

Holiday Inn Fort Worth South
100 Altamesa East Blvd.
Fort Worth, TX 76134
(817) 759-4610

Westin Beechwood Fort Worth
3300 Championship Parkway
Fort Worth, TX 76177
(817) 961-0800

Marriott Dallas/Fort Worth Airport South
4151 Centreport Drive
Fort Worth, TX 76155
(817) 358-1700

Irving

Dallas Marriott Las Colinas
223 West Las Colinas Blvd.
Irving, TX 75039
(972) 831-0000

OMNI Mandalay Las Colinas
221 East Las Colinas Blvd.
Irving, TX 75039
(972) 556-0800

Embassy Suites DFW Airport, South
4650 West Airport Freeway
Irving, TX 75062
(972) 790-0093

Harvey DFW Airport
4545 West John Carpenter Freeway
Irving, TX 75063
(972) 929-4500

Holiday Inn Select DFW Airport North
4441 Highway 114 at Esters Blvd.
Irving, TX 75063
(972) 929-8181

Holiday Inn Select DFW Airport South
4440 West Airport Freeway
Irving, TX 75062
(972) 399-1010

Marriott DFW Airport North
8440 Freeport Parkway
Irving, TX 75063
(972) 929-8800

El Paso

Camino Real Hotel
101 South El Paso Street
El Paso, TX 79901
(915) 534-3060

Marriott El Paso
1600 Airway Blvd.
El Paso, TX 79925
(915) 774-6947

Houston

Doubletree Hotel at Allen Center
400 Dallas Street
Houston, TX 77002
(713) 759-0202

Four Seasons Houston
1300 Lamar Street
Houston, TX 77010
(713) 650-1300

Hyatt Regency Houston
1200 Louisiana Street
Houston, TX 77002
(713) 654-1234

Marriott Medical Center Hotel
Houston
6580 Fannin Street
Houston, TX 77030
(713) 796-0080

Renaissance Houston Hotel
6 Greenway Plaza East
Houston, TX 77046
(713) 629-1200

Adam's Mark Hotel Houston
2900 Briarpark Drive
Houston, TX 77042
(713) 978-7400

Best Western Park Place Suites
1400 Old Spanish Trail
Houston, TX 77054
(713) 796-1000

Hilton Houston Southwest
6780 Southwest Freeway
Houston, TX 77074
(713) 735-6106

Holiday Inn Astrodome
8111 Kirby Drive
Houston, TX 77054
(713) 790-1900

Holiday Inn Hotel & Suites Galleria
7787 Katy Freeway
Houston, TX 77024
(713) 681-5000

Intercontinental Houston
2222 West Loop South
Houston, TX 77459
(713) 627-7600

Marriott West Loop Galleria
1750 West Loop South
Houston, TX 77027
(713) 624-1512

Holiday Inn Intercontinental
15222 John F. Kennedy Blvd.
Houston, TX 77007
(281) 449-2311

Houston Marriott Hobby Airport
9100 Gulf Freeway
Houston, TX 77017
(713) 943-7979

Marriott Houston Airport
18700 JFK Blvd.
Houston, TX 77032
(281) 443-2310

Marriott North Greenspoint
Houston
255 North Sam Houston
  Parkway East
Houston, TX 77060
(281) 875-4000

Sheraton North Houston Hotel
15700 JFK Blvd.
Houston, TX 77032
(281) 969-1225

Wyndham Greenspoint
12400 Greenspoint Drive
Houston, TX 77060
(281) 875-2222

San Antonio

Adam's Mark San Antonio
Riverwalk
111 Pacan Street. East
San Antonio, TX 78205
(210) 354-2800

Four Points by Sheraton—
Riverwalk North
110 Lexington Avenue
San Antonio, TX 78205
(210) 223-9461

Hilton Palacio Del Rio
200 South Alamo Street
San Antonio, TX 78205
(210) 222-1400

Holiday Inn Riverwalk
217 North Saint Mary
San Antonio, TX 78205
(210) 272-2512

Hyatt Regency San Antonio
123 Losoya Street
San Antonio, TX 78205
(210) 222-1234

La Mansion Del Rio
112 College Street
San Antonio, TX 78205
(210) 518-1000

Marriott Rivercenter
101 Bowie Street
San Antonio, TX 78205
(210) 223-1000

The Westin Riverwalk
420 West Market Street
San Antonio, TX 78205
(210) 224-6500

Menger Hotel
204 Alamo Plaza
San Antonio, TX 78205
(210) 223-4361

OMNI San Antonio
9821 Colonnade Blvd.
San Antonio, TX 78230
(210) 691-8888

Hilton San Antonio Airport
611 Northwest Loop 410
San Antonio, TX 78216
(210) 377-4610

UTAH

Ogden

Holiday Inn Express Hotel
& Suites
2245 South 1200 West
Ogden, UT 84401
(801) 392-5000

Ogden Marriott
247 24th Street
Ogden, UT 84401
(801) 627-1190

Salt Lake City

Grand America Hotel
555 South Main Street
Salt Lake City, UT 84111
(801) 258-6790

Hilton Salt Lake City Center
255 Southwest Temple
Salt Lake City, UT 84101
(801) 328-2000

Holiday Inn—Downtown
999 South Main Street
Salt Lake City, UT 84111
(801) 359-8600

Hotel Monaco Salt Lake City
15 West 200 South
Salt Lake City, UT 84101
(801) 595-0000

Little America Hotel
500 South Main Street
Salt Lake City, UT 84101
(801) 596-5800

Marriott Salt Lake City—Downtown
75 South West Temple
Salt Lake City, UT 84101
(801) 531-0800

Sheraton City Centre Hotel Salt Lake
City
150 West 500 South
Salt Lake City, UT 84101
(801) 532-3344

Wyndham Hotel Salt Lake City
215 West South Temple
Salt Lake City, UT 84101
(801) 531-7500

Salt Lake City Marriott University Park
480 Wakara Way
Salt Lake City, UT 84108
(801) 581-1000

Hilton Salt Lake City
5151 Wiley Post Way
Salt Lake City, UT 84116
(801) 539-1515

VERMONT

Smugglers' Notch

Smugglers' Notch Resort
4323 Vermont Route 108 South
Smugglers' Notch, VT 84111
(800) 521-0536

Stowe

Topnotch at Stowe Resort & Spa
4000 Mountain Road
Stowe, VT 05672
(802) 253-6413

Trapp Family Lodge
700 Trapp Hill Road
Stowe, VT 05672
(802) 253-8511

VIRGINIA

Alexandria

Hilton Alexandria Old Town
1767 King Street
Alexandria, VA 22314
(703) 837-0440

Radisson Hotel Old Town
901 North Fairfax Street
Alexandria, VA 22314
(703) 683-6000

Sheraton Suites Alexandria
801 North Saint Asaph Street
Alexandria, VA 22314
(703) 836-4700

Embassy Suites
1900 Diagonal Road
Alexandria, VA 22314
(703) 684-5900

Hilton Alexandria Mark Center
5000 Seminary Road
Alexandria, VA 22311
(703) 845-1010

Arlington

Marriott Crystal City
1999 Jefferson Davis Highway
Arlington, VA 22202
(703) 920-3230

Marriott Key Bridge
1401 Lee Highway
Arlington, VA 22209
(703) 524-6400

Four Points By Sheraton Washington
D.C.—Pentagon
2480 South Glebe Road at I-395
Arlington, VA 22206
(703) 682-5500

Hyatt Arlington at Key Bridge
1325 Wilson Blvd.
Arlington, VA 22209
(703) 525-1234

Crystal Gateway Marriott
1700 Jefferson Davis Highway
Arlington, VA 22202
(703) 920-3230

Doubletree Hotel Crystal
City
300 Army Navy Drive
Arlington, VA 22202
(703) 416-4100

Embassy Suites
1300 Jefferson Davis Highway
Arlington, VA 22202
(703) 979-9799

Hilton Crystal City at National
Airport
2399 Jefferson Davis Highway
Arlington, VA 22202
(703) 418-6800

Hyatt Regency Crystal City
2799 Jefferson Davis Highway
Arlington, VA 22202
(703) 418-7230

Ritz-Carlton Pentagon City
1250 South Hayes Street
Arlington, VA 22202
(703) 415-5000

Sheraton Crystal City
1800 Jefferson Davis Highway
Arlington, VA 22202
(703) 769-3945

Sheraton National Hotel
900 South Orme Street
Arlington, VA 22204
(703) 521-1900

Herndon

Hilton Washington Dulles Airport
13869 Park Center Road
Herndon, VA 20171
(703) 478-2900

Hyatt Dulles
2300 Dulles Corner Blvd.
Herndon, VA 20171
(703) 713-1234

Norfolk

Norfolk Waterside Marriott
235 East Main Street
Norfolk, VA 23510
(757) 628-6440

Radisson Hotel Norfolk
700 Monticello Avenue
Norfolk, VA 23510
(757) 627-5555

Sheraton Norfolk Waterside
Hotel
777 Waterside Drive
Norfolk, VA 23510
(757) 622-6664

Hilton Norfolk Airport
1500 North Military Highway
Norfolk, VA 23502
(757) 466-8000

Richmond

Marriott Richmond
500 East Broad Street
Richmond, VA 23219
(804) 643-3400

OMNI Richmond
100 South 12th Street
Richmond, VA 23219
(804) 344-7000

The Jefferson Hotel
101 West Franklin Street at
   Adams Street
Richmond, VA 23220
(804) 788-8000

Embassy Suites Hotel Richmond—
The Commerce Center
2925 Emerywood Parkway
Richmond, VA 23294
(804) 672-8585

Holiday Inn Select Koger Center
1021 Koger Center Blvd.
Richmond, VA 23235
(804) 897-1405

Sheraton Richmond West
6624 West Broad Street
Richmond, VA 23230
(804) 285-2000

Holiday Inn Richmond Airport
5203 Williamsburg Road
Sandston, VA 23150
(804) 222-6450

Wyndham Hotel Richmond Airport
4700 South Laburnum Avenue
Richmond, VA 23231
(804) 226-4300

Virginia Beach

Doubletree Virginia Beach Hotel
1900 Pavilion Drive
Virginia Beach, VA 23451
(757) 422-8900

Holiday Inn Executive Center
5655 Greenwich Road
Virginia Beach, VA 23462
(757) 499-4400

Holiday Inn Sunspree Resort
39th & Oceanfront
Virginia Beach, VA 23451
(757) 428-1711

Ramada Plaza Resort Oceanfront
5700 Atlantic Avenue
Virginia Beach, VA 23451
(757) 428-7025

The Cavalier
Oceanfront at 42nd Street
Virginia Beach, VA 23451
(757) 425-8555

Virginia Beach Resort Hotel &
Conference Center
2800 Shore Drive
Virginia Beach, VA 23451
(757) 481-9000

Williamsburg

Holiday Inn Patriot & Conference
Center
3032 Richmond Road
Williamsburg, VA 23185
(757) 565-2600

Kingsmill Resort & Conference
Center
1010 Kingsmill Road
Williamsburg, VA 23185
(757) 253-3948

Colonial Williamsburg Hotel
P.O. Box 1776
Williamsburg, VA 23187
(757) 220-7600

Marriott Williamsburg
50 Kingsmill Road
Williamsburg, VA 23185
(757) 220-2500

WASHINGTON

Spokane

Doubletree Hotel Spokane City
Center
North 322 Spokane Falls Court
Spokane, WA 99201
(509) 455-9600

Westcoast Grand Hotel at the Park
West 303 North River Drive
Spokane, WA 99201
(509) 459-6111

Westcoast Ridpath Hotel
515 West Sprague Avenue
Spokane, WA 99201
(509) 459-6111

Westcoast River Inn
700 North Division Street
Spokane, WA 99202
(509) 323-2572

Doubletree Hotel Spokane Valley
1100 North Sullivan Road
Veradale, WA 99037
(509) 922-6229

Bellevue

Bellevue Hilton
100 112th Avenue Northeast
Bellevue, WA 98004
(425) 455-3330

Best Western Bellevue Inn
11211 Main Street
Bellevue, WA 98004
(425) 455-5240

Meydenbauer Center
11100 Northeast 6th Street
Bellevue, WA 98004
(425) 450-3721

Doubletree Bellevue Center
818 112th Avenue Northeast
Bellevue, WA 98004
(425) 455-1515

Doubletree Hotel Bellevue
300 112th Avenue, Southeast
Bellevue, WA 98004
(425) 455-1300

Hyatt Regency Bellevue
900 Bellevue Way Northeast
Bellevue, WA 98004
(425) 462-1234

Seattle

Aljoya Conference Center
3920 Northeast 41st Street
Seattle, WA 98005
(206) 268-7091

Crowne Plaza Hotel Seattle
1113 6th Avenue
Seattle, WA 98101
(206) 464-1980

Elliott Grand Hyatt Seattle
721 Pine Street
Seattle, WA 98101
(206) 774-6300

Four Seasons Olympic
411 University Street
Seattle, WA 98101
(206) 287-4051

Hilton Seattle
1301 6th & University
Seattle, WA 98111
(206) 695-6036

Renaissance Madison
515 Madison Street
Seattle, WA 98104
(206) 583-0300

Sheraton Seattle Hotel & Towers
1400 6th Avenue
Seattle, WA 98101
(206) 389-5735

The Edgewater
2411 Alaskan Way, Pier 67
Seattle, WA 98121
(206) 269-4565

West Seattle Hotel
1112 Fourth Avenue
Seattle, WA 98101
(206) 264-6125

Warwick Hotel Seattle
401 Lenora
Seattle, WA 98121
(206) 443-4300

Westin Seattle
1900 5th Avenue
Seattle, WA 98101
(206) 727-5876

Embassy Suites Hotel Seattle—
North
20610 44th Avenue West
Lynnwood, WA 98036
(425) 775-2500

Doubletree Guest Suites Seattle
16500 Southcenter Parkway
Seattle, WA 98188
(206) 575-8220

Doubletree Hotel Seattle Airport
18740 International Blvd.
Seattle, WA 98188
(206) 433-1881

Embassy Suites Hotel Seattle—Tacoma
International Airport
15920 West Valley Highway
Seattle, WA 98188
(425) 227-8844

Hilton Seattle Airport & Conference
Center
17620 Pacific Highway South
Seattle, WA 98188
(206) 244-4800

Marriott Sea-Tac Airport
3201 South 176th Street
Seattle, WA 98188
(206) 241-2000

WEST VIRGINIA
Charleston

Holiday Inn Charleston House
600 Kanawha Blvd. East
Charleston, WV 25301
(304) 344-4092

Marriott Town Center Charleston
200 Lee Street East
Charleston, WV 25301
(304) 345-6500

White Sulphur Springs

The Greenbrier
300 West Main Street
White Sulphur Springs, WV 24986
(304) 536-1110

WISCONSIN
Green Bay

Regency Suites
333 Main Street
Green Bay, WI 54301
(920) 432-4555

Lake Geneva

Grand Geneva Resort & Spa
7036 Grand Geneva Way Highway
   50 & Highway 12
Lake Geneva, WI 53147
(262) 248-8811

Interlaken Resort & Country SPA
West 4240 Highway 50
Lake Geneva, WI 53147
(262) 248-9121

Madison

Best Western Inn on the Park
22 South Carroll Street
Madison, WI 53703
(608) 257-8811

Hilton Madison Monona
Terrace
9 East Wilson Street
Madison, WI 53703
(608) 255-5100

Madison Concourse Hotel &
   Governor's Club
One West Dayton Street
Madison, WI 53703
(608) 257-6000

Sheraton Madison Hotel
706 John Nolen Drive
Madison, WI 53713
(608) 251-2300

Marriott Madison West
1313 John Q. Hammons Drive
Middleton, WI 53562
(608) 831-2000

Milwaukee

Hilton Milwaukee City Center
509 West Wisconsin Avenue
Milwaukee, WI 53203
(414) 271-7250

Holiday Inn City Center Milwaukee
611 West Wisconsin Avenue
Milwaukee, WI 53203
(414) 273-2950

Hyatt Regency Milwaukee
333 West Kilbourn Avenue
Milwaukee, WI 53203
(414) 276-1234

Pfister Hotel
424 East Wisconsin Avenue
Milwaukee, WI 53202
(414) 273-8222

Ramada Inn Civic Center
633 West Michigan Street
Milwaukee, WI 53203
(414) 272-8410

Wyndham Milwaukee Center
139 East Kilbourn Avenue
Milwaukee, WI 53202
(414) 291-4761

WYOMING

Casper

Holiday Inn Casper
300 West F Street
Casper, WY 82601
(307) 234-5362

Parkway Plaza Hotel & Convention
Centre
123 West East Street
Casper, WY 82601
(307) 235-1777

Radisson Hotel Casper
800 North Poplar Street
Casper, WY 82601
(307) 266-6000

Jackson Hole

Jackson Hole Resort Lodging
P.O. Box 510
Jackson Hole, WY 83025
(307) 733-3990

Jackson Lake Lodge
P.O. Box 250
Moran, WY 83013
(307) 543-3005

Snake River Lodge & Spa
7710 Granite Loop Road
Teton Village, WY 83025
(307) 732-6000

Snow King Resort
P.O. Box SKI
Jackson, WY 83001
(307) 733-5200

Speakers Bureaus in the United States

State	Company	Phone	Web site
AL	Sycamore International, L.L.C.	(256) 765-0000	http://www.sycamoreinternational.com/contact_us.htm
AZ	Gold Stars Speakers Bureau	(520) 742-4384	http://www.goldstars.com
AZ	New Information Presentations	(480) 967-6070	http://www.newinformation.com/
AZ	Look Who's Talking Speakers Bureau	(480) 722-2525	http://www.lookwho.com/ http://www.dirgroup.com/
AZ	Merestone Unique Speakers Bureau	(480) 945-4631	http://www.UNIQUESPEAKERSBUREAU.COM/ http://www.merestone.com/mainpage/uniqspek.html
AZ	Equanimity, A Life Balance	(602) 765-9984	http://www.alifebalance.com
CA	Agency for Speakers & Entertainers	(760) 323-4204	http://www.challengetomorrow.com/agency/index.html
CA	Jostens Speakers Bureau	(925) 831-1229	http://www.jostensspeakersbureau.com/
CA	World Class Speakers Bureau	(818) 991-5400	http://www.speak.com
CA	Bernstein & Associates, Inc.	(858) 459-8553	http://www.ibaspeakernet.com/
CA	Clean Comedians	(714) 670-1929	http://www.cleancomedians.com/
CA	That's Entertainment International	(714) 693-9300	http://www.teientertainment.com/

State	Company	Phone	Web site
CA	BMI—Barnes Marketing Inc.	(949) 768-2942	http://www.barnesmarketing.com/speaking/index.html
CA	SPEAKER SERVICES: Speakers, Authors and Entertainers for Free and Fee	(310) 822-4922	http://www.speakerservices.com/
CA	Nationwide Speakers Bureau	(310) 273-8807	http://www.nationwidespeakers.com/
CA	Prime Time Speakers Bureau	(707) 765-5959	http://www.primetimespeakers.com/
CA	Speakers Corner	(310) 230-2242	http://www.speakerscornerbureau.com http://www.FindMeASpeaker.com
CA	Black Speakers On-line	(310) 671-7136	http://www.blackspeakers.net/
CA	Extreme Connection	(415) 331-0416	http://www.extremeconnection.net/
CA	Patterson & Associates	(818) 882-8700	http://www.pattersonandassociates.com
CA	Blanchard Speakers Bureau	(760) 489-5005	http://www.kenblanchard.com/speakers/index.cfm
CA	Keynote Speakers Inc.	(650) 325-8711	http://www.keynotespeakers.com
CA	LectureAgent.com	(415) 453-7357	http://www.lectureagent.com/
CA	Speak Inc. Speakers & Trainers Bureau	(858) 457-9880	http://www.speakinc.com/index_alt.html
CA	Great Speakers!	(707) 463-1081	http://www.GreatSpeakers.com/
CA	Dynamic Speakers, Inc.	(818) 889-1134	http://www.dynamicspeakers.com/
CA	O.C. Speakers Bureau	(310) 313-6764	http://www.ocspeakers.com/
CA	Key Speakers Bureau	(949) 675-7856	http://www.keyspeakers.com
CA	Mulligan Management Celebrity Look-Alikes	(818) 752-9474	http://lookalikes.net/home.html
CA	Allstar Alliance	(760) 597-4000	http://www.allstaralliance.com/speakers/bureau.htm

State	Company	Phone	Web site
CA	Hudson Agency	(925) 935-2005	http://www.speakersearch.com/html/aboutframes.html
CA	Hall Star Speakers & Talent	(661) 943-4589	http://www.hallstar.net/about.html
CA	Speakers Platform Prometheon	(415) 920-9027	http://www.speaking.com/
CA	Convention Connection & Speakers R Us	(310) 454-3164	http://www.speakersrus.com http://www.conventionconnection.net
CA	Golden Gate International Speakers Bureau	(760) 345-2861	http://www.ggisb.com/
CA	Sacramento Speakers Bureau International	(916) 962-7422	http://www.sacspeakers.com
CA	SS—Speakers Source	(818) 776-1244	http://www.speakerssource.com/
CA	Strictly Speakers—C.D. Lilly, Inc.	(760) 340-1652	http://www.strictlyspeakers.com/ http://www.cdlilly.com
CA	BASA—Bay Area Speakers Bureau	(510) 655-9494	http://www.bay-area-speakers.com/
CA	Steven Barclay Agency	(707) 773-0654	http://www.barclayagency.com/
CA	Keynote Resource	(805) 966-6465	http://www.keynoteresource.com/
CA	Bay Area Speakers	(650) 759-3628	http://www.bayareaspeakers.com
CA	America's Top Performers & Aviation Speakers Bureau	(949) 498-2498	http://www.aviationspeakers.com/
CA	Speakers Bureau Unlimited & Strickly Speakers	(909) 244-1885	http://www.lillygribow.com http://www.strictlyspeakers.com/ http://www.capcityspeakers.com/
CA	SBSB—Santa Barbara Speakers Bureau	(805) 682-7474	http://www.speakingpros.com
CA	Damon Brooks Associates	(805) 604-9017	http://www.damonbrooks.com

State	Company	Phone	Web site
CA	BigSpeak / Consciousness Unlimited Speakers Bureau	(805) 569-0654	http://www.BigSpeak.com, http://www.consciousU.com
CA	International Celebrity Images	(818) 780-4433	http://www.international celebrityimages.com/
CA	SME: Sports Marketing & Entertainment Inc.	(310) 207-2233	http://www.smenet.com/key note_list.php
CA	Bravo Speakers Bureau	(707) 935-6723	http://www.bravospeakers bureau.com/
CA	American Governance & Leadership Group	(909) 336-1586	http://www.americangover nance.com/speakers express.html
CA	Blue Feather Management	(858) 292-8994	http://www.visionaryvoices. com
CA	Allen Agency, Inc.— Speaker Booking Service	(310) 456-0049	http://www.speakerbooking. com/
CA	RTA—Roth Talent Associates	(530) 792-0162	http://www.rothtalent.com/
CA	SG Celebrity Productions	(818) 776-9200	http://www.sgcelebrityprod uctions.com/contact.html
CA	Speak Out—Institute for Democratic Education and Culture	(510) 601-0182	http://www.speakersand artists.org/
CA	ChristianYouthSpeaker s.com		http://www.christianyouth speakers.com/
CA	African American Speakers Bureau! (AASB)	(877) 467-1735	http://www.aasb.net/
CA	Athletic Appearance	(619) 282-1482	http://www.athleticappear ance.com/frameset.php? page=3
CA	Celebrity Talent International		http://www.celebritytalent. net
CA	EXCELLENCE IN PRESENTATIONS	(916) 687-8486	http://www.galaxymall.com/ services/leadership_training
CA	INNOVATION NETWORK	(805) 886-1491	http://www.thinksmart.com
CA	JUSTICE FOR ALL SPEAKERS	(818) 762-4422	http://www.justiceforall speakers.com

State	Company	Phone	Web site
CA	SAN DIEGO SPEAKERS NETWORK	(760) 476-2788	http://www.speakersnet.com/
CA	Zaring–Cioffi Entertainment, LLC	(661) 294-9999	http://www.zcentertainment.com/
CA	CCT, Inc.—Contracted Computer Training	(310) 827-0303	http://www.treelinetraining.com/
CO	Integrity International Speakers Bureau	(720) 842-0600	http://www.integrityisb.com
CO	Lecture Management Bureau	(719) 380-9909	http://www.lecturemanagement.com
CO	Brooks International Speakers Bureau	(303) 825-8700	http://brooksinternational.com/ http://www.hirepublicspeakers.com/
CO	Taylor Made Events & Speakers	(303) 979-9373	http://www.taylormadeevents.com
CO	Rickie Hall & Associates Speakers Bureau	(303) 444-4508	http://www.rickiehall.com/
CO	JWA Entertainment & Speakers Bureau	(303) 469-3313	http://www.jwa-e.com
CO	Ascend Coaching	(303) 979-0319	http://www.AscendCoaching.com/speakers.html
CO	TAYLORED TRAINING	(303) 733-6171	http://www.tayloredtraining.com
CO	TreeLine Training	(800) 288-1962 (303) 544-1930	http://www.treelinetraining.com/
CT	Speakers Home Exclusive	(203) 226-0199	http://www.speakershome.com/
CT	The Motivators	(203) 454-7203	http://www.motivatorsconference.com/HTML_pgs/Speakers/speaker.htm
CT	Tanya Bickley Enterprises	(203) 966-5216	http://www.bickley.com/authors.html
CT	Goodman Speakers Bureau	(860) 687 1116	http://www.goodmanspeakersbureau.com
CT	Wolfman Productions	(800) 735-4933	http://www.wolfmanproductions.com
CT	Best Bookings Agency	(203) 740-9134	http://www.bestbookings.com/

State	Company	Phone	Web site
CT	Magicorp Productions		http://www.magicorppro ductions.com/index2.html
CT	STEINER TALENT	(213) 319-0050	http://steinertalent.com/ about.html
CT	SPEAKERS' CORNER	(203) 929-4295	http://www.thespeakers corner.net
DC	National News Speakers' Bureau	(202) 638-7468	http://www.Nationalnews speakers.com/
DC	Leading Authorities, Inc.		http://www.leading authorities.com
DC	Du Plain International Speakers Bureau	(202) 244-3338	http://www.duplain.com/
DC	Accuracy in Media Speaker's Bureau	(202) 364-4401	http://www.aim.org/
DC	Podium Prose	(856) 428-9475 (202) 857-9793	http://www.podiumprose. com/
DC	PLAYERS INC., NFL Players Association	(202) 463-2200	http://www.playersinc.com/
DC	United States Holocaust Memorial Museum Speakers Bureau	(202) 314-7824	http://www.ushmm.org/ museum/speakers/ content.php
DE	LLUMINARI, INC.	(302) 631-2672	http://www.lluminari.com/ all_speakers.htm
FL	Superstars-Speakers Resource Bureau	(904) 264-1515	http://www.superstars-inc.com/
FL	American Speakers Bureau	(407) 826-4248	http://www.speakersbureau. com/ http://www.amotivational speakersbureau.com/
FL	Happy Talk International	(386) 441-819	http://www.HappyTalk.org/
FL	Incredible Speakers Bureau	(407) 297-1090 (321) 947-2099 877-Speakwell	http://incrediblespeakers. com/
FL	Florida Speakers Bureau, Inc.	(813) 948-3222	http://www.trainingforum. com/Speakers/fsb.html
FL	Dick Hall Productions Inc.	(914) 747-9010	http://www.dhall.com
FL	Access to Experts Speakers Bureau	(305) 535-8199	http://accesstoexperts.com/

State	Company	Phone	Web site
FL	Commanding View	(727) 791-7338	http://www.commanding-view.com/consultants/coach.asp
FL	Global Connections Speakers Bureau	(954) 972-5515	http://www.global connections.com/
FL	Pro Legends Speakers Bureau NFL ALUMNI	(954) 630-2100, ext. 210	http://www.nflalumni.org
FL	EXPERT Speakers Bureau	(352) 438-0261	http://www.expertspeaker.com/ http://www.expertmagazine.com/
FL	Richard Lutz Entertainment Agency	(402) 475-1900	http://www.lutzagency.com/index.htm
FL	Golfpodium / Sportspodium	(561) 776-9112	http://www.golfpodium.com/
FL	T. Skorman Productions	(407) 895-3000	http://www.TalentAgency.com/
GA	Wow! Solutions, Inc.	(770) 781-2355	http://www.wowspeakers.com/contact.htm
GA	SpeakerConnect USA	(770) 338-8388	http://www.speaker connectusa.com/
GA	The Speaker's House	(770) 844-1370	http://www.speakershouse.com/
GA	PEAK Speakers	(678) 587-9911	http://www.peakspeakers.com/
GA	The Robinson Agency	(770) 736-0775	http://www.therobinson agency.com/
GA	Corporate Talent Discoveries	(404) 355-0990	http://www.ctdiscoveries.com/speakers/
GA	STARS, a division of Orchestrated Events	(770) 438-2204	http://www.orchestrated events.com
GA	The Family Business Speakers Bureau	(866) 738-7529	http://www.efamilybusiness.com
GA	Packaging University Speakers Bureau		http://www.packaging university.com/pkg speakersexpertscon.htm http://www.womenin packaging.org/packaging-speakers.html
GA	Your Event Solution	(770) 945-2160	http://www.4yes.com/Speakers/Speakers.htm

State	Company	Phone	Web site
HI	Hawaii Speaker Bureau	(808) 672-0775 (808) 672-0777 (808) 674-9331	http://www.hawaiispeaker sbureau.com
IA	Midwest Speakers Bureau	(515) 974-8305 (515)-974-8304	http://www.speakernow.com /index2.shtml
IA	Kelling Management Group Speakers Bureau	(515) 402-8255	http://www.kellingmgt. com/
ID	Speaker Spotlight		http://www.speakerspotlight. com/
IL	Lanktree Sports Celebrity Network Inc.	(312) 755-9539 (312) 266-9583	http://www.lanktreesports. com/
IL	Burns Sports Celebrity Services Inc.	(847) 866-9400	http://www.burnssports. com
IL	National Speakers Bureau	(847) 295-1122	http://www.nationalspeakers. com
IL	George O'Hare's All Occasions Speakers Bureau	(630) 323-3565	http://www.allspeak.com/
IL	Ibach & Associates	(847) 590-5302 (847) 922-6686	http://www.www.ibach sportspr.com
IL	Sterling International Speakers Bureau	(847) 577-5000	http://www.sterlingspeakers. com/index.htm
IL	Capitol City Speakers Bureau	(217) 544-8552	http://www.speakingof sports.com/
IL	celebrityFOCUS Sports Marketing Services	(847) 291-0095	http://www.celebrityfocus. com
IL	GR-PR	(630) 789-8555	http://www.gr-pr.com
IN	Americas Best Speakers	(866) 237-8776 (317) 547-4679	http://www.americasbest speakers.com/
IN	Professional Speakers Network	(317) 873-9797	http://www.tillergroup.com
IN	Spotlight Speakers & Entertainment	(317) 377-0250	http://www.spotlightwww. com/
IN	International Entertainment Bureau	(317) 926-7566	http://pages.prodigy.net/ jleonards/
IN	IASB International Assn. of Speakers Bureaus	(317) 297-0872	http://igab.org/
IN	Roland Enterprises Unlimited Bureau	(317) 566-0417	http://www.ustalentnet work.com

State	Company	Phone	Web site
IN	ARREC—Charisma Pros	(317) 462-4245	http://www.charismapros. com/
KS	Five Star Speakers & Trainers	(913) 648-6480	http://www.fivestarspeakers. com
KS	The Bureau of Lectures and Concert Artists, Inc.	(785) 843-9197	http://assemblyline.com/ BOLhome.html
KY	Program Resources	(502) 339-1653	http://www.program resources.com
KY	McKinney Associates	(502) 583-8222	http://www.mckinney speakers.com
KY	Bluegrass Speakers Bureau	(859) 269-2921	http://www.bluegrass speakersbureau.com/
LA	insideSPEAKERS	(504) 569-7930	http://www.insidespeaker. com
MA	Speakers Guild, Inc.	(508) 888-6702	http://www.speakersguild. com
MA	American Program Bureau	(617) 965-6600	http://www.apb-speakers. com
MA	Jodi Solomon Speakers Bureau Assoc Div.	(617) 266-3450	http://www.jodisolomon speakers.com/
MA	MasterMedia Speakers Bureau	(800) 453-2887	http://www.mastermedia speakers.com/
MA	Lordly & Dame, Inc., & Strategic Events Intl.	(617) 482-3593	http://www.lordly.com/ http://www.strategic eventsintl.com
MA	Loretta LaRoche Speakers Network	(508) 746-3998	http://www.lorettalaroche. com/abt_speakers.htm
MA	AEI—American Entertainment International	(617) 731-8521	http://www.aeispeakers. com/
MA	Cassidy & Fishman	(508) 485-8996	http://www.cassidyand fishman.com/
MA	Athlete & Artist Business Collaborative	(617) 916-1202	http://www.collaborative speakers.com
MA	The Lecture Bureau	(617) 492-0355	http://www.thelecturebureau. com/
MA	Learning Circle	(978) 443-0784	http://www.learningcircle. com/ (under construction)
MD	Speakers Worldwide Inc.	(301) 654-1091	http://www.speakersworld wide.com

State	Company	Phone	Web site
MD	InterSpeak	(301) 896-9700	http://www.inter-speak.com
MD	The Sandra Ford Agency	(410) 626-0965	http://www.sandraford agency.com
MD	WEDGEWOOD PRO- DUCTIONS	(301) 621-9600	http://www.wwproductions. com/
ME	Tuller Group Maine Speakers Bureau	(207) 829-4008	http://www.thetullergroup. com/greatspeakers.html
ME	Soldier Creek Associates	(207) 236-7077	http://www.soldiercreek. com/main.html
ME	Entertainment Resources, Inc.		http://www.entertainmaine. com/services.htm#book
MI	Speak Up	(810) 982-0898	http://www.speakup speakerservices.com/
MI	The Yes! Network Bureau	(248) 383-2000	http://www.yesmidwest. com/
MI	Business Speakers Bureau	(616) 455-9637	http://www.business speakersBureau.com
MI	Universal Speakers Bureau	(231) 933-1176	http://www.universal speakers.com
MI	Kivana Productions, Inc.	(586) 826-8201	http://www.kivana.com/ acts/SpeakerMotiv.html
MI	Entertainment Connection	(810) 559-3600	http://www.entertainconnec tion.com/convention.htm
MN	Preferred Speakers	(952) 920-9161	http://www.preferred speakers.com/
MN	The Speakers Bureau Inc.	(612) 942-6768	http://www.thespeakers bureau.com
MN	Podium Professionals	(651) 739-1111	http://www.speakers- bureau.org/
MN	Sensational Meetings, Inc.	(612) 861-5408 (877) 861-5408	http://www.sensational meetings.com
MN	WorkandWellness.com		http://www.workandwell ness.com/
MN	MASSMAN & ASSOCIATES	(320) 259-7108	http://www.massmanasso ciates.com/speakers.htm
MN	THE BARRY AGENCY	(612) 550-0513	http://www.thebarryagency. com/
MO	AMU Speakers Bureau	(800) 255-6734, ext. 6628	http://www.amuniversal. com/ups/speakers/index. htm

State	Company	Phone	Web site
MO	TalentPlus Inc. Speakers Bureau	(314) 421-9400	http://www.talent-plus.com/
NC	Speakers Network, Inc.	(704) 342-0095	http://www.thespeakers network.com/home.asp
NC	The Powerhouse Speakers' Bureau	(704) 548-1131	http://www.powerhouse speakers.com/
NC	Pinnacle Speakers Bureau	(919) 676-8158	http://www.pinnaclespeakers bureau.com
NC	Total Access Speakers Bureau & Lecture Agents Inc.	(800) 532-1413	http://www.totalaccess speakers.com/
NC	CONTENT EVOLU- TION LLC	(919) 942-4941	http://www.contentevolution. net
NC	Wisse, Hollmann & Co.	(919) 832-2323	http://www.whandco.com
NE	Prism Speakers Bureau	(402) 423-1741	http://www.prismspeakers. com
NE	Richard Lutz Entertainment Agency	(402) 475-1900	http://www.lutzagency.com/ index.htm
NH	Get Ahead Pro Speakers Bureau	(800) 943-7747	http://www.getaheadpro.com
NJ	Eagles Talent Connection, Inc.	(973) 313-9800	http://www.EaglesTalent. com/
NJ	W. Colston Leigh Inc.: Leigh Bureau	(908) 253-8600 (908) 253-6033	http://www.leighbureau. com/lbw/
NJ	SRN Business Speakers, Consultants, and Trainers	(201) 963-7764	http://www.srnbusiness. com/
NJ	A Vision in Motion, a unique speakers bureau	(800) 883-4147	http://www.avisioninmotion. com/
NJ	STI Supreme Talent International	(201) 307-0604	http://www.supremetalent. com
NJ	DISTINCT CONCEPTS		http://www.distinctconcepts. com
NJ	ISM	(201) 610-0200	http://www.ismsports.com
NJ	JR ASSOCIATES	(609) 921-6605	http://jrmeetings-speakers. com/
NM	Class Services, Inc.	(505) 899-4283	http://www.classervices.com

State	Company	Phone	Web site
NM	Rodney Stewart & Associates	(505) 822-1113	http://www.rodstewart speakers.com/speakersbure au.html
NV	Silver State Speakers Bureau	(775) 829-0606	http://www.thesilvergroup. com/silver–5.html
NV	American Dreams Speakers Bureau	(702) 732-1971	http://www.usdreams.com
NV	Celebrity Speakers & Entertainment Bureau, Inc.	(702) 367-0331	http://www.speak.com
NV	Las Vegas Executive Speakers Bureau	(702) 889-2657	http://www.LVSpeakers. com/
NV	Motivational-speakers.com	(866) 546-0831	http://www.motivational-speakers.com/
NV	Nationwide Entertainment Services Celebrity Speakers Bureau	(702) 451-8090	http://www.entertainment services.com http://www.celebrityspeakers bureau.com
NV	Geary Eindels Enterprises, Inc.	(702) 222-2300	http://www.corporate comedy.com
NY	Authors Unlimited	(212) 481-8484	http://www.authorsun limited.com/info.html
NY	HUMOR Project Speakers Bureau	(518) 587-0362 (518) 587-8770	http://www.humorproject. com/programs/speakersb. php
NY	Global Entertainment Network East., Inc.	(631) 262-1757	http://www.entertainment pros.com
NY	Motivational and Celebrity Speakers Resource Center	(716) 835-7730	http://speakerresource.com/ 2001/
NY	Harry Walker Agency, Inc.	(646) 227-4900	http://www.HarryWalker. com/
NY	Program Corporation of America	(914) 428-5840, ext. 40	http://www.speakerspca. com/
NY	Empire Entertainment Inc.	(212) 343-0956	http://www.empireentertain ment.com/
NY	The Learning Partnership USA	(212) 687-4141	http://www.tlp.org
NY	Nili London International, LLC (NLI) Speakers Bureau	(845) 708-7884	http://www.nililondon.com/

State	Company	Phone	Web site
NY	IMG New York	(212) 774-6735	http://www.imgspeakers.com/news.asp
NY	Greater Talent Network	(212) 645-4200	http://www.greatertalent.com/
NY	Royce Carlton Inc.	(212) 355-7700	http://www.roycecarlton.com
NY	ICM Artists LTD.	(212) 556-5602	http://www.icmtalent.com/
NY	Jeri Charles Associates	(845) 758-4447	http://www.lecturenow.com/
NY	Celebrity Direct, Inc.	(212) 541-3770	http://www.celebrity-direct.com/speakers.htm
NY	Standpoint Healthcare Speakers		http://www.standpointinc.com/
NY	Soapbox, Inc.	(646) 486-1414	http://www.soapboxinc.com
NY	The Chelsea Forum, Inc.	(212) 945-3100	http://www.chelseaforum.com/
NY	Speakers and Entertainment	(914) 271-5825	http://www.se-speakers.com/
NY	All American Speakers Bureau, LLC	(607) 273-0878	http://www.allamerican speakers.com
NY	A&L Speakers/ Nubian Speakers	(212) 353-9114	http://www.donpedrocookies.com/A&L_speakers_and_consultants_pg1.html
NY	Global Talent Associates	(212) 921-8500	http://www.globaltalent assoc.com
NY	ORMA—Operation Role Models of America, Inc.		http://www.ormaspeakers.org
NY	Power Performers Speakers Bureau	(315) 735-9667	http://www.power performers.com/
NY	Ray Bloch Productions	(202) 347-1010	http://www.raybloch.com/performers.html
NY	Triumph Sports Memorablia and Promotions, Inc.	(718) 477-4050	http://www.football spectacular.com/ http://www.triumphsports.com http://www.getinthegame.com
NY	WASHINGTON SQUARE ARTS	(212) 253-0333	http://www.washington squarearts.com/

State	Company	Phone	Web site
NY	Women's Sports Foundation's Athletes' Speaker Service	(516) 542-4700, ext. 158	http://www.womenssports foundation.org
OH	Speakers Unlimited	(614) 864-3703	http://www.speakers unlimited.com/
OH	Speakers Network	(614) 442-3300	http://www.speakers-network.com
OH	Intermediaries Speakers Bureau, div. N.E. Fried & Associates, Inc.	Calif: (760) 633-4444; Ohio: (614) 766-9800	http://www.nefried.com/ speakers/spkfrmain.cfm
OH	Professional Speakers Bureau International	(614) 841-1776	http://www.terrificspeakers. com/
OH	The Meeting Connection	(614) 888-2568	http://www.the-meeting-connection.com/
OH	Sensational Speakers	(614) 865-0051	http://www.sensational speakers.com/
OK	Gary Good Entertainment & Speakers Bureau	(405) 840-2020	http://www.inervision.com/
OK	Impact Unlimited Speakers Bureau	(918) 749-1749	http://impactunlimited speakers.com/
OK	RICHARD DELA-FONT AGENCY	(918) 455-9000	http://www.delafont.com/ fast_index.htm
OR	Voices, Inc.	(503) 631-7477	http://www.voicesinc.com
OR	Speakers Connection	(503) 233-5977	http://www.speakers connection.com/
OR	Diverse Solutions Speakers Bureau	(503) 245-5588	http://www.diverse-solutions-inc.com/speakers.html
OR	Great Women Speakers	(503) 631-7477	http://www.greatwomen speakers.com/
PA	21st Century Speakers, Inc.	(570) 842-3300	http://www.speakersaccess. com/
PA	Imagination Plus Bureau	(412) 276-0122 (877) 610-6284	http://www.imagination-plus.com/SpkrBur/ spkrpg1.html
PA	ExpertsWhoSpeak	(814) 774-5070	http://www.expertswho speak.org/
PA	RWS Speakers Bureau	(800) 796-3323	http://www.realworld success.com/speakers.html

State	Company	Phone	Web site
PA	Koeberle & Associates Sports and Entertainment Marketing	(412) 788-9550	http://www.kasports.com/celebrity.htm
SC	Speakers International	(843) 361-2433	http://www.speakersinternational.com/
SC	SHEILA GRANT'S INTL. CELEBRITY NETWORK	(843) 722-1950	http://www.icnlive.com/
TN	Ambassador Speakers Bureau	(877) 425-4700, (615) 352-3291	http://www.ambassadoragency.com/
TN	Executive Speakers Bureau	(901) 754-9404	http://www.executivespeakers.com
TN	Great Keynote Speakers / Great Speakers and Trainers	(615) 883-2005	http://www.greatkeynotespeakers.com/ http://www.salesspeakersandtrainers.com
TN	Premiere Speakers Bureau	(615) 261-4000	http://www.premierespeakers.com http://www.corporatespeakers.net
TN	SpeakersQuest	(305) 946-8449	http://www.SpeakersQuest.com/text/membership.htm
TN	Nashville Speakers Bureau	(615) 236-1072	http://www.nashspeakers.com
TN	Everest Speakers Bureau.com	(865) 609-0231	http://www.toddrgreene.com/ http://www.everestspeakersbureau.com http://www.footballspeakers.com
TN	BookASpeaker.com	(865) 429-0252	http://www.BookASpeaker.com/ http://www.insightproject.info
TN	Abacus Speakers Bureau—Barber & Assoc.	(865) 546-0000	http://www.abacusspeakers.com/
TN	Issues Lecture Agency	(615) 320-7679	http://issueslectureagency.com/issues.html
TN	Christian Speakers & Artists Agency	(615) 771-9400	http://www.christianspeakers.com/ http://www.christianartists.com/

State	Company	Phone	Web site
TN	Sports Stars USA	(865) 546-9839	http://www.sportsstarsusa. com/ http://www.abacusspeakers. com/
TN	Lessons In Learning	(615) 273-1070	http://www.lessonsin learning.com/resource_ network/speakers.html
TX	Awesome Speakers	(210) 341-4600	http://www.awesome speakers.com/index.htm
TX	International Speakers Bureau	(214) 744-3885	http://www.isbspeakers.com http://www.international speakers.com/
TX	Personalities & Promotions International	(972) 361-5400	http://www.ppimarketing. com/p_search.asp
TX	Gail Davis & Associates, Inc.	(817) 283-3821	http://www.gdaspotlight. com/index_flash.htm http://www.gaildavisandasso ciates.com/index_flash.htm
TX	Connect the Dots, Inc.	(281) 379-1060	http://www.connectdots.com/
TX	The ESI Group	(972) 578-1900	http://www.theesigroup. com/speakers/index.jsp
TX	Leading Legacy Speakers Bureau	(214) 663-4600	http://www.leadinglegacy speakersbureau.com
TX	Grabow & Associates Bureau	(972) 250-1162	http://www.grabow.biz
TX	American Speakers Association—Bureau	(713) 914-9444	http://www.american speakers.com/
TX	Garrett Speakers International Inc.	(972) 513-0054	http://www.garrettspeakers. com/
TX	Odenwald Connection, Inc.	(972) 496-3902	http://www.odenwaldconnec tion.com/od03001.htm
TX	Ken-Ran Entertainment	(972) 690-6099	http://www.kenran.com/ speakers.html
TX	Space Agency	(281) 333-9500	http://www.thespaceagency. org/
TX	Speakermatch / Simply Speaking, Inc.	(866) 372-8768	http://www.simplyspeaking. com
TX	Motivational and Inspirational Speakers Bureau	(936) 890-6338	http://www.motivational-inspirational-corner.com/ motivational_inspirational_ speakers_bureau.html

State	Company	Phone	Web site
TX	Simply Speaking & Speaker Match	(512) 372-8989	http://www.speakermatch.com http://www.simply-speaking.com/
TX	American Training Associates Int'l.	(512) 346-4177	http://www.amertraining.com
TX	Diversity Speakers	(972) 864-5516	http://www.diversityspeakers.com
TX	MMEA: Marshall Maxwell Entertainment Agency	(713) 522-3514	http://www.marshallmaxwell.com/
TX	Frog Pond Speakers Bureau	(800) 704-3764	http://www.frogpond.com/authorsprofile.cfm
UT	Champions For Life Speakers Bureau	(801) 266-8483	http://www.a-motive.com
UT	Franklin Covey Co.		http://www.franklincovey.com/speakers
UT	Financial Forum—Your Complete Speakers Bureau	(435) 750-0062	http://www.financialspeakers.com
VA	Living History Associates, Ltd.	(804) 788-1493	http://lhaltd.com/speakers/cheatham/
VA	Keppler Associates, Inc. .	(703) 516-4000, Ext. 208	http://www.kepplerassociates.com
VA	Washington Speakers Bureau	(703) 684-0555	http://www.washingtonspeakers.com
VA	Speakers Plus! Worldwide Speakers Bureau	(757) 312-9589	http://www.speakersplus.com
VA	All-Star Agency	(703) 503-9438	http://www.allstaragency.com
VA	Clifford Agency	(703) 847-9711	http://www.cliffordagency.com
VA	OCTAGON	(703) 905-3300	http://www.octagon.com/
WA	Seattle Speakers Bureau—Diamond Productions	(425) 869-1444	http://www.propertymanagementnw.com/speaker/index.html
WA	MJM Speakers Bureau	(509) 443-0184	http://www.mjmspeakers.com
WA	Amplify! Professional Speaker Services	(206) 784-7315	http://www.amplifybureau.com/aboutus.htm
WA	Seattle Bookings	(206) 329-3095	http://www.seattlebookings.com/

State	Company	Phone	Web site
WA	JW Speaker's Bureau LLC	(425) 455-4515	http://www.jwspeakersbureau.com
WA	MPRESS Speakers Bureau	(425) 861-7779	http://www.speakerlinks.com http://www.call4speaker.com http://meetingsrus.com/
WA	MFS Speakers Bureau	(425) 444-4625	http://www.madeforsuccess.com/SpeakersLineup.asp
WI	Speakers & Events-R-Us	(262) 245-6543	http://www.speakersandeventsrus.com
WI	Mortgage Speakers Bureau, Foundation Marketing, Inc.	(715) 426-3647	http://www.mortgagespeakersbureau.com/
WI	Ad Cetera Sports Marketing	(414) 967-7767	http://www.www.dukeroufusgym.com/adcetera.html
WI	Class Act Performing Artists and Speakers, Inc.	(262) 249-0700	http://www.class-act.com/
WI	Speakers Direct	(262) 781-5398	http://www.speakersdirect.us/
WI	PeopleTalk Speakers' Bureau	(888) 290-9558	http://www.peopletalk2000.com/
WI	Contemporary Issues Agency	(800) 843-2179	http://www.ciaspeakers.com

Speakers Bureaus Outside the United States

Country	Bureau	Phone	Web site
Australia	Claxton Speakers & Trainers Bureau	011-61-9909-0033	http://www.claxtonspeakers.com/
Australia	IMG Sydney	(61) (29) 285-1653	http://www.imgspeakers.com.au
Australia	IMG Melbourne	(61) (39) 658-6812	http://www.imgspeakers.com.au
Australia	Speakers Solutions		http://www.speakersolutions.com.au http://www.voicesofintegrity.com

Country	Bureau	Phone	Web site
Australia	Global Speakers & Entertainers Pty. Ltd.	011-61-9956-6956	http://www.global speakers.com.au/
Australia	Celebrity Speakers	011-61-2–9251-1333	http://www.celebrity speakers.com.au/index. asp
Australia	EnterTrainers & Speakers	011-61-2–9299-0644	http://www.espeak. com.au/
Australia	The Learning Partnership Pty.	011-61-2–9233-4141	http://www.tlp.org
Australia	Sydney Office Saxton Speakers Bureau: Harry M. Miller	011-61-2-9231-1900	http://www.saxton.com. au/about.html
Australia	Ovations International Pty. Ltd.	011-61-2–9818-6622	http://www.ovations. com.au/
Australia	Speakers Network International	011-61-29-953-3399	http://www.speaker seeker.com/
Australia	Melbourne Office Saxton Speakers Bureau	011-61-3–9813-2199	http://www.saxton.com. au/
Australia	ICMI SPEAKERS & ENTER-TAINERS OLYMPIC COMMUNI-CATORS	011-61-3–9529-3711	http://www.icm.net.au/
Australia	Great Expecta-tion Speakers & Trainers Bureau	011-07-3844-2277	http://www.greatexpecta tion.com.au/
Australia	Australian Speak-ers Bureau	618 -9388-0211	http://www.Australian Speaker.com
Belgium	European Speakers Bureau	011-32-02-646-1383	http://www.european speakers.com/ indexx.html
Brazil	Palestrarte Speak-ers Bureau	011-5511-5044-656	http://www.palestrarte. com.br/
Canada	Speakers' Corner	(902) 492-8000	http://www.ardenneinter national.com/speakr.htm
Canada	Creative Bound, Inc. Speakers Bureau	(613) 831-3641	http://www.creative bound.com

Country	Bureau	Phone	Web site
Canada	Momentous Speakers Bureau		http://www.momentum learningsystems.com/ bureau.html
Canada	Voices of Experience, div. of Quandary Solutions	(780) 430-9494, ext. 121	http://www.quandary solutions.ab.ca/ speakers/home.html
Canada	Atlantic Speakers Bureau	(506) 465-0990	http://www.atlantic speakersbureau.com/
Canada	Idea Connection Speakers Bureau	(705) 438-5795	http://www.ideacon nection.com/
Canada	CanSpeak Presentations	(705) 741-2992	http://www.canspeak. com/
Canada	Ethos Enterprises Inc.	(416) 399-9223 (905) 473-6841	http://www.ethos.on.ca/
Canada	Pro Speak International Speaker's Bureau	(905) 770-1886	http://www.prospeakers. com/
Canada	Brickenden Speakers Bureau Canadian Speakers	(905) 713-3222	http://www.brickenden. com/
Canada	Outspoken1 Inc.	(905) 713-8962	http://www.outspoken1. com/
Canada	Sports Celebrity Marketing S.C.M. Inc.	(905) 873-8405	http://www.sportscelebs. com
Canada,	Global Speakers Agency	(800) 360-1073	http://www.global speakers.com
Canada	Canadian Speak- ers & Writers Service Ltd.	(416) 921-9691	http://www.KEYSpeakers. com/
Canada	The Celebrity Speakers Intl. Lecture Bureau	(416) 921-4240	http://www.celebrity speakersintl.com/
Canada	Speakers' Spotlight	(416) 345-1559	http://www.speakers.ca/
Canada	David Lavin Agency— Speakers Bureau Int'l	(416) 979-7979	http://www.thelavin agency.com/

Country	Bureau	Phone	Web site
Canada	Speakers Gold		http://www.speakers gold.com
Canada	The Knowledge Bureau, A Division of Evelyn Jacks Productions, Inc.	(204) 953-4760	http://www.knowledge bureau.com/skc/ aboutus.asp
Canada	Success Source International & Dimension 11 Consulting Ltd.	(306) 586-2315 (306) 352-4677	http://www.dimension–11.com/bureau.htm
Canada	MCP Talent	(306) 382-0330	http://www.mcptalent.com
Canada	One Step Beyond Worldwide	(403) 678-5255	http://www.adventure-speakers.com/
Canada	Pinpoint. A Maxibit® Group Company	(877) 541-9177	http://getspeakers.com/
Canada	TALKShop! International	(403) 245-0550	http://www.talkshop speakers.com/
Canada	CanSpeak Presentations	(780) 944-9898	http://www.canspeak. com/
Canada	A-Z Events Inc./Int'l Speakers Bureau of Canada	(604) 931-7635	http://www.a-zevents. com/speaker/index.htm
Canada	NSB—National Speakers Bureau	(604) 734-3663	http://www.nsb.com
Canada	CanSpeak Presentations Ltd.	(604) 986-6887	http://www.canspeak. com/
Canada	CanSpeak	(604) 986-6887	http://www.canspeak. com/
Canada	Reboot Communica-tions, Ltd.	(250) 388-6060	http://www.rebootworld wide.com/keynote.htm
Canada	ProSPEAK International Speakers Bureau	(866) 267-7325 (250) 384-8424	http://www.prospeak. com/

Country	Bureau	Phone	Web site
France	Glamour Speakers	066-356-3933	http://www.glamour speakers.com/index. cfm?lng=en http://www.glamour speakers.com
Ireland	Creative Concepts & Promotions		http://www.ccpireland. com/html/speakers.asp
Netherlands	Nederlandsgroots tesprekersbu- reau—Speakers Academy	011-31-10-433-33- 22	http://www.speakers academy.nl/
New Zealand	Celebrity Speakers (NZ) Ltd.	011-64-9–373-4177	http://www.celebspeakers. com/Templates/ about_us.cfm http://www.csnz.co.nz/ Templates/index.cfm
New Zealand	Speakers New Zealand	64-9–537-5375	http://www.speakers. co.nz
United Kingdom	Speakers Agency	44-1295-760-692	http://www.speakers agency.com/
Scotland	David John Associates	0141-357-0532	http://www.davidjohn associates.co.uk/ presenters.html
Scotland	Tailored Talks	44 (0)1324-832856	http://www.tailoredtalks. com/
Scotland	Open Minds (International Masterclass Speakers)	44-1875-870075	http://www.open- minds.net/
South Africa	Speakers of Note		http://www.speakersof note.co.za/
South Africa	Conferences Speakers International	011-27-11-465- 4447	http://www.conference speakers.co.za/
South Africa	Atlantic Seminars & Cape Speakers International	27 (021) 557-4000	http://www.atlanticnet. co.za/ & http://www.atlanticnet.co .za/cape_speakers.htm
Spain	Nueva Economía Fórum—New Economy Forum Speak- ers Bureau		http://www.nueva economiaforum.com http://www.foronuevae conomia.com

Country	Bureau	Phone	Web site
Spain	Speakers Bureau SL	93 323 8543	http://www.speakers bureau.es
United Kingdom	Excel Speakers	01224 325720	http://www.excelspeakers. com/
United Kingdom	Absolute Speakers	(0845) 458-2581	http://www.absolute-speakers.co.uk/
United Kingdom	Emerald Speakers	+44 0151 630 2489	http://www.Emerald-Speakers.com
United Kingdom	Arena Entertainment	0113 239 2222	http://www.arenaenter tainments.co.uk/ speakers.html
United Kingdom	Commercial Casting	020 7372 0009	http://www.commercial casting.com
United Kingdom	Creative Concepts	08707 404008	http://www.creative-concepts.co.uk/home.htm
United Kingdom	Cunningham Management	0181 233 2824	http://www.cunningham-management.co.uk/ index1.html
United Kingdom	Dave Winslett Associates	0181 668 0531	http://www.davewinslett. com/presenters.htm
United Kingdom	Fammous Faces	01752 844 567	http://www.famousfaces. co.uk/
United Kingdom	Fanfare 3000	0181 429 3000	http://www.fanfare.co.uk
United Kingdom	M & CT Event Management	01531 890 790	http://www.mctevent. co.uk/
United Kingdom	MTC Manage-ment & Media	020 7935 8000	http://www.mtc-uk.com/
United Kingdom	Nic Picot Entertainment	0181 421 2700	http://www.nicpicot. co.uk/
United Kingdom	Performing Artistes	020 7224 0107	http://www.performing artistes.co.uk, http: www.f4group.co.uk
United Kingdom	PVA Entertain-ment Consultants	0117 950 4504	http://www.pva.ltd.uk/ home.htm
United Kingdom	SELECT Speakers Ltd.	01600 712 387	http://www.selects peakers.com/
United Kingdom	Kudos Communi-cations Speak-ers Bureau International	01784 430461	http://www.speakers bureau.co.uk

Country	Bureau	Phone	Web site
United Kingdom	Speakers Corner Associates Ltd.	01753-651-700	http://www.speakerscorner-pinewood.co.uk/
United Kingdom	Speakers UK	0845-458-3707	http://www.speakers-uk.com/
United Kingdom	TLC Casting	020-7659-2337	http://www.tlccasting.com/
United Kingdom	Trading Faces, Ltd.	020-7287-0866	http://www.tradingfaces.co.uk/
United Kingdom	Lipton Parker Entertainments Ltd.	011-44-208-508-7744	http://www.link-connect.co.uk/~link101575/page2.htm#KEYNOTE%20SPEAKERS
United Kingdom	Norman Phillips Agency, Ltd.	011-44-021-308-1267	http://www.normanphillips.co.uk/homepage.htm
United Kingdom	Parliament Communications Ltd.	011-44-1202-242424	http://www.parliamentspeakers.com/index2.asp
United Kingdom	Gordon Poole Agency Ltd.	011-44 1275-463222	http://www.gordonpoole.com
United Kingdom	City Speakers International	020-7247-1193	http://www.cityspeakersinternational.co.uk
United Kingdom	Speakers for Business	011-44-207-929 5559	http://www.sfb.co.uk/cgi-bin/main.cgi?p=home
United Kingdom	Speakers Corner	020-8866-8967	http://www.speakerscorner-uk.com/
United Kingdom	After Dinner Speakers & Comedians Ltd.		http://www.comedians.co.uk
United Kingdom	Power Promotions	0151-230-0070	http://www.powerpromotions.co.uk
United Kingdom	GNP Management Speakers		http://www.gnp.co.uk/speakers.htm
United Kingdom	Norwich Artistes		http://www.norwichartistes.co.uk
United Kingdom	Celebrity Speakers International Limited	441-75-374-7400	http://www.speakers.co.uk/ http://www.csaspeakers.com/
United Kingdom	Easyspeakers	44-020-7870-7883	http://www.easyspeakers.com/

Country	Bureau	Phone	Web site
United Kingdom	Jillie Bushell Associates (JBA) Ltd.	44-0171-582-3048	http://www.jilliebushell.com
United Kingdom	The Learning Partnership Ltd.	011-44-207-371-4141	http://www.tlp.org
United Kingdom	JLA—Jeremy Lee Associates	011-44-207-240-0413	http://www.jla.co.uk/
United Kingdom	Business Speakers Bureau Ltd.	(020) 7224-4040	http://www.bsb-world.com/ http://www.afterdinner-speakers.com/
United Kingdom	IMG London	(44) (208) 233-5000	http://www.imgspeakers.com/contact.asp
United Kingdom	The London Speaker Bureau	011-441-181-748-9595	http://www.london speakerbureau.co.uk
United Kingdom	Ace Entertainments (North West)		http://www.ace-entertainments.co.uk
United Kingdom	L E O Management & Agency	01942-701942	http://www.agents-uk.com/256
United Kingdom	M & CT Event Management	01531-890790	http://www.mctevent.co.uk
United Kingdom	Now You're Talking—Conference Key	(01442) 831865	http://www.nyt.co.uk/
United Kingdom	MBN Promotions	0161-926-9569	http://www.mbnpro motions.co.uk
United Kingdom	Taylor Made Speakers	01905-767465	http://afterdinner speakers.org/
United Kingdom	Interphiz Ltd.	011-44-01273 479900/479911	http://www.interphiz.com/
United Kingdom	Speakers Agency Ltd.		http://www.thespeakers agency.com/
United Kingdom	Celebrity Model Management	(01628) 675529	http://www.cmmol.net/

Corporate Training
Companies

Company	Specialty	City	State	Web site	Phone
Executive Leadership Skills	Organization and leadership development, team building	Madison	AL	http://www.executive leadershipskills.com	(334) 514-7325
Proven Training Solutions	Managerial & supervisory training and customer Service Training	Phoenix	AZ	http://www.proventraining.net	(623) 566-1579
Scottsdale Seminars	Business writing, time & priority management, project management	Phoenix	AZ	http://www.scottsdale seminars.com	(480) 585-7058
Training for Excellence	Presentation Skills Training, train the trainer & employee performance	Phoenix	AZ	http://www.wetrain.biz	(403) 289-4215
University Associates, Inc.	Train-the-trainer, organization development & change management	Tucson	AZ	http://www.university associates.com	(877) 247-6362
4 Hour Training	Short yet highly effective training programs in management and customer service	San Rafael	CA	http://www.4hourtraining.com	(415) 479-5102
Advanced Marketing Instruction	Sales training & coaching and sales & marketing strategies	LaGrange	CA	http://ami.home.mind spring.com	(706) 812-8822
American School of Mortgage Banking	Mortgage loan processor, underwriter and originating	Tustin	CA	http://www.asmb.com	(800) 343-5549
Applied Learning Solutions, Inc.	Design of custom software application training, product knowledge training and job-specific procedure training	San Francisco	CA	http://www.anythingbut dull.com	(415) 701-7600
Bev Anderson Associates	Training facilitation skills workshops and coaching	Woodside	CA	http://www.bevanderson.com	(650) 529-9159

Company	Description	City	State	Website	Phone
Chapman University	Business skills and certifications and information technology training	Orange	CA	http://www.chapman.edu/enhance	(949) 585-2997
Diversified Solutions & Finance	Strategic planning, financial analysis and financial training	Redondo Beach	CA	http://www.DSF-Training.com	(818) 887-2255
Donna Earl Training	Customer service, management effectiveness & emotional intelligence	San Francisco	CA	http://www.DonnaEarlTraining.com	(415) 929-8110
Honig IdeaGuides	Creativity & idea generation, meeting management & teambuilding	San Rafael	CA	http://www.ideaguides.com	(415) 479-5102
Megamind Training Institute	Computer security training, programming training & development training	San Jose	CA	http://www.megamind.org	(831) 662-9164
NEXT TURN Consulting and Training	Management/team development & time management	South San Francisco	CA	http://www.nextturnconsulting.com	(800) 845-7484
PERSONAL STRENGTHS PUBLISHING	Motivation, mediation skills for managers and conflict management	Carlsbad	CA	http://www.personalstrengths.com	(800) 624-7347
Power Communication	Leadership	Santa Rosa	CA	http://chancemassaro.com	(707) 526-9196
Project Management Practice Inc.	Project management concepts training, Microsoft project training & project management coaching	San Francisco	CA	http://www.pmpractice.com	(877) 585-9909
Richard Chang Associates, Inc.	Organizational development, performance management and measurement/scorecards	Irvine	CA	http://www.richardchangassociates.com	(949) 727-7477

Company	Specialty	City	State	Web site	Phone
San Diego Training & Conference Center	Facilities rental, computer lab rental & meeting space/conference center	San Diego	CA	http://www.sandiegotacc.com	(619) 235-8600
Seaport Conference Center	Computer labs, classrooms and meeting rooms	Redwood City	CA	http://www.seaportcenter.com	(650) 363-1390
Silicon Valley Training Technologies	Training consulting, e-learning & multimedic development and instructional design & development	San Jose	CA	http://www.svtt.com	(408) 452-7888
Stapleton Communications	Business writing training, oral presentations training & freelance business writing	Glendale	CA	http://www.stapcomm.com	(626) 806-4427
Strategic Action Associates	Creative strategic thinking & planning and breakthrough leadership training & facilitation	Danville	CA	http://StrategicAction.com	(925) 820-8838
Succession Planning Partners	Assessment, planning and implementation	Santa Rosa	CA	http://publicpartners.net	(707) 526-9196
The MARBEC Company LLC	Sexual harassment prevention on-site training seminars and hiring & firing on-site training seminars	Cottonwood	CA	http://www.legalpitfalls.com	(303) 617-3769
The Opportunity Thinker	Innovation tools: Six thinking hats & lateral thinking, high-stakes meeting facilitation training	Glendale	CA	http://www.LyndaCurtin.com	(818) 507-6055
The Quest Team, Inc.	Sales & marketing training—high-tech industries, sales & marketing consulting	San Jose	CA	http://www.questteam.com	(408) 261-3498

Company	Description	City	State	Website	Phone
The Training Clinic	Train the trainer, training design & delivery and new employee orientation	Seal Beach	CA	http://www.thetrainingclinic.com	(800) 937-4698
Value Creation Partners	Operations improvement, Six Sigma and Process mapping & redesign	Concord	CA	http://www.valuecreationpartners.com	(925) 459-8755
Life Learning Institute	Work-life balance & improving employee productivity	Cottonwood	CA	http://www.lifelearninginstitute.com	(530) 347-1000
InQ Educational Materials, Inc.	Team building and thinking skills tools	San Francisco	CA	http://www.inq-hpa.com	(800) 338-2462
LearnCom	Management, human resources & safety training	Irvine	CA	http://www.learncom.com	(800) 459-5573
Direct Hit Marketing, Inc.	Laser-focused seminar & conference mailing lists, database marketing	Lafayette	CO	http://www. Directhit marketing.com	(303) 666-0798
Employee Development Systems Inc.	Communication & interpersonal skills, performance management and professionalism	Denver	CO	http://www.edsiusa.com	(800) 282-3374
Enlightened Leadership Int'l, Inc.	Integrated process/product team development, change management and talent selection & development	Greenwood Village	CO	http://www.enleadership.com	(800) 798-9881
Hartmann Software Group	Information technology training & software consulting services	Denver	CO	http://www.hartmannsoftware.com	(303) 377-9333
Human Dimension	Executive coaching & development and management & team development	Denver	CO	http://www.humandimension.org	(303) 887-4891
IAS Training	Sales training seminars	Lakewood	CO	http://www.iastraining.com	(800) 248-7703

Company	Specialty	City	State	Web site	Phone
Innovative Training, Inc.	Job/task specific technician training, entry-level technical training and upgrading technical skills/knowledge	Denver	CO	http://intraining.com	(800) 304-5380
MGT Performance Improvement, LLC	Business management, project management, and team building	Denver	CO	http://www.MGTPerformance.com	(303) 863-8263
Career T.E.A.M.	Job readiness training, motivational training & customer service training	Hamden	CT	http://www.careerteam.com	(860) 584-9787
LJL Seminars	Presentation, public speaking, and communication skills seminars	Strattford	CT	http://www.LJLSeminars.com	(800) 606-4855
Right Source Learning	Technical training, technically equipped classroom rentals and staffing for technical demonstrations & presentations	Norwalk	CT	http://www.rightsource.com/learning	(800) 462-0102
Creative Learning Solutions, Inc.	Management consulting, team development, and diversity training	Newark	DE	http://www.CLSolutionsInc.com	(302) 738-4173
Goeins-Williams Associates, Inc.	Consulting, training, and professional speaking	Wilmington	DE	http://www.goeinswilliams.com	(302) 655-4404
Professional Staffing, Employee Training & Development	Team building, professional development, and communication skills	Wilmington	DE	http://www.professionalstaffinginc.com	(302) 652-3519
Anthony Robbins & Associates	Sales effectiveness, personal & organizational development	Tampa	FL	http://www.AnthonyRobbinsDC.com	(301) 865-8292

Company	Description	City	State	Website	Phone
For Your Instructors Inc.	IT Trainer placement, IT out-sourcing & soft skills training	Kissimmee	FL	http://www.fyitrainers.com	(866) 636-8601
Hathaway & Associates, Inc.	Business systems analysis, requirements engineering and testing software systems	Tampa	FL	http://www.thehathaway.com	(813) 973-3046
Liaison Professional Meeting Services	Meeting planning/seminar planning services, event planning and hotel/motel negotiations	Orlando	FL		(352) 357-9598
Plum International, Inc.	Competency systems, leadership development & competency development tools	Ft. Lauderdale	FL	http://www.pluminternational.com	(800) 870-9490
Sales Training Consultants	Sales, management, and customer service training	Ft. Lauderdale	FL	http://www.salestrainingconsultants.com	(800) 940-1230
Scarecrow Workshops	Supervisor/manager development, interpersonal "soft" skills and innovative leadership	Jacksonville	FL	http://www.scarecrowworkshops.com	(904) 379-9865
TDC International	Negotiation skills and sales training	Miami	FL	http://www.tdcinternational.com	(305) 279-8531
The Blakeslee Group, Inc.	Management/leadership development, team development and customized training	Boynton Beach	FL	http://www.theblakesleegroupcom	(800) 490-6040
The Sky's The Limit Consulting, Inc.	Business & life coaching, interpersonal skills training and facilitation	Estero	FL	http://www.theskysthelimitconsulting.com	(941) 275-3258

Company	Specialty	City	State	Web site	Phone
The Temple Group	Training & development, compensation management and human resources management	Orlando	FL	http://www.oliversystem.com	(888) 535-4168
SemCo Enterprises, Inc.		Orlando	FL	http://www.semcoenterprises.com	(407) 830-5400
Bianco Hopkins & Associates, Inc.	Custom training program development, e-learning strategy & development and presentation coaching	Norcross	GA	http://www.biancohopkins.com	(770) 368-0828
Business Training Experts	Management, supervisory and leadership training	Atlanta	GA	http://www.BusinessTrainingExperts.com	(800) 541-7872
Classroom Resource Group, Inc.	Classroom rentals	Atlanta	GA	http://www.classroomresourcegroup.com	(877) 620-8684
ClientQuest Inc.	Sales training, customer service training, & public speaking	Atlanta	GA	clientquest.net	
Competitive Solutions, Inc.	Leadership/management training, team training and executive coaching and consulting	Alpharetta	GA	http://www.competitive-solutions.net	(800) 246-8694
Cypress Media Group, Inc.	Business & technical writing and media relations	Atlanta	GA	http://www.cypressmedia.net	(770) 640-9918
EuroQuest	Quality management and information security	Atlanta	GA	http://www.euroquest.net	(800) 355-3876
Fuddwhacker Consulting	Motivational keynotes—humor, team building workshops and interpersonal skills seminars	Atlanta	GA	http://www.fuddwhacker.com	(770) 645-9473
Gee Wiz, LLC	Training, corporate coaching, and executive coaching	Atlanta	GA	http://www.geewizwow.com	(678) 441-9449

Company	Description	City	State	Website	Phone
HRcertification.com	Mandated compliance training for HR professionals (COBRA, ADA, FMLA, etc.), compensation training and HR management training	Atlanta	GA	http://www.HRcertification.com	(678) 366-3959
Leadership Strategies, Inc.	Facilitation training, meeting facilitation, and strategic planning	Atlanta	GA	http://www.leadstrat.com	(800) 824-2850
Pervado, Inc.	Performance effectiveness, documentation services, and workplace learning	Atlanta	GA	http://www.pervado.com	(678) 592-5959
Roger Reece Seminars	Interpersonal communication skills training, leadership training, and time/stress management training	Atlanta	GA	http://www.rogerreece.com	(770) 645-9473
The PAR Group	Influencing skills, sales skills, and leadership & teamwork	Atlanta	GA	http://www.thepargroup.com	(800) 247-7188
Advanced Practical Thinking Training	Creativity, meeting management, and decisionmaking	Des Moines	IA	http://www.aptt.com	(800) 621-3366
Innova Training & Consulting, Inc.	Innovation, teamwork, and thinking skills	Des Moines	IA	http://www.innovatraining.com	(800) 621-3366
Resources Unlimited	Leadership training materials, creativity & innovation training and workplace assessments	Johnston	IA	http://www.resourcesunlimited.com	(800) 278-1292
Seed Planters Training & Develop. Ctr.	Team building, leadership development, and adventure education	Waterloo	IA	http://www.seedplanters.org	(319) 433-1300
PCKeys Technology Solutions	Computer training project management training & room rentals	Boise	ID	http://www.pckeys.com	(208) 331-3121

Company	Specialty	City	State	Web site	Phone
Accelerated Learning Group	Graphic design, digital video, and web design	Chicago	IL	http://www.learngroup.net	(678) 380-9065
Centrax Corporation	Custom e-learning development, 3D animation & simulation development and consultation on e-learning strategies	Chicago	IL	http://www.centrax.com	(312) 946-9360
Coovert & Associates, Inc.	Leadership development, experiential education, Myers-Briggs type indicator	Plainfield	IL		(815) 577-2912
Corporate Learning Institute	Change management, adventure programming, and training & development	Lisle	IL	http://www.corplearning.com	(800) 203-6734
Corporate Training Consultants, Inc.	Training audits, strategic training planning, & on-the-job training	Schaumburg	IL	http://www.enhancedtraining.com	(847) 885-1880
Human Synergistics	Team-building, organizational culture assessment and individual & leadership development surveys	Arlington Heights	IL	http://HSCar.com	(847) 590-0995
InfoWorks International, Inc.	Project management training, management training, and negotiation skills training	Lake Bluff	IL	http://www.infoworksonline.com	(800) 236-0506
MFK Consulting, Inc.	Purchasing & corporate law for non-lawyers, contract writing & negotiation for non-lawyers and construction law for contractors, design professionals, and suppliers	Chicago	IL	http://www.mfkconsulting.com	(773) 227-9500

Company	Description	City	State	Website	Phone
MicroTek	Computer and non-computer classrooms, e-tech and related training services	Oakbrook Terrace	IL	http://www.mclabs.com	(714) 377-3719
Performance Partners	Stress & leadership management and powerful communication skills	Frankfort	IL	http://www.performancepartnersinc.net	(815) 464-5472
QualiFine Industries, Inc.	MINITAB software training, Hertzler systems software training and computer training, facility rental	Roseville	IL	http://www.qualifine.com	(888) 317-4820
SP3 International	Performance consulting in sales, service, and leadership and territory, major account & business strategies	Napierville	IL	http://www.sp3international.com	(630) 420-9592
Thomas Enterprises	Technology training/mentoring and SMB technology support	Chicago	IL	http://www.tei-tech.com	(773) 651-9851
Training Coordination Professionals	Meeting & conference room rentals and professional event coordination	Chicago	IL	http://www.trainingcoordination.com	(773) 914-2015
ADVANCED SYSTEMS	Executive performance coaching, youth self-leadership and customized training, development & facilitation	Valparaiso	IN	http://www.perpetualsuccess.com	(219) 759-5601
Perpetual Technologies, Inc.	Database administration & design, software design & development, and IT training	Indianapolis	IN	http://www.perptech.com	(317) 824-0393
Alliance Training and Consulting, Inc.	Leadership/management development, customer service training and training and presentation skills	Overland Park	KS	http://www.alliancetac.com	(877) 385-5515

Company	Specialty	City	State	Web site	Phone
Accelerated Leadership	Leadership, communication, and teamwork	Jeanerette	LA	http://altrainer.com	(888) 632-5419
Earle Company	Leadership, communication, and business coaching	Baton Rouge	LA	http://www.EarleCompany.com	(225) 293-3783
Washauer Seminars	Sales training, customer service, and public speaking courses	Baton Route	LA	http://www.washauerseminars.com	(800) 553-0745
1 X 1 Companies	Raising retail revenues at the upper end and sales & management training	Lenox	MA	http://www.onexone.com	(877) 663-9663
APR Testing Services	Employee selection training and diagnostic educational testing	Boston	MA	aprtestingservices.com	(617) 244-7405
Atlantic Consultants	Management and team building training	Wellesley	MA	http://www.atlanticconsultants.com	(781) 235-7555
Bercume Associates	Performance management, leadership development and human resources	Shrewsbury	MA	http://www.bercumeassociates.com	(888) 781-1881
CRG Associates	Leadership & management training, trainer & facilitator development, and team development	Ashland	MA	http://www.crgassocs.com	(508) 881-9364
Double Eagle Communications, Inc.	DiSC® classic profile for understanding ourselves & others and behavioral styles selling skills course	Worcester	MA	http://www.doubleeaglecomm.com	(888) 772-4637
FRONTLINE Training & Consulting	Sales, customer service, and communication skills training	S. Egremont	MA	http://www.frontlinetraining.com	(413) 644-0180

Company	Description	City	State	Website	Phone
FUSION	Marketing and promotion resource to public seminar companies	Boston	MA	http://www.sellmoretraining.com	(978) 443-5943
Habart Training Solutions	E-Learning development, corporate training consulting, and corporate training	Waltham	MA	http://www.htsconsultants.com	(781) 209-1062
IMA Associates	Business writing & communication, management & team development	Stoughton	MA	http://www.tregistry.com/ima.htm	(781) 297-2024
Institute for Advanced Professional Studies	On-site training: software development & ITT, needs assessment & course development	Boston	MA	http://www.iaps.com	(617) 742-2777
Interaction Associates	Facilitation, leadership, and collaboration	Boston	MA	http://www.interactionassociates.com	(617) 234-2725
Jim Schaffer & Associates	Advanced sales training and change management workshops	Newton	MA	http://www.jimschaffer.com	(617) 332-9105
M. Salmon & Associates, Inc.	SuperNetworking; to drive more revenue, reach the right people & land your dream now	Framingham	MA	http://www.salmonsays.com	(508) 877-8861
Matthew Ferrara Seminars, Inc.	Technology seminars for real estate professionals	Methuen	MA	http://www.mfseminars.com	(888) 832-2473
Partnering Consultants	Project & change management consulting and facilitation	Newton	MA	http://partneringconsultants.com	(617) 558-1615
Pinnacle Performance Improvement Worldwide	Executive management, and organization deveopment	Wayland	MA	http://www.ppiw.com	(508) 358-8070

Company	Specialty	City	State	Web site	Phone
Sideris Consulting Group, Inc.	Instructor-led training in Oracle10g, 9i, 8i & Java, and courseware materials in Oracle, Java, Linux, Microsoft, CompTIA, A+, Net+	Newton	MA	http://www.sideris.com/	(300) 748-7300
The Victoria Group, Inc.	ISO 9001 and ISO 14001 Management Systems & management system audit	Methuen	MA	http://www.VictoriaGroup.com	(978) 681-8404
Warner Sales Architects	Customer-centric selling, cold call coaching, and self management workshops	Belmont	MA	http://www.warnersalesarchitects.com	(617) 489-4528
Applied Performance Strategies, Inc.	Presentation skills, supervisory training, and creating respectful workplaces	Columbia	MD	http://www.aps-online.net	(410) 715-0800
Creative Visions Consulting	Leadership development, supervisory training, and creating professional & personal prosperity	Frederick	MD	http://www.cvc-inc.com	(866) 322-8263
The Lett Group	Etiquette, international communication skills, and international protocol	Silver Spring	MD	http://www.lettgroup.com	(888) 933-3883
The Pincus Group	Presentation/speech training, media training, and crisis communications training	Silver Spring	MD	http://www.thepincusgroup.com	(301) 908-3896
Travis Consulting Associates, Inc.	Performance management, team building, and MBTI & DISC personality profile	Baltimore	MD	http://www.travisusa.com	(410) 667-9055

Company	Description	City	State	Website	Phone
AchieveMax, Inc.	Change and time management and creativity	Grand Blanc	MI	http://www.AchieveMax.com	(800) 886-2629
Lanista Tech-Knowledgies	Working together to achieve more—teamwork essentials, moving ahead in business & your life, mommies in the workplace—how to survive work & home	Lathrup Village	MI	http://Lanista.com	(248) 423-4201
Noumena Corporation	Tcl/Tk and Unix/Linux	Dexter	MI	http://www.noucorp.com	(734) 426-1066
rtlf	Consulting, staffing, and training	Birmingham	MI	http://www.rtlf.com	(248) 910-8921
Workplace Results, LLC	Leadership development, supervisory training, and team building	Saline	MI	http://www.workplaceresults.com	(734) 429-5249
Computer Training International Inc.	Customized training, instructional design, and training rollouts	Minneapolis	MN	http://www.computertraininginternational.com	(612) 378-0665
Dream Chasers Ltd	Setting & achieving goals, productivity & performance and sales	Tracy	MN	http://www.dream-chasers.net	(877) 385-6461
Executive Development Inc.	Strategic & tactical decision analysis, problem solving & root cause analysis and team start-up training	Minneapolis	MN	http://www.FocusTools.com	(952) 595-8000
Impression Management Professionals	Presentation, communication, and negotiation skills	Minneapolis	MN	http://www.impressionmanagement.com	(952) 921-9421
Meiss Education Institute	Team building, coaching, and leadership training	Minneapolis	MN	http://www.MeissEducation.com	(952) 446-1586

Company	Specialty	City	State	Web site	Phone
TEC Trainer Inc.	Onsite electricity & motor controls training simulators and onsite pneumatic & pick and place training simulators	Jordan	MN	http://www.tectrainer.com	(612) 708-4910
Psychological Associates	Leadership through people skills and effective selling through psychology	St. Louis	MO	http://www.q4solutions.com	(800) 345-6525
Sam Black Consulting	Sales and customer service training, business development/telemarketing training	St. Louis	MO	http://www.samblack.com	(314) 567-3764
M5 Corp	Technical management, managing technical professionals and people management skills for technicals	Bozeman	MT	http://www.m5corp.com	(800) 700-7524
Bristlecone Learning, LLC	Strategic change management, leadership development, and mediation	Raleigh	NC	http://www.bristlecone learning.com	(919) 684-3255
Business & Technology Management	Project management, leadership, and communications training	Greensboro	NC	http://www.BTMgt.com	(336) 292-1288
CCG, Inc.	Leadership & culture development, alignment of leadership & culture with strategy and executive team development	Greensboro	NC	http://www.ccgteam.com	(336) 294-8793
Human Resource Directions	Workplace assessments as people management tools, managing within the law, and effective performance management	Raleigh	NC	http://www.tregistry.com/hrd.htm	(919) 848-5995

Company	Description	City	State	Website	Phone
Hurley TechComm, Inc.	Designing & teaching writing modules, scientific writing & editing, and technical writing & editing	Wilmington	NC	http://www.hurleytechcom.com	(910) 233-7670
Interactive Consulting Services, Inc.	Training, meeting facilitation, and executive coaching	Raleigh	NC	http://www.changingwork.com	(919) 387-6666
International Technology Solutions, Inc.	Information technology training services, training program management, and learning management system	Wake Forest	NC	http://www.itsinc-us.com	(800) 876-5010
IVORY MANAGEMENT GROUP, INC.	Motivational keynotes, leadership development, and hospitality consulting	Durham	NC	http://www.ivorymanagement.com	(919) 596-1326
Qualifying.org, Inc.	MBTI and linked instrument qualifying and training, application-oriented training with assessments and integration of multiple development methodologies	Winston Salem	NC	http://www.qualifying.org	(336) 774-0330
SmarTrack	Leadership training, sales/marketing training, and keynote speaking	Raleigh	NC	http://www.smartrack.net	(919) 562-2280
The Adventure Solution	Experiential learning, experiential training and experiential facilitation	Raleigh	NC	http://www.theadventuresolution.com	(919) 684-3255
The Assessment and Development Group International Inc.	Management development and human resource assessment	Pinehurst	NC	http://www.2oms.com	(800) 919-9220

Company	Specialty	City	State	Web site	Phone
Ability-Alliance LLC	Process improvement implementation coaching, organizational transformation training, and organizational transformation seminars	Windham	NH	http://www.abilityalliance.Com	(603) 898-1555
Blended Solutions, LLC	Computer training, NET programming, and health and safety training	Manchester	NH	http://www.blendedsolutions.net	(603) 622-6191
BridgeWorks Business Solutions, LLC	Leadership development, business strategy, and organizational alignment	Wilmot	NH	http://www.yourbridgeworks.com	(800) 564-4008
Entelechy, Inc.	Customizable management & supervisory training, customizable sales & customer service training	Merrimack	NH	http://www.unlockit.com	(603) 424-1237
Human Capital Solutions, LLC	Culture as business driver, workforce planning & development, executive team development	Derry	NH	http://www.humancapitalize.com	(866) 434-4042
Paul Charles & Associates	Marketing communication, promotional copywriting and books	Londonderry	NH	http://www.paulcharles.com	(603) 537-1190
All the World's a Stage	Presentation skills, sales presentations, and technical presentations	Princeton	NJ	http://www.savvypresentations.com	(609) 683-8824
ON LINE SERVICES	Computer training, consulting, and business analyst	Denville	NJ	http://www.onlineservicesinc.com	(973) 625-2175
Productivity Resource Group, Inc.	Productivity enhancement, work/life balance, and leadership development	Montclair	NJ	http://www.productivityresource.com	(973) 748-5100

Company	Description	City	State	Website	Phone
Solutions Provided	Executive coaching, sales performance, and Board of Director development	Point Pleasant	NJ	http://www.solutions provided.com	(732) 701-1661
Workforce Solutions, Inc.	Sales, coaching & customer service workshops, value-centered assessments	Lambertille	NJ	http://www.workforceinc.com	(609) 397-3797
Johnson Advisory Group	Outsourced training records management, small business technical services and Web-based employee learning management systems	Rio Rancho	NM	http://www.johnsongroups.com/advisory	(505) 270-4228
Johnson Solutions Group	Customer service, technical writing, and training development	Rio Rancho	NM	http://www.johnsongroups.com/solutions	(505) 270-4230
Practical Management, Inc. (PMI)	Train the trainer, management & supervisory programs and course design	Las Vegas	NV	http://www.practicalmgt.com	(800) 444-9101
Turning Point International Inc.	Customer service, leadership, and communication	Las Vegas	NV	http://www.turningpoint intl.com	(702) 896-2228
ASME	Engineering and online learning	New York	NY	http://www.asme.org/education	(800) 843-2763
Buz Larson	Cluster strategy	New York	NY	http://www.larson.bm	(212) 751-6520
ELM Associates	Customer service, supervision & management skills, and technical skills	Albany	NY		
Executive Coach Academy	Training in executive and corporate coaching and seminars in 360 feedback facilitation	New York	NY	http://executivecoach academy.com	(212) 501-7666

Company	Specialty	City	State	Web site	Phone
Hebert Performance Training	Customer service, train the trainer skills, and management development	Liverpool	NY	http://www.heberttraining.com	(888) 282-7291
Interactive Employment Training, Inc.	Online discriminatory harassment prevention training, online diversity training, and workplace law compliance training	Jericho	NY	http://www.hrtrain.com	(888) hr-train
Langevin Learning Services	Train the trainer, instructional design, and presentation skills	Ogdensburg	NY	http://www.langevinonline.com	(800) 223-2209
PC Learn Seminar & Conference Center	Hosting large training events, technical training events, and seminars & conferences	New York	NY	http://www.nycconferencecenter.com	(646) 336-4408
Sequent Learning Networks	Product management & product development training and product management and marketing consulting	New York	NY	http://www.sequentlearning.com	(212) 673-5454
Synergy Solutions International	Sales, management & presentation skills training, training & development consulting, and curriculm design	Syosset	NY	http://www.synergysolutionsint.com	(516) 921-3887
T. T. Mitchell Consulting	Leadership, diversity, and management	Liverpool	NY	http://www.ttmitchellconsulting.com	(315) 622-5922
Tec-Ease, Inc.	Geometric dimensioning & tolerancing, print reading, and manufacturing mathematics	Cherry Creek	NY	http://www.tec-ease.com	(888) 832-3273

Company	Description	City	State	Website	Phone
The Ford Group	Organizational development, management & leadership development, and human resource management	Rome	NY	http://www.fordgroup.com	(315) 339-6398
TrainersDirect	Management training seminars and organizational development consulting	New York	NY	http://www.trainersdirect.com	(518) 891-9238
Training Dynamics	Customer service, presentation skills, and business writing	White Plains	NY	http://www.trainingdynamicsweb.com	(914) 948-8065 x11
Training-NYC	Advanced office & business software training, audio/visual software training, and advanced software training	New York	NY	http://www.training-nyc.com	(646) 209-2333
Webucator	NET, Java, and Macromedia	Syracuse	NY	http://www.webucator.com	(315) 391-6371
Cannon Advantage	Decisionmaking, strategy, and marketing	Chagrin Falls	OH	http://www.cannonadvantage.com	(216) 408-9495
Cleveland Institute of Electronics	Electronics and computer technology	Cleveland	OH	http://www.cie-wc.edu	(800) 243-6446
ContactPointe, Training Administration Services	Facility management, student registration, and virtual classroom hosting	Columbus	OH	http://www.contactpointe.com	(949) 481-6974
Fink, Inc.	Supervision training, sales training, and team problem-solving training	Cincinnati	OH	http://www.think-fink.com	(513) 324-6279
Headwinds Ltd.	Human performance improvement, high performance leadership & team training, high performance business strategic planning	Walton Hills	OH	http://www.headwindsltd.com	(216) 662-3462

Company	Specialty	City	State	Web site	Phone
Technicomp, Inc.	Quality skills training, blueprint reading, and internal auditing	Cleveland	OH	http://www.technicomp.com	(800) 735-4440
Training Services & Solutions, Ltd	Manufacturing process employee training, employee job skill enhancement & assessment, and on-the-job CNC training	Miamisburg	OH	http://www.trngsrvcs.com	(937) 312-1698
Character of Excellence, LLC	Corporate training, executive coaching, and keynote speeches	Edmond	OK	http://www.characterofexcellence.com	(877) 263-2761
Center for Individual & Organizational Effectiveness (C4IOE)	Corporate training & organizational development, nonprofit consulting, and social enterprise/social ventures	Pittsburgh	PA	http://www.c4ioe.com	(724) 360-3150
ComputerEase	Windows PC training, Macintosh training, and custom onsite training	Philadelphia	PA	http://www.karinrex.com	(215) 393-7640
High Probability Selling	Sales training, insurance, and real estate sales training	Philadelphia	PA	http://www.highprobsell.com	(800) 394-7762
Job Training Systems, Inc.	Maitenance training self-study books, plant operations training self-study books, and industrial training books	Unionville	PA	http://www.jobtraining.com	(610) 444-0868
Lausanne Institute	Management, communications, and management sciences	Kennett Square	PA	http://lausanne.cc	(610) 444-9013
Mission Control	Individual & team productivity, work-life balance, and aligning employee actions with management priorities	Yardley	PA	http://www.missioncontrol.com	(925) 228-5977

Company	Description	City	State	Website	Phone
MVS Training, Inc.	Custom onsite mainframe, e-learning, and technical book sales	Pittsburgh	PA	http://www.mvs-training.com	(800) 356-9093
Premier Performance Network	Six Sigma training, organization consulting, and Six Sigma implementations	York	PA	http://www.premierperformance.net	(440) 926-2375
ProTechTraining.com	Enterprise IT technology instructor-led training, self-paced and life online e-learning and content development, LCMS integration, project management/PMI	Pittsburgh	PA	http://www.protechtraining.com	(800) 373-9188
Richard M. DiGeorgio & Associates	The strategic business management workshop, developing internal change agents and making mergers & acquisitions successful	Wasington Crossing	PA	http://www.change-management.net	(215) 369-0088
SIRCO Consultants, Inc.	Finance for non-financial managers	West Chester	PA	http://www.sircoconsultants.com	(610) 388-0969
The Center for Professional Innovation & Education	Pharmaceutical technical training, biotechnology & bio-pharma training, and medical device training	Wayne	PA	http://www.cfpie.com	(610) 688-1708
The Writing Center, Inc.	Effective business writing training, effective technical writing training, and writing effective proposals training	West Chester	PA	http://www.writingcenter.com	(610) 436-4600
TrainingBuz.com	Training products, consulting services, and predesigned courses	Philadelphia	PA	http://www.trainingbuz.com	(215) 463-4155

Company	Specialty	City	State	Web site	Phone
Transfers of Learning, LLC	Leadership & team development, technical & soft skills training development & delivery, and enhanced employee effectiveness programs	Coatesville	PA	http://www.transfersof learning.com	(877) 819-2881
Winds of Change; Holistic Education and Leadership, Center	Stress & change management, leadership, and executive coaching	Portsmouth	RI	http://www.ServiceGuru. com	(401) 683-6406
Anne Bruce, Speaker/Author	Personal growth/self-development, leadership, and motivation	Charleston	SC	http://www.annebruce.com	(214) 507-8242
Facilitator4hire, Inc.	Meeting facilitation, facilitation skills training, public & private in-house courses	Westminster	SC	http://www.facilitator4hire. com	(678) 296-7527
Fitzgerald Addison Group LLC	Management skills, managing change, and performance management	Hilton Head	SC	http://www.Fitzgerald AddisonGroup.com	(646) 298-4242
KnowledgeLabs News Center	Internet for business (strategy, security, spam, viruses, e-business), leadership and marketing & media	Singapore	SG	http://keynotepresenter. com	(659) 790-8324
Design Management Alliance	Training and development	Gean Station	TN	http://www.designmgt. com	(865) 993-0077
Integrated Management Resources	Senior leadership training, hiring/development assessments, and communications training	Knoxville	TN	http://www.integratedman agementresources.com	

Company	Description	City	State	Website	Phone
TLD-Training and Leadership Development	Professional development workshops, special learning events, and motivational speaking	Knoxville	TN	http://www.tldconsultants.com	(865) 588-4290
Adams Six Sigma	Six Sigma, strategic planning, and team building	Lake Jackson	TX	http://www.adamssixsigma.com	(979) 297-5198
Adkins & Associates	Workplace conflict, leadership, and presentation skills	Ft. Worth	TX	http://www.trainingspeaking.com	(817) 370-8746
Bassham, Rayl & Associates	Professional development training, training product sales, executive coaching & consulting	Carrollton	TX	http://www.bassham-rayl.com	(214) 731-9608
BFCI Learning Systems	Equipping leaders to be champions of change, workforce performance development, and organizational development & cultural change	El Paso	TX	http://www.bfci.com	(915) 276-8587
Business Management Consultants	Project management training, project management consulting, and project management organizational development	Houston	TX	http://www.bmc-online.com	(281) 440-0455
CertTest Training Center Inc.	Professional certification classes and career advancement in management & compliance	Grapevine	TX	http://www.CertTest.com	(817) 424-0024
EduCorp Training & Consulting, Inc.	Technical training, professional skills training, and course development	Grapevine	TX	http://www.educorptraining.com	(800) 668-0943
Expressively Speaking	Presentation & influence, conflict management, and executive development	Austin	TX	http://www.expressivelyspeaking.com	(888) 992-6700

Company	Specialty	City	State	Web site	Phone
International Training Consultants, Inc.	Off-the-shelf training modules and train the trainer resources and leadership assessment	Kemah	TX	http://www.trainingitc.com	(800) 998-8764
Roberts & Roberts Associates	Managing accelerated projects, negotiating skills, and multi-tasking management skills	Dallas	TX	http://www.R2Assoc.com	(800) 545-8975
The Leader's Institute	Public speaking training/presentation skills, leadership training, and team building	Dallas	TX	http://www.leadersinstitute.com	(800) 872-7830
The Lyon Group	Management training, organizational development, and workforce performance	Houston	TX	http://www.lyon-group.com	(877) 637-6443
Cook & Williams Communications Inc.	Sales & marketing training, business process improvement, and strategic planning	Charlottesville	VA	http://www.cookandwilliams.com	(434) 245-9167
Dr. Elliott B. Jaffa	Management, professional development and associations	Arlington	VA	http://ejaffa.home.mindspring.com	(703) 931-0040
Management Concepts	Leadership & management, project management, and federal financial management	Vienna	VA	http://www.managementconcepts.com	(703) 790-9595
StarrSmith, Inc.	Human resources, training, and instructional design	Leesburg	VA	http://www.starrsmith.com	(703) 779-2995
The Potomack Group, LLC	ISO management systems, leadership coaching, and globalization consulting	Vienna	VA	http://www.potomack.net	(540) 338-9076

Company	Description	City	State	Website	Phone
TRAINING SOLUTIONS, Inc.	Management development, team building, and assessment and 360	Chantilly	VA	http://www.training solutions.com	(703) 318-0838
Wealth in Diversity Consulting Group, Inc.	Cultural diversity, change management, and leadership & management in health care	Cambridge	VT	http://www.wealthin diversity.com	(802) 644-5140
Bob Mendonsa & Associates	Leadership development, HR compliance training, and ethics training	Bellevue	WA	http://www.trainingplus. com	(425) 827-6861
Business Writing That Counts!	Online and on-site strategic writing workshops and virtual coaching on business writing	Seattle	WA	http://www.Drjuliemiller. com	(425) 485-3221
LifeTime Media	Software for training administration	Mercer Island	WA	http://www.ltmedia.com	(800) 567-7741
Quality Media Resources, Inc.	Diversity, harassment prevention, and conflict management	Bellevue	WA	http://www.qmr.com	(800) 800-5129
Richardson Co. Training Media	Management training toolkits, employee training toolkits, and harassment prevention training toolkits	Tacoma	WA	http://www.rctm.com/app /View/about_us.jsp	(800) 488-0319
Corporate Resource Development, Inc.	Sales, customer service, and personality accountability	Milwaukee	WI	http://www.crdinfo.com	(414) 422-1689
Laurel and Associates, Ltd.	Training program design, train the trainer programs, and leadership training	Madison	WI	http://www.laureland associates.com	(608) 255-2010
Personal Effectiveness Plus	Time management, goal setting, and personal coaching	Wauwatosa	WI	http://www.gainingtime. com	

Company	Specialty	City	State	Web site	Phone
Phoenix Training & Development	Sales, presentation skills, and management	London	United Kingdon	http://www.phoenix-training.co.uk	020 7234 0480
IMARKA	Communication, marketing, and management	Brasschaat	Belgium	http://www.imarka.com	+32 3 653 30 73
PTP Training & Marketing Ltd	Management, sales, and customer care training	Leicester	Leicestershire	http://www.ptp.co.uk	0116 268 0066
TL Olson & Associates Inc.	360 Degree Feedback	Calgary	AB, Canada	http://www.360feedbackcanada.com	(403) 247-1342
Black Isle Consultants	Executive training, presentation skills, and media relations	Toronto	ON Canada	http://www.black-isle.com	(416) 927-1880
CANTRAIN DEVELOPMENT CORPORATION	Management & leadership training, service & quality improvement training, and Web-based soft skills training	Toronto	ON Canada	http://www.thetrainingbank.com	(416) 698-8230
Rovell Enterprises Ltd.	E-learning, technical training & manufacturing processes, distance education & distributed training	Kanata	ON Canada	http://www.rovell.com	(613) 599-9975
The Lachlan Group	Executive/management education seminars, executive/management team building, and strategic planning & implementation process	Toronto	ON Canada	http://www.lachlangroup.com	(905) 841-2268
JED New Media Inc.	e-learning off-the-shelf business skills, e-learning custom, and translation/adaptation	Montreal	QE Canada	http://www.jedlet.com	(514) 289-1800

Professional Associations for Networking and Education

Academy of Management
P.O. Box 3020
Briarcliff Manor, NY 10510
Phone: (914) 923-2607
Web site: www.aom.pace.edu

Members: Professors who research and teach management as well as doctoral students in management and business professionals interested in principles of management.
AM*: August

Academy of Security Educators and Trainers
P.O. Box 802
Berryville, VA 22611
Phone: (540) 554-2547
Web site: www.suite2000.com/aset

Membership: 400 individuals
AM: Spring

Accrediting Council for Continuing Education & Training
1722 N. Street, NW
Washington, D.C. 20036
Phone: (202) 955-1113
Web site: www.accet.org

Members: 230 institutions and 700 branches
AM: Fall

*AM = Annual Meeting

AFSM International
1342 Colonial Blvd.—Suite 25
Ft. Myers, FL 33907
Phone: (941) 275-7887
Web site: www.afsmi.org

Members: Executives and managers in the high-technology services/support industry.
AM: Fall

Alliance for Nonprofit Management
1899 L Street, NW, Suite 600
Washington, D.C. 20036
Phone: (202) 955-8406
Web site: www.allianceonline.org

Members: Individuals devoted primarily to helping nonprofit organizations increase their effectiveness and impact.
AM: Summer

American Academy of Ambulatory Care Nursing
P.O. Box 56
Pitman, NJ 08071
Phone: (856) 256-2350
Web site: www.aaacn.org

Members: Registered nurses engaged in the care of ambulatory patients
AM: April

American Association of Industrial Management
293 Bridge Street, Suite 506
Springfield, MA 01103
Phone: (413) 737-8766
Web site: www.americanassocofind mgmt.com
Members: Manufacturers, insurance companies and banks, town and city governments, universities and hospitals

American Association of Law Enforcement Trainers
121 N. Court Street
Frederick, MD 21701
Phone: (301) 668-9466
Web site: www.aslet.org
Members: Represents law enforcement trainers, educators, and administrators
AM: January

American Association of Managing General Agents
9140 Ward Parkway
Kansas City, MO 64114
Phone: (816) 444-3500
Web site: www.aamga.org
Members: Independent insurance managers with contractual authority to perform managerial functions on behalf of insurance companies and syndicates
AM: Spring

American College of Healthcare Executives
One N. Franklin Street, Suite 1700
Chicago, IL 60606
Phone: (312) 424-2800
Web site: www.ache.org
Members: Healthcare executives
AM: Spring

American Council on Schools & Colleges
13014 N. Dale Mabry, Suite 363
Tampa, FL 33618
Phone: (813) 926-5446

Members: Represents private schools, institutes, trade schools, in-house training programs, consultants, publishers, other suppliers, vendors, and support organizations

American Dog Trainers Network
161 W. 4th Street
New York, NY 10014
Phone: (212) 727-7257
Web site: www.canine.org
Members: 300 individuals

American Healthcare Radiology Administrators
P.O. Box 334
Sudbury, MA 01776
Phone: (978) 443-6911
Web site: www.ahraonline.org
AM: Summer

American Management Association International
1601 Broadway
New York, NY 10019
Phone: (212) 903-8327
Web site: www.amanet.org
Members: Devoted to all types of management education

American Society for Engineering Management
P.O. Box 820
Rolla, MO 65402
Phone: (573) 341-2101
Web site: www.awir.org
Members: Engineering management professionals from academic, industrial, and governmental organizations to promote the development of engineering management
AM: Fall

American Society for Public Administration
1120 G Street, NW, Suite 700
Washington, D.C. 20005
Phone: (202) 393-7878
Web site: www.aspanet.org
Members: Dedicated to advancing excellence in public service and public management
AM: Spring

American Society for Training & Development
1640 King Street
Alexandria, VA 22313
Phone: (703) 683-8100
Web site: www.astd.org
Members: Professional society of trainers and human resource development professionals

American Technical Education Association
North Dakota State College of Science
800 N. Sixth Street
Wahpeton, ND 58076
Phone: (701) 671-2240
Web site: www.ateaonline.org
Members: Composed of post-secondary institutions, businesses, and industrial concerns. Involved in expanding and improving the quality of technical education at the secondary level
AM: Spring

Analytical Laboratory Managers Association
1201 Don Diego Avenue
Santa Fe, NM 87505
Phone: (505) 989-4683
Web site: www.labmanagers.org
Members: University, industrial, and government laboratories
AM: Fall

APICS—The Educational Society for Resource Management
5301 Shawnee Road
Alexandria, VA 22312
Phone: (703) 354-8851
Web site: www.apics.org
Members: Professionals in the field of resource management
AM: Fall

ARMA International—The Association for Information Management Professionals
4200 Somerset Drive, Suite 215
Prairie Village, KS 66208
Phone: (913) 341-3808
Web site: www.arma.org
AM: Fall

Association for Career & Technical Education
1410 King Street
Alexandria, VA 22314
Phone: (703) 683-3111
Web site: www.avaonline.org
Members: A federation of state vocational associations
AM: Winter

Association Chief Executive Council
8421 Frost Way
Annandale, VA 22003
Phone: (703) 280-4622
Members: Chief executive officers of trade and professional associations
AM: Monthly

Association for Correctional Research & Information Management
1129 Rivara Circle
Sacramento, CA 95864
Phone: (916) 487-9334
Web site: www.happenings.com

Association for Data Center, Network & Enterprise Systems Management
742 E. Chapman Avenue
Orange, CA 92866
Phone: (714) 997-7966
Web site: www.afcom.com
Members: Managers of corporate and institutional computer facilities
AM: Sprint

Association for Information & Image Management International
1100 Wayne Avenue, Suite 1100
Silver Spring, MD 20910
Phone: (301) 587-8202
Web site: www.aiim.org
Members: Users and manufacturers of equipment, supplies, and services for the document management industry
AM: Spring

Association for Information Media & Equipment
134 Sunflower Avenue
Clarksdale, MS 38614
Phone: (662) 624-9355
Web site: www.aime.org

Members: Association of producers and distributors of educational films and video, companies who provide related equipment and services, and others who use information media materials and equipment
AM: Spring

Association for Public Policy Analysis & Management
Box 18766
Washington, D.C. 20036
Phone: (202) 261-5788
Web site: www.appam.org
Members: Individuals with an interest in the teaching, research, or practice of public policy analysis
AM: Fall

Association for Volunteer Administration
320 W. Sabal Palm Place, Suite 150
Longwood, FL 32779
Phone: (407) 834-6688
AM: Fall

Association of Information Technology Professionals
315 S. Northwest Highway
Park Ridge, IL 60068
Phone: (847) 825-8124
Web site: www.aitp.org
Members: System professionals
AM: Fall

Association of Internal Management Consultants
1200 19th Street, NW, Suite 300
Washington, D.C. 20036
Phone: (212) 687-9463
Members: Individuals engaged in the practice of internal management consulting with five or more years experience and operating at a senior or project leader level
AM: Spring

Association of Management Analysts in State & Local Government
c/o Fels Center of Government
University of Pennsylvania
Philadelphia, PA 19104
Phone: (215) 898-8216

Members: Promotes administrative specialization of management analysis, primarily among state and local governments
AM: Spring & Fall

Association of Management Consulting Firms
380 Lexington Avenue, Suite 1700
New York, NY 10168
Phone: (212) 551-7887
Web site: www.amcf.org
Members: Professional management consulting firms
AM: Fall

Association of Productivity Specialists
521 Fifth Avenue, Suite 1700
New York, NY 10175
Phone: (212) 286-0943

Association of Professional Energy Managers
143 S. Citrus Street
Orange, CA 92868
Phone: (800) 543-3563
Web site: www.apem.org
Members: Individuals responsible for energy production, consumption, or management decisions, including professional consultants, in all types of organizations

Association of Proposal Management Professionals
P.O. Box 668
Dana Point, CA 92629
Phone: (909) 659-0789
Web site: www.apmp.org
AM: Spring

Association of Sales Administration Managers
P.O. Box 1356
Laurence Harbor, NJ 08879
Phone: (732) 264-7722
Members: Independent consultants and corporate employees providing sales and marketing services

Association of School Business Officials International
11401 North Shore Drive
Reston, VA 20190
Phone: (703) 478-0405
Web site: www.asbointl.org
Members: School district–level business executives, professors of business and education, students, and businesspeople of school-related firms
AM: Fall

Association of University Related Research Parks
1730 K Street, NW, Suite 700
Washington, D.C. 20006
Phone: (202) 828-4167
Web site: www.aurrp.org
Members: Serves as a central clearing house for the exchange of information on the planning, construction, marketing, and management of university-related research parks and technology incubators
AM: Summer

Athletic Equipment Managers Association
P.O. Box 2093
Ann Arbor, MI 48106
Phone: (734) 477-9073
AM: Spring

Automotive Trade Association Executives
8400 Westpark Drive
McLean, VA 22102
Phone: (703) 821-7072
Members: Executives of state and local automobile dealer associations
AM: Winter & Summer

Automotive Training Managers Council
13505 Dulles Technology Drive, Suite 2
Herndon, VA 20171
Phone: (703) 713-1113
Web site: www.atmc.org
Members: Automotive aftermarket manufacturing and distributing concerns, each represented by a training department executive
AM: Spring & Fall

Building Owners & Managers Association International
1201 New York Avenue, NW, Suite 300
Washington, D.C. 20005
Phone: (202) 408-2662
Web site: www.boma.org
Members: Building owners, developers, managers, service companies, investors, brokers, and third-party management firms
AM: June

Building Owners & Management Institute International
1521 Ritchie Highway
Arnold, MD 21012
Phone: (410) 974-1410
Web site: www.bomi/edu.org
Members: Developers, fee managers, multinational corporations, and governments
AM: June

Business Forms Management Association
319 S.W. Washington, Suite 710
Portland, OR 97204
Phone: (503) 227-3393
Web site: www.bfma.org
Members: Form designers, analysts, systems managers, and IS managers
AM: May

Center for Management Advisors
111 E. Wacker Drive, Suite 990
Chicago, IL 60601
Phone: (312) 729-9900
Web site: www.cpaselect.com/center
Members: CPAs

Christian Management Association
P.O. Box 4090
San Clemente, CA 92674
Phone: (949) 487-0900
Web site: www.cmaonline.org
Members: Managers of churches and Christian organizations
AM: February

CLMA—Leadership in Clinical Systems Management
989 Old Eagle School Road, Suite 815
Wayne, PA 19087
Phone: (610) 995-9580
Web site: www.clma.org
Members: Laboratory executives and their suppliers
AM: Fall

Club Managers Association of America
1733 King Street
Alexandria, VA 22314
Phone: (703) 739-9500
Web site: www.cmaa.org
Members: Managers of leading private membership clubs
AW: Winter

College Athletic Business Management Association
19090-398 Laurel Park Road
Rancho Dominguez, CA 90220
Phone: (310) 637-0670
Web site: www.cabma.com
Members: Business and ticket managers, directors of athletics and their assistants, fundraisers, facilities managers, systems managers
AM: January

Communications Managers Association
1201 Mt. Kemble Avenue
Morristown, NJ 07960
Phone: (973) 425-1700
Web site: www.cma.org

Communications Media Management Association
P.O. Box 227
Wheaton, IL 60189
Phone: (630) 653-2772
Web site: www.cmma.net
Members: Individuals managing communications media departments in business and education
AM: Spring & Fall

Construction Financial Management Association
29 Emmons Drive, Suite F–50
Princeton, NJ 08540
Phone: (609) 452-8000
Web site: www.cfma.org
Members: Accountants, controllers, financial managers, and CPAs in the construction industry concerned with financial management tax, technology, and risk management issues
AM: May

Construction Management Association of America
7918 Jones Branch Drive, Suite 540
McLean, VA 22102
Phone: (703) 356-2622
Web site: www.cmaanet.org
Members: Firms and individuals that provide total management of a construction project from conception through completion as a professional service
AM: Fall

Cost Management Group
10 Paragon Drive
Montvale, NJ 07645
Phone: (201) 573-9000
Web site: www.imanet.org

Council of Logistics Management
2805 Butterfield Road, Suite 200
Oak Brook, IL 60523
Phone: (630) 574-0985
Web site: www.clm1.org
Members: Individuals concerned with transportation, warehousing inventory, materials, logistics and/or physical distribution management
AM: Fall

Decision Science Institute
Georgia State University
College of Business
35 Broad Street
Atlanta, GA 30303
Phone: (404) 651-4005
Web site: www.decisionsciences.org

Members: Business school faculties and management specialists who use quantitative and behavioral techniques to apply theories of administrative decision making
AM: Fall

Driving School Association of America
111 W. Pomona Blvd.
Monterey Park, CA 91754
Phone: (323) 728-2100
Web site: www.californiadrivingsch.net

Members: Professional, state-licensed driving schools in the United States and Canada, as well as spokespersons of state associations
AM: November

Employment Management Association
1800 Duke Street
Alexandria, VA 22314
Phone: (703) 548-3440
Web site: www.shrm.org

Members: Employment and human resource executives or those interested in employment and staffing
AM: Spring

Environmental Industry Association
4301 Connecticut Avenue, NW,
Suite 300
Washington, D.C. 20008
Phone: (800) 424-2869
Web site: www.envasns.org
AM: Spring

Evangelical Training Association
110 Bridge Street
Wheaton, IL 60189
Phone: (630) 668-6400
Web site: www.ETAWorld.org

Members: Active member seminaries and colleges present courses using ETA materials to prepare students for professional church leadership and to train church volunteers
AM: Odd years – February

Federal Managers Association
1641 Prince Street
Alexandria, VA 22314
Phone: (703) 683-8700
Web site: www.fedmanagers.org

Members: Managers and supervisors in all federal agencies
AM: Spring & Fall

Financial Management Association
College of Business Administration
University of South Florida
Tampa, FL 33620
Phone: (813) 974-2084
Web site: www.fma.org

Members: College professors of financial management and corporate and organizational financial officers
AM: Fall

Fraternal Field Managers Association
P.O. Box 404
Wheaton, IL 60189
Phone: (630) 871-2554
Members: Sales managers of fraternal life insurance societies

Fulfillment Management Association
60 E. 42nd Street, Suite 1146
New York, NY 10165
Phone: (815) 734-5821
Web site: www.fmanational.org

Members: Direct mail fulfillment, marketing, and circulation executives
AM: Monthly

GAMA International
2901 Telestar Court
Falls Church, VA 22042
Phone: (703) 770-8184
Web site: www.gamaweb.com

Members: Field managers within the life insurance industry
AM: Spring

Golf Course Superintendents Association of America
1421 Research Park Drive
Lawrence, KS 66049
Phone: (785) 841-2240
Web site: www.gcsaa.org
AM: Winter

Groundwater Management Districts Association
P.O. Box 905
Colby, KS 67701
Phone: (785) 462-3915
Web site: www.gmda.nrc.state.ne.us

Members: Districts, consulting organizations, and individuals concerned
with the management and conserva-
tion of water resources
AM: Winter

Health Care Resource Management Society
P.O. Box 29253
Cincinnati, OH 45229
Phone: (513) 520-1058
Web site: www.hcrms.com

Members: Resource management professionals employed in the health
care/hospital field

Healthcare Financial Management Association
Two Westbrook Corporate Center,
Suite 700
Westchester, IL 60154
Phone: (708) 531-9600
Web site: www.hfma.org

Members: Individuals directly or
indirectly associated with financial
management in healthcare
organizations
AM: June

Healthcare Information and Management Systems
230 E. Ohio Street, Suite 500
Chicago, IL 60611
Phone: (312) 664-4467
Web site: www.himss.org

Members: CIOs, Information Systems,
Management Engineering, Clinical
Systems and Telecommunications
AM: Feb.-March

Hospitality Sales & Marketing Association International
1300 L Street, NW, Suite 1020
Washington, D.C. 20005
Phone: (202) 789-0089
Web site: www.hsmal.org
AM: June

Institute of Behavioral & Applied Management
Wilkes University
Wilkes-Barre, PA 18766
Phone: (717) 408-4706

Members: Educators and other professionals interested in organizational
behavior and management theory
AM: Fall

Institute of Certified Professional Managers
James Madison University
Harrisonburg, VA 22807
Phone: (540) 568-3247
Web site: www.jmu.edu/icpm

Members: Professional supervisors
and managers
AM: Spring

Institute of Certified Records Managers
P.O. Box 8188
Prairie Village, KS 66208
Phone: (800) 422-2762
Web site: www.lcrm.org

Members: Professional records managers and administrative officers
who specialize in the field of
Records and Information
AM: Fall

Institute of Management Consultants
2025 M Street, NW, Suite 800
Washington, D.C. 20036
Phone: (202) 367-1134
Web site: www.imcusa.org

Members: Individual management consultants
AM: April/May

Institute of Real Estate Management
430 N. Michigan Avenue
Chicago, IL 60611
Phone: (312) 329-6000
Web site: www.irem.org

Members: Individuals and companies
that manage real estate in the United
States and abroad
AM: Fall

International Association for Exhibition Management
5001 Freeway, Suite 350
Dallas, TX 75244
Phone: (972) 458-8002
Web site: www.laem.org

Members: Managers of shows, exhibits, and expositions; associate members are industry suppliers
AM: June & December

International Association of Association Management Companies
414 Plaza Drive, Suite 209
Westmont, IL 60559
Phone: (630) 655-1669
Web site: www.laamc.org

Members: Companies engaged in the management of two or more organizations on a professional client basis
AM: February

International Association of Assembly Managers
635 Fritz Drive
Coppell, TX 75019
Phone: (972) 255-8020
Web site: www.iaam.org

Members: Managers of auditoriums, arenas, convention centers, stadiums, and performing arts centers representing the most prominent sports, entertainment, and convention facilities
AM: Summer

International Association of Correctional Training Professionals
P.O. Box 471264
Lake Monroe, FL 32747
Phone: (407) 321-3215
Web site: www.iactp.org

Members: 450 individuals
AM: Spring & Fall

International Association of Culinary Professionals
304 West Liberty Street, Suite 201
Louisville, KY 40202
Phone: (502) 581-9786
Web site: www.iacp.com

Members: Indviduals employed in, or providing services to, the culinary industry (cooking schools, cooking educators, cooking students, culinary specialists, caterers, and food writers)
AM: Spring

International Association of Healthcare Central Service Material Management
213 W. Institute Place, Suite 307
Chicago, IL 60610
Web site: www.iahcsmm.com

Members: Persons serving in a technical, supervisory, or management capacity in hospital departments responsible for the management and distribution of supplies
AM: May

International City/County Management Association
777 North Capitol Street, NE, Suite 500
Washington, D.C. 20002
Phone: (202) 289-4262
Web site: www.jcma.org

Members: Local government administrators
AM: Fall

International Council for Small Business
3674 Lindell Blvd.
St. Louis University
St. Louis, MO 63108
Phone: (314) 977-3628
Web site: www.icsb.org
AM: June

International Customer Service Association
401 N. Michigan Avenue
Chicago, IL 60611
Phone: (312) 321-6800
Web site: www.icsa.com

Members: Customer service management professionals
AM: Fall

International Facility Management Association
One E. Greenway Plaza, Suite 1100
Houston, TX 77046
Phone: (713) 623-4362
Web site: www.ifma.org

Members: In-house member or manager of a department responsible for facility planning, design, or management
AM: Fall

International Management Council
7502 Maple Street
Omaha, NE 68134
Phone: (402) 330-6310
Web site: www.imc-ymca.org
Members: Provides individuals with
  opportunities to develop their leadership and management skills through
  a network of shared experiences and
  education
AM: Spring

**International Personnel Management
  Association**
1617 Duke Street
Alexandria, VA 22314
Phone: (703) 549-7100
Web site: www.ipma-hr.org
AM: Fall

**International Publishing Management
  Association**
1205 W. College Street
Liberty, MO 64068
Phone: (816) 781-1111
Web site: www.ipma.org
Members: Professional association for
  corporate publishing (creation, production, distribution) professionals
  who work for educational institutions, government, and private
  industry
AM: Spring

**International Society for Intercultural
  Education, Training & Research**
883 SW Canyon Lane, Suite 110
Portland, OR 97225
Phone: (503) 297-4622
Web site: www.seitarusa.org
Members: Individuals concerned with
  understanding the interaction
  between peoples of different national,
  cultural, racial, and ethnic back-
  grounds
AM: Spring

**International Society for Performance
  Improvement**
1400 Spring Street, Suite 260
Silver Spring, MD 20910
Web site: www.ispi.org

Members: Performance technologists,
  training directors, human resource
  managers, instructional technologists,
  human factors practitioners,
  and organizational development
  consultants
AM: Spring

**International Society for the
  Performing Arts**
P.O. Box 909
Rye, NY 10580
Phone: (914) 971-1550
Web site: www.ispa.org
Members: Executives and directors
  of concert and performing halls,
  festivals, performing companies
  and artist competitions, govern-
  ment cultural officials, artists'
  managers
AM: Semi-annual June & December

**International Society of Facilities
  Executives**
200 Corporate Place, Suite 2B
Peabody, MA 01960
Phone: (978) 536-0108
Web site: www.isfe.org
Members: Professional organization
  for senior facilities executives
  with ultimate responsibilities for
  their corporate and institutional
  assets

International Ticketing Association
250 W. 57th Street, Suite 722
New York, NY 10107
Phone: (212) 581-0600
Web site: www.intix.org
Members: Box office managers,
  treasurers, marketing and systems
  directors, and other administrators
  from the performing arts and
  sports fields, performing arts
  center

LOMA
2300 Windy Ridge Parkway,
  Suite 600
Atlanta, GA 30339
Phone: (770) 951-1770
Web site: www.loma.org

Members: Sponsors education, training, employment development programs, networking, and research to promote effective management in life and health insurance companies and other related organizations
AM: Fall

Materials Handling and Management Society
8720 Red Oak Blvd., Suite 201
Charlotte, NC 28217
Phone: (704) 676-1184
Web site: www.mhia.org/mhms
Members: Professional society of individuals interested in advancing the theory and practice of the management and handling of all types of material
AM: Semi-annual Spring & Fall

Medical Group Management Association
104 Inverness Terrace East
Englewood, CO 80112
Phone: (303) 799-1111
Web site: www.mgma.com
Members: Represents medical group practice
AM: Fall

Mineral Economics and Management Society
P.O. Box 721
Houghton, MI 49931
Phone: (906) 487-2771
Members: Professional society for mineral, energy, and natural resource economics, managers, consultants, financiers, policy analysts, geologists, engineers
AM: Spring

National Association of Credit Management
8840 Columbia 100 Parkway
Columbia, MD 21045
Phone: (410) 740-5560
Web site: www.nacm.org
Members: Charter member credit executives
AM: Spring

National Association of Flood & Stormwater Management Agencies
1299 Pennsylvania Avenue, NW, 8th Fl.-W
Washington, D.C. 20004
Phone: (202) 218-4122
Web site: www.nafsma.org
Members: State, county, and municipal organizations concerned with the management of water resources in metropolitan areas
AM: Fall

National Association of Postal Supervisors
1727 King Street, Suite 400
Alexandria, VA 22314
Phone: (703) 836-9660
Web site: www.naps.org
AM: Aug./September

National Association of Professional Organizers
P.O. Box 140647
Austin, TX 78714
Phone: (512) 454-8626
Members: Time, productivity, and organization management consultants
AM: Spring

National Association of Purchasing Management
P.O. Box 22160
Tempe, AZ 85285
Phone: (480) 752-6276
Web site: www.napm.org
AM: May

National Association of Resident Management Corporations
4524 Douglas Street, NE
Washington, D.C. 20019
Phone: (202) 397-7002
AM: Summer

National Association of Scientific Materials Managers
Biology Dept.
Northeastern University
360 Huntington Avenue
Boston, MA 02115
Phone: (617) 373-2260
Web site: www.denison.edu/naosmm

Members: Stockroom managers, supervisors, and other support personnel, mainly in university, industry, and commercial research laboratories, who purchase scientific equipment
AM: July/August

National Association of Service Managers
P.O. Box 712500
Santee, CA 92072
Phone: (619) 562-7004
Web site: www.nasm.com

Members: Service managers in all industries

National Association of Workforce Boards
1201 New York Avenue NW, Suite 350
Washington, D.C. 20005
Phone: (202) 289-2950
Web site: www.nawb.org

Members: Private industry councils and private employers concerned with employment and training policies in the context of economic development and education
AM: February

National Basketball Trainers' Association
400 Colony Square, Suite 1750
Atlanta, GA 30361
Phone: (404) 875-4000
Members: All athletic trainers in the NBA
AM: June

National Business Incubation Association
20 E. Circle Drive, Suite 190
Athens, OH 4571
Phone: (740) 593-4331
Web site: www.nbia.org

Members: Small business incubator managers and developers as well as those interested in tracking the industry
AM: Spring

National Classification Management Society
994 Old Eagle School Road, Suite 1019
Wayne, PA 19087
Phone: (610) 971-4856
Web site: www.classmgmt.com

Members: Information security professionals concerned with identifying and assigning a security classification to information and materials needing protection in the national interest
AM: Summer

National Contract Management Association
1912 Woodford Road
Vienna, VA 22182
Phone: (703) 448-9231
Web site: www.ncmahq.com

Members: Individuals concerned with various forms of contracting with federal, state, and local governments and industry

National Council of Agricultural Employers
1112 16th Street, NW, Suite 920
Washington, D.C. 20036
Phone: (202) 728-0300
Web site: www.agemployees.org

Members: Growers and producers who employ agricultural laborers, as well as processors and organizations related to the agriculture business
AM: Semi-annual Summer & Winter

National Council of Social Security Management Association
106 Plaza Drive, Suite A
Vallejo, CA 94591
Phone: (707) 643-2577
Members: Managers and supervisors of Social Security field offices and teleservice centers
AM: November

National Credit Union Management Association
4989 Rebel Trail, NW
Atlanta, GA 30327
Phone: (404) 255-6828

Members: Credit unions whose assets total more than $5 million

National Environmental Training Association
5320 N. 16th Street, Suite 114
Phoenix, AZ 85016
Phone: (602) 956-6099
Web site: www.ehs-training.org
Members: Trainers of personnel in the field of air and noise pollution, solid and hazardous waste control, water supply, and wastewater treatment, and occupational safety and health
AM: April

National Institute of Management Counselors
P.O. Box 193
Great Neck, NY 11022
Phone: (516) 482-5682

National Institute of Packaging, Handling & Logistics Engineers
6902 Lyle Street
Lanham, MD 20706
Phone: (301) 459-9105
Web site: www.erols.com/niphie
AM: Semi-annual Spring & Fall

National Institute on Park and Grounds Management
730 W. Frances Street
Appleton, WI 54914
Phone: (920) 733-2301
Web site: www.tpo.org/pgm
Members: Managers of parks, campuses, and other large outdoor areas
AM: Fall

National Management Association
2210 Arbor Blvd.
Dayton, OH 45439
Phone: (937) 294-0421
Web site: www.nmal.org
Members: Mid-level and supervisory management personnel united to professionalize management
AM: Fall

National Property Management Association
1108 Pinehurst Road
Dunedin, FL 34698
Phone: (727) 736-3788
Web site: www.npma.org
Members: Specialize in asset management for federal, state, and local government agencies; industry; educational institutions and nonprofit organizations
AM: Summer

National Safety Management Society
4915 Auburn Avenue
Bethesda, MD 20814
Phone: (800) 321-2910
Web site: www.nsms.ws
Members: Membership is open to anyone with management responsibilities
AM: October

National Training Systems Association
2111 Wilson Blvd., Suite 400
Arlington, VA 22201
Phone: (703) 522-1820
Web site: www.trainingsystems.org
Members: Companies in the simulation and training industry and training support services
AM: Winter

Newspaper Association Managers
c/o New England Newspaper Association
70 Washington Street
Salem, MA 01970
Phone: (978) 744-8940
Members: Managers of state, regional, national, and international press associations
AM: August

North American Performing Arts Managers & Agents
459 Columbus Avenue, Suite 133
New York, NY 10034
Phone: (888) 745-8759
Web site: www.napama.org

Members: Professional managers, agents, or personal representatives and businesses and individuals related to the industry
AM: December

North American Transportation Management Institute
2200 Mill Road
Alexandria, VA 22314
Phone: (703) 838-7952
Members: Those in the industry and related organizations concerned with training and certification
AM: Spring

Paper Industry Management Association
1699 Wall Street, Suite 212
Mt. Prospect, IL 60056
Phone: (847) 956-0250
Web site: www.pima-online.org
Members: Managers of paper mills
AM: June

Product Development & Management Association
236 Route 38 West, Suite 100
Moorestown, NJ 08057
Phone: (856) 231-1578
Web site: www.pdma.org
Members: Professional interest in improving the management of product innovation
AM: Fall

Professional Association of Health Care Office Managers
461 E. Ten Mile Road
Pensacola, FL 32534
Phone: (850) 474-9460
Web site: www.pahcom.com
Members: Managers of medical practices
AM: May

Professional Baseball Athletic Trainers' Society
400 Colony Square, Suite 1750
Atlanta, GA 30361
Phone: (404) 875-4000
Members: Athletic trainers in major league baseball
AM: December

Professional Convention Management Association
2301 S. Lake Shore Drive, Suite 1001
Chicago, IL 60616
Phone: (312) 423-7262
Members: Convention managers, CEOs, meeting planners, and suppliers representing 1000 organizations
AM: Winter

Professional Football Athletic Trainers Society
400 Colony Square, Suite 1750
Atlanta, GA 30361
Phone: (404) 875-4000
Members: Athletic trainers in the NFL
AM: June

Professional Managers Association
P.O. Box 77235
Washington, D.C. 20013
Phone: (202) 874-1508
Members: Federal employees in management positions and management officials

Professional Services Management Association
99 Canal Center Plaza, Suite 250
Alexandria, VA 22314
Phone: (703) 739-0277
Web site: www.psma.org
Members: Business managers, owners, and principals of professional service firms
AM: Fall

Professional Society for Sales & Marketing Training
P.O. Box 995
Fayatteville, GA 30214
Phone: (770) 719-4768
Members: 170 individuals
AM: September

Project Management Institute
4 Campus Blvd.
Newtown Square, PA 19073
Phone: (610) 356-4600
Web site: www.pmi.org
AM: November

Radiology Business Management Association
1550 South Coast Highway, Suite 201
Laguna Beach, CA 92651
Phone: (888) 224-7262
Web site: www.rbma.org
AM: Semi-annual – June & October

Religious Conference Management Association
One RCA Dome, Suite 120
Indianapolis, IN 46225
Phone: (317) 632-1888
Web site: www.rcmaweb.org
Members: Responsible for planning and/or managing meetings, seminars, conferences, conventions, assemblies, or other gatherings for religious organizations
AM: January

Roundalab
355 N. Orchard, #200
Boise, ID 83706
Phone: (208) 377-1232
Web site: www.roundalab.org
Members: Individuals who teach round dancing at any phase
AM: June

School Management Study Group
P.O. Box 4865
Pocatello, ID 83205
Phone: (208) 233-6822
Members: School and college administrators interested in improving educational institutions

Section for Women in Public Administration
American Society for Public Administration
1120 G Street, NW, Suite 700
Washington, D.C. 20005
Phone: (202) 393-7878
Web site: www.homestead.com
Members: Develops programs and projects which promote the full participation and recognition of women in all levels and areas of public service
AM: Summer

Society for Advancement of Management
College of Business
6300 Ocean Drive
Texas A & M University—Corpus Christi
Corpus Christi, TX 78412
Phone: (361) 825-6045
Members: Management executives
AM: March

Society for Foodservice Management
304 W. Liberty Street, Suite 201
Louisville, KY 40202
Phone: (502) 583-3783
Web site: www.sfm-online.org
Members: Executives who are responsible for noncommercial food service, such as employee cafeterias, colleges and universities, and heathcare facilities
AM: Fall

Society for Information Management
401 N. Michigan Avenue
Chicago, IL 60611
Phone: (312) 644-6610
Web site: www.simnet.org
Members: IS executives and senior executives responsible for management of the business enterprise
AM: Fall

Society of Insurance Trainers and Educators
2120 Market Street, Suite 108
San Francisco, CA 94114
Phone: (415) 621-2830
Web site: www.connectyou.com
Members: Education and training personnel, personnel directors, and those responsible for the training function in insurance
AM: June

Society of Medical-Dental Management Consultants
3646 E. Ray Road, Suite B16-45
Phoenix, AZ 85044
Phone: (480) 763-9403
Web site: www.smdmc.org

Society of Roller Skating Teachers of America
6905 Corporate Drive
Indianapolis, IN 46278
Phone: (317) 347-2626

Special Interest Group for Computer Personnel Research
C/O Association for Computing Machinery
1515 Broadway, 17th Floor
New York, NY 10036
Phone: (212) 626-0607
Web site: www.acm.org/sigcpr

Members: Computer professionals, educators, MIS managers, and human resources specialists
AM: April

Sports Turf Managers Association
1375 Rolling Hills Loop
Council Bluffs, IA 51503
Phone: (712) 366-2669
Web site: www.sportsturfmanager.com

Members: Individuals involved in the management and maintenance of sports turf areas at schools, parks, professional stadiums, race tracks, etc.
AM: December

State Risk and Insurance Management Association
101 E. Wilson Street
Madison, WI 53707
Phone: (608) 266-1866
Web site: www.strima.org

Members: State government risk and insurance managers

Training Directors' Forum
50 S. 9th Street
Minneapolis, MN 55402
Phone: (612) 340-4912
Web site: www.lakewoodpub.com

Members: 2500 individuals
AM: May

Training Media Association
198 Thomas Johnson Drive, Suite 206
Frederick, MD 21702
Phone: (301) 662-4268
Web site: www.trainingmedia.org

Members: Training Media Distributors. Concerned with preventing unauthorized copying of training media.
AM: February

Travel Professionals Association
5221 S. Puritan Avenue
Tampa, FL 33611
Phone: (813) 876-0286

Turnaround Management Association
541 N. Fairbanks Court, Suite 1880
Chicago, IL 60611
Phone: (312) 822-9700
Web site: www.turnaround.org

Members: Financial advisors, operational consultants, crisis managers, corporate executives, attorneys, accountants, appraisers, commercial lenders
AM: Spring & Fall

United Professional Horsemen's Association
4059 Iron Works Parkway, Suite 4
Lexington, KY 40511
Phone: (859) 231-5070

Members: Professional trainers
AM: January

United States Fencing Coaches Association
P.O. Box 274
New York, NY 10159
Phone: (212) 532-2557

Members: Fencing teachers who conduct clinics and workshops to train fencing instructors
AM: Summer

United States Professional Tennis Registry
P.O. Box 4739
Hilton Head, SC 29938
Phone: (843) 785-7244
Web site: www.usptr.org

Members: Certified and registered tennis teaching professionals in 120 countries
AM: February

United Thoroughbred Trainers of America
P.O. Box 7065
Louisville, KY 40257
Phone: (502) 893-0025
Web site: www.thebackstretch.com

Members: Licensed thoroughbred horse trainers united to elevate the standards of the professional trainer's vocation and to promote interest in the sport of thoroughbred racing

University Council for Education Administration
University of Missouri, Columbia
205 Hill Hall
Columbia, MO 65211
Phone: (573) 884-8300
Web site: www.ucea.org

Members: Major universities
AM: October

Veterinary Hospital Managers Association
48 Howard Street
Albany, NY 12207
Phone: (518) 433-8911
Web site: www.uhma.com

Members: Individuals involved in veterinary practice management
AM: November

Walking Horse Trainers Association
P.O. Box 61
Shelbyville, TN 37162
Phone: (931) 684-5866

Members: Works for unity in the horse industry and sponsors continuing research
AM: December

Women in Management
P.O. Box 9560
Springfield, IL 62791
Phone: (217) 544-2706
Web site: www.wimonline.org

Members: Professionals in corporate, academic, not-for-profit, government, or entrepreneurial sectors of management

World at Work
14040 N. Northsight Blvd.
Scottsdale, AZ 85260
Phone: (480) 951-9191
Web site: www.worldatwork.org

Members: Individuals responsible for the compensation and benefits in their organization
AM: May

Young Presidents' Organization
451 S. Decker Drive
Irving, TX 75062
Phone: (972) 650-4600
Web site: www.ypo.org

Members: Company presidents under age 50 whose companies employ at least 50 individuals and have either $7 million in annual sales or $140 million in total assets

Public Seminar Companies

24/7 University
4201 Wingren Drive, Suite 202
Irvin, TX 75061
Phone: (972) 717-9170
Fax: (972) 717-1481
E-Mail: dhinkle@247university.com
Web site: www.247university.com
Topics: Career development, customer service, executive development, sales training, personal development
Staff Size: 6
Contact: Delwin Hinkle, Chairman/CEO

Acclivus Corporation
14500 Midway Road
Dallas, TX 75244
Phone: (972) 385-1277
Fax: (972) 386-6720
E-Mail: Ron.Gajewski@acclivus.com
Web site: www.acclivus.com
Topics: Sales training, customer service/client relations, negotiation skills, presentation skills, coaching
Staff Size: 60
Contact: Randall K. Murphy, President

Achieveglobal
8875 Hidden River Parkway
Suite 400
Tampa, FL 33637
Phone: (813) 631-5560
Fax: (813) 631-5796
E-Mail: Lisa.Fagan@achieveglobal.com
Web site: www.archieveglobal.com

Topics: Leadership, sales training, customer service/client relations, coaching, teams/team building
Staff Size: 900
Contact: Lisa Fagan, Director, Business, Development & Global Accounts

Advance Consulting, Inc.
582 Virginia Drive
Tiburon, CA 94920
Phone: (415) 435-3001
Fax: (415) 435-3007
E-Mail: advanceinfo@advanceconsulting.com
Web site: www.advanceconsulting.com
Topics: Consulting services, communication skills, customer service/client relations, conflict management, coaching
Staff Size: 30
Contact: Suzanne Saxe, President

Advanstar Communications
201 E. Sandpointe Avenue,
Suite 600
Santa Ana, CA 92707
Phone: (714) 513-8603
Fax: (714) 513-8611
E-Mail: rwheeler@advanstar.com
Web site: www.elearningexpos.com
Topics: Events/Magazines
Staff Size: 1000
Contact: Ruth Wheeler, Group Show Director

Allearnatives
10592 Perry Highway, Suite 201
Wexford, PA 15090
Phone: (724) 934-9349
Fax: (724) 934-9348
E-Mail: info@allearnatives.com
Web site: www.allearnatives.com
Topics: Telework/telecommuting, team skills/development, communication skills, work-life balance, e-policy/culture
Staff Size: 3
Contact: Debra Dinnocenzo, President

Alpha Genesis
25 West Eighth Street, Suite 300
Holland, MI 49423
Phone: (616) 820-2211
Fax: (616) 820-2215
E-Mail: jbrooks@agenesis.com
Topics: CBT developers, instructional systems design
Staff Size: 36
Contact: James W.F. Brooks, Managing Partner

American Arbitration Association
335 Madison Avenue, 10th Floor
New York, NY 10017
Phone: (212) 716-5800
Fax: (212) 716-5906
Web site: www.adr.org
Topics: Construction advocacy, unions, labor-management relations, advanced advocacy, and drug & alcohol problems in the workplace

American Management Association
1601 Broadway
New York, NY 10019
Phone: (212) 586-8100
Fax: (212) 903-8168
Web site: www.amanet.org
Topics: Finance, research & design, sales & marketing, insurance risk

American Marketing Association
250 S. Wacker Drive
Chicago, IL 60606
Phone: (312) 648-0538
Web site: www.ama.org
Topics: Research, services, new products, sports marketing, and marketing

American Productivity & Quality Center
123 N. Post Oak Lane
Houston, TX 77024
Phone: (713) 681-4020
Web site: www.aoqc.org
Topics: Total quality management, benchmarking, customer satisfaction, and zero defects

Applied Research Corporation
304 Amboy Avenue
Metuchen, NJ 08840-2442
Phone: (732) 549-8891
Fax: (732) 549-9179
E-Mail: jmargolis@arclead.com
Web site: www.arclead.com
Topics: Assessing talent, executive development, management skills/development, coaching, personal development/growth
Staff Size: 36
Contact: Jan Margolis

ASTD
1640 King Street
P.O. Box 1443
Alexandria, VA 22313-2043
Phone: (703) 683-8100
Fax: (703) 683-8103
E-Mail: tsung@astd.org.
Web site: www.astd.org
Topics: Membership association for workplace learning and performance professionals
Staff Size: 140
Contact: Tina Sung, President/CEO

Baygroup International
2200 Larkspur Landing Circle
Larkspur, CA 94939
Phone: (415) 464-4400
Fax: (415) 464-4405
E-Mail: Baygroup@baygroup.com
Web site: www.baygroup.com
Topics: Negotiation skills, conflict management, sales skills, communication skills, management skills/development
Staff Size: 50
Contact: Paul Hennessey, Executive Vice President

Being First, Inc.
1242 Oak Drive DW2
Durango, CO 81301
Phone: (970) 385-5100
Fax: (970) 385-7751
E-Mail: beingfirst@beingfirst.com
Web site: www.beingfirst.com
Topics: Transformational change, change leader development, change consultant development
Staff Size: 8
Contact: Dean Anderson, President

Better Communications, Writing Solutions
1666 Massachusetts Avenue, Suite 14
Lexington, MA 02420
Phone: (781) 862-3800
Fax: (781) 862-8383
E-Mail: workshops@bettercomm.com
Web site: www.writetothetop.com
Topics: Coaching, sales training, management skills/development, customer service/client relations, presentation skills
Staff Size: 12
Contact: Deborah Dumaine, President

Booher Consultants, Inc.
2051 Hughes Road
Grapevine, TX 76051
Phone: (817) 416-8866
Fax: (817) 318-6521
E-Mail: mailroom@booher.com
Web site: www.booher.com
Topics: Writing, presentation skills, communication skills, customer service/client relations, personal development/growth
Staff Size: 12
Contact: Dianna Booher, President/CEO

Brookings Institution
Center for Public Policy Education
1775 Massachusetts Avenue, NW
Washington, D.C. 20036
Phone: (202) 797-6000
Web site: www.brookings.edu
Topics: Conferences on public policy and executive education seminars

Business Training Library
745 Craig Road, Suite 210
St. Louis, MO 63141
Phone: (314) 432-3077, Ext. 106
Fax: (314) 567-4783
E-Mail: info@bizlibrary.com
Web site: www.bizlibrary.com
Topics: Computer skills (desktop & technical), HR/Legal issues, communication skills, management skills/development, sales and service training
Staff Size: 20
Contact: Dean Pichee, President/CEO

BVS Performance Systems
4060 Glass Road, NE
Cedar Rapids, IA 52402-2509
Phone: (319) 393-1193
Fax: (319) 393-1435
E-Mail: rkaron@bvsinc.com
Web site: www.bvsinc.com
Topics: Builds and delivers knowledge management systems
Staff Size: 34
Contact: Roy Karon, President

Cahners Tracom Group
8773 South Ridgeline Blvd.
Highlands Ranch, CO 80129-2345
Phone: (303) 470-4900
Fax: (303) 470-4901
E-Mail: nguy@cahners.com
Web site: www.cahnerstracom.com
Topics: Communication skills, teams/team building, sales training, management skills/development, conflict management
Staff Size. 36
Contact: John R. Myers, President

Career Systems International, Inc.
900 James Avenue
Scranton, PA 18510
Phone: (800) 577-6916
Fax: (570) 346-8606
E-Mail: hq@csibka.com
Web site: www.careersystemsintl.com
Topics: Career development, retention, executive development, employability, mentoring/coaching
Staff Size: 12
Contact: Dr. Beverly Kaye, President

Career Track
9757 Metcalf Avenue
Overland Park, KS 66212
Phone: (800) 944-8503
Web site: www.careertrack.com
Topics: Management issues, con-
sumer issues, communications,
and motivation

Center for Creative Leadership
One Leadership Place
P.O. Box 26300
Greensboro, NC 27438-6300
Phone: (336) 288-7210
Fax: (336) 288-3999
E-Mail: downingk@leaders.ccl.org
Web site: www.ccl.org
Topics: Leadership, executive devel-
opment, teams/team building,
coaching, creativity
Staff Size: 800
Contact: Kris Downing, Group
Director

Center for Effective Performance,
Inc.
2300 Peachford Road, Suite 2000
Atlanta, GA 30338
Phone: (770) 458-4080
Fax: (770) 458-9109
E-Mail: sleibler@cepworldwide.com
Web site: www.cepworldwide.com
Topics: Train the trainer, instructional
systems design, management
skills/development, facilitation
skills, technology-based training
solutions
Staff Size: 30
Contact: Seth Leibler, President

Charthouse International Learning
221 S. River Ridge Circle
Burnsville, MN 55337
Phone: (612) 890-1800
Fax: (612) 882-7375
E-Mail: Patrick@charthouse.com
Web site: www.charthouse.com
Topics: Customer service/client
relations, creativity, change man-
agement, employee recruitment
selection/staffing, organizational
change

Click2learn
110 110th Avenue NE, Suite 700
Bellevue, WA 98004
Phone: (425) 637-5885
Fax: (425) 637-1508
E-Mail: Kevin.oakes@click2learn.
com
Web site: www.click2learn.com
Topics: CBT developers, technical
skills training, career development,
management skills/development,
sales training
Staff Size: 400
Contact: Kevin Oakes, President

Columbia Executive Education
Columbia University
2880 Broadway, 4th Floor
New York, NY 10025
Phone: (212) 854-3395
Fax: (212) 316-1473
Web site: www.gsb.columbia.edu
Topics: Marketing Analysis

Comprehensive Loss Management,
Inc.
15800 32nd Avenue N., Suite 106
Plymouth, MN 55447
Phone: (763) 551-1036, Ext. 101
Fax: (763) 551-1030
Web site: www.clmi-training.com
Topics: Management consulting
services, custom multimedia
product for unique client spec-
ifications, pre-packaged safety
& ergonomics training, & com-
pliance programs
Contact: Rick Pollock

Conference Board
845 Third Avenue
New York, NY 10022
Phone: (212) 759-0900
Fax: (212) 836-9740
Web site: www.conference-board.
org
Topics: Compensation, management, development, communications, human resources,
strategic management, financial
briefings and conferences, and
business ethics

Core Media Training Solutions
1771 NW Pettygrove Street
Portland, OR 97209-2539
Phone: (503) 952-0012
Fax: (503) 223-9654
E-Mail: tcrane@cmts.com
Web site: www.cmts.com
Topics: Consulting, assessment of accident prevention process, on-site instruction, Web-based training, and custom production
Staff Size: 17
Contact: Doug Crane

Cornelius and Associates
631 G Harden Street
Columbia, SC 29205
Phone: (803) 779-3354
Fax: (802) 254-0183
E-Mail: info@cornelius.com
Web site: www.corneliusassoc.com
Topics: Teams, organizational change, communication skills/development, supervisory skills
Staff Size: 20
Contact: Edwin T. Cornelius, III

Crisp Learning
1200 Hamilton Court
Menlo Park, CA 94025-1427
Phone: (650) 323-6100
Fax: (630) 323-5800
E-Mail: crisplearning.com
Web site: www.crisplearning.com
Topics: Management and supervision, customer service and sales, personal productivity, human resources, communication, career and life planning
Staff Size: 40
Contact: Michael Crisp, CEO

Crkinteractive, Inc.
One Dundee Park, Suite 4
Andover, MA 01810
Phone: (978) 474-8657
Fax: (978) 474-8659
E-Mail: info@crkinteractive.com
Web site: www.crkinteractive.com
Topics: Sales training, customer service/client relations, coaching, management skills/development, leadership
Staff Size: 27
Contact: Len D'Innocenzo, CEO

CRM Learning
2215 Faraday Avenue
Carlsbad, CA 92008
Phone: (760) 431-9800
Fax: (760) 931-5792
E-Mail: sales@crmlearning.com
Web site: www.crmlearning.com
Topics: Organizational change, quality customer service, communication, teams, management skills/development
Staff Size: 52
Contact: Peter Jordan, President

Custom Learning Systems Group, Ltd.
#200, 2133 Kensington Road NW
Calgary, Alberta, T2N 3R8
Canada
Phone: (403) 245-2428
Fax: (403) 228-6776
E-Mail: info@customlearning.com
Web site: www.customlearning.com
Topics: Customer service/client relations, leadership, management skills/development, presentation skills, change management
Staff Size: 9
Contact: Brian Lee

Development Dimensions International
1225 Washington Pike
Bridgeville, PA 15017-2838
Phone: (412) 257-0600
Fax: (412) 257-2785
E-Mail: info@ddiworld.com
Web site: www.ddiworld.com
Topics: Supervisory training, leadership, employee recruitment, executive development, customer service/client relations

Disney Institute
P.O. Box 10,000
Lake Buena Vista, FL 32830
Phone: (407) 824-7997
Web site: www.disneyinstitute.com
Topics: Business Management: Disney's approach to people management, quality service, and creativity. Teachers/educators: graduate credits and teacher certification. Young people's programs. Group convention workshops.

Dove Consulting
600 South Highway 169
Suite 1630
Minneapolis, MN 55426
Phone: (952) 595-8689
Fax: (952) 595-8550
Web site: www.consultdov.com
Topics: Management skills/
    development, leadership, sales
    training, coaching, business
    knowledge
Staff Size: 130
Contact: Dr. Stephen Cohen

Eagle's Flight
Creative Training Excellence, Inc.
4925 Xerxes Avenue South
Minneapolis, MN 55410
Phone: (612) 285-5665
Fax: (612) 286-5666
E-Mail: info@eaglesflight.com
Web site: www.eaglesflight.com
Topics: Leadership, communica-
    tion skills, management skills/
    development, teams/team
    building, personal development/
    growth
Staff Size: 110
Contact: Sue Krautkramer,
    President

ebb Associates, Inc.
P.O. Box 8247
Virginia Beach, VA 23450
Phone: (757) 363-1950
Fax: (757) 363-1951
Web site: www.ebbweb.com
Topics: Teams/team building,
    communication skills, facili-
    tation skills, organizational
    change, personal development/
    growth
Contact: Elaine Biech, CEO

Electrolab Training Systems
P.O. Box 320
335 University Avenue
Belleville, ON K8N 5A5
Canada
Phone: (613) 962-9577
Fax: (613) 962-0284
E-Mail: btait@electrolab.ca
Web site: www.electrolab.ca

Topics: Safety training, behavior-
    based safety training and con-
    sulting, supervisory/HRD training,
    technical skills training
Staff Size: 35
Contact: Barbara Tait, General
    Manager

Employment Learning Innovations,
Inc.
2675 Paces Ferry Road, Suite 470
Atlanta, GA 30339
Phone: (770) 319-7999
Fax: (770) 319-7905
E-Mail: info@eliinc.com
Web site: www.eliinc.com
Topics: Employee/labor relations,
    management skills/develop-
    ment, communication skills,
    supervisory skills, executive
    development
Staff Size: 32
Contact: Stephen Paskoff,
    President

Enlightened Leadership
International, Inc.
7100 E. Belleview Avenue, Suite
G–11
Englewood, CO 80111
Phone: (303) 729-0504
Fax: (303) 729-0552
Web site: www.enleadership.com
Topics: Change management,
    leadership, management
    skills/development, organi-
    zational change, teams/team
    building

Franklin Covey Company
2200 West Parkway Blvd.
Salt Lake City, UT 84119
Phone: (800) 827-1776
Fax: (801) 817-4205
Web site: www.franklincovey.
    com
Topics: Time & project management,
    leadership management, communi-
    cation skills, organizational change,
    sales training
Staff Size: 1,200
Contact: Stephen Covey, Executive
    Vice President

Frontline Group
52 Vanderbilt Avenue, 7th Fl.
New York, NY 10017
Phone: (212) 972-4899
Fax: (212) 972-4855
E-Mail: kdaley@communispond.com
Web site: www.communispond.com
Topics: Communication skills, sales
skills, supervisory skills, manage-
ment skills/development, personal
development/growth
Staff Size: 400
Contact: Kevin Daley, CEO

Gilmore & Associates
1300 Bloor Street West, Suite 700
Toronto, ON M5S 1N5
Canada
Phone: (416) 926-1944
Fax: (416) 926-1351
Web site: www.gilmore-opening
monds.com
Topics: Change, continuous improve-
ment, leadership, teams, sales
Staff Size: 20
Contact: Blake Gilmore, CEO

Great Circle Learning
687 South Collier Blvd.
Marco Island, FL 34145
Phone: (941) 389-2000
Fax: (941) 389-0569
Web site: www.gclearning.com
Topics: Critical thinking, leader
guide pro, management skills/
development, leadership, career
development
Contact: Richard Michaels, President

Hawthorne Associates
60 Washington Street
Suite 203
Salem, MA 01970
Phone: (978) 745-4878
Fax: (978) 745-2553
Web site:
www.hawthorneassociates.com
Topics: Strategic planning, mar-
keting, public relations, trade
show support and design, & copy
writing
Staff Size: 5
Contact: Christine Sullivan, President

Herrmann International
794 Buffalo Creek Road
Lake Lure, NC 28746
Phone: (828) 625-9153
Fax: (828) 625-1402
Web site: www.bdi.com
Topics: Thinking style preference
assessment & interpretation, personal, management & executive
development/growth, strategic
thinking, creativity & team thinking, product design & human
interface, learning style/curriculum
assessment & development
Staff Size: 9
Contact: Ann Herrmann-Hehdi, CEO

**HAS Learning & Performance
Solutions**
1520 South Beverly Gloenn Blvd.
Suite 305
Los Angeles, CA 90024
Phone: (310) 286-2722
Fax: (310) 286-2724
E-Mail: ekeeps@has-lps.com
Web site: www.has-lps.com
Topics: Technical skills training,
instructional design, trainer
training, performance consulting,
blended learning, & performance
solutions
Staff Size: 8
Contact: Harold Stolovitch

Human Resource Executive
747 Dresher Road, Suite 500
Horsham, PA 19044-0980
Phone: (215) 784-0910
Fax: (215) 784-0870
E-Mail: bcorsini@trp.com
Web site: www.workindex.com
Topics: Magazine
Staff Size: 60
Contact: William Corsini, Group
Publisher

Human Synergistics International
39819 Plymouth Road, Suite C-8020
Plymouth, MI 48170-8020
Phone: (800) 622-7584
Fax: (734) 459-5557
E-Mail: info@humansyn.com
Web site: www.humansyn.com

Topics: Organizational change, teams/team building, executive development, management skills/development, personal development/growth
Staff Size: 29
Contact: Gerry Clarke

The Humor Project, Inc.
480 Broadway, Suite 210
Saratoga Springs, NY 12866
Phone: (518) 587-8770
Web site: www.humorproject.com
Topics: Humor as a positive power and humor in business

Huthwaite, Inc.
15164 Berlin Turnpike
Purcellville, VA 20132
Phone: (540) 882-3212
Fax: (540) 882-9004
E-Mail: jelsey@huthwaite.com
Web site: www.huthwaite.com
Topics: Sales training, negotiation skills, coaching, consulting/measurement, management skills/development
Staff Size: 62
Contact: John Elsey, President

Inscape Publishing
6465 Wayzala Blvd., Suite 800
Minneapolis, MN 55420
Phone: (763) 765-2265
Fax: (763) 765-2278
E-Mail: info@inscapepublishing.com
Web site: www.inscapepublishing.com
Topics: Instrumented learning. Communication skills, management skills/development, team/team building, personal development/growth
Staff Size: 35
Contact: Jeffrey Sugerman, President

IIR
708 3rd Avenue
New York, NY 10017
Phone: (212) 661-3500
Fax: (212) 599-2192
E-Mail: register@iirusa.com
Web site: www.iir.org

Topics: Sales training, project management, leadership, management skills/development, diversity
Staff Size: 3500
Contact: Chris Maybury, World CEO

Institute for Professional Education
P.O. Box 756
Arlington, VA 22216
Phone: (703) 527-8700
Web site: www.ipeseminars.org
Topics: Statistics, management, research design, simulation modeling, forecasting, and the applied art of artificial intelligence

Interaction Associates, Inc.
20 University Road, Suite 400
Cambridge, MA 02138
Phone: (415) 241-8000
Fax: (415) 241-8010
Web site: www.interactionassociates.com
Topics: Coaching, change management, facilitation skills, leadership, teams/team building
Staff Size: 100
Contact: Trina Soske, President

Integrated Learning Solutions
2720 W. Calle Cuero de Vaca
Tucson, AZ 85745
Phone: (520) 624-9575
Fax: (520) 624-9576
E-Mail: ann@annboland.com
Topics: Sales & marketing strategy, tactics & execution, product viability analysis, business plan development, market research & interpretation
Contact: Ann Boland, President

IWCC Training In Communications
30 East Beaver Creek Road, Suite 209
Richmond Hill, ON L4B 1J2
Canada
Phone: (905) 764-3710
Fax: (905) 764-3712
E-Mail: iwcc@iwcc-com.com
Web site: www.iwcc-com.com
Topics: Writing skills, presentation skills, proposal writing, communication skills, facilitation skills
Staff Size: 22
Contact: Jean Findlater

J. A. Drago
P.O. Box 445
Western Springs, IL 60558
Phone: (708) 784-9300
Fax: (703) 784-9301
Web site: www.jadrago.com
Topics: Strategic problem solving, key introductions, business brokering, board development
Contact: Joseph Drago, President

Jonesknowledge.com™, Inc.
9697 East Mineral Avenue
Englewood, CO 80112
Phone: (303) 792-3111
Fax: (303) 784-8597
E-Mail: homara@jonesknowledge.com
Web site: www.jonesknowledge.com
Topics: Instructional systems design, E-learning platform software
Staff Size: 120
Contact: Heather O'Mara

Kepner-Tregoe, Inc.
Research Road
P.O. Box 704
Princeton, NJ 08542
Phone: (609) 921-2806
Web site: www.ketner-tregoe.com
Topics: Technology, training the trainer, problem solving, people management, management involvement, and project management

Lakewood Conferences
50 South 9th Street
Minneapolis, MN 55402
Phone: (612) 333-0471
Web site: www.vnulearning.com
Topics: Training and development, customer-service training, and human resources

Langevin Learning Services
P.O. Box 1221
Ogdensburg, NY 13669
Phone: (800) 223-2209
Web site: www.langevin.com

Learning Resources (Pty.) LTD
12 Lonsdale Building
Lonsdale Way, Pinelands
Cape Town Western Cape, South Africa 7405
Phone: 27-21-531-2923
Fax: 27-21-531-2944
E-Mail: ricky@learning-resources.com.za
Topics: Learning products and services to businesses in Southern Africa
Staff Size: 80
Contact: Ricky Robinson, Managing Director

LMA Consulting Group
1848 Charter Lane
Lancaster, PA 17601
Phone: (717) 509-8889
Web site: www.lmasystems.com
Topics: Business ethics, performance coaching, performance management, situational leadership, effective performance appraisals, performance coaching

Lore International Institute
1130 Main Avenue
Durango, CO 81301
Phone: (970) 385-4955
Fax: (970) 385-0659
E-Mail: impact@lorenet.com
Web site: www.lorenet.com
Topics: Executive development, sales training, coaching, leadership, communication skills
Staff Size: 66
Contact: Linda Simmons, VP Operations & Business Development

Mail Advertising Service Association Int'l
1421 Prince Street, Suite 200
Alexandria, VA 22314
Phone: (703) 836-9200
Web site: www.mfsanet.org
Topics: Technical seminars on machines used in lettershops

Management 21
111 10th Avenue South
Nashville, TN 37203
Phone: (615) 871-4321
Fax: (615) 871-9821
E-Mail: info@management21.com
Web site: www.management21.com
Topics: Organizational change, strategic
planning, leadership, customer ser-
vice/client relations, instructional
systems design
Staff Size: 11
Contact: Ron Galbraith, President

Management Concepts, Inc.
8230 Leesburg Pike, Suite 800
Vienna, VA 22182
Phone: (703) 790-9595
Fax: (703) 790-1371
Web site:
www.managementconcepts.com
Topics: Acquisition/contracting,
project management
Staff Size: 100
Contact: Thomas Dungan III,
President

Management Team Consultants,
Inc.
1010 B Street, Suite 403
San Rafael, CA 94901
Phone: (415) 459-4800
Fax: (415) 459-5151
E-Mail: mtc@interviewedge.com
Web site: www.interviewedge.
com
Topics: Selection interviewing,
diversity
Staff Size: 6
Contact: Jim Kennedy, President

Market Data Retrieval
16 Process Drive
Shelton, CT 06484
Phone: (800) 243-5538
Web site: www.schooldata.com
Topics: Direct marketing for educational marketing; how to design a
promotional piece; integrating
various marketing arms to work
together

Medical Learning Inc.
245 East Sixth Street, Suite 502
St. Paul, MN 55101-1918
Phone: (651) 292-3400
Fax: (651) 224-4694
E-Mail: mrogge@medlearn.com
Web site: www.medlearn.com
Topics: Technical skills/knowledge
updating, quality training, publica-
tions, new methods/procedures,
organizational change, online testing
Staff Size: 45
Contact: Michael Rogge

Mica Management Resources
229 Yonge Street, Suite 400
Toronto, ON M5B 1N9
Canada
Phone: (416) 366-6422
Fax: (416) 362-6422
E-Mail: info@micaworld.com
Web site: www.micaworld.com
Topics: Leadership, creativity, manage-
ment skills/development, organiza-
tional change, employee
recruitment/selection staffing
Staff Size: 60
Contact: Don McQuaig, President

Mind Resources (Pty.) LTD
Level 5, 285 Clarence Street
Sydney NSW 2000
Australia
Phone: 011 029-299-0699
Fax: 011 029-299-0799
E-Mail: Fiona@mindresources.net
Web site: www.mindresources.net
Topics: Provides learning resources to
the corporate, industrial, and govern-
ment sectors within Australia, New
Zealand & Southeast Asia
Staff Size: 20
Contact: Fiona Barry, Managing
Director

National Seminars Group
6901 W. 63rd Street
Shawnee Mission, KS 66202
Phone: (913) 432-7755
Web site: www.natsem.com
Topics: Communications, leadership,
productivity, and lifestyle

NTL Institute
300 North Lee Street, Suite 300
Alexandria, VA 22314-2630
Phone: (800) 777-5227
Web site: www.ntl.org
Topics: Human relations training,
   management and personal development, consultation skills, organization development, and training
   of trainers

ODR
2900 Chamblee-Tucker Road
Building 16
Atlanta, GA 30341
Phone: (770) 455-7145
Fax: (770) 455-8974
E-Mail: odr2@odr.odrnet.com
Web site: www.odrinc.com
Topics: Organizational change
Staff Size: 10
Contact: Daryl Conner, CEO

Omega Performance Corporation
8701 Red Oak Blvd., Suite 450
Charlotte, NC 28217
Phone: (704) 672-1400
Fax: (704) 672-1416
E-Mail: jgutierrez@omega-
   performance.com
Web site: www.omega-
   performance.com
Topics: Credit management, sales
   training, customer service/client
   relations, management skills/
   development
Staff Size: 75
Contact: Juan F. Gutierrez, President

Oy Rastor AB
Wavulinintie 3
00210 Helsinki, Finland
Phone: 358-9-615-181
Fax: 358-9-615-18200
E-Mail: rastor@rastor.fi
Web site: www.rastor.fi
Topics: Management training, manage-
   ment consulting, technical training by
   distance learning, publishing of man-
   agerial books & magazines
Staff Size: 50
Contact: Yrjo Junkkari, President

Paradigm Group
140 Sherman Street
Fairfield, CT 06430
Phone: (203) 255-6855
Fax: (203) 255-2615
E-Mail: office@paradigmgroupinc.com
Web site: www.paradigmgroupinc.
   com
Topics: Sales training & management,
   customer service/client relations,
   coaching, management skills/
   development, employee recruit-
   ment/selection staffing
Staff Size: 10
Contact: Dennis McCarthy

Paradigm Learning, Inc.
2701 N. Rocky Point Drive
Suite 400
Tampa, FL 33607
Phone: (813) 287-9330
Fax: (813) 287-9331
E-Mail: cathyr@paradigmlearning.com
Web site: www.paradigmlearning.com
Topics: Business/financial literacy,
   organizational change, teams/team
   building, leadership, project
   management, E-business
Staff Size: 48
Contact: Catherine Rezak, President

Partners In Change, Inc.
2547 Washington Road
Suite 720
Pittsburgh, PA 15241
Phone: (412) 854-5750
Fax: (412) 854-5801
E-Mail: mail@partners-in-change.com
Web site: www.partners-in-change.
   com
Topics: Performance consulting, perfor-
   mance assessment, change manage-
   ment, organizational change
Staff Size: 8
Contact: Dana Robinson, President

Performance Express
3730 Ridge Mill Drive
Hilliard, OH 43026
Phone: (614) 527-4421
Fax: (614) 527-4417
E-Mail: mark@performanceexpress.
   com

Topics: Mid-upper-level leadership & change management online, management & business acumen development for technical employees & professionals, advanced IT & engineering learning applications
Contact: Mark Luciano

Peliculas Mel, SA
Uruapon 17 Col. Roma
Mexico D.F. 6700
Phone: 52-5-207-3725
Fax: 52-5-207-3608
E-Mail: elias@peliculasmel.com.mx
Web site: www.peliculasmel.com
Topics: Sales training, communication skills, safety, leadership, supervisory training
Staff Size: 23
Contact: Elias Lasky London, General Director

Personal Decisions, Inc.
2000 Plaza VII Tower
45 S. 7th Street
Minneapolis, MN 55402
Phone: (612) 339-0927
Web site: www.personneldecisions.com
Topics: Management, leadership, and human resources

Pharmaceutical Training Institute
708 Third Avenue, 4th Floor
New York, NY 10017
Phone: (212) 661-3500
Fax: (509) 351-2296
E-Mail: hko@iirusa.com
Web site: www.pharmatraining.org
Topics: FDA compliance, career development, total quality management, executive development
Staff Size: 20
Contact: Heej Ko, Vice President

Pope & Associates, Inc.
1313 E. Kemper Road, Suite 350
Cincinnati, OH 45246
Phone: (513) 671-1277
Web site: www.popeandassociates.com
Topics: Diversity management training, consulting pairs training, self- development, and self-development for women

Porter Henry & Company, Inc.
360 Lexington Avenue, 20th Floor
New York, NY 10017
Phone: (212) 953-5544
Fax: (212) 953-5899
E-Mail: sales@porterhenry.com
Web site: www.porterhenry.com
Topics: Sales skills, sales management skills/development, sales technical skills/knowledge updating, sales quality customer service, account management training
Staff Size: 26
Contact: Richard Holmes, Executive Vice President

Provant, Inc.
5255 N. Edgewood Drive, Suite 125
Provo, UT 84604
Phone: (801) 654-7622
Fax: (801) 818-8520
E-Mail: jzenger@provant.com
Web site: www.provant.com
Topics: Leadership & management development, building winning cultures, technical & job-skills development, project management, recruitment & retention
Staff Size: 1700
Contact: John Zenger, Vice Chairman

Provant Media
4601 121st Street
Urbandale, OA 50323-2311
Phone: (888) 776-8268
Fax: (515) 327-2570
E-Mail: custsvc@provantmedia.com
Web site: www.provantmedia.com
Topics: Compliance issues, employee recruitment, selection/staffing, management skills/development, leadership, diversity
Staff Size: 36
Contact: Laura Tarrant, Vice President & General Manager

Psychological Associates, Inc.
8201 Maryland, Suite 300
St. Louis, MO 63105
Phone: (314) 862-9300
Fax: (314) 862-0477
E-Mail: pa@q4solutions.com
Web site: www.q4solutions.com

Topics: Management skills/development, sales skills, teams, organizational change, executive development
Contact: Victor R. Buzzotta, Chairman

Quality Media Resources, Inc.
10929 SE 23rd Street
Bellevue, WA 98004
Phone: (425) 455-0558
Fax: (425) 462-7087
Web site: www.qmr.com
Topics: Harassment, workforce diversity, customer service, leadership skills, coaching, mentoring & conflict management
Contact: Robert Rosell, President

R. Thomas Consulting & Training
2872 Woodcock Blvd., Suite 220
Atlanta, GA 30341
Phone: (770) 234-0222
Fax: (770) 234-0226
E-Mail: info@rthomasconsulting.com
Web site: www.rthomasconsulting.com
Topics: Diversity, executive development, culture assessment, staff training
Staff Size: 7
Contact: Hal Jones, Vice President

Rainmaker Associates
62 Central Street
Byfield, MA 01922
Phone: (978) 465-1145
Fax: (978) 462-0331
Web site: www.rainmakerassoc.com
Topics: Total sales effectiveness, employee recruitment selection/staff, sales training, coaching, change management
Contact: Don Weintraub, President

Realchange Network, Inc.
1840 San Miguel Drive, Suite 203
Walnut Creek, CA 94598
Phone: (925) 284-8787
Fax: (925) 284-8725
Web site: www.realchange.com

Topics: Global/virtual teams development, cross-cultural change management, organizational change, leadership renewal, learning expectations
Contact: Christian Forthomme, President

Ridge Associates, Inc.
The Textile Building
119 N. Fourth Street, Suite 501
Minneapolis, MN 55401
Phone: (612) 376-7720
Fax: (612) 376-7722
E-Mail: info@ridge.com
Web site: www.ridge.com
Topics: Communication skills, management skills/development, teams, sales skills, professional trainer development
Staff Size: 40
Contact: James Bolton, CEO

Right Management Consultants
100 Prospect Street
South Tower
Stamford, CT 06901
Phone: (203) 326-3880
Fax: (203) 326-3890
E-Mail: toni.lucia@right.com
Web site: www.right.com
Topics: Career development, coaching, executive development, leadership, organizational change
Staff Size: 230
Contact: Toni Lucia, Managing Principal

Saba Software, Inc.
2400 Bridge Parkway
Redwood Shores, CA 94065
Phone: (650) 696-3840
Fax: (650) 696-1630
E-Mail: info@saba.com
Web site: www.saba.com
Topics: Customer service/client relations, new methods/procedures, organizational change, software systems (learning management & learning networks), Internet services
Staff Size: 30
Contact: Grant Ricketts, Vice President Business Development

A. E. Schwartz and Associates
P. O. Box 228
Waverly, MA 02179
Phone: (617) 926-9111
Fax: (617) 926-0660
Web site: www.aeschwartz.com
Topics: Management, sales, and
customer service

Sales Momentum
9280 E. Thompson Peak Parkway
Suite 36
Scottsdale, AZ 85255
Phone: (480) 513-0900
Fax: (480) 513-0706
Web site: www.salesmomentum.
com
Topics: Sales training, coaching/
sales
Contact: Richard Ruff

Siamar LTD
Rua Adib Auada 289-G Vianna
06710-700 Cotia, SP – Brazil
Phone: 55-11-4613-5500
Fax: 55-11-4613-5510
E-Mail: nickmartino@siamar.
com.br
Web site: www.siamar.com.br
Topics: General management, sales
motivation, customer relations,
quality, industrial safety and
related subjects.
Staff Size: 42
Contact: Nick Martino

Situation Management Systems,
Inc.
195 Hanover Street
Hanover, MA 02339-2292
Phone: (781) 826-4433
Fax: (781) 826-2863
E-Mail: info@smsinc.com
Web site: ww.smsinc.com
Topics: Influence and negotiation
skills, management skills/develop-
ment, personal development/growth,
project management, organization
consulting
Staff Size: 20
Contact: Sherri Malouf, President

Six Sigma Qualtec, Inc.
1295 West Washington Street
Suite 215
Tempe, AZ 85281
Phone: (800) 247-9871
Fax: (480) 586-2586
E-Mail: srust@ssqi.com
Web site: www.sixsigmaqualtec.com
Topics: Six sigma, problem solving,
total quality management
Staff Size: 70
Contact: John Lopez-Ona, CEO

Skillpath
6900 Squibb Road
Mission, KS 66201-2768
Phone: (913) 362-1207
Fax: (913) 362-9145
E-Mail: rcox@skillpath.net
Web site: www.skillpath.com
Topics: Soft skills and technical
skills training
Staff Size: 300
Contact: Ronald L. Cox, CEO

Snider Associates
2 Canal Park
Cambridge, MA 02141
Phone: (617) 947-1170
Fax: (617) 761-3691
E-Mail: andy@sniderassociates.com
Web site: andy@sniderassociates.
com
Topics: Defining strategies for successful technology initiatives,
facilitation to align teams for technology changes, assistance in
selecting and integrating vendors,
developing on-going support for
technology efforts, project management
Staff Size: 10
Contact: Andy Snider, President

Summit Training Source, Inc.
2660 Horizon Drive SE
Grand Rapids, MI 49546
Phone: (616) 949-4343
Fax: (616) 949-5684
E-Mail: info@safetyontheweb.com
Web site: www.safetyontheweb.
com

Topics: Safety training, technical skills
training, CBT development
Staff Size: 46
Contact: Valerie Overhuel, President

Swan Consultants, Inc.
420 Lexington Avenue
New York, NY 10170
Phone: (212) 682-0606
Web site: www.swanconsultants.
com
Topics: Interviewing skills

The Ariel Group
792 Massachusetts Avenue
Arlington, MA 02139
Phone: (781) 648-9470
Fax: (781) 648-5551
E-Mail: info@arielgroup.com
Web site: www.arielgroup.com
Topics: Presentation skills, leadership,
coaching, creativity
Staff Size: 12
Contact: Kathy Lubar

The Baron Group
57 Wilton Road
Westport, CT 06880
Phone: (203) 227-7907
Fax: (203) 221-8411
E-Mail: tbt@barongroup.com
Web site: www.barongroup.com
Topics: Sales training, coaching,
problem solving, communication
skills, negotiation skills
Staff Size 6
Contact: Eric Baron, CEO

The Bob Pike Group
7620 West 78th Street
Edina, MN 55439
Phone: (952) 829-1954
Fax: (952) 829-0260
E-Mail: bpike@bobpikegroup.
com
Web site: www.bobpikegroup.
com
Topics: Coaching, facilitation skills,
presentation skills, teams/team
building, train the trainer
Staff Size: 25
Contact: Robert W. Pike, CEO

The Brooks Group
1903 Ashwood Court, Suite C
Greensboro, NC 27455
Phone: (336) 282-6303
Fax: (336) 282-5707
E-Mail: sales@thebrooksgroup.com
Web site: www.brooksgroup.com
Topics: Sales training, time manage-
ment, presentation skills, personal
development/growth, leadership
Staff Size: 21
Contact: William T. Brooks, CEO

The Clark Wilson Group, Inc.
4900 Nautilus Court North
Suite 220
Boulder, CO 80301
Phone: (800) 537-7249
Fax: (303) 581-9326
E-Mail: info@wcginc.com
Web site: www.clarkwilson.com
Topics: 360 feedback programs,
executive development, leadership,
management skills/development,
teams/team building
Staff Size: 14
Contact: Daniel J. Booth, President

The Forum Corporation
One Exchange Place
Boston, MA 02109
Phone: (617) 523-7300
Fax: (617) 973-2001
E-Mail: jhumphrey@forum.com
Web site: www.forum.com
Topics: Leadership, management
skills/development, sales training,
customer experience development,
customer service/client relations
Staff Size: 350
Contact: John Humphrey

The Heim Group
P.O. Box 1745
Pacific Palisades, CA 90272
Phone: (310) 459-3178
Fax: (310) 459-2083
Web site: www.heimgroup.com
Topics: Gender differences in communi-
cation & work styles, communication
skills, executive development,
teams/team building, consulting
Contact: Pat Heim, President

The Ken Blanchard Companies
125 State Place
Escondido, CA 92029
Phone: (760) 489-5005
Fax: (760) 489-1332
E-Mail: hollygreen@kenblanchard.
com
Web site: www.kenblanchard.com
Topics: Leadership, management
skills/development, teams/team
building, customer service/client
relations, coaching
Staff Size: 225
Contact: Holly Green, President

The Marcom Group Ltd.
20 Creek Parkway Building 11304
Boothwyn, PA 19061-3132
Phone: (610) 859-8989
Fax: (610) 859-8106
E-Mail: Marcomltd@aol.com
Web site: www.marcomltd.com
Topics: Regulatory compliance
& training (OSHA), safety
training
Staff Size: 16
Contact: Don Leonard, President

The Masie Center
P.O. Box 397
Saratoga Springs, NY 12866
Phone: (518) 587-3522
Fax: (518) 587-3276
E-Mail: info@masie.com
Web site: www.masie.com
Topics: E-Learning, new methods/
procedures, organizational
change
Staff Size: 10
Contact: Elliott Masie, President

The Profit Ability Group, Inc.
27 Chesterton Lane
Chesterfield, MO 63017
Phone: (636) 527-7111
Fax: (636) 527-7227
Web site:
www.theprofitabilitygroup.com
Topics: Financial skills training,
business skills training
Contact: Raymond Halagera,
President

THINQ Learning Solutions
2620 Augustine Drive, Suite 145
Santa Clara, CA 95054-2908
Phone: (888) 931-3311
Fax: (408) 727-8544
E-Mail: general@learningsolutions.com
Web site: www.learningsolutions.com
Topics: LMS infrastructure software,
portal to content provider
Staff Size: 380
Contact: Susan Dawson, Vice President

Tompeterscompany!
101 Commerce Blvd.
Loveland, OH 45140-7727
Phone: (513) 683-4702
Fax: (513) 683-8958
E-Mail: info@tompeters.com
Web site: www.tompeters.com
Topics: Leadership development, lead-
ership communication, executive
development, organizational change,
innovation & self-branding,
teams/team building
Staff Size: 70
Contact: Boyd L. Clarke, CEO

Training Magazine
50 South Ninth Street
Minneapolis, MN 55402-3118
Phone: (612) 333-0471
Fax: (612) 333-6526
E-Mail: smarmolejo@trainingmag.com
Web site: www.trainingsupersite.com
Topics: Magazine publishing, confer-
ences, newsletter

Triad Performance Technologies, Inc.
30101 Northwestern Highway, Suite
201
Farmington Hills, MI 48334
Phone: (248) 737-3300
Fax: (248) 737-0333
E-Mail: teda@triadperform.com
Web site: www.triadperform.com
Topics: Instructional systems design,
technical skills training, CBT
developers, change management,
organizational change
Staff Size: 42
Contact: Theodore D. Apking,
President

Ulysses Learning
249 Williamson Road
Suite 200
Mooresville, NC 28117
Phone: (704) 943-5800
Fax: (704) 892-0833
E-Mail: info@ulysseslearning.
   com
Web site: www.ulysseslearning.
   com
Topics: Customer service/client
   relations, coaching, sales train-
   ing, supervisory training, CBT
   developers
Staff Size: 30
Contact: Mark Brodsky, President

Vital Learning Corporation
9415 F Street
Omaha, NE 68127-1215
Phone: (800) 243-5858
Fax: (402) 592-7142
E-Mail: sales@vital-learning.com
Web site: www.vital-learning.com
Topics: Sales training, supervisory
   training, customer service/client rela-
   tions, personal development/growth,
   E-learning
Staff Size: 20
Contact: Karl G. Gnau, President

VNU Business Media
50 South Ninth Street
Minneapolis, MN 55402-3165
Phone: (800) 328-4329
Fax: (612) 340-4759
E-Mail: pjones@vnulearning.com
Web site: www.vnulearning.com
Topics: Magazine publishing,
   conferences/expos, newsletters
Staff Size: 100
Contact: Stacey Marmolejo

Walters Speakers Services
P.O. Box 1120
Glendora, CA 91740
Phone: (626) 335-8069
Web site: www.walters-intl.com
Topics: Speak and Grow Rich, How
   to Be a Better Speaker, How to Have
   Audience Involvement

Zimmerman Communi-Care
   Network, Inc.
20550 Lake Ridge Drive
Prior Lake, MN 55372
Phone: (952) 492-3888
Fax: (952) 492-5888
Web site: www.dzimmerman.com
Topics: Motivation, mastering change,
   relationships

Index

About the Author

Paul Karasik is one of America's leading sales and management consultants. He is the president of The Business Institute,
a sales and management training and consulting organization.
Paul has devoted 18 years helping America's professionals and
businesspeople achieve their goals. He is the creator of eight
sales and management programs.

Paul's client list reads like a *Who's Who* of American business. His client list includes: Prudential, Mercedes Benz,
AT&T, IBM, New York Life, and Shell Oil.

Paul is the author of seven all-time business classics, *Sweet
Persuasion* and *Sweet Persuasion for Managers, Seminar Selling
for Financial Services, Brilliant Thoughts, How to Market to High-
Net-Worth Households,* and *22 Keys to Sales Success.*

He is a frequent speaker and seminar leader at conferences,
sales rallies, and advanced sales and marketing programs both
nationally and internationally. Paul is the founder of the
American Seminar Leaders Association. To learn more go to
www.paulkarasik.com.